Choosing Project Success

A Guide for Building Professionals

J.F. McCarthy

PARETO
BUILDING IMPROVEMENT

Choosing Project Success—A Guide for Building Professionals

Notice: This book is designed to provide information to assist building professionals. It is sold with the understanding that the publisher and author are not engaged in rendering legal, accounting, architectural, or engineering professional services. Such topics as discussed herein are for example or illustrative purposes only. If you need professional assistance, you should use the services of an appropriately qualified professional where you can explore the unique aspects of your situation and received specific advice tailored to your circumstances.

It is not the purpose of this guide to reprint all information that is otherwise available to building professionals, but to complement, amplifying, supplement other texts and resources. You are urged to read all available material and learn as much you can about building, and tailor the information to your specific circumstances

Every effort has been made to make this guide is complete and accurate as possible. However there may be mistakes, both typographical and in content. Therefore this text should be used only as a general guide, not the ultimate source of information.

The author and Pareto - Building Improvement shall have no liability or responsibility to any person or entity with respect to any loss or damage is caused, or alleged to have been caused, directly or indirectly by the information contained in this book

Library of Congress Control Number 2007909768

Published by:
Pareto - Building Improvement
1220 Bristol
Westchester, IL 60154

Publisher's Cataloging-in-Publication
(Provided by Quality Books, Inc.)

    McCarthy, J. F. (Joe F.)
      Choosing project success : a guide for building
    professionals / J.F. McCarthy.
      p. cm.
      Includes index.
      ISBN-13: 9-7809-799969-0-0
      ISBN-10: 0-9799969-0-2

      1. Construction industry--Management. 2. Project
    management.   I. Title.

    HD9715.A2M33 2008   690'.068
                    QBI07-600330

Printed in United States of America

Table of Contents

Acknowledgements

Throughout history heroes made and did things. They built, expanded, and explored new horizons, going where no one had gone before. The 20th century changed hero jobs from doing things to talking about doing things. Also there was a transition from an understanding of human nature, the physical world, and right and wrong that was formerly considered so obvious that it didn't need to be stated—to relative values and fashionable intellectual theories conceived in the dark halls of universities that whither in the sunlight of real people doing real things.

The writer lived in the second half of this century of transitions, and built things when building things was unfashionable. But buildings needed to be built, and it is a most enjoyable way to spend one's days. The enjoyment of building is to create something good where nothing was before. Then you stand back and look and say, "That is good" and "I did it"—but moments later you start to think, "How can I do it better next time."

This is a description of how to build well and how to build better. Over 30 years those I worked for, or with, gave suggestions and corrections. I made an effort to listen, implement the improvements, see the results, and try again. I was also influenced by my father who grew with, shaped, and became an authority in the field of academic marketing during this same time. I see small traces of his thinking in mine. But his larger influence is an approach and way of thinking that made me see the construction industry as sophisticated and as capable of excellence and improvement as any other endeavor.

Deepest thanks to all who helped, many of whom did so without knowing—seeds planted in stubborn soil bearing later fruit. I thought about this for 30 years, then sat down and wrote it out. The contributions are from many, but the responsibility is all mine.

Preface

This book helps working professionals in the building business, who have already achieved success, to improve and go further. Building owners, facility managers, owner's representatives, lenders and insurers, designers, general contractors, subcontractors, and vendors all need the same knowledge—to "play with the same deck of cards"—so communication and cooperation are possible.

Each building task is complex and constantly changing, and mastery of one trade can well occupy an entire career. No one can master them all. This book is not trade education—"hands on, how to descriptions"—for the many required building tasks. But, what this book does share with trade education is a focus on results. We want to know what works, why it works, and how we can make it work better. Classroom theories that cannot be used now, or Do not work at all, have no place here.

And the results must start right now. Starting a new job, assignment to an unfamiliar project type, or responsibility for implementation of a new technology where you must instantly be the manager of subjects of which you are ignorant, is familiar to many.

Classroom education may not be a solution. Classes may not be available when and where you need them. Or the time demands of your present job, family, church, or sports limit classroom attendance possibilities.

This book solves these problems. All chapters can be read anywhere in less than an hour—no classrooms, tests, or papers. Previous education or knowledge of the subject is not assumed or required. Although the entire book is needed to understand all parts of the building process, and there is a flow that aids understanding, single chapters can be read in any order if you need to answer a question right now. Read a few chapters over the weekend, and be ready on Monday morning.

This book provides the information needed to plan a project successfully, to hire and manage the right people, to answer their questions, and to check their results. Use this book to make project success the norm, and you can manage better, faster, and easier, starting now.

Introduction

Construction projects can and should be routinely successful. Failed projects should be as rare as projects destroyed by natural disaster.

However, many projects are attempted in ways that make failure all but certain. If you accept failure as normal, "project management" can make a career of managing that failure. (Failing projects take more management time, which means more management fees.) With this approach, the efforts of competent, skilled, hard working, well meaning people can be wasted. Slow motion and well-documented failure will be the usual outcome. This approach is similar to "get rich quick schemes" and "weight loss without exercise programs," and it is just as effective.

This book describes a different approach. It makes success the normal outcome for construction projects. The approach starts with an attitude and a point of view—believing project success is possible and choosing it. Next, the approach adds a little humility—to see the world as it is, not as you wish it were. Finally, add facts, followed by knowledge, and then judgment. Management tools work within, and only within, this framework to successfully organize this effort.

These facts and knowledge are known by few, but are not hard to understand. The contents of this book provides information that will place you in the top few percent of people in the building business—including those with years of schooling and fancy degrees and certificates. Ordinary people, who think right and keep trying, achieve extraordinary things everyday. This book shows you how.

Part I: Observing Well, Thinking Right

Observing Clearly, with Organization, and Increasing Focus

Introduction

Observing Well, Thinking Right

It is now fashionable (1) to skip the facts and move directly to management or to "let the little people handle the details" and (2) to suggest that facts do not exist or are too much trouble—"it's all too complicated," "nuanced," or can not be "precisely known for sure." This is nonsense and rubbish.

There is light and dark, hot and cold, gravity exists, and stone has had the same properties for hundreds of millions of years and water for billions. Facts are the building blocks of information, and information of knowledge. Increasing useful facts decreases uncertainty and makes correct judgments clearer and more certain.

Facts must be true and believed by others to be true, which means they must be reproducible—others can check and measure and get the same results. This means that you must present your facts in a way others can easily check. Once presented, checked, and accepted, they are facts and further discussion can and should cease—so you can move on to other tasks.

But there is a subjective component of facts as well. Facts are always scarcer than we would like, so we need to fill in the blanks, which brings bias. And everyone has bias, (yes, everyone who is alive has a bias—and that means you) which makes it difficult to know what to observe, how to observe, and how precisely to observe. Bias cannot be eliminated, but it can be recognized and managed. So even though you might not see entirely clearly, at least you are looking in the right direction, and at the right objects.

Organization is required to convert this huge overwhelming volume of facts into usable knowledge. This organized knowledge permits communication and cooperation with others.

Time, and the impact of time, is ever present and persistent. It initially comes free, but has costs and impacts that affect all aspects of project planning and execution. But it is frequently given little or late attention, or completely ignored—with disastrous results and no possibility of full recovery. Managing time is critical to project success.

Part I is about thinking right. All possible useful fact building blocks are obtained and organized so you can communicate with others, and the path to project success can begin.

1.1 Observation is For a Purpose

Qualitative and quantitative observation are both necessary

"Facts are stubborn things, and whatever may be our wishes, our inclinations, or the dictate of our passions, they can not alter the state of facts and evidence."—John Adams

"The world is filled with knowledge almost empty of understanding."
"There are things that intelligence alone can seek but never find. These things instinct alone could find but it will never seek them."—Louis Sullivan

Observations Vary by the Purpose of the Observer

Observation is noticing and describing things and characteristics of things for a purpose. The purpose determines what can, should, and will be observed.

The parties who build parts of a building see different things in the completed structure and can and do observe differently:

The earthwork contractor sees volumes and grades of earth, possible placement of equipment and haul roads.

The foundation contractor sees the foundation, methods of forming, shoring, and temporary drainage. Most of these are concealed from view, or even removed from the site after completion of the foundation.

The bricklayer sees types, numbers, and configurations of bricks, blocks, reinforcing, mortar, and possible methods of scaffolding.

The window contractor sees the type and quantity of windows, and probable method of anchorage and sealing windows.

The interior designer sees colors, textures, lights, and shadows.

Each party's observation is correct for its own purpose. But if each party made and used only his own observations, there would be a "Tower of Babel"—each speaking his own language, unable to communicate with others. The purpose is not just to perform earthwork or install foundations, brick, and windows, and decorate them, but to build a complete building.

For this purpose, observations are required that can be made, organized, and used many different ways by many people. These observations must be able to be organized in many ways to convert data (facts) to information (knowledge), which is necessary for our purpose—successful completion of the project.

Quantitative Observation Involves Measurement

Quantitative observation is possible of:

- Length, width, height, thickness, and volume
- Weight
- Force, power, energy, and light
- Indivisible units such as people
- Money
- Time

Each party can measure these quantities, understand them, and use them. Use of standard quantities makes communication possible—establishing facts that all agree are facts. These quantitative observations (facts) are the necessary starting point for all knowledge and decision-making, and must be maintained throughout the decision-making process. But facts alone will not produce knowledge. Qualitative observation is also necessary.

Qualitative Observation Involves Impressions, with Support

Qualitative observations are impressions which are supported by information that is less complete and precise than one would want. This is so because some of what would be useful information is not available, or the subject is too complex and subjective to permit quantitative measurement.

Everyone needs and uses impressions, feelings, intuitions, and instincts in daily life. Use in the business world is also required. But because business is people working together to take measurable inputs to produce measurable outputs in a mutually agreeable way, convincing support—though incomplete—is required to communicate and gain agreement with others. "It is so because I feel it is so," lacks any supporting information that others could check, and has no useful purpose in the business world. On the other hand, recognizing only observations that can be quantitatively measured misses many of the observations people use every day in the real world.

> For example, the impression that there are difficult and corrupt cities that discourage legitimate business activity is widely accepted. Some documentation is possible—length of time and cost to obtain permits—but others such as bribes paid are concealed as much as the perpetrators can manage. The mix of hard data- time and cost of permits, and the occasional conviction for bribery constitutes the less than complete, but generally accepted, support for this impression.

> Similarly, the impression that some work forces are motivated and some are not is also widely accepted. Productivity, and changes in productivity, rate of defects, absenteeism,

higher than normal use of sick and personal days, quantity of employee suggestions, are not measures of motivation itself, but are considered supporting indication of motivation.

The qualitative observations and the supporting data must be both true and generally believed to be true, if they are to be accepted and used by others.

> Which pickup truck is "best" can be described by the manufacturer's detailed description of size, weight, engine, transmission, load capacity, and other information on features. Although this information is available to all, it is not generally accepted as support for the selection of the "best" truck. Many buyers are blindly loyal to one brand of truck for life. Because the support for "best" truck is not generally accepted, it cannot be used when communicating with others.

Quantitative and Qualitative Observations Must Work Together

Both quantitative and qualitative observations are necessary to make the most informed decisions. When building a construction project, the most obvious, basic, quickly and cheaply available quantitative facts are obtained, and then a qualitative reaction to these facts is made. This two-step process is repeated with increasing detail for both the quantitative and qualitative observations until the qualitative and quantitative reasonably agree. These ideas are illustrated in the following example:

Starting a four-story office building in Chesterton, PA

1. Basic quantitative observations:

    A four-story office building is proposed for a 3.6-acre site at the southwest corner of Main Street and First Avenue in Chesterton, PA. The project budget has been established, financing obtained, and a desired completion date established.

2. Qualitative observation:

    Chesterton and the surrounding county both claim jurisdiction for permits and inspections, so these activities will need more time and effort. The site is in a congested, built-up area with slow access roads, so access, staging, hoisting, and storage of materials will take more time and money to properly manage.

3. Additional quantitative observation:

    The structure is to be a conventional structural steel building, but the owner of the building is an affiliate of a foreign company engaged in manufacture and erection of aluminum and glass atriums and skylights. Their product is to be used on this building, but it has never been installed in this country.

4. Additional qualitative observation:

The unfamiliar atrium and skylight product will require all parties to learn the system and the implications for their work. The construction personnel may want changes to the structure or the mechanical system for unanticipated structural, heating and cooling loads, and unusual hoisting. The financing personnel may have insurance impacts and financing restrictions. The government permitting agencies may have code evaluation difficulties. This requires time and effort, and the conclusion could be that the system is unfeasible at this location at this time with the budget available.

Summary

Qualitative and quantitative observations together are necessary for informed decisions. First, quantitative observations (facts) are obtained that are agreed to be facts, and therefore permit communication. Then, qualitative impressions are obtained that are partially supportable and are believed to be true. Quantitative facts permit and encourage qualitative observation. Qualitative facts give meaning and insight, and suggest further areas where quantitative facts can be obtained. Quantitative and qualitative observation together can produce knowledge, which is the start of excellence and normal project success.

1.2 Precision and Variation in Observations

Choosing the best achievable level of detail

"Men who wish to know about the world must learn about it in its particular details."—Herakleitos

Variation is Everywhere, Precision Nowhere. Manage variation to be "Precise Enough"

Precision refers to the acceptable variation from a stated (perfect) value or point. For example "this 10-foot long board is straight plus or minus one inch." Exact precision (perfection) never exists in the real world. One can, with effort, move closer to perfection but because variation exists in all things and people, exact precision is never reached. A measurement may at first appear precise, but a new, finer measuring tool will show the object's variation.

Precision for a Purpose

The purpose determines the level of precision required. So, the purpose must first be clearly defined. Without a clear purpose, the range of precision possible is too vast to permit selection of the right level of precision for your project. Setting an arbitrarily high standard—"let's just get the best"—is not achievable and will fail.

Once the purpose is clearly defined, common sense, industry standards, and a determination of what is available at an acceptable price will guide selection of an appropriate level of precision, as shown by the following examples:

When traveling from a house on the east side of the country to a factory on the west side of the country, arrival is achieved at the parking lot. A spot on the east side of the lot, or 400 feet away on the west side is close enough.

You are re-grading earth on a square site measuring 1,000 feet on each side, and this requires raising some parts 6 feet and lowering some parts 4 feet. Final achieved grades within feet or inches of the specified grades are precise enough.

Wood and steel framing is sometimes considered exact at within 2 inches, and sometimes within 1/4 of an inch, while cabinet and millwork construction gaps of 1/4-inch gap in finished work would be unacceptable.

Pump and pump motor alignment require 1/1000-inch shims to make the pump and motor run without excessive vibration and wear.

These hugely different levels of precision seem appropriate and obvious because the purpose was defined. Location in the factory parking lot would not be measured to the same 1/1000 of an inch that would be appropriate for the pump alignment. All of these examples may be viewed as precise enough for the intended purpose. But if finer measuring tools—a better ruler, a magnifying glass, or a microscope—were used, the variations would be apparent, and the variation might be unacceptable, depending on how much precision is needed.

Variation Exists in All Things and People

Manufacturing methods are usually similar in industries, and there are accepted industry standards for tolerances.

Steel mills are factories stretching for miles producing around the clock, every day for years. The steel companies have agreed how much variation will be allowed. For a 30-foot wide flange beam, sometimes referred to as an "I" beam, the industry has agreed that 3" out of line is "straight enough."

Rough lumber such as 2" x 4"s is produced by giant timber companies and small mills with a few employees. The wood products industry has agreed on allowable variation. For a 2" x 12", 16 feet long, the industry has agreed that 1-1/2" out of line is "straight enough."

Some tolerances have improved and may continue to improve over the years. But they will *not* change their specifications in time for your project. This may sound obvious, but expectations and specifications that assume these tolerances do not exist, or will be changed by writing specifications on a piece of paper, are common.

Human variation exists in all activities. A professional baseball pitcher, for example, may be talented, skilled, and trained, but can rarely pitch a no-hitter. Similarly, human variation and achievable levels of precision in construction must be recognized and managed in the construction process.

Realizing the Optimal Level of Precision

Seeking more precision takes effort and usually costs money. If a more precise product costs more, some think it is "better." But this is not necessarily so. Precision that is greater than what the user can see, measure, or needs is not harmful to the installed work, but it is wasted—such as measuring a car's location in a factory parking lot to 1/1000 of an inch.

A common approach is to seek a level of precision in components that is far in excess of what is required, or maybe possible, in the hope that this greater precision of one component will somehow overcome the lesser precision of other components—producing a completed project achieving the desired level of precision. But good intentions and "just hoping" will not make it so. The requested precision will not always be available at an acceptable cost. And one precise component can never increase the precision of another component. The lowest level of precision in all components that achieves your purpose is the optimal level. More precision (at the same cost) will neither hurt nor help. But there usually is a cost— higher purchase cost for unnecessarily precise materials, schedule delay costs to wait for these less common materials, or elimination of otherwise desirable vendors from consideration.

How Much Precision Can the Project Afford?

Increased precision usually takes effort, time, and money, which are all limited. An illustrative description of the effort required for various levels of precision is as follows:

100 man-hours to achieve 67% precision, being wrong 33% of the time, is considered unacceptable.

200 man-hours to achieve 90% precision, being wrong 10% of the time, is considered acceptable for only some purposes.

300 man-hours to achieve 95% precision, being wrong 5% of the time, might initially seem that "we could do better" until the cost and feasibility is evaluated. Then, this level of precision may look "ok."

400 man-hours to achieve 97% precision, better, but at a great cost for the improvement.

500 man-hours to achieve 98% precision, cost becomes excessive for almost all purposes.

600 man-hours to achieve 99% precision, seldom used because of the excessive cost.

Note: If an entire industry increases precision over time, the costs will decline, maybe hugely. But our purpose is to build a project here and now with the men and materials available, so future possibilities cannot be considered.

Getting the Best From the Level of Precisions that Fits Your Purpose

Determining how good is "good enough"

Some logical steps should be followed:

1. Define the purpose the project will serve.

2. Determine the precision of the components and capability of labor now available in the market at an acceptable cost.

3. Rule out the levels of high precision and the levels of low precision that are inappropriate for the purpose. Start the selection of the remaining levels by working bottom up, not top down. Define the lowest available precision of components that will achieve the purpose

as the minimum standard, then define the highest standard achievable for this project, but not necessarily the upper limit.

The level of 95% is now the most frequently selected level of "good enough" for projects, lower levels of precision are offered by many. Higher levels require effort, time, and cost that are only used for "whatever it takes, cost is no object" projects such as manned space travel. In this case there is usually a third party, such as the taxpayer, paying the bill.

Making the Building Appear More Precise with "Tolerant Fit"

Once you have determined the desired level of precision for your project, you can then make the completed project appear more precise than the components for little or no additional cost. This is done with "tolerant fit," which designs more "give and go" in the assembly of the components. This approach takes the components that are available and assembles them in such a way that their lack of precision is less apparent, as illustrated by the following examples:

> A doorframe that butts to a finished wall can appear incorrectly installed with an 1/8 inch gap. If a gripping frame that overlaps the same wall is used, wall misalignment of up to 3/8" can be completely hidden.

> A door release electric strike designed to operate at 24 volts can be damaged or fail to operate if the supplied voltage varies. If the same strike is designed to operate from 8 to 32 volts, supplied voltage can vary and the strike will still appear to function perfectly.

The completed building appears more precise and functions more precisely than the actual precision of the individual components. "Tolerant fit" results from clever selection of components and assemblies of components that "look like we meant it that way."

Communicating the Precision Used
Mean what you say and be consistent

When you have selected a level of precision for a purpose, you communicate this selection by writing all measurements with that level of precision, and no more. Everyone is entitled to believe, and will believe that if you write 12-1/8 inches, you have, and intend to continue to achieve 1/8-inch accuracy. All measurements for a purpose, since the parts must fit together, should have the same level of precision.

Also, it is clearer if all measurements for a purpose are written in exactly the same format. For clear communication, the measurements in the form 12-1/8" (inches only) should not be arbitrarily changed to 1' 0-1/8" (feet and inches), even though the measurements are equal.

Summary

Perfection does not exist in the real world, and precision is not in itself a virtue. The optimal level of precision is the level that fits your purpose. This level is protected and made to appear more precise with a tolerant fit. This achieves excellence and the appearance of high precision, which helps make project success normal.

1.3 Find the Boundaries of "Workable Approaches" That Could Fit the Job

Approximating project size, difficulty, ingredients, opportunities, and obstacles

"It requires a very unusual mind to undertake the analysis of the obvious."—Alfred North Whitehead

"When searching for the truth be ready for the unexpected, for it is difficult to find and puzzling when you find it."—Herakleitos

Finding the Probable Workable Approach

A "workable approach" is one that can and probably will achieve the workable purpose with the grade of materials, cost, and time required. Determining the "workable approach" to a job is similar to getting the right tool for a task. However, it is quite different in timing and impact. If the wrong tool is selected, the right tool can be quickly substituted, and the consequences will probably be minor. If the wrong project approach is selected, the error will be noticed at the middle or end of the project, when partial or total failure is admitted. "I can do anything, just let me get started," or "Do it like we did last time" will frequently end in delay, cost overruns, or failure.

Determining a workable approach is 95% hard work—counting, measuring, checking, and organizing. But, you must know the approximate size, scope, look, and feel of the project before you can approximate an approach and know what to count and measure.

Creating such an approach is a five-step process:
1. Evaluate the project to find the probable range of workable approaches.
2. Evaluate the ingredients for problems and opportunities.
3. Count and measure everything, and place in an organized format.
4. Develop a workable approach using this information.
5. Check each ingredient for the particular project.

Steps one and two are discussed below.

Determine the Scale and " Look and Feel" and Nature of Your Project

Start with your intuitive judgment of about how big and difficult the project is, but keep an open mind since you may be wrong. The following broad categories are starters:

Epic—Unprecedented size, unproven techniques, vast time frames. Examples include: The Great Wall of China, the Great Pyramids of Egypt, the Cathedrals of Medieval Europe (taking up to 300 years to complete), the Panama Canal, and the first man on the moon.

Massive—One of the largest projects under construction in the world, techniques difficult but have been previously completed, time frames are over five years but within one person's lifetime. Examples include the Hoover Dam, the tunnel under the English Channel, and the Three Gorges Dam in China.

Large—Large size (but many similar projects are also underway at other remote locations), techniques completed many times, completion under 5 years. Examples include an 80-story office building, a lock and dam, a refinery, and a suspension bridge.

Medium—Size similar to many completed projects in the surrounding area, techniques off the shelf, completion in one to 5 years. Examples include a 6-story suburban office building, a new public school, and a highway cloverleaf interchange.

Small—Size identical to projects completed and underway in the area, techniques off the shelf or field fabricated with supply house material, completion under one year. Examples include single-family homes, office tenant build-outs, and chain store construction.

Although this is a progression from large to small, it is not a progression from hard to easy. All projects require similar intuitive thought and detailed analysis. The short time frames of smaller projects, in fact, make recovery from project approach errors more difficult.

Qualitative as well as quantitative impressions are needed to find the best "workable approach." Since this is done before the project starts—before design, cost estimates, or detailed evaluations are made—the estimate of quantities for each project ingredient is an approximation based on specific knowledge from prior projects. These quantitative impressions coupled with intuition ask the questions:

"What is probably going to be a challenge on this project?"

"Where are the opportunities for improvement?"

"What project is this most similar to?"

"Could we look at this project in a different way?"

"Does this feel about right?"

This is the last opportunity to resolve the quantitative and qualitative impressions and to view the project in a different light—to reduce the time, cost, and effort of the approach—and still achieve the intended result. For example, a government office building will require the most effort, cost, and time; a custom-designed, private office building will require a medium amount; and an adaptation of a previously completed private office design will require the least amount. Three approaches may produce the same building, but have vastly different costs and times of completion.

Early clear thinking can produce large benefit, but it must be early. Once the approach is chosen, management and field forces will be assigned and vendors contracted, effort, cost, and time can then not decrease easily or much.

Project Ingredient Evaluation—Verifying That the Estimated Approach Will Probably Work

Estimating an approach is a valuable start, but most projects are too large and complex for any one to grasp entirely at once. An estimated approach must be verified and adjusted by individually evaluating the availability of each ingredient for a project's specific time, price, and location. Assumptions must all be checked with information and knowledge specifically gathered for this project.

What is required and available is influenced by the price to be paid, time available, and normal variation (such as plant shutdowns, material or labor shortage, or the arbitrary whim of governing authorities). Since these can change instantly, even identical projects in different places or times can have very different ingredient effort, time, and cost. Specific estimates by component must be obtained. Every single ingredient is necessary for project completion, so no detail can be entirely missed or misunderstood.

Project Ingredients

Labor

The quantity of labor—of the character and capacity required for the project—must be estimated. Skilled labor is limited at a specific location, price, and time, so an approximation of the amount of each labor type—unskilled, skilled, technical, and management—for the project must be made to ensure sufficient labor can be available. If the "required" field labor is unacceptably expensive, more mechanized on-site production, or subcontracted off-site component production, may be substituted to lower cost. If there is a shortage of available labor, wages can be raised, or additional compensation offered to attract more labor—re-attracting skilled labor temporarily employed in other pursuits, or attracting skilled labor from outside the normal geographical area. Training of the available, insufficiently skilled labor is another option, but takes time and money. There are limits, and once reached, more time and/or money must be allocated, or the project must be deemed unfeasible.

There are also limits to the density of labor on the job site at one time. Increases in the density will reduce productivity and increase accidents. Increasing labor by adding shifts will increase cost. "We can always add more people" is not always true.

Material

The quantities of each required material must be estimated. All materials are scarce at some price, time, and place, so quantities and availability must be estimated for the specific project. Water for human use, construction cleaning, and concrete mixing will be scarce and expensive for desert projects. Water is available at city projects by turning on the tap. Basic materials such as steel, cement, copper, oil, and aluminum vary wildly in price and availability, due to variations in demand, plant shutdowns, and short-term manipulation of prices. Manufactured equipment can have even greater variation.

Outside companies—designers, subcontractors, and vendors

Designers, vendors, and subcontractors are required on all projects. At a given price level, a limited group will be available. These groups' capabilities for technical expertise, and capacity for quality and quantity of delivery must be estimated. Their size provides some guidelines as explained below:

1. One-man shop—Furnishes proposals, does the work, and does the books with no other employees. May be extremely responsive, somewhat limited in technical innovation, and strictly limited in quantity of output.

2. Small shop—One person oversees everything and can do all or most tasks, but has employees. Same as one-man shop, but fewer restrictions on technical innovation, and greater output is possible.

3. Medium size shop—One or two owners who each may be able to perform only some of the tasks. Valued and skilled long-term employees may perform all functions of the business. This size shop is limited to the number of employees owners know personally and interact with daily or many times per week. Management can be by the force of the owners' personalities, with little formal structure. Can be responsive and innovative and has ability to expand output beyond normal capacity. Geographical reach may be limited.

4. Large shop—One or many owners who perform few or no on-line tasks. More than one key employee can perform each key task. Formal management structure restricts responsiveness and innovation. Can have major management failures and quality control deficiencies that are not promptly detected. Capable of large quantities of output with long geographical reach.

Small firms cannot do all that large firms do. The large firms cannot do well what the small firms do. The vast majority of subcontractors and vendors are small- and medium-sized shops. The smallest firm suitable for the project tends to be the best fit. An evaluation of the firms available must be made so the assignment of tasks to firms matches their execution capability. There may be many names in the phone book, but few or no optimal firms may be available for a specific project at a specific time.

Time

Possible construction times to achieve optimal quality and cost must be estimated and compared with the desired cost. Every project has a small range of completion times that can be achieved with maximum productivity and performance standards. If a project "must" be done by a time that is unfeasible with the available straight time labor at an acceptable cost, an alternate time or cost premium must be selected. "Drop-dead" times usually mean that costs must increase or performance standards decease, or both.

There are also limits to the time of material installation—governed by chemical cure times. Concrete cures in 28 days. "High early" concrete can achieve (for additional cost) the design strength earlier than 28 days, but will not be fully cured to properly accept chemical coatings and adhesives. Similarly, the coatings and adhesives have cure times between coats that can be shortened somewhat, but not eliminated.

Obstacles Can Kill a Project

Major forces must be considered

War surrounding a job site, war or revolution in a remote country that supplies an important component of the project, trade disruptions between countries, destruction of a plant producing a required material, labor strikes, and catastrophic weather can radically affect project completion. Although wars surrounding the job site are unlikely for most projects, disruptions in other countries that increase the cost or delay or prevent delivery of critical components are quite common. Oil prices, exotic hardwood, or granite and marble are materials subject to price swings or reduced availability. Although the time of disruption cannot be predicted, recognition that a project includes such materials allows alternate plans to manage the disruption—such as stockpile early, or have contingency plans for alternate materials.

Government forces (taxes, fees, regulation, and permissions) can raise costs

The impact (in time and cost) of government regulations on a project must be estimated. Permits, zoning, land use, and "access" fees are only partly specified by written regulation. A reasonable person can determine the probable impact of the regulations. However, the government is also political, so a reasonable interpretation may not be enough. A portion of the fees can also be arbitrary. Example: a politically influenced tax on the project, completely unrelated to any regulation or government service rendered. In predictability and project impact, these fees are similar to bribes paid to corrupt politicians. Additional time, money, and increased risk of further arbitrary demands are possible and could delay or prevent the completion of the project.

Any interaction with the government will take time and have a cost. If multiple successive approvals are required—first environmental approval, then zoning approval, then building approval—the time and money required could rapidly escalate out of control rendering the project unfeasible at the time and cost required.

Innovation can have extra costs too

If portions of the building, such as structural or mechanical systems, have never been built before in the project area, additional expertise, time, and money must be allowed to learn the system and learn the implications on the other parts of the building. Substantial redesign of other building components, which are necessary to accommodate the innovative portion, will have cost and time implications. If multiple innovative systems interact on one project, such as a new curtain wall system and a new structural system, both of which require regulatory approval, then significant impacts in management, technical expertise, time, and money must be anticipated.

Summary
A workable approach will probably succeed—with hard work

Approximating the quantity and availability of ingredients—and the magnitude of obstacles for a project—helps select a workable approach. These approximations are compared to the project's "required" ranges for products, costs, and time. The project approach, design, the ingredients are then refined with increasing precision until what is "required" is within the range of what is available—a workable approach.

Once the selected workable approach makes timely and cost effective availability of the project ingredients probable, then talented, motivated, and hard working project personnel can make project success highly likely.

1.4 Bias Affects All People and Projects

Manage prejudice, put experience to work

*"Nothing is easier than self-deceit. For what each man wishes,
that he also believes to be true."—Demosthenes*

*"Becoming more familiar with a subject does not significantly reduce people's
tendency to exaggerate how much they actually know about it."—Baruch Fishhoff*

"We are all ignorant, just on different subjects."—Mark Twain

Everyone Has One Nature, Motivation, and Direction

Everyone is biased

Bias is the influence of instincts, previous experience, and purpose on the execution of a task. All human beings are biased in some way.

On a business level, people are biased against hostile and unpredictable superiors who may withhold benefits or fire them. The same is true with suppliers and vendors who have not performed as promised—be they inferior goods, late deliveries, or changing prices. On a job site level, people may have a preference for a particular brand and model of tools because of superior productivity, less down time, and a comfort level produced by past use.

Bias can be viewed as good if someone is "experienced" or bad if someone is "prejudiced." Prejudice is experience that fails to recognize that your point of view may have been a little wrong—changed conditions now make it a lot more wrong. Prejudice also fails to recognize that although your viewpoint is right for your purpose, a different viewpoint may be equally right for a different purpose.

The person who claims to be unbiased has not identified or recognized his bias, and therefore cannot manage it. He is either inexperienced, uninformed, or an arrogant fool poised to make the next big mistake. Your task here is to identify and admit your bias, then manage it—use experience well and control the prejudice.

If you are a hammer, everything looks like a nail

Everyone sees their world through the lens of their previous experience and present purpose. This determines the point of view from which all observations are made. Achievement of the purpose is evaluated by incentives, personal satisfactions and dissatisfactions. A concrete cement finisher is judged by how many square feet is finished per day at an acceptable quality. A project manager/estimator is judged both by estimates that gain the contract, and completion of the project at a cost less than the estimate.

Incentives are hard quantifiable goals and rewards: production targets to be met, job retention or bonuses to be received. Satisfactions are the reasons you are doing the job to start with—you like to work with your hands, like to build things, like to be outside, like doing new things, or like the people you work with. Dissatisfactions are the things you complain about—meaningless paperwork, arbitrary changes, bosses who won't listen, or inadequate tools.

Incentives, satisfactions, and dissatisfactions are mixed together in the real world—production goals are met, you keep your job, you have pride in work well done, and the boss is off your back—all at the same time. To clearly recognize your bias, the incentives, satisfactions, and dissatisfactions must be evaluated one at a time. Incentives are how the purpose is defined, how success will be measured, and what you get if you succeed. Satisfactions include why you are doing the job, what you like about it, and what makes you proud. Dissatisfactions include what you want to minimize or avoid as much as possible. Once each is recognized, and mixed together, management becomes possible.

"Follow the money" or how people get paid (or profit), is often identified as the main motivator and influence on a person's point of view, but this is seldom true. People have one nature and one speed. "I do it because this is what I am," "I feel this is the right thing to do," "I have always done it this way, and it works"—all matters of personal pride and satisfaction—usually come before money. People act the way they want to act as long as they can make enough money to continue acting that way.

Managing the Bias

Recognizing your bias—to control it

Recognition of your bias is the first and largest step towards managing it. Questions such as:

> "What tasks take up most of your day?"

> "What gives you satisfaction with your job?"

> "How is your work evaluated?"

> "How are you rewarded and paid?"

help to understand your point of view.

These questions also help to understand that people spending their days on very different tasks, with different satisfactions and rewards, will have different points of view and bias that are valid for their purpose.

For example, if pouring and finishing concrete floor slabs requires and is evaluated for high production levels, the foreman will tend to be focused on rapid installation of the largest, easiest parts of the slab.

Missing electrical conduit that should be embedded in the slab will require costly rework, or boxing out portions of the slab—requiring uneconomic Comebacks. But his bias towards high production might make him actually believe that he is 95% complete; however, rework and comebacks make the job far less complete. A project manager who is motivated to finish not just the concrete, but also the entire job for less than his estimate will be very sensitive to the costly rework. He will manage his potential bias because he recognized it.

Managing the bias
Two heads are better than one

After you recognize your bias, the next step in managing the bias is to have another person, with a different bias, evaluate the same situation.

A common business example is the requirement for two signatures on a check. This simple act of two people thinking "is this payment right?" helps avoid incorrect payments and fraud.

The same idea is used if a foreman—biased to show lots of production—reports the labor hours expended, while an estimator or project manger—biased to show low costs—reports the amount of work executed. The agreement of these two that the concrete slab is acceptably complete can be further reinforced by the agreement of others—the plumber and electrician agree that all the required items are embedded in the slab and the floor-covering contractor accepts the slab.

Summary
Recognize and manage your bias, and put your experience to work

Recognizing your bias and putting measures in place to manage it are extremely important. A slight adjustment in attitude can increase communication and understanding, and can help avoid costly mistakes. Once the negative aspects of bias are controlled, the benefits of the positive aspect of bias—experience—can be put to work. Your talent, training, and experience, if controlled, can produce the judgments and intuition necessary to develop and execute workable approaches that will probably succeed.

1.5 What to Observe, How to Observe

Standard units of measure permit communication

"Talk of things, not ideas."—Justice Oliver Wendell Holmes

"A definition is not getting into his mind—not what he meant, but what those words would mean in the mouth of a normal speaker of English, using them in the circumstances which they were used."—Justice Oliver Wendell Holmes

What to Observe

Observations are "facts" that are relevant to the purpose of the project for the project participants. Single facts may be recognized by all but no collection of facts will be equally recognized by all. Which facts are collected should be determined by the purpose of the collector.

"Outsiders" will observe one way

Prior to the start of a project, "outside" observers of a vacant site might have entirely different purposes and views, for example:

The neighborhood children may see their favorite play area.

The neighborhood adults may see the vacant land as a park-like setting that is good for bird watching or dog walking.

A politician may see the future tax increases that will come if a building is built on vacant land.

An architect may see the artistic benefit that a building might make to the neighborhood.

All of these are relevant and real to the observer, but basically irrelevant to the builders of a building.

Project participants will observe another way

Prior to the start of a project, the parties building the building might have entirely different purposes and views, for example:

> The excavator will see grades, possible haul roads, and staging areas for trucks and machines.

> The utility contractor will see the existing water, sewer, gas, electrical and phone services, and consider the street crossings, temporary shoring, and excavation necessary to bring utilities to the site.

> The steel erector will see crane access and truck staging to determine a sequence of erection.

> The painting and floor-covering contractors will see areas to receive their materials, unloading and storage areas, the quality of the surfaces to receive their material, and provisions for heat and humidity control.

Use Standard Units of Measurement to Permit Communication

The first step in useful observation is to clearly define the purpose of the project—intended use, quality standards, acceptable costs, and time of construction. If the purpose is not clearly defined, what and how to observe cannot be determined.

Observations that are relevant to the purpose of the project, and that can be used equally well by all the participants, must first be sought. Single facts that have multiple uses permit communication. Concrete descriptions of the physical characteristics of a project, not its meaning or value, must first be obtained.

To get these single facts for communication, standard units of measurement must be used, as explained below.

Use a measurement device that is available and familiar to the parties

The more available and familiar the device, the more parties can use it, and the better the communication.

> *Good Examples:*
> Rulers and tape measures that are available at hardware stores and lumber yards—used by all since grade school

> Man-hours—clocks are available to all

> *Bad Examples:*
> Truck load, bucket, pail, shovelfull, crew day—the size of each is not standard, consistent, or known to all, particularly those not in the trade

Use standard units of measure

Standard units of measure communicate to all, including non-specialists, with no further explanation.

> *Good Examples:*
> Inches, feet, yards, meters, pounds, kilograms, gallons, cubic feet—all can be measured with standard measuring devices

> *Bad Examples:*
> Carton, skid, pallet, load, roll, and unit—all differ by product, industry, and change over time

Standard measured quantities can be used for multiple purposes

Many contractors can use the square footage of the building floor area: for example, the concrete flat work, floor covering, ceiling, and roofing contractors. If instead of square feet, they used cubic yards of concrete, rolls of carpet, cartons of ceiling tile, or squares of roofing, no communication would take place. The small effort needed to use standard units of measure, instead of the measures commonly used by the supply house, permits you to communicate and work with others.

What to Observe and in How Much Detail

Since single facts must be used by many parties for many purposes, only observations that have multiple uses are made. Similarly, only as much detail as will permit multiple uses should be observed. Observation of more facts or more detail than is needed produces clutter and confusion and is harmful.

Area is a good measure

Areas that will receive some operation or treatment are useful measures. Details of about 1 square foot, or at most 1/10 of a square foot, are commonly measured.

> *Good Examples (and their applications):*
> Area of the site—clearing, grading, landscaping, and paving
> Floor area—steel deck, concrete, floor covering, ceilings, roofing
> Wall area—masonry, curtain wall, drywall, plaster, painting, and decorating

> *Bad Examples:*
> Pipe surface area—no operation or treatment performed by area (pipe insulation and pipe painting are by lineal foot)
> Door area—doors are indivisible units and are counted, not measured, in area

Linear measures are common—length, width, height, thickness

Linear measures that will receive some operation or treatment are measured. Measurement for the purpose of communication and planning is usually in whole feet, no fractions. (Actual installation of each work item will have higher precision, but the shared figures for communication will not.)

Good Examples:
Lineal feet of electrical conduit, or mechanical pipe, pipe insulation, pipe painting—useful for different tasks on the same object
Height of building—Useful for scaffolding, hoisting, elevators, curtain wall masonry, painting
Length and width of site—Useful for sewer, water, electrical power, and fencing

Bad Examples:
Lineal feet of ceiling tile wall angle and saw-cut concrete control joint, and caulk joint—Useful to the installing trade only
Lineal feet of masonry mortar joint, or total length of slats in window blinds—Have no use to anyone

Weight

Weight is used extensively to design the building, then to check the engineering on select components. (Such as selecting anchorage devices for curtain wall, and elevator rail support.) Weight is also necessary for selection of equipment and methods for material handling, such as cranes, hoists, trucks, carts, and rigging devices. Otherwise there is no reason to measure weight. Units of tons, or hundreds of pounds, are used—with 10 pounds the smallest useful increment.

Good Example:
Weight of materials—for hoisting, shoring, and transport

Bad Example:
Weight of the completed building—has no purpose

Indivisible units

Only units and levels of detail that are recognized and have a purpose for multiple parties are used. Usually the unit is also a recognized manufactured unit.

Good Examples:
Doors—Doors are installed, painted, and may have security devices
Light fixtures—ceiling preparation and electrical work

Bad Examples:
Wire nut connectors, or flange bolts, are only useful to the installing trade

Who Measures What?

First: select boundaries of the observation for a purpose

If you are estimating the man-hours to lay a quantity of carpet, the time must include all tasks, delivery and unloading, installation, clean up and rubbish removal, and callbacks. The tendency is to focus on the installation only, but the entire effort is the relevant period. Use of man-hours in pay periods, cross-checked by evidence of completion, such as inspection reports, will help.

In another case, mechanical piping measurement must be broken down by category, all of the pipe used on the project is too large for anyone to grasp, and different types or locations of piping will be useful to different groups of people. For example, the piping can be identified by type (sanitary sewer, storm sewer, domestic water, natural gas, chilled water, and steam) or by location (location on the site and floor of the building). Both identifications or other identifications can be used, as long as the identification has use for multiple parties.

Establishing boundaries that define the beginning and end of a task, or a recognized area or system, will work. For example: start lighting rough in—lights are illuminated.

Second: Observation must be able to be checked and reproduced by another party.

If you state that an opening is 16'-3" wide, another person can measure it. If you say 100 man-hours were expended on the job, time cards signed by others can sometimes be checked.

Third: You can use verification from independent sources.

If the roofer says he is complete, and the manufacturer's roofing inspection performed and guarantee has been furnished, he probably is.

Summary

Observing single facts permit communication. Communication permits both essential coordination between trades, and can be used to control bias—so agreed facts can be produced and used throughout the project.

Observing single facts that are understood by many is the necessary first step to useful knowledge. Organization of the relevant facts will help determine meaning, value, and assist selection of courses of action. These will be discussed in chapter 1.7.

1.6 Time is Continuous and Has Costs and Impacts

The measure of time, the cost of time, lost opportunities, momentum

"The river stepped into is not the river in which we now stand."—Herakleitos

"A thing is only worth so much time."—Michael Dirda

Time is "free", but has "costs"

Time is always passing. It cannot be "requested" or stopped. It is not purchased like other resources, but it does have costs and impacts. Since it is "free" but has "costs," time is measured both directly and by its impact.

Standard time measurement units are recognized by all, but...

Time is measured directly using conventional standard units such as seconds, minutes, hours, days, weeks, months, years, decades, centuries, and millennia. Just like a ruler, this is an objective counting of time. These standard units of time measure are objective facts that are recognized by all, but they give no meaning or purpose to the time measured.

Conventional Time Measurement Periods—For a Purpose

Conventional time periods group the standard time measurement units for a purpose. Examples of conventional time measurement periods include the following:

Employee pay periods—daily, weekly, bimonthly, monthly. The length of pay periods is customary by country, time, and industry. Once established, these periods strongly affect how productivity is measured. Labor cost information by pay period will be used unless there is a reason (foresight and money) to measure labor another way. These pay periods have meaning to the employee, personnel managing the project, and accountants.

Accounting periods—weekly, monthly, quarterly, and annual accounting periods are established by custom, accounting regulation, corporate law, and tax law. The start and end of each period is fixed and will not change for any project. The accountant will know the costs by accounting period, and the project personnel will know work executed by time periods defined by the project tasks. Management effort is required to reconcile costs expended by accounting period and work executed by project time periods. If this reconciliation is not done, the accountant's report will tend to get more attention by the company owners, even though the report is not an accurate representation of the project.

Seasons—weather conditions change by season: extremely high heat, freezing temperatures, extremely dry conditions, heavy rains, and high winds are familiar to all who work outside (although not to many office personnel). The seasons will dictate the desirable and possible times to perform activities. Therefore, they become another system of measuring time—and are very meaningful to those doing the work.

Time periods that have meaning to multiple project participants should be sought

An accountant may choose a customary period, such as a financial quarter, and state, "This is the answer—I know I am right—I checked my work and the books balance." The field personnel who installed the work may state, "I was there—I know when we started and when we finished." They may both be right for their own purpose, but because common time periods were not used, communication does not occur.

The weekly time period is the longest time period that is common to both the accountant and the personnel doing the work. It is, therefore, the period that should be used by all, so that communication happens. The accountant should not try to communicate with quarter or year-end figures, nor the project personnel with seasonal or project task completion figures. Using the week will permit both to agree on single objective facts. Agreement on a collection of facts, discussed in the project schedule below, is then possible.

Relevant Time Periods Established by Project Participants

Drop dead dates

"Drop-dead" completion dates exist for projects that are definitely fixed in time. Projects to serve the Olympics, a political election, or part of a war are examples that have no use or value after a specific time. Most projects with drop-dead dates really mean, "We need it done by this date as long as you won't charge me any more." These often cease to be drop-dead dates once costs are known.

Project funding dates

Project funding will have both time for the funding review process to start, and time to complete the funding process once started. Both governments and companies will have fiscal years (usually different than calendar years), and authorize a fixed expenditure at the beginning of that year. Financial lending institutions will adjust lending policies one to four times per year, and loan committees will approve specific loan applications every week, two weeks, or month.

Project schedule dates

A project schedule is a statement of the intended sequence and duration of activities to complete a project, at an acceptable time and cost. The objective time periods that each project participant's use must be reconciled into project milestones. Milestones describe events that have meaning to all, but do not exactly match any participant's conventional time periods. Examples of milestones are: project start, structure complete, weather enclosure complete, heating and cooling complete and producing a climate controlled environment, project complete. This requires an effort to prorate fractions of weeks to match the exact dates of the milestones.

The Cost and Value of Time

The "cost in money" directly caused by time

Time causes costs—personnel and equipment cost money every second they are assigned to a project. The personnel could be assigned to another project or terminated, and the equipment could be assigned to another project or sold.

The owner of the project will also incur costs continually, both on the cost of his personnel involved with the project, and on the continual interest cost on his construction loan. Cost will also occur because of the "lost opportunity" cost of not receiving the income and benefits of the completed project.

Lost opportunities caused by time (not to decide is to decide)

Each sequence of activities, such as designing, obtaining required manufactured products, and constructing a building takes a minimum amount of time. If selection of an approach is started sufficiently early, all options are possible and can be considered. Passage of time will progressively eliminate possible options. For example, an innovative new custom design is possible with unlimited time, but as available time is progressively reduced, a custom but uninnovative design, or reuse of a previously completed design, may become the only available options, by default. And the more rushed options may be both less desirable and more expensive.

Increasing momentum increases productivity

Every activity has an established pace and feel. For construction projects, the fastest pace that the cure times of materials permit, and that can be maintained without causing a loss of productivity, is usually the most desirable pace. The reason this is true is that the personalities attracted to construction want to move, to get things done. They want to see a lot of material in place fast. Give them this satisfaction and they will be more content and have fewer problems and expressed dissatisfactions, which increases productivity.

High productivity expectations increase momentum

High productivity demands and expectations increase productivity. The saying "If you want something done fast, give it to a busy person" illustrates that once productivity is high, it tends to stay high.

Attention of project participants focuses on fast moving projects. If there is no time to wait and see what others do, they act—not react. Full attention is devoted to the job. A few repetitions of "Too late. It's poured" and "Get moving or we will bury you" focuses the mind on rapid execution of essential tasks. Speed also permits focus on only the important and relevant, avoiding entirely the trivial and unimportant. Petty nonessential grievances and disputes that would have occurred if there was more time than necessary to complete the task never materialize. Communication is improved, the number of items requiring consideration reduced, and disagreements minimized.

Momentum increases productivity, reduces cost, and improves communication. (And you can have a good time doing it.)

Summary

Time should be measured with standard units and in standard periods that permit communication among project participants. Measuring the value and cost of time—cost of assigned personnel and equipment, lost opportunities caused by passing time, and productivity increasing momentum—can all benefit the project. Management of time can only bring these benefits if recognized early and measuring is started when planning the project.

1.7 Organization of Observations Requires Organizational Structure

Change facts into information, information into knowledge

"So out of the ground the Lord God formed every animal of the field and every bird of the air, and brought them to the man to see what he would call them: and whatever the man called every living creature, that was its name."—Genesis

"A horse! A horse! A kingdom for a horse!"—King Richard the III

(In 1591 King Richard the III of England was in battle. A nail in his horse's shoe came out. He lost the horseshoe, the horse, the battle, his kingdom, and his life.)

Once useable observations produce single objective facts, organization helps a reasonable person change the observations (facts) into information (knowledge) to make informed decisions.

Number of observations can get unmanageable

The number of observations needed and made for all purposes on a project vastly exceeds the capacity of any person's memory. For example, ordering wall framing lumber requires the following steps:

1. Estimate the required quantity.
2. Obtain a price from the supply house.
3. Make a notation of quoted price.
4. Determine precise quantity of each size and material to be ordered.
5. Determine the portion of the entire order that can be stored and used at the job site without double handling.
6. Place the order.
7. Make notation of order placed and balance of order to be placed.
8. Place balance of the order.
9. Receive order and place it in required location
10. Determine that received count matches ordered count.
11. Determine if any material is defective.

12. Notify supply house of defects.
13. Notate defective materials on shipping ticket.
14. Receive replacements for defective material.
15. Determine count is correct
16. Determine if all material is correct.
17. Receive invoice for material.
18. Match invoice with delivery ticket for first shipment and for the second shipment of re-
    placement materials.
19. Pay invoice.
20. Record invoice in accounting system.

Twenty steps are required to obtain the wall framing material. If any step is missed, performance will suffer (e.g. payment for material never received, installation of defective material, avoidable double handling of material, late payment to the supply house, loss of job cost control). And ordering wall framing material is just part of framing the walls. And walls are just one part of all framing, and framing is just one part of the building. The number of required observations on a small building project completed in 3 months might be 5,000. Larger projects can easily have hundreds of thousands of observations.

If 100,000 or even 5,000 material orders, delivery tickets, and invoices are dumped on a person's desk with the instructions "Make sense of this and get it right; it is very important" the average person will give up. The unusually hard working would struggle and achieve, at best, second-rate results. With organizational structure, such failures can be avoided.

Establishing the Purposes for an Organizational Structure

An organizational structure, filters, sorts, and sets in order observations for a purpose.
Establishing the purpose must come first:

Possible purposes for your organizational structure

Build an excellent product—common to all projects

Make a profit—almost always a stated purpose, but frequently not accompanied by the necessary action

Get paid and pay your bills on time—common to all successful projects

Manage a vast number of tasks with many participants—a need common to all projects, but found on few

Documentation for project owner accounting—accounting for construction cost by owner requirements, such as by department, by financial year, or by different depreciation periods for shell, core, and tenant development

Documentation for financing—if the project is financed by a construction loan, accounting and documentation will have to meet the lender's requirements

Satisfy government regulation—do it well enough to avoid government interference, a purpose by default

Process improvement—documentation of ongoing activities so quality can be improved or costs reduced for future projects—exists, but it's rare

Selecting your purposes—many sound nice, but only a few are achievable

Clear, complete, and realistic purposes of the project are required before a good organizational system can be selected. If the purpose is not selected before the start of the project, catch up later is not possible. Many of the required observations will not have been made. And the time to make them has passed. If purposes are too ambitious—demands exceeding the capabilities or time available for execution—the system will be too cumbersome for effective use and multiple failures will occur.

Organizational System Characteristics That Work

Organizations systems that will work (and be used) have these characteristics:

The system structure is immediately apparent without explanation.

Data entry personnel with little training can enter observations successfully.

Observations recorded in the system can be verified.

The system purpose will tend to be realized due to the structure of the system, even if the purpose is not immediately apparent.

Many people can use an observation for many different purposes.

Observations can be reordered for multiple purposes, without re-entry of data.

Filter out "useless" characteristics

Useful observations must have the following characteristics:

They have a purpose for more than one party.

They are in standard units of measurement.

All observations that do not have these characteristics are useless, and must be discarded before sorting and setting in order.

"Sort and set in order" characteristics

Three sortings of observation are usually the limit of the patience of most people. It is also the limit of what is necessary to get the result. (For example, it is usually true that one can locate a person anywhere in the country with three phone calls.)

Two levels of organization are useful for construction projects

Sort by the objective facts of the observation—alphabetically by name, number such as street address or age, or time order of occurrence. Phone books, dictionaries, employee listings, and job site activity logs are examples. The purpose is only to record information for easy recall. No assistance in transforming this information into knowledge is provided by this organizational structure.

An employee list, for example, with name, trade, job assignment, and dates of employment could be sorted by name and date to answer the question, "did this guy work for us two years ago," or could be sorted by date, job assignment, and trade to answer the question, "How many electricians did we have on that job last July?" This is useful information that is obtained only by sorting, without further data entry. It cannot answer the questions, "Was this a good employee?" or "Was the staffing of that job about right?" But it does answer some of the questions that must be answered.

A system that is structured for, and assists, a defined purpose. The structure of these "good" systems resemble the purpose they serve—making use obvious and achievement of the intended result probable.

An example in the construction industry is the Construction Specification Institute system for organizing projects. This system uses a numeric system (1–16) to organize the project by trade and by the usual sequence of installation. The purpose is to build a project—make a detailed checklist of all required tasks, order these tasks, and define their relation to other tasks. The Construction Specification Institute system headings are as follows (There are hundreds of more detailed sub headings.):

> Division 1 General Requirements (e.g. administration, contracts, and insurance)
> Division 2 Site Construction (e.g. earthwork, drainage)
> Division 3 Concrete
> Division 4 Masonry
> Division 5 Metals (e.g. structural steel, ornamental railings)
> Division 6 Wood and Plastics (e.g. wood framing of the structure, wood cabinets)
> Division 7 Thermal and Moisture Protection (e.g. roofing and waterproofing)
> Division 8 Doors and Windows
> Division 9 Finishes (e.g. walls, ceilings, flooring, painting)
> Division 10 Specialties (e.g. lockers, mailboxes, flagpoles)
> Division 11 Equipment (e.g. kitchen, church, prison, appliances and fixtures)
> Division 12 Furnishings (e.g. furniture, artwork, theater seating)
> Division 13 Special Construction (e.g. swimming pools, ice rinks, dog kennels)
> Division 14 Conveying Systems (e.g. elevators, escalators)
> Division 15 Mechanical (e.g. heating, plumbing, fire sprinklers)
> Division 16 Electrical

With the exception of the mechanical and electrical trades, who work continuously throughout the project, this is a listing in order of installation. The order of the organization system is the same as the order of construction. This makes "building it in heads before actually building it" or "building it on paper" easier and therefore more likely to succeed. In other words, the organizational structure encourages and helps good planning.

(This 16-section format, that has proved workable for some 40 years, has been revised into a 50-section format. Some of the changes recognize new project work areas, such as telecommunication, which was formerly installed only by the phone company monopoly. Much of the useful structure was retained, but some was lost. For example, earthwork was moved from division 2 to 31—thus moving it out of the order of installation making the format less helpful for "building it in your head and on paper." Also, 50 sections is too large a number for most people to grasp and remember.)

Organizational Structures That Are Not Useful to the Project

Organization by arbitrarily defined structure may be imposed by the owner of the project, or by the construction company itself. Organization by geographic region, department, or customer account, for example, lacks clarity. The Midwest region in the United States has been variously defined as a half dozen states surrounding the Great Lakes, all states between the Appalachian and Rocky Mountains, and all states west of the Appalachian Mountains plus Japan. Department definition is not standard across companies, nor is the responsibility and authority. Customer account can mean anything from a certain product or project type for the customer, to anything that can evolve out of the customer relationship.

These organizational structures are unrelated or even contrary to the purpose of the project, but they can be imposed very forcefully. If employee compensation, or continued employment, depends on achieving profitability goals for region, department, or customers, quality and timely completion of an individual project will be secondary and poor results may follow.

Summary

These organizational principles can be applied on all project sizes. They work for back of the envelope, limited check lists, and sophisticated computer systems. The principles for all systems remain the same:

- Define the purpose of the project
- Observe and establish objective facts
- Filter the facts
- Sort and set the facts in order in an organizational system that serves the project purpose

The purpose of this organizational structure is to change data (facts) into information (knowledge) so that communication and informed decision-making are possible, as is explained in the following chapters.

Part II: Purpose Definition, Personnel Organization, Management Tools
Know What You Are Supposed to Do and How You Will Do It

Introduction

What is the purpose of your project? This simple and essential question is frequently answered late, partially, or not at all, which guarantees failure. If you do not know what you want, how will you know if you get it? If you cannot answer this question then stop. You do not have a project.

The definition of the project purpose must include three parts: (1) product (including grade of material and essential features), (2) cost, and (3) time (of start, execution, and completion). All three parts are interactive and must be determined at the same time. These three parts must be defined before you can determine feasibility and start the project, and they must be used throughout the execution of the project to make sure you are achieving this purpose. Miss one of the three and failure is certain. Properly define all three and success is possible and (with hard work) probable.

The project personnel must then be organized to achieve this defined purpose. It starts with recognizing the nature of people. And then uses a very flat (few management layers) organizational structure that helps distribute knowledge to all project personnel. Then these personnel are made responsible for self control—they know what they're supposed to do, what they're doing right now, if they're achieving the required result, and how to make the necessary corrections.

Lastly there are tools—project management, estimating, and scheduling—that can assist these efforts. But these are only effective with a defined purpose and effectively organized personnel. A fancy software package is not a magic bullet. Scheduling programs do not keep projects on schedule, people do. These are tools—essential, effective, and powerful—but tools that can only produce results by right-thinking, properly organized, project personnel.

A defined purpose, effective personnel organization, and use of management tools by these personnel are the framework for project success.

2.1 Define a Workable Purpose

Project success can and should be normal

"You have got to be careful if you do not know where you are going cause you might not get there."—Yogi Berra

Achieving excellent and predictable performance, project success, must start with defining a workable purpose. This must be followed by establishing a workable approach that makes achieving this purpose highly probable. Failure to define the purpose *before* the start of the project usually ensures failure to achieve the purpose.

Defining a Workable Purpose Includes the Use of the Project and the Reason for the Project

Getting it right the first time means knowing what "it" is. To begin a project, one must know the purpose—consisting of use to be served and the reason for the project. The definition of intended use and reason, including grade of materials, time, and likely cost, must be set to determine if the project is feasible. Once a feasible purpose is defined, workable approaches can be selected to achieve this purpose, and success will be possible. Hoping to get lucky later is not a plan. Starting a project with the thoughts "we can work that out later" or "we just need to get some ideas and input" makes partial or complete failure probable.

Use of the completed project—why you are building

State the project's intended use.

Examples:
- Apartment building
- Church
- Manufacturing facility
- Retail store
- Vacation home
- Interstate highway
- Municipal sewage treatment plant

Specify few uses—one is best

Some projects legitimately have multiple uses such as an office warehouse or a hi-rise facility combining retail, office, and residential space. Most mixed-use facilities, however, do *not* have a legitimate use. Instead they represent cloudy and confused thinking that must be corrected before the project proceeds. Some examples include: an owner's manufacturing facility that will also house his antique car collection, or a church that wishes to add rental retail facilities in a portion of the building to make income to "help out with the expenses." A good project should serve only the essential and necessary use.

A mixed-use facility will cost more and take more time to build than either of the single uses. This is true, first, because each use will have unique site development considerations such as parking, truck access, site lighting, storm drainage, structural systems related to clear spans and floor loading capacities, floor to floor heights, heating, ventilation, air conditioning, and electrical systems. Second, it is usually true that the more complicated and expensive requirement of one use gets imposed to some degree on the other uses. Further, there are usually additional design considerations, such as firewalls that separate the two uses. All these will increase the cost of a mixed-use project.

Contributing to the design problems of a mixed-use project is the fact that different companies and different personnel usually specialize in each type of project. For example, one type of company and set of personnel would perform road construction, and a different set would perform interior construction of hi-rise residential units. Neither is adequately suited to do the others' work. For more similar uses, such as an office warehouse, similar differences in firm and personnel capabilities exist. A single company will typically try to perform both, but one or more of the tasks will be performed at a less than optimal level.

If multiple uses are essential in a project, then proceed knowing that additional time, cost, and management effort will be needed. If multiple uses for the project are not essential, or you are not willing to pay the cost and time premium necessary, make the hard decision—before starting—and delete the unnecessary part of a project.

What Is the Project Reason—Why You Are Building It?

The reason for the project is defined by the most important characteristics sought—expressed in both qualitative and quantitative terms, for grade of material, cost, and time.

For example:

- Apartments
  Apartments built for investment, to achieve a 7% return on investment for market rate housing in a specified area. The grade of materials will be the lowest acceptable for the market area, and a minimal time of construction to minimize construction financing costs is required.

- Manufacturing facility
  This manufacturing facility requires precision and consistency of the manufacturing processes, and will require rapid manufacturing line change—overs, so grade of materials and reliability of mechanical systems cannot be compromised. Construction cost is not critical, and time may or may not be critical, depending on the prevailing market demand for the product to be manufactured.

- Hotel interior construction
A "new" image is required every three years, so the selected finishes and furnishings cannot be compromised. Construction in the slow season with minimum down time is required to minimize revenue loss. Cost is of medium importance, and short-term image means long-term material durability is of no concern.

- Government projects
Allocating of political favors to certain persons or groups can be a primary purpose, so a high cost is desired (more favors to pass out). Grade of materials and functional use may be of little concern. Time of construction is only important to produce a big show around election time.

Truthful statements are critical

Truthful statement of some reason(s): "the highest cost is best," "grade of materials doesn't matter," and "time of completion isn't important" are awkward and usually must be disguised for public consumption. But truthful internal statements must be made to define the reason for the project. Such statements can best be made by the highest-ranking decision maker(s), even if guided by subordinates, but they must be made. Subordinates telling the boss what he wants to hear, then telling him the bad news later avoids defining the reason, and will fail.

Be definite only when you mean it

State definitely only the essentials with both qualitative and precise quantitative definitions. For the qualities that are not essential, state a range or qualitative description only. The fewer definite statements made, the more achievable the project. Three definite statements are usually the limit for achievable projects.

State requirements only if necessary for your purpose. Requiring the highest grade of materials, at an impossibly low price, in an impossibly short time, because "if we start high, we can always go down from there" is a failure to decide. A demanding, unnecessary requirement will compete with necessary requirements, and the necessary requirements may lose.

Set your priorities

After establishing all of the essentials of the project, and listing all of the characteristics that need to be achieved, you must rank each in the order of importance. You cannot have it all and everything is not equally important. Set your priorities now. Your failure to set priorities at the start of the project will let somebody else decide as the project unfolds, and your goals may not be achieved!

This is true first because the project will proceed without turning back from the starting requirements. To make a mid-project correction, and start over from a clean slate, requires a person who is willing to say that they were completely wrong at the beginning. The need for such people always exceeds the supply. Second, once the project is underway, time constraints have been established and the clock is running. There is usually not time to completely start over. Finally, the project participants can only partially change their point of view of the project purpose, reason, and approach. They will have vested interests, partial work done they wish to salvage, and attitudes that cannot be changed easily or completely. Midcourse use and reason correction is a patch and repair operation that cannot achieve excellent results.

A forceful personality with better communication skills, a more competent company, or someone with a quicker response will be heard first and better. Decisions will be made randomly and you will begin giving up on the wrong things. This will produce, at best, mediocre results and failure to achieve some or all of your goals.

Summary

Define the project purpose—consisting of the use and reason, and specifying grade of material, cost, and time—before starting. Make definite requirements only when you mean it and can pay for them, otherwise provide a range or qualitative description. Set priorities and rank requirements in order of importance. Do not proceed with the project until the use and reasons are established and ranked. Ranking helps ensure that all-important points are considered.

Mid-project correction of use and reason cannot produce excellent results. A clear definition of purpose before the start of a project makes determination of a workable approach and project success possible.

2.2 Determine a Workable Approach

An intuitive understanding, a framework for facts, count everything, observe
the limits, implications and impacts, and then refine the approach

*"Human felicity is produced not so much by great pieces of good fortune that
seldom happen, as by little advantages that occur ever day."—Benjamin Franklin*

*"When you first do a thing it is hard and messy. Others
following can make it look easy."—Pablo Picasso*

An intuitive understanding—then count and measure

Determining a workable approach builds the project in your head and on paper, before touching a shovel. A workable purpose must precede a workable approach, or you will have no way of knowing if your approach will achieve this purpose. If you do not know where you are going, you cannot know how to get there, or that you have arrived. Although this is obvious common sense, it is frequently omitted, and the project partially or completely fails.

Determining a workable approach consists of understanding the project, counting all the building blocks, then organizing the building blocks into relationships and sequences to achieve your purpose. Knowledge gives power, and knowledge requires both intuition and experience—and facts.

Obtaining, organizing, and analyzing facts takes the most time and effort. The process is 5% inspiration (fun, intuitive understanding of what the project might be) and 95% perspiration (work, counting, checking availability). Without intuitive understanding, you won't know what to count. Without counting the facts, problems and opportunities for improvement and innovation cannot be known, and the results cannot be checked.

First a framework for facts—use racks for storage and organization of information

An organizational structure for information gathered must be set at the very start of the project. It will have these characteristics:

1. It identifies all required work items.
2. It organizes a place for all facts.

3. It avoids your personal point of view, and itemizes all work items and facts with equal consideration, weight, and detail.

Such a framework will be used for all projects, regardless of the size, scope, or nature. At the start of the project, all racks will be empty. The racks stay the same for the entire project, and get fleshed out with additional information.

Without such an organizational system at the start of the project, important facts and observations will be temporarily or permanently misplaced. Constant rework and reorganization of facts that are not properly stored exceeds the attention span of almost all project participants. People will give up and shoot from the hip.

One such system that fulfills these requirements is the CSI (Construction Specification Institute) system. This system uses an organizational structure that is in the approximate order of normal construction of a project. This helps building the project in your head and on paper. It is the most common organizational system now in use. Other systems, such as the Army Corps of Engineers system, also work.

You should not attempt to design your own organizational system. It is a far more difficult task than it appears, and will require the participation of many people, with many different points of view. Also, you will tend to make an organizational system from your point of view, emphasizing what you know best and are most accustomed to, and this is usually very different from the requirements of a whole project.

One example of this bias occurs when a carpentry contractor attempts to grow into a general contractor. Their usual organizational system for approaching a project is very heavy on the carpentry items, and may miss entire portions of the other 85% of the project. Many such contractors have gone out of business because of these missed costs.

Having an organizational system that counts everything in place at the beginning of the project is critical to all following steps. Even the smallest item must be identified, so that its implications are not overlooked. For example, window blinds can increase or decrease the solar heat gain into or heat loss out of a building. These heat gains and losses affect the heating, ventilation, and air-conditioning system size, which can in turn, affect the size of the electrical service. Although blinds may be only a fraction of a percent of the project value and seem trivial, "leave it to the decorator later," they cannot be overlooked without consequence. All projects have many similar examples.

Use the Intuition and Organized Facts to Design a Workable Approach

Designing a workable approach is a circular three-step process.

1. Developing a qualitative, intuitive understanding of the nature of the project, and its building blocks.
2. Counting the building blocks, and obtaining the facts about the building blocks (purchasing methods, engineering and fabrication, distribution and shipping, and costs).
3. Determining the implications and impact of this information on your understanding of the nature of the project.
4. Go back to step one and repeat the three steps above until done.

This circular process is repeated with increasing information, understanding, and precision. In the real world, determining a workable approach is neither starting with a blank slate, and determining everything from scratch, nor is it slight modifications of: "what we did last time." An approximate project type that closely resembles the present project is selected from a file of past efforts—recognizing it will change—and this approximation is probably partially or maybe even completely wrong. The building blocks of the selected project are listed and counted, and the possible project type is confirmed, modified, or rejected. Continuing this circular process eventually develops a workable approach to a new project.

What to Count

All of the work items listed in the rack framework must be counted, as well as the building blocks that make up the work items. Full itemization that is understood and usable by all is needed. So, this is a mechanical counting, but in a manner that communicates effectively. The following guidelines may be helpful:

1. Count physical things and systems of things. For example, cubic yards of concrete, square feet of ceiling tile, or lineal feet of piping in sanitary waste risers, using standard units of measure.
2. Show relevance of all project participants. "What about me? Where's my stuff?" must be answered. The work of all project participants of even very small consequence must be identified and counted. Listing of all categories in the CSI organizational system will identify most of these people, but you should also check by people, not just the organizational structure. Do not forget about your own people.
3. If a contract is awarded or a purchase order is issued to a vendor, count their stuff. If a dedicated work group is working on an item, count their stuff.
4. If an outside party, owner, architect, financial institution, or a government agency is identified as important for the project, count their stuff. If parties do part of a task in succession, count each parties' tasks.
5. Break into bite size pieces. Long tasks must be able to be subdivided into tasks with maximum two-week onsite work duration. Tasks must be able to be broken down into parts of the project (floors) and systems (sanitary waste, phone and data cabling). The task subdivision must be able to be organized into milestones that are un-missable and indisputable. For example, weather enclosure of a building, permanent electrical power on, heated and air-conditioned air is being delivered—not "we are two thirds complete."
6. Analyze things not ideas. Count objects that can be seen and touched. Use standard units of measure, so communication is possible.

Building blocks to be counted, measured, and checked

The common building blocks that are widely recognized and used are listed below.

People

The capacity, skill, and experience to perform a task are critical to selecting good people. But, character, disposition, and tendencies of people must also be recognized. Although it is frequently stated: "We can always add more people." This is not always true. Every employer states that getting good help is a large problem. Good help is always in short supply.

Capital—Money

Capital is the owner's and contractor's available money to perform a project. The owner's capital is the long-term ability to pay for the work as it is completed, and finally pay the entire amount. The contractor's capital is the money required between the owner's payments.

Material

Materials are generic stock products not made to order for the job. Materials typically have no serial numbers, and no project specific product data. Materials are abundant at one price, location, and time, and scarce at others. This should be figured in.

Equipment

Equipment is a product made to order for each job, frequently has serial numbers, and has job specific technical data. Equipment made to order requires a sequence of ordering, engineering, fabrication, and shipment. Each step takes time and costs money and should be accounted for.

Companies—Subcontractors and Suppliers

A company consists of an assembled work force with shared knowledge, tools and equipment, and capital. If a company has patents on a process, or has specialized high value equipment that is paid for and still serviceable, an advantage exists. For the vast majority of companies, this advantage does not exist. The people are the most important ingredient, and they are usually only one or two deep. So account for them in your framework.

Information

When building products were simpler, everything necessary was known about them from past use, and information was not considered a building block. Now, with proprietary products containing sophisticated systems, chemicals, and computer-controlled mechanical electrical components, specific information for each product for each project is required. Information always has a cost, and is always in short supply. Even parties who want to assist you may not fully know about their products or services. Competitors will attempt to prevent you from gaining the necessary information. Future outcomes cannot be completely known. Facts, information, and knowledge are always in short supply.

Identify constraints, obstacles

Constraints include changing economic conditions that may affect prices of material, or the availability of capital. Politicians may restrict or block all or parts of a project. Non-rational decision-making by the owner, designer, and/or government agencies can lead to obstacles. And force majeure—such as adverse weather conditions or strikes that affect the ability to secure materials and equipment, or to work at the job site—and plant shutdowns or discontinuation of required products can be constraints. Innovative new products or systems will take additional time and effort, and may have unforeseen implications on other parts of the project or be impossible to use.

The possibility of all these constraints exists at all times. But a general notion of possibilities doesn't permit action. The specific probability of the building blocks must be determined—using information obtained for this project. If a constraint is probable, concrete steps must be taken to ensure the constraint can be managed, or alternate fallback positions must be included in your project approach.

Observe the Implications and Impacts

Production Limits

Job site density

Job site material and personnel density affect the speed materials can move from the point of entry to the point of installation. As the job site becomes obstructed, either with material or a larger number of workers, productivity can decline. There is a point where productivity nearly stops, and reorganization of material, or moving material off site, must be done before production can continue.

A 5000 sf medical office building example and some guidelines:

A 50' x 100' one-story, medical office is to be constructed 15' off one side of a 200' x 300' site.

Machine operation circle of required area

A group of machines working together will require an unobstructed work area, a circle, to achieve maximum safe productivity. The circle for a truck delivering 50' roof joists, and a crane setting the joists is:

Crane work circle with boom extended	70 feet
8-foot wide truck on a 12-foot wide haul road	12 feet
50-foot joist	50 feet
Total circle of machine operation	132 feet
Given the building and set back:	
Building	50 feet
Building set back	15 feet
Total circle of machine operation, building, set back	197 feet

Since the site is only 200 feet wide, the 197 feet listed above means only one group of these machines can operate on this side of the site. Two sets of machines would be able to operate at one time if both could and would remain in one position. In this example, if the water and sewer were being installed in the front, and the joists were being set from the side, two groups of machines would be possible. More groups are not possible without severe reductions in productivity, and possibly safety.

Drawing circles of machine operation, sized to the equipment being used, on a site plan can determine the maximum number of machine groups possible.

Hand construction circle of worker operations—400-800 sf (square feet) per man

Materials such as framing, piping, conduit, and ceiling grid have common maximum hand installed lengths of 8–12'. The circle of workers' operations is:

Average reach of one arm	3 feet
Average material length	10 feet
Transportation space-walkway	3 feet
Total circle of worker operations	16 feet

Most rooms are squares not circles, so the 16-foot circle would fit in a 16 x 16 foot room, which has an area of 256 square feet.

Maximum workers of this type in a 5,000 sf building

Total building area	5,000 sf
Permanent obstructions—walls, cabinets, plumbing fixtures	
15 % of total building	-750 sf
Stored materials, tools and equipment	
20% of total building	-1,000 sf
Unobstructed area of total building	3,250 sf

With 256 sf of unobstructed work area required per man, about 12 men could work at once. This means about one man per 400 sf of total building area (both obstructed and unobstructed) for perfect conditions. Obstructions, stored material, and coordination will always be less than perfect, so planning areas might be double—about 800 sf of total building area per man.

Area for materials requiring cure time—800-1,600 sf per man

Materials requiring cure time such as concrete floors, floor tile, and carpet have installations rates of 400–800 sf per man per day. The cure times of the materials, concrete or adhesives require the entire work areas to be available for the entire day. Areas required are therefore double the circle of worker operations calculated above.

Long Narrow Operations

Long narrow operations such as installation of pipelines or high voltage electrical lines require a fixed group of machines and men, but encounter conditions producing variable production rates. If a crew produces rapidly and catches up to the next crew, they have nothing else to do and can only wait, with no production. To maintain maximum production 2–5 days of buffer should be allowed between crews or the next natural break or termination point. In this case, the maximum site density is determined using a length 2–5 times the daily production.

Time Limits

Limits to hours worked in a week

For continuous trade production requiring skill and judgment, 40 hours is a sustainable workweek achieving both full productivity, and minimal injuries. A 50-hour workweek has productivity declines after the first week, accelerating until the end of week 6. At week 6 the productivity of the 50-hour week is the same as a 40-hour week, and the 10 hours of overtime is wasted. At 60 hours, productivity declines start the first week. Incorrect work, requiring removal and rework, and personal injuries accelerate, making the 60-hour week less productive than the 40-hour week within 2 weeks.

Cure time of materials

Many installed materials involve a chemical reaction that has a fixed cure time. For example, concrete will set in several hours to 1/2 day, but will not be fully cured to receive adhesive type materials or other coatings for 28 days. Painting will require a minimum of 12-hour cure time between coats. Selection of specialized products, such as high early strength cement, can accelerate these times, but not eliminate them. So these times must be accounted for.

Moisture reduction time

Many materials have a higher presence of moisture at the time of installation than is acceptable for successive operations. For example, earthwork can be entirely submerged during portions of the earthwork operation, but must be dry before foundation installation. Concrete is a product that is made with water, but following application of coatings, paints, or installation of moisture sensitive products such as wood doors, millwork, and ceiling tile, the partially finished product requires a far lower presence of moisture for acceptable installation and long-term serviceability.

Removal of some of this moisture will take place naturally when exposed to the prevailing weather, but requires and can be accelerated by the use of mechanical heating and cooling. Minimum moisture extraction times will be at least weeks and probably months. Moisture removal time can be accelerated, at a cost, but cannot be eliminated.

Crew size by task requirements or maximum efficiency

The smallest crew size suitable for a task will tend to achieve optimal productivity. Weight, length, and height of specialized pieces of equipment or operations, where men must be stationed at multiple points, can dictate minimum crew sizes. In the absence of these specialized requirements, a crew size of 5 has frequently been found to be the largest practical productive crew size. This permits an individual capable of understanding and performing the task with limited supervision to oversee a few competent individuals, and possibly one or two of less than desired competence, or trainees.

Sequence of operations—work with the normal and customary or pay a premium

There are normal required sequences of operation. When designing a workable approach, you must decide on a material before ordering it, obtain the technical information to ensure suitability, order it before it will be fabricated, and have it fabricated before it will be shipped. On the job site, you must dig the hole before you can build the structure, or before you can install the roof. Alteration of the normal sequences is possible in only some cases, and alteration will always require more management time.

Time to obtain material and train personnel

The time to obtain the materials and equipment must be specifically determined for each building block for this project. The time for training of employees must be realistically assessed.

Training for some very limited specific tasks that require no judgment or response to changing conditions can be performed within two weeks—fast food workers, for example. Training a competent individual in one additional specific skill can also be done in hours, days, or at most two weeks. The training time for a trade apprenticeship is 4 years. College education is 4 years. Some professional education requires 2–4 years after a 4-year college education. And at the conclusion of these educations students are only beginning to learn and are not yet experienced and not fully capable of working on their own.

With these time constraints, it is unreasonable to anticipate significant retraining of personnel for any specific project with the expectation of producing competent, skilled personnel, capable of reacting with judgment to changing conditions. For a specific project you must take people as you find them, and plan accordingly.

A Cycle of Refinement to Achieve a Workable Approach

Selecting a possible project approach, counting (listing) all the building blocks, and evaluating results within a logical sequence of operation is repeated with increasing precision using our three-step process. When doing this process, one should first rule out any unacceptable options, and do not attempt to work top down. Going for the best and working down until an acceptable approach is found, sounds easy, but it is easy to talk yourself into a totally unacceptable option.

A useful decision-making aid is calculating break even between two decisions. If two options are being evaluated, determine when the options have equal cost. For example, if use of a machine costing $500 per hour or hand labor costing $100 per hour is being considered, the break even point is when the machine can produce 5 times as much per hour as the hand labor. If two options are close, using the more customary, normal, and comfortable will tend to produce the better results. If the breakeven calculation is tremendously lopsided, the right decision is also suggested.

The cycle of selecting a possible approach, counting and evaluating can stop when:

1. All building blocks are within an achievable range of grade of material, time, and cost.
2. The building blocks can be arranged in a sequence that is achievable.
3. You have control of every critical project constraint, or have planned for an alternate fallback position.

You should stop when you have considered all available information

Once you have achieved a workable approach, the process can continue to be repeated with increasing precision, and will provide some benefit to the completed project. However, once no further information is available, no significant further improvement can be made. Stop talking and build it.

Summary

Determining a workable approach must be preceded by a workable purpose. If you do not know where you are going, you cannot figure out how to get there. An organizational system—storage racks for facts—must also be in place to handle the large quantity of facts the project will require, without exceeding the participants' tolerance for detail.

The workable approach is then determined by intuitively understanding the project and selecting a possible approach, counting the building blocks, determining the impact of this information, and then repeating the process until a workable approach is reached. All work items, even small items must be identified, counted, and specific determinations of cost, time, and effort necessary to secure materials must be made. Job site constraints of density, work hours, cure time, and moisture control as well as constraints by politicians, major natural disasters, material, equipment, and labor availability must be identified and be determined to be within achievable limits. With a workable approach, project success is possible. With hard work by competent people, success is then probable.

2.3 The Nature of People

The nature of people must be included in project planning

"One must talk about everything according to its nature, how it comes to be and how it grows. Men have talked about the world without paying attention to the world or their minds, as if they were asleep or absent minded."—Herakleitos

"If you don't like my peaches, don't shake my tree."—Moms (Jackie) Mabley

Building is a people business. Although the final result is a physical object, a project is built by the knowledge, skill, and effort of people. Success, failure, opportunities, and problems focus on the nature, character, and capacity of people. The owners of the project must overcome their ego and define a workable purpose. The management of the project must overcome their egos also and perform the work necessary to develop a workable approach. The trade personnel must know what they are supposed to do, know if they are doing it, and know when they are done.

Most failed projects are caused either by a failure to define a workable purpose or a workable approach. Almost all cost overruns are caused by low trade productivity, not material or equipment problems. "Watch your labor" is a "given" to experienced managers. Failure to understand human nature and work with it, "as it is" is a cause of many of these problems. Expectations and demands that cannot possibly be achieved with the people available will result in failure. This chapter (and the next two chapters) will look at the nature of people and how they can be managed better.

Work is part of people's identity—they need to be proud of their work

Work occupies the largest part of workers' waking hours. It partially defines who they are. And, if they are to feel good about themselves, they need to feel that their work is worthwhile. People need to see that their part of a project fits into the whole, and have a natural tendency to see their part as the indispensable contribution that makes the whole possible. People need to feel they are part of something big and important. But not all contribute to the effort equally.

- 5% understand how a project works, and can and will make it happen.
- 10% understand how the project works, but just watch and do not make things happen.
- 75% want to be part of the project and feel proud. They may understand their portion in

great detail, but do not understand how the whole project works, or even quite how their part fits with the whole.

- 5% are bad actors, troublemakers, and a drag on the project. Maybe this job is not right for them—maybe no job is right for them. Get rid of them or contain them in a job where they cannot affect others.

Character is unusually important

Character in construction is more critical than in many other industries. This is so because the project starts with many undefined conditions, and will encounter other unforeseen conditions. It is impossible to specifically define each and every condition and activity with precision at the start of a project. Only a shared understanding of how one can and should behave in reaction to these changed conditions—character—will permit successful execution.

Character has the following attributes:

1. Principles matter more than their personal gain. They must see themselves as part of something bigger than themselves.
2. They feel personally responsible for their actions.
3. They understand a deal.
4. They will stick with it when the going gets tough.

For our purposes, character is focused on the activities at work, not necessarily at home. Although people of moderate habits tend to possess the desired character more frequently, gamblers, skirt chasers, and two-fisted drinkers may possess character, while deacons in the church with religious pictures in their office, may not.

Natural tendencies—how they relate to people

Some people like to work with people and need to work around people and in groups, and do not work well independently. (Working with people must be distinguished from very people-oriented operators such as politicians and some self-serving sales people who really only see people as place holders in a power relationship. If one person leaves a position, their replacement will fill the place just as well for the people-oriented operators).

Other people work with things, numbers, or written documents, and do not feel the need or desire to relate continually with people.

How They Figure Things Out

Things or ideas—visual, verbal, number people

The first important distinction about most people in construction is that they work in the world of things, not ideas. They must see, touch, and move things around to understand them. Talking about them, writing about them, making counts of them are not the first natural way construction people figure things out. (Architects and engineers tend to be more on the opposite end, working in the world of ideas, drawings, numbers, symbols, and quite frequently cannot even recognize the things they are describing when they see them in the real world.)

All people make decisions in the way that work for them and are, therefore, more comfortable. Some are visual thinkers. Others are verbal thinkers, or number thinkers, or symbol thinkers. (Symbol thinkers are found in mathematics and philosophy, and are rare in construction.)

Speed of Decision

People make decisions at different paces. Some people can only decide quite rapidly, and if they linger over a decision their thinking becomes muddy. Others have to think about it, sleep on it, think about it a different way, and continue for days or even weeks before reaching a comfortable decision.

Time Horizons

People have natural time horizons, which are nearly impossible to change in the short run, and very difficult to change at all. For example:

- Immediate Time Horizon—Some workers can only understand the task that they are doing at that time and have no concept of what might come next.
- 2–4 Hours—These workers understand their tasks and the forces that are required to do their task, such as parts or systems from other people.
- 1–2 Weeks—These workers understand their tasks and how they fit with related tasks.
- Entire Project—These workers know how projects in general should work, and how this specific project will work.
- Their Career and Longer—These workers understand larger principles and possibilities that are not apparent from the immediately available facts, and can undertake tasks and project types that have never been done before.

A time horizon of two weeks minimum is required for any management position, such as a foreman or assistant superintendent. Time horizon of an entire project or longer is required for management positions that are attempting continuous improvement.

Know and Work with Their Nature

Everyone has one nature, tendency, and speed. People can make decisions usually in one, sometimes in a couple of ways. No one is good at everything. All decision-making processes work well for some activities and not for others, but all are necessary for some part of a project. For example, a detail-oriented accountant would not be a good superintendent and vice versa. Similarly, people working in the world of things cannot be compelled to keep detailed paperwork records or write long verbal reports. And, an office person might be completely useless at field tasks. Recognize the natural tendencies of the people, use them where their talents will produce the best results, and do not plan for unreasonable expectations—given their tendencies.

Change is Possible—But Only a Little and Slowly

Capacity

The skills, knowledge, talent, and training to do a specific assigned task are, of course, critical. This usually receives proper attention and focus. However, it is frequently the only item receiving any attention at all—excluding character, natural tendencies, and time horizons.

Motivation

Some people cannot be motivated at all. Posters, incentives, cheerleading sessions will be wasted on people who have no tendency or need to be proud of their work. Fortunately, the vast majority of workers need to be proud of their work and can be motivated if you can show that their efforts are part of a bigger picture. Recognition and appreciation is always appreciated, and an effective motivator. Management has to genuinely believe that all tasks are really important, and show this belief in their actions. You will not fool them with a pat on the back and some nice words if they see you do not mean it and act it.

This trust doesn't happen naturally in the work place, but can be developed with effort. It will take weeks, months, or years to build the trust and the system of feedback and control where the workers will really believe that they are part of something good and big. It can also be destroyed in a single event, lasting even minutes.

Summary

Building is a people business, and people have different strengths and weaknesses. Trade skills such as carpenters, plumbers, and electricians are usually recognized. Character, method and time of decision making , are less frequently recognized. The time horizons for planning are frequently overlooked. And since longer time horizons are required for higher management positions, promoting someone with a short time horizon can guarantee failure.

People can change only a little and slowly–usually not in time for the project. Match people as they are to the task needed. The culture of a company, training, and experience can improve a person, but not completely change their nature.

2.4 Managing People with Rules and Incentives

Rules enforce minimum standards, incentives execute all possibilities

"The law is like a single bed blanket on a double bed with two people in bed on a cold night."—Robert Penn Warren

"People act first, then the laws are made up to fit them."—Robert Penn Warren

"Prohibition is better than no liquor at all."—Will Rogers

The activities of a group, such as a company, the staff of a project, or a crew require communicated goals, expectations of behavior, boundaries, rewards and consequences. Rules and incentives are two different ways to encourage people to achieve these tasks and objectives. Rules enforce minimum standards and are always needed. Incentives can encourage all possibilities, and are required to achieve excellence and continuous improvement.

For example, when driving a car, there are lane marking lines, directional arrows, and stop signs. These are necessary rules and must be followed, but following them will not make you a good driver, or get you where you want to go when you want to get there. Signs such as "20 mph when school children present" or "bridge slippery when wet" try to guide judgment, but help only a little. Good, safe driving does not come only from rules alone, but also judgment produced by experience, and influenced by the situation. If your goal is safe and defensive driving, you may slow down or move over when you sense a dangerous driver near you. But, you many exceed the speed limit on the way to the hospital if you have a passenger requiring urgent medical attention. Rules are a necessary starting point, incentives finish the job.

Rules—Recognized Customs, Boundaries, and Instructions for Task Execution

Recognized customs

First is the type of rules that are not intended to achieve tasks, but are really customs where many ways will do equally well. You just need to pick one and change it as infrequently as possible. Examples include: red light means stop and green light means go, drive cars on the right side of the street, pay periods end on Sunday, and pay day is on Tuesday.

Boundaries

Second are rules that define a playing field, boundaries of behavior, and the minimum standards of behavior. These consist primarily of "thou shalt nots." They intend to keep us from doing bad things, but do not tell you how to execute a specific task. Examples include: no company tools or vehicles can be taken for personal use, no drugs or alcohol at the job site, report injuries immediately. The Ten Commandments are examples of this second type of rule, relying heavily on "thou shalt nots." After we received these commandments 3,500 years ago, most people can follow most of them, most of the time. But excellence has not yet been achieved.

Instructions for task execution

The third type of rules is detailed directions on how to execute a specific task. Use of this type of rule requires the belief that some higher authority can specify all the exact steps to do the task. These rules are enforced by catching people doing something wrong and punishing them. This will work only if the task is repetitive without variation, and requires no judgment. The results can never be better than the original intent. And, because of human imperfection, the results will always be somewhat less than expected.

Incentives—Goals and Rewards

Incentives, by contrast, use a stated goal and feedback to accomplish a task. This requires that (1) a goal be stated, (2) everyone understands the goal, (3) everyone has the ability to decide how to reach it, (4) everyone knows when they have accomplished it, and (5) everyone get a reward at completion. This is a process of assisting and encouraging people to do something right, and then giving them rewards. Because there is individual latitude in execution of the task, the final result can be superior to the original expectation.

For example, a stated goal might be to "finish on time and on budget," but in the real world, goals are seldom this simple. A more realistic example is a restoration and reconstruction of an enclosed pedestrian bridge between two buildings. The technical concerns are maintaining existing electrical power and communication during construction, installing a trouble free new roof while keeping the existing adjacent roofs water tight, and providing the highest level of cosmetic finishes both interior and exterior. There are two owner representatives you must keep happy—one cares about mechanical systems, and one cares about finish material appearances and fast execution. This owner has six other similar bridges needing restoration, and you want to perform this project in such a way that you also negotiate and perform the additional work. Coming close to budget is important, but getting the next six jobs is more important.

These are the goals. You know when you have achieved the goals when you complete the first project well and close to budget, and get the next six projects.

Communication of Rules and Incentives—Gravity Flow of Information

Communication flows by "gravity" downward from superiors to subordinates, but must be moved upwards with effort. For example, in a downtown hi-rise building, superiors can have the parking attendant park their cars in the lower level garage, pass the security guard on the way to the elevators, and pass the receptionist on the way to their offices. It is not uncommon for the car parking personnel to call the security guard, to call the secretary, and communicate who was in the party, what they were discussing, and their mood at the time. The superior may not know this is happening, or even these people's names.

This one-way flow of information restricts the knowledge of the subordinates from reaching the superiors. For example, if the parking lot attendants knew that a fence around the parking lot had been broken and criminals were entering and vandalizing cars, they may want to let management know, but the effort might be too great—or they might fear being blamed.

Information flows downward by gravity, because the subordinates rely on the superiors for continued employment, raises, and satisfactory employment conditions. Also, most people are not used to being asked about what they want. For example, with a house purchase, mortgage, car purchase, school for their children, taxes, and medical care choices, you can chose from preset options, but not specify exactly what you want. Variations exist and everyone has to pick and choose and craft an acceptable solution from the options available.

But, simple picking from existing options is not enough—you must work with and around the rules, and consider options not covered by rules at all. Most of what employees learn is learned by example from those around them including equals, subordinates, and superiors. They respond to incentives to achieve their goal. They need to be able to check their results against the stated intended purpose. They will watch and mimic what you do, more than listen to what you say.

A Workable Approach Defines the Rules and Emphasizes Incentives

Stating the workable purpose means that everyone can know what is supposed to happen, and will have a standard against which to check if they are achieving it—the first requirement for incentives. The definition of workable purpose communicates the goal in a way everyone can understand—the second requirement for incentives. Counting everything, and finding a workable plan (described in the previous section) both defines the rules and provides the means for everyone to know when they have accomplished it—the third requirement.

A definition of the workable purpose and approach requires continuous management involvement—working with others—or it will not happen at all. Management's effort setting goals, determining methods to achieve these goals, and counting everything communicates by example and gravity that this is real and important.

Finally, with a purpose that can be achieved, and the information to determine it is achieved, everyone can verify that their part fits in the whole. Making the incentives that match with their success the same as yours will enforce creditability throughout the entire process.

Summary

Rules that are conventions and boundaries are needed to define the playing field and enforce minimum standards for behavior. Set them early, and leave them alone. Incentives can produce results that exceed expectations. Whenever possible, incentives should, therefore, be emphasized over rules that are detailed directions on how to execute a specific task.

Management's work with others to define the workable purpose and approach provides the information for others to work by incentives. Since management has the same goals and incentives, it also communicates by example and gravity what management says is real, and believable.

2.5 Managing People and Information

Reduce the clutter, write or draw facts, talk about judgments

"Knowledge is an absolute mastery of details, and since of details there is no end, ours is always an imperfect and superficial knowledge."—Le Duc de La Rochefoucauld

"Eyes are better informers than ears."—Herakleitos

Define your terms

Definition of all terms is required for understanding and communication, if you do not know what you mean no one else will either. Single items by one trade usually are understood by common trade names, and only the grade and quality needs to be stated. Four-inch cast iron hub pipe, of a specific grade, needs no further definition. However, assemblies and systems need definition in every case.

The terms "General conditions," "Special conditions," "Rough carpentry," "Finishes," "Equipment," and "Special systems" just to name a few, have no commonly accepted definitions. Further, for any work item waste, sales tax, shipping, payroll taxes, tools and equipment, vehicle expense, supervision, and home office overhead may or may not be included. There are contradictory attempts at industry standard definitions, but even these are unknown to many and used by few.

The importance of definition applies also to the previous discussions about observation, organization of observations, and determining the workable approach. But, is discussed here because the importance becomes more noticeable when you are organizing and communicating the previously obtained information.

Definitions are required—if you do not do it, it won't get done. But, you alone cannot change everyone much or soon. So the practical rules that help are: (1) Use standard industry terms that communicate to all when possible. (2) Use a consistent method to allocate burdens (as described above: waste, sales tax, shipping, etc.) to every line item, and have this allocation visually evident in all presentation material. (3) Use an organizational structure recognized by many such as the CSI system. (4) Define only the remaining terms not defined by steps 1–3, but define them in as many places as they first occur. Even with these steps, frequent and repeated communication will be necessary.

Every person in a management or supervisory position handles 15,000–20,000 tasks in a year. Every task is required, and therefore important. But no single person can remember this volume of tasks. And no group possessing individual collections of 15,000–20,000 tasks can possibly communicate or even function.

People can only think of one thing at a time and, usually in western culture, only for seven seconds—then they have to think about it in a different light, or from a different angle. People can think of, at most, a group of seven related things at a time, but many people can only think of about three. After that they must bundle things into groups. There are two distinct approaches required to manage the inevitably large volume of facts.

Facts—write or draw, then talk

For information that is objective (facts) write or draw the fact, and put it in an organizational structure that is available to all. For some people you must follow up the written or drawn facts with additional talk, but you should not talk without first writing or drawing.

All facts are entered individually and put into racks for information storage. Get them stored and out of the way, but not lost. This has the advantage that everything urgent and non-urgent can be addressed in the order you chose. Also, the facts will be stored and available for all, so people who process information at different paces can come back in their own time. People who prefer written communication, or verbal, or numbers, or touching and feeling physical things, can all make the same facts real and understandable in their own way. In this way, all of the facts can be available to all in a way that is usable to different processing styles.

Judgments—talk then write

Judgments, intuitions, impressions, and people judgments must be discussed, not written, except, the conclusion of the judgment that will be used in action can be written. Reading detailed written descriptions of subtle information is a limited skill not shared by the full range of people with different information processing styles. So, it should be avoided. Writing well about judgments is yet a rarer skill. But a project requires the judgment of many, so alternate methods of communication usable by all are required. Subtle communication is possible by all within personal verbal communication. And this is the appropriate and effective manner to discuss and analyze judgments and impressions.

By writing the facts and talking about the judgments, clutter can be reduced, and you can choose to focus on the important, not merely the urgent. Further, when the facts are fully identified, organized, and available all will be equally informed. Ignorant statements, wild baseless conjecture, and analysis of impossible options will be substantially eliminated. The discussion about judgments will focus on the few crucial areas required for determination of the workable approach. Since the participants are informed, the discussions are shorter and conclusive. The conclusion of these discussions, but little of the discussions themselves, can and must be documented in writing.

A successful example

Effective use of these principles occurs with the following project estimating process: (1) the plans and specifications (facts) are provided to all estimating personnel, (2) estimators perform quantity surveys (facts) and request vendor pricing or sub proposals where required (soliciting facts), (3) a preliminary scope and nature of the project emerges (facts and preliminary judgments), (4) job site walkthrough with owner and architect is conducted, and the owner's, architect's, and estimator's impressions and feelings are verbally communicated (some facts and some judgment), (5) estimator completes estimate (judgment and some facts). Here the facts come first and occupy over 95% of the time. All can gather facts and form independent preliminary judgments in their own way and time—followed by discussion of these judgments with others.

An unsuccessful example

The alternate unsuccessful, but frequently used approach is: (1) Owner sends request for proposal describing the project in the most favorable light (judgment). (2) The plans and specifications are distributed at the job site walkthrough—differing in part from the request for proposal description. Without time to even unroll the plans, ignorant questions are asked (an attempt at judgment in the absence of facts). (3) The estimators return to their offices and complete steps 2 and 3 described in the successful example above. (4) The estimator questions the architect and owners by phone and in writing (request for facts). (5) The estimator completes the estimate in the absence of any substantial meeting of the minds with the architect and owner (unresolved attempt at judgment). Judgments are made without facts and initial judgments can be altered only partially and with difficulty. Ignorant judgments will later produce errors and arguments.

Summary

Managing people and information involves facts and judgment. The facts are many and each is important. Facts must be organized into racks for storage, and made available to all- with sufficient time for all to analyze them in their own way and at their own pace. Facts, therefore, must be presented in writing, not verbally. Judgments have to be discussed, not written because all can understand subtle and complicated nuances in person, but few can process the same information well in writing, and fewer still can write this information. Facts and judgments are both required. Obtaining, and processing facts comes first and occupies over 95% of the time and is done in writing. Judgments follow the facts, and are discussed verbally with conclusions documented in writing.

2.6 Managing People with Organizational Structures

Knowledge and decision must be distributed to the project site

"In the ordinary business of life, industry can do anything that genius can do, and very many things it can not."—Henry Ward Beecher

All companies require structures to organize personnel. A chart of a company's formal organization, which resembles a chart of the team pairings for a basketball tournament, is often drawn—and most recognize that this chart neither represents the real lines of communication nor has much to do with how things are accomplished.

Where facts are found and stored—and judgments and decisions are made—defines the real organizational structure. A top down, command and control structure restricts judgment and decisions to the upper levels of the organization, which provides specific instructions to the lower levels. A distributed knowledge system requires facts to be known, and judgments and decisions made, at all levels.

The top down command and control, and distributed knowledge organizational structures are compared below. Two unworkable structures to avoid, the bureaucratic and matrix structures, are also discussed.

Mechanization reduces required manpower—sophisticated products require increased knowledge

The days when construction was a place for strong backs and weak minds—and construction sites looked like anthills—are gone. The number of workers required for a task has been reduced by mechanization. For example, a large piece of earth moving equipment can do the work of 50 men with wheelbarrows and shovels. Trade worker knowledge requirements have increased because of more proprietary and sophisticated products that require knowledge and experience to install. For example, in 1940 paint and varnish products were mixed on the job with recipes—just like baking a cake. These coatings required no special knowledge to mix or apply and achieved only adequate performance. Paints and other coatings are now sophisticated in formulation, application, and performance. These are factory mixed and require specific knowledge and training, and sometimes certification, about surface preparation and application techniques.

Another requirement for knowledge is caused because computers are built into many construction components. For example, heating and air conditioning units will contain a microprocessor. Knowledge of this computer system is required to make the unit run. If the entire building is controlled by an energy management system, integration of the unit into this system can require significant additional knowledge and experience.

Although there are still unskilled positions in construction, there is no trade or class of work that is unskilled—all require some knowledge and judgment.

Construction organizations must have few layers

Construction companies are almost all family-owned enterprises that are less than three generations old. Construction has unsteady work volume, peaks and valleys, so management must stay lean. Deep benches and top heavy organizational structures can seldom survive very long. One management level, such as project mangers and superintendents, above those executing the work is a common limit. Very large companies may have one additional vice president level. Additional levels will soon produce loss of control with disastrous outcomes.

An illustration of the workability of flat organizational structures is the development of special projects divisions. Special project divisions are developed at some construction firms who typically perform very large projects, but wish to also perform small projects. To achieve the speed and responsiveness required for these smaller projects, layers of management are slashed to one, and rules reduced or eliminated. That this reduction is necessary and does work is a negative comment on the larger multi-layered structure. This is reinforced when the larger project personnel are temporarily without work and attempt to move to the special project division. Cost overruns of up to several times the project value frequently result, and firings follow.

Organizational structures are flat also because project management is highly focused, with few external considerations. For example, a common trade union rule for termination requires 20 minutes notice and delivery of a pay check—thus eliminating many of the functions of the human resource department. A finance department—since the project is financed by the owner—also has reduced work.

Projects are in many locations, so are judgments and decisions

Construction projects are in locations remote from the contractor's office, so travel times make the management and control that could exist in a factory unfeasible. Judgment and decision must be made at the job site level. As the knowledge required to execute tasks increases, the amount of job site decisions and judgments increase. Shorter decision times caused by accelerated schedules further add to the need for job site decision and judgment.

Centralized and Distributed Systems Compared

The centralized and distributed systems for organizations have similar principles to the rules and incentives for people discussed in the previous chapter. The centralized system works by rules—the upper level makes them and the lower level follows them. The knowledge of the subordinate ranks is lost and wasted. The centralized system cannot possibly be better than the instructions of the top levels and, because of variation in human performance, will always be less.

The distributed system realizes that the people closest to the work know it best. Facts, judgments, and decisions must be made on all levels. Establishment of a workable purpose and approach is essential and must precede the execution of the work. This requires the involvement of many, but cannot succeed without the commitment and leadership of the highest levels. Clear communication of this workable purpose and approach gives context so all can understand how their part fits into the whole. It also gives a concrete way for each person to check that they are doing their job right as they are doing it—and self correct when required.

A comparison: Ford's centralized system—Toyota's distributed system

A comparison to illustrate the two systems can be found with the early years of the Ford Motor and the Toyota Companies. Ford Motor began manufacturing cars—the Model A in 1903 and the Model T in 1908—when America had large geographical area and population that could afford to purchase and benefit from an automobile. The available work force was typically lower income people used to working for wages and doing what they were told. Ford Motor's response was to set up a system of detailed instructions on an assembly line producing a basic model in any color you want—as long as it is black. Large quantities of this uniform product were sold.

In contrast, Toyota began making automobiles in 1937. After the manufacturing interruption of World War II, Toyota made only 1,008 passenger cars in 1950 (Ford was making 7,000 cars per day at this time). High volumes were not immediately possible, and more variation in the product was required.

Further, the Toyota workers were typically farmers who tended their own small farms and were, therefore, used to seeing the whole picture, and making all the parts work together. They were not accustomed to simply taking directions. The Toyota approach became a flexible operation with a higher degree of worker decisions expected and included in the process. Mass customization of rapidly changing and improving products was the goal and result.

Construction by nature is done in small batches, usually batches of one. So, the Toyota mass customization model with distributed decision-making is vastly more suitable to construction than the Ford model mass production of central command and control. Yet the command and control model is frequently used in construction, with the expected inferior results.

Management Structures that Do Not Work and Must be Avoided

Bureaucratic management structures guarantee no results will be achieved

Bureaucratic structures have rigid job titles and responsibilities, rigid rules, and perform processes and procedures rigidly. Protection of the organization and the employees in the organization is the goal. Achieving results is of little or no importance.

A bureaucratic model is used by government agencies. Unfortunately, this type of thinking frequently creeps into private firms. There are some "program managers," "construction managers," or "owner's representatives" who are full-fledged construction bureaucrats—watching and finding fault with others, but accomplishing nothing themselves. A natural human tendency to feel "there ought to be a law against that" produces this kind of thinking. Yet that there are still criminals indicates that laws do not guarantee success.

The bureaucrat believes:
- The process matters—results do not
  Although bureaucrats say they are trying to achieve results, their actions say the opposite.

They are only concerned with processes and procedures. This is particularly difficult for people in construction to believe since everything in construction is judged by results.

- Rules rule
  Bureaucrats who have never accomplished anything believe they can tell everyone else how to do everything. For this they write rules—many and complicated.

- Rules apply only to others
  Bureaucrats believe rules apply to others, never to them. Even those who are quite decent in their personal lives never see this position as inconsistent and unfair.

- No bureaucrat is personally responsible for anything ever
  Everything is depersonalized. Things are done by the organization, agency, or by specialists, or analysts, not by real people with real names. Real people do not act this way.

- Punish them all
  Rules are enforced by coercion—physical threats (jail), penalties (taxes, fines, firing, demotions). Incentives are rarely used.

- Slow them down, stop them if you can
  Waiting, slowing all activities, fabricating delays, waiting them out, or stopping all accomplishments is the standard operating procedure. And this again is not done for any reason, or to accomplish some alternate result, but only because this is what bureaucrats do.

- Speak a foreign language
  Use of jargon and pointless complexity when mangling the English language is used to hide that they have little to say, or that what they have to say would be unacceptable if plainly spoken.

- We want more
  More money, more time, more staff, more authority. Whatever the reason, or even without a reason, the bureaucrat's answer is always, "We want more".

Since the bureaucratic structure does nothing to achieve results, and since everything in construction is organized to achieve results, all parts of the bureaucratic model should always be completely avoided. Even a few bureaucratic procedures can compete with those trying to get results, and use up all the oxygen in the room.

Matrix structures
You cannot serve two masters—A house divide against itself can not stand.

A matrix structure requires parties to report to more than one boss. An example is a company that has four regions. The functions of the company are divided into three departments, each with its own head: project management, field operations, and accounting and finance. If a person trying to execute a project reports both to the head of the northern region and to the head of each of the other three departments, immense time would be taken up in communication, resolution of power struggles, and personality conflicts. A similar conflict is common between heads of field and office operations in companies with only one region.

The matrix structure can appear to function in the short run if there is vast profit to allow for these inefficiencies. But a lean and well-run organization cannot function under a matrix structure. One master alone must be selected.

Summary

Construction companies have few layers of management—usually one, sometimes two. All construction operations require knowledge at all levels and for all trades. Sophisticated products require knowledge to install, and the project's remote locations and fast pace require increased decision-making at the job site. A distributed organizational structure with facts, judgments, and decisions made at all levels is therefore required. This must be accompanied by clear communication of the workable approach and purpose. Bureaucratic and matrix structures cannot succeed, and must be avoided.

2.7 Feedback and Control

Achieves short-term correction and long-term improvement

Feedback obtains information about the present execution of a task, and control uses this feedback information to make necessary adjustments. In the short run, feedback and control are used to check the work as it is being preformed—to ensure the workable approach is achieving the purpose—and to make required adjustments in real time. In the longer run, it is used to make approach improvements for future similar projects.

Checking and Adjusting the Execution of the Workable Approach

Feedback and control—The top-down approach

The company's organizational structure governs the type of feedback and control system that can be used. A top-down command and control organizational system restricts information, knowledge, and judgment to the upper levels of the organization. Those doing the work will have imperfect knowledge of what they are supposed to do, so mistakes will be made, sometimes frequently and persistently. Feedback consists of finding defective work, and tearing it out and doing it over—or discovering cost overruns have occurred. This feedback may be in the form of a very elaborate job cost accounting system requiring and producing many reports, but no control is achieved. You are just documenting and fixing past failures. With knowledge only that a mistake was made, but not how it was made, improvement for future projects is not possible. Excellence and continuous improvement are therefore not possible with this approach.

Feedback and control—the distributed knowledge approach

With a distributed knowledge organizational system, excellence and improvement are possible. When facts, decisions, and judgments are made by those doing the work—and a workable approach has been established and communicated—self control is possible.

Self control

Self control requires:

1. You know what you are trying to do.
2. You know what you are doing right now.

3. You have the ability to change 2 into 1.

This can only be done in a distributed knowledge system—where facts, judgments, and decisions are made by those doing the work. Self control is greatly enhanced when those doing the work help develop the workable approach. They understand how it was developed, feel ownership, and believe it will work. With the expertise of all built into the approach, it is usually completed with only minor corrections. Required minor corrections noticed early can be corrected early, and therefore stay minor.

Feedback for Process Improvement

Continuous process improvement is necessary to maintain the long-term health of a construction company. Construction is, however, a short-term discontinuous process, with many things going on at once. So, getting continuous process improvement is challenging.

Traditionally, record keeping in construction has been poor. This is partially because the personnel attracted to construction do not tend to be interested in record keeping. Also, the discontinuous nature of the process—with no identical, and few quite similar projects—makes standard record keeping (alone) of limited value when seeking detailed information on specific tasks.

Many process improvement techniques that work in manufacturing—where the processes are more continuous and long-term—cannot work in construction. But what can work for construction is as follows:

1. Check what you can when you can.
    The project has many tasks starting and stopping at different times, so checking the project as a whole produces no information on specific tasks. If you are doing one task right, and another task of equal size wrong, you may get the impression that both tasks are being performed "average." You must get into more detail. You can occasionally find one activity that a crew is performing exclusively for days or weeks, and use this as a productivity benchmark. Noting the factors that change productivity—travel time to the work area, congestion at the work area, scaffold, ladders or hoists required—this benchmark can be used for future projects. And once the productivity of one task is known, others can be found. For example, if 500 man-hours were spent on two tasks in the last week, and your benchmark task is known to have taken 300 man-hours, the other task must have taken 200 man-hours.

2. Break the project into short time periods to find periods of good and bad performance.
    Another approach is to break the schedule into sections to find the portions where you are performing well and poorly. Two-week periods are most useful. This will lead to suspicions about the performance of some tasks that merit further investigation. Determining if your suspicions are correct will require further investigation. This approach requires detailed information on the manpower, materials, and equipment estimated and allocated for each task—so estimated can be compared with actual. This can be done manually, but this clerical effort is usually found too burdensome. Scheduling computer programs can provide this same information automatically.

3. Study three tasks and make improvements.
   Select the three tasks with the greatest possibilities for improvement, and review the tasks in detail. Are the right trades and crew sizes assigned? Is the right equipment used and positioned correctly? Ask the personnel (including subcontractors and material vendors) doing the task and the preceding and following tasks about delays, breakdowns, and possibilities for improvement. Based on this information, make the required changes to the work approach to achieve the needed improvements.

4. The cycle of continuous improvement.
   Check the results of these changes, evaluate again, and pick three more tasks for improvement. This is a circular process of continuous improvement—check how you are doing real time, get the facts, make a judgment about what these facts mean, get more facts to see if your judgment is correct, and make an improvement. Once this is part of normal operations and has been repeated hundreds or thousands of times, repeating patterns emerge. Rates of productivity can be determined within seconds of entering a job site. This is not intuition, but "experience" produced from facts and judgments.

These are simple techniques that do not use fancy statistics, charts and graphs, and computer programs, but they work. This simplicity is required first because knowledge is always in short supply. Limited knowledge limits the analysis of this knowledge. It is also required because real time improvement by the people doing the work is required for the best results—and this requires speed. Having others take the information and later make a report provides stale information too late for use.

A benefit to these simple techniques is that every one can understand them. Applied knowledge, real world judgment, and common sense stay in the mix. But simplicity is not a reason not to document your efforts—the facts obtained, judgments made, improvements attempted, and the results. Without written documentation, you cannot communicate with others, nor will you long remember how improvements were realized.

Summary

Feedback and control are used to obtain information about the work as you are doing it—to see how close you are getting to your goal—and to make necessary corrections. This same information can also be used to improve your approach to future projects. Feedback must be both facts (man-hours, units of work) and judgments (crew size, equipment selection, positioning of equipment). Feedback and control are a continuous cycle of facts, judgments, and more facts to check the judgments, then improvement. Control and improvement can only be realized in a distributed knowledge system, not in a top-down management system.

2.8 Project Management

Purpose driven, focused, and fast

*"From the way a war is planned, one can forecast its outcome. Careful
planning will lead to success and careless planning to defeat. How much
more certain is defeat if there is no planning at all."—The Art of War*

*"People will expend any effort and go to any length to avoid
critical thought and hard work."—Mark Twain*

Project management is not a new innovative field. It shares most activities with general management, but has a different focus and emphasis because of a project's short, fixed time frame. A project has a definite start and end—temporary always and short is best. In contrast, management in general is as continuous as possible—long production runs of great profitable products are desirable. Because the project is temporary and short, project management uses special tools and techniques to get each unique project right the first time, and built fast. Project management also minimizes or eliminates some areas of management such as finance. When done properly, mid-project change and "value engineering" are reduced or eliminated.

Project management can focus on a single purpose, with defined cost and time

"Project management" is usually said to have been developed because of the demands of big and complicated projects. But this is not correct. There were many large and complicated projects thousand of years before "project management." For example, the Great Wall of China is a structure so extensive that it can be seen from space. The Appian Way is a road constructed by the ancient Romans for thousands of miles throughout Europe. The Palace of Versailles in France was constructed on a swamp, used the finest decorative techniques of the time, and employed 35,000 workmen on-site. The Great Pyramids of Egypt are massive structures with probable astronomical significance. Some of the great Cathedrals of Europe took 300 years to construct. More recently, the Panama Canal was both large and had unique engineering challenges. The Brooklyn Bridge also used pioneering techniques, such as marine caissons. All of these projects were constructed before project management was developed. And all of them are standing now.

How project management came to be and developed

Management has been studied and documented for thousands of years. Books on running farms, monasteries, and military organizations have been available for many years. For example, *The Art of War*, written about 500 B.C., describes the management of military enterprises. *The Rule of St. Benedict,* written about 1,500 years ago, describes the management of a monastery. In these cases, the person actually doing the work described the management techniques. St. Benedict was the founder of the Benedictine order and the abbot of a monastery. The authors of *The Art of War* were working generals. These books are still in print today.

The study of management by a person not doing the work arose in the early twentieth century. Taylor, with his time and motion studies, developed "management" as a separate topic. The man with a clipboard and a stopwatch was not actually doing the factory's line production work. The separate field of "project management" is frequently said to have started with the construction of a nuclear submarine in the late 1940s in America. Although project management did begin at this time, it did not begin just because of the complexities of building a nuclear submarine.

The factors that gave rise to project management

The first was the growing wealth and expansion of America following victory in World War II. Europe and Japan were both devastated and required years to rebuild. There was a huge domestic expansion in the United States—booming production and little competition—so there was less pressure to compete.

Included in this boom in America was the GI Bill, which permitted many more people to complete a college education. If not for college, many would have worked in factory production or the trades. This helped produce the notion of people spending more time in the office and less time on the shop floor or job site, because thinking and talking is more important than actually making and doing. In the building and engineering areas, similar trends existed for architects and engineers. They began to spend less and less time at the job site, with most of their time spent in the office. This trend continued through the second half of the twentieth century until many younger architects and engineers seldom went to a job site, and were unable to execute any task on a professional level once there.

Another development was the tendency for people to view themselves as more important than they formerly did. These perceived elevated values of the individual (theoretical book learning, and assumed intelligence) produces a situation where everyone wants to be the manager, but nobody wants to do the work. Lack of field knowledge can divorce these people from common sense, and the real physical world.

Finally, within large or cumbersome organizations populated by these new managers where quick execution of new tasks is counter to the organization's nature and culture, rapid project execution was unfeasible. A way to divorce yourself from this management structure is to make project management a "special temporary exception" to the rules and procedures of the organization. Nothing is as permanent as a temporary exception, especially when it works.

What Project Management Is Not—General Management with Parts Missing

Because project management focuses on a single purpose with a defined cost and time, many aspects of management that are needed in a company as a whole are not needed in a focused project, and are omitted.

First, strategic planning is absent. Since you have already decided to do the project, the portion of strategic planning that determines that a project is a good idea has been done and is not open for further discussion.

Second, finance is substantially irrelevant because you have already decided to do the project at a specific cost level. Money management of the project is a concern, but the main focus is usually to finish as quickly as possible and minimize finance (interest) costs. Inventory is not a concern because the project scope is fixed and the components are known. The only concern is getting these necessary components, and no more, to the project as needed. No inventory is kept for future stock. Finally, promotion and advertising are substantially eliminated. There may be some promotion for the company performing the project—using the project as an example—but because the project will stand-alone and will not be repeated, ongoing advertising to promote the project is omitted.

What Project Management Is—For a Specific Purpose with a Defined End

Project management is a system to execute a single purpose within a specified time and cost. The project management structure is divorced from the rest of a company's management burden, rules, and structures. The project management structure is extremely flat, with one person usually capable of making all decisions. Unless there is a deviation from the agreed cost or time, no outside approval of decisions is required. The project is a stand-alone profit center with its own cost and record keeping systems.

Because of the intense focus on cost and speed for a single purpose, four tools and techniques, though not unique to construction, are more heavily used and highly developed. These are: (1) the cost estimate and the related development of the workable approach, (2) information systems to track the procurement of the building blocks (permissions, materials, and equipment), (3) job costing with intense focus on labor productivity, and (4) scheduling tools to check that the relationships of the building blocks suggested in the workable approach will probably work before starting, and continues to work while executing the project. It is the focus on these four activities and the exclusion of many general management functions that defines the difference between general management and project management.

Project Manager's Skills and Knowledge

For project management, you must have a defined purpose, a workable approach, and a count of all components. A project manager must have a theoretical knowledge of the tasks being executed and must have a workable knowledge of how they are actually done. The project manager must have all information about the building blocks, cost, availability, sequence, and time to obtain and install. This means, without exception, the project manager must have one or two areas of expertise, including some field exposure. Some have come up through the trades. Some have come up with education in subjects such as civil engineering, and then some field experience. Others have related architectural engineering training plus field experience. A one-year field experience minimum, if diverse and well supervised, is required. Three years is more realistic, since a new hire will be given repetitive low-level tasks. Whatever career path is followed, a project manger must have a time horizon that is at least a little longer than the project duration. Finally, a project manager must have at least some authority to hire, fire, and purchase, or he is just a technician, not a manager.

If all of these conditions are not met, the project manger will not achieve the purpose. Printing up business cards saying "Project Manager" without the knowledge and authority to actually manage anything, will produce nothing. Paper shufflers or keyboard pounders—with charts and reports who are not capable, qualified, and obsessed with actually building the project—should get out of the way and let someone who is take over.

Value Engineering and Change Management Are Patch-Up Techniques

Value engineering and change management are two techniques frequently presented as beneficial project management services. These techniques have rare legitimate use, and are more commonly for patch and repair of poor or absent initial planning.

Value engineering is used when a project is substantially designed, but then pricing finds it is over the owner's acceptable cost. The contractor then offers alternate products, systems, or methods of construction that achieve the same result at a lower cost. If these suggestions still do not achieve the acceptable costs, the contractor then offers suggestions for scope reductions. Since the purpose of this exercise is cost reduction, the contractor knows the architect and engineer will probably not be paid extra to make the very substantial required drawing revisions, so corners will be cut. But the additional management time and loss of field productivity to execute the incompletely redesigned work will increase cost. So, full credit cannot be provided and the work suffers.

Change management is an administrative process where the owner is progressively restricted from making changes as the project is designed, priced, and constructed. The real need for mid-project change due to change in technology or market conditions is extremely rare in all industries, and substantially absent from most. But arbitrary changes by big egos, who want to throw their weight around to show who is boss, are common.

For example, if a factory is being constructed to produce a chemical, and a previously unknown vastly superior chemical is brought on line by a competitor, the project in progress must be radically changed (mid-project change) or abandoned (the original purpose of the project is no longer worthwhile). This could be called a change. But complete ignorance of a competitor's developments is rare, so care must be used. For example, for a high rise condominium the most saleable mix of one, two, and three-bedroom units is always initially a guess. What is true will be verified by presales. This is not mid-project change since the need for flexibility is a known project requirement. Late project alteration in the mix of units should have been built into the original design and not called change at all.

Value engineering and change management techniques are needed because of a failure to (1) define a purpose, and (2) establish a workable approach to achieve this purpose (that includes standards of quality, time, and cost). These are, therefore, patch and repair techniques caused by the failure to plan correctly. As patch and repair techniques, they will achieve less than optimal results. And, you will pay for the removal cost plus more than retail for the rework.

In most projects, the owner, and designers, will have already invested substantial time and made commitments to others they can only partially reverse. Change orders lead to the owner and/or the architect attempting to get money back from the contractor, rather than not give it to him in the first place. Not an easy job! For most projects, value engineering and change management will be completely eliminated with a workable purpose and a workable approach.

Summary

Project management is a subset of general management, which reflects the project focus on rapid execution of a single task with a fixed duration. Many areas of general management such as strategic planning, finance, and advertising are eliminated. Use of the tools of cost estimating to develop the workable approach, and information systems to track the procurement of the building blocks, are typical. Job costing, particularly labor productivity, and scheduling are emphasized. Project management executed properly eliminates mid-project change and value engineering.

2.9 Productivity

The largest opportunity for cost and schedule reduction

"Send one boy to do a job and it will get done in one day. Send two boys and it will get done in one day. Send three boys and it will not get done at all."—Lord Snowdon

"Watch your labor" is a priority for all experienced project managers. Labor productivity is the greatest source of profit increase or decrease for most projects. It can also provide the earliest warning of other problems, such as poor selection of construction equipment.

One third of the work day is actually productive work

Productivity is measured as the percentage of the work time spent moving material *once* (from the point of entrance at the job site to point of installation) and installing it *correctly* so no rework is required. It doesn't matter whose fault it is—any work that does not fit this description doesn't count. For example, double handling of material doesn't count. Incorrect installation of material, which must be removed or reworked, doesn't count. You may go home very tired at the end of a day having worked very hard, and having accomplished nothing. You can be a competent, hard working, well-meaning worker and still have low productivity.

Construction trades average about 32% productive time. That is, 32% of their workweek is transportation and correct installation of their work, and 68% is non-productive "waste." The cause of which is listed below:

- Waiting 29%
- Traveling 13%
- Instruction 8%
- Tools and materials transportation 7%
- Late starts/early quits 6%
- Personal breaks 5%

Reducing this unproductive time is the largest opportunity for increased project speed and profit. Further, it should be noted that the nonproductive parts—waiting, traveling, and instructions—are only partially within the control of the trade whose productivity is being measured. Improvement also requires design of a workable approach by management. The trades people can improve productivity somewhat themselves, but not greatly without management's commitment and effort.

Studies of productivity typically are done by management studying the productivity of trade employees, but management productivity must be considered as well. Field supervision, field office personnel, home office personnel, designers, and owners all spend time that has costs. Obtaining information, processing changes, meetings, and documentations should be substantially minimized, and in most cases entirely avoided. Small and mid-sized projects can and should be done with virtually no changes. Large projects should have few changes. Therefore, the time spent obtaining information, processing, and documenting changes is considered unproductive time. Nonproductive management time of up to 90% is not uncommon. Further, management's failure to do their job correctly or on time further reduces trade labor productivity.

Increasing Productivity

Having information available when needed is crucial

Having a workable approach and counting all of the building blocks will produce significant immediate improvements in productivity. With knowledge of what you are building, all of the components and building blocks, a sequence of operations and time of completion, then most instruction and much of waiting are eliminated. Information produces the single largest increase in productivity. When talented, hard working, motivated personnel know what to do they can and will do their best.

Reducing travel time

The next largest source of productivity improvement is managing travel time from the site entrance to the work area. For materials, this trip should be made only once in the job. For personnel, it should only be made once per shift. This requires a clear path of travel, unencumbered by obstructions, and storage space for the materials in the immediate work area. To achieve this, all materials must be ordered for short installation durations. A few days would be ideal for productivity, but two weeks is more achievable—the limit of the delivering vendor's tolerance. Note: The tendency to stock the entire job to save a few hundred or a few thousand dollars in delivery charges can produce tens or hundreds of thousands of dollars in increased labor cost caused by lower productivity.

The means of transport must also be appropriately selected. Travel on foot, manpowered carts, machine-powered transportation devices (carts, trucks, forklifts), or hoisting devices (lifts, cranes, and temporary elevators) must be selected carefully. Especially designed or modified transportation devices for the particular task or job site can greatly increase productivity, and ensure a single trip from the job site entrance to the work area.

Finally, in the immediate work area there must be the necessary support services, such as electrical power, heat, water, toilets, break areas, rubbish bins, and communications. Trade personnel will then have no reason to leave the work area.

Reducing mobility restriction in the work area

A clean, unobstructed work area is necessary to achieve maximum productivity. Any moving of material (double handling) is a reduction in productivity. This requires short ordering durations for materials, as described above. Where possible, leaving some material on carts for minor relocation will help further. The number of men assigned to a work area must be below the density limits.

Next, the work area must be properly manned so that all men and machines have unobstructed circulation space. Hoisting devices for high work must be properly selected. Fully stocked gang boxes for tools and equipment storage in the immediate work are also essential.

If the work is in an occupied space, or extremely congested, such as a mechanical room, careful scheduling must be considered, including the use of multiple shifts. A 50% time premium may seem high, but if it can produce a 300% increase in productivity, the cost can be justified.

Lead By Example and Momentum

Additional productivity improvement is gained by example and momentum—by selecting a "pushing trade." Choose a trade that is a significant portion of the project work, and preferably one that has work that has large installed dimensions. Examples include the concrete structure, HVAC ductwork, or on civil projects, large underground piping. Choose an aggressive subcontractor or your own management personnel for this trade. Give them the opportunity to move fast, and push them.

The other trades on the project will see the example, and will first react as, "If he can do it, I can do it too" and second, since the pushing trades work is large, they know they must keep up with them, or get ahead of them, or their productivity will suffer greatly by having to work around the large installed work.

Summary

Since field productivity averages 32%, close to a 300% increase of productivity is reasonably achievable. Information, reduced travel time, and an unobstructed work area can produce much of this improvement. Management must use a workable approach, and owners must participate in this approach, to eliminate changes.

2.10 Estimating Project Costs to Determine and Confirm the Workable Approach

Focus on cost to balance with grade of material and time of construction

"According to the ancients, the truly great in warfare are those who not only win but win with such ease and ingenuity that their wisdom and courage often go unrecognized. Such men do their best to ensure that the victory will be theirs before they commence fighting, placing themselves in an invulnerable position and not missing any opportunity to defeat the enemy. The winner does everything to ensure success before he fights. The loser rushes into combat without adequate preparation."—The Art of War

"The science of war may be summarized under these headings:
1. *Measurement of distances*
2. *Estimation of expenses*
3. *Evaluation of forces*
4. *Assessment of possibilities*
5. *Planning for Victory"—The Art of War*

Estimating costs builds on the cost part of the workable approach. The approach to the job, grade of material, and time of construction all affect costs. The acceptable target costs in the workable approach affect the possible approaches, materials, and time. So, the costing must be done as part of the approach development and confirmation process—with back and forth, and give and take between approach and costs. Estimating involves detailed counting and arithmetic, but it is not just bean counting. It is part of building the project on paper and in your head to determine the approach. The organization of the information in the estimate is the start of project planning and is later used in project management.

The Estimate Starts with an Organizational System—So You See the Big Picture and Nothing Is Missed

The first step in preparing an estimate is establishing an information organizational system, which contains all work items. If all work items are in the estimate, but not precisely estimated correctly, mid-project feedback and control makes correction possible and success still probable. If a work item is not in this original estimate, additional management time and probably cost will be incurred later. And timely completion at the required cost will become less likely—full recovery is usually not possible.

A reusable template is required

You cannot visualize an entire project in your head, so you do not start with a completely blank slate every time. A reusable organizational framework for the type of project your firm builds is required. The Construction Specification Institute (CSI) 16-section classification system is a common and useful framework. All 16 sections must be included in your reusable framework, even if some of the sections may not apply to all your projects. Additional subsections should be added for the detail common to your type of work, but must be limited (there are about 10,000 subcategories in the CSI format and you will not use many of these items in your entire career). The effort to make a specific determination that a section does not apply, or is not shown but maybe should apply, or is shown and needs to be counted and costed forces thought on the scope of the project. The estimate summary sheet containing the 16 sections and your selected subsections should be limited to one page, or it becomes difficult to see how the pieces fit together to form a project you understand. (Summary items will, of course, be supported by more detailed estimates on supporting pages.)

Breakdown costs into—labor, material, and subcontractors and vendors

Once all components are identified in the organizational system, these components are measured and counted. Each component is broken down into three parts—labor (forces on your own payroll), material (you purchase directly from a supply house, but it is not custom manufactured for the job), outside vendors (including equipment and material made to order for the job, and subcontractor costs). The three-part breakdown is useful to permit easy adjustments of the preliminary baseline unit costs—and these three categories behave differently. Labor productivity may change labor costs but not material costs. A sudden increase in material prices will not affect labor productivity or cost. Also, this breakdown resembles the way a project is contracted, managed and paid, so this breakdown serves as the starting point of future accounting and project management. People get weekly pay checks, material vendors get paid shortly after material delivery, and subcontractors get paid at agreed times after milestones are reached. This component breakdown is also customary, and is therefore widely recognized and accepted.

The components are counted in the order they are installed. This is a pipe-by-pipe, stick-by-stick, brick-by-brick count. Not square foot, ballpark figures, or plugged cost for assemblies. You cannot buy 1,000 square feet of electrical work from an electrician, so do not measure electrical work by square foot. To permit communication and help see how the parts fit together, standard unit of measure must be used. Measure square feet, not sheets, rolls, or bundles. Measure cubic yards, not truckloads or bags.

Complete and comprehensive is very important—precision is less important

The estimate is calculated in a very short time: days, weeks, or for very large projects, months. This limits the information available, and the possibilities that can be explored. Your organizational system and component counts must be fully complete and make one fully possible workable approach. That is the best that can be expected during the estimate preparation. It must be a good possible way to build the project, but it may not be the best way. If, when building the project, personnel with a different point of view and more time find a faster or more efficient approach that will alter component quantities, productivities, and cost, then this improved approach should be selected.

The counted and measured quantities of physical objects can and should be precise from the start—get it done right so it is out of the way and you can move on. But, the unit costs assigned will be at first very imprecise. As the estimate is completed, and the time, approach, and productivity that affects costs is refined with the workable approach, precision of unit costs will increase, but will still be approximate. The precision of the unit costs is limited by available information, and there is always less information than you would really like.

The Item's Cost Components

Labor Cost Estimating

Estimate using base line unit costs—man hours first, then money

Labor unit costs must first be estimated in man-hours, not money. (Cost in money is calculated by multiplying your burdened labor rates times these estimated man-hours.) Baseline labor rates from your cost library (cost libraries are discussed below) are entered to start. This makes the estimated cost usable for variable wage rates, in different time periods, or in different regions. Adjustments for the trade type and crew size assigned to the task can be made. It also makes it easy to adjust for job site-specific productivity variations.

Adjust baseline costs for productivity

Job site productivity adjustment is influenced by travel time from the site entrance to the work area, and mobility at the work area, as restricted by high, confined, or congested spaces. Productivity is also affected by time—the pace of the project. Productivity will increase with increased pace to a point, then decrease as the pace increases further. Productivity will decease rapidly with project change or lack of required information. Using these considerations, estimated modifications to the project's baseline productivity are entered. Start with a productivity modifier for the entire project (125%, or 75% of baseline productivity), which can be further modified for individual work tasks, or later again modified for the entire project. Start with your best, but imprecise estimate, and continue to increase the precision as the workable approach is refined. Modification to labor productivity is the largest and most common adjustment to labor baseline costs. Changing labor rates by assigning the same task to a different trade with a different labor rate can also be done.

Material Cost Estimating

Material estimating starts with counting and measuring the physical components in standard units of measure, not money. Baseline unit costs in money from your cost library are then entered and multiplied by the measured quantities. Material cost includes the cost of the material, vendor delivery charges, and sales tax. (Initial entries are from your cost library, but must later be verified for this project.) To this burdened material cost, waste factors must be added. For components that are completely divisible into any sized unit, such as earthwork or concrete that can be obtained in a 1/2 cubic yard unit, a percentage waste factor based on historical knowledge can be added, usually under 5%. For components that come in standard sizes, specific knowledge of the dimensions and delivery possibilities must be known, and an appropriate waste factor used. For example, carpet typically comes in 12' wide rolls. If you are carpeting a corridor that is 7' wide, 5' of every 12' roll will be wasted.

Adequate precision is acceptable for estimates—higher precision is required later when ordering

The component counts are part of securing the information that will refine the workable approach. Therefore, they are initially less precise than the built result. For example, if a roof slopes from 12' to 14' uniformly, the walls under the slope would average 13' high. Estimating 13' high framing material is acceptable for an estimate. But, since material only comes in 12' and 14' lengths, the 12' and 14' lengths must be counted when ordering the material. Specific verification of the material unit costs for the project and determination of waste factors are the largest and most common modification to material baseline unit costs.

Subcontractor and Vendor Cost Estimating

Increased knowledge of their work decreases required adjustment to baseline costs

If you hire a subcontractor or vendor, then you are responsible for them. And you must estimate their work as if you were doing it with your own forces. You must perform a detailed count and costing of each of their components with the labor, material, and vendor/subcontractor component breakdown. And, in addition, you must obtain project specific subcontractor quotations.

Detailed estimates are required first to understand the nature of the subcontractor's work and second, to keep them honest and catch mistakes. Finally, their estimated labor determines the limits and opportunities for improvement to your workable approach for their work item. And their labor can only be known for sure every time if you estimate it yourself. This estimated labor figure will also be used later to develop the project schedule.

Adjustments to the baseline subcontract costs are more limited than the adjustment possible to labor and material, since you are also getting lump-sum quotations. But this dual internal estimate and lump-sum quotation approach will tell you if you are getting good quoted prices or, if not, why, and what you can do about it.

Complete Your Costing of the Permanent Project—Then Cost the Temporary Construction and Activities

Detailed count and costing is first performed on all the components of the permanent project. These components are shown by plans and specifications. Once what you are building is measured, counted and costed, you then move to the activities that are not part of the permanent project, and are not shown on the plans, but are required for construction. These cost items, general and special conditions, and soft costs will be discussed in the next chapter.

Making a Cost Library—to Establish Baseline Unit Costs

Baseline costs must be internally generated from actual job experience. This is not difficult, and can be done by anyone with a working knowledge of the trade. If a tradesman who has never performed an estimate wants to assemble costs about the trade he knows, he already has sufficient information to start. Labor hours worked, materials used, and equipment for the past few jobs, or the past few months, can be used to calculate a starting point for unit costs. An experienced estimator with an existing cost library moving into a new and unfamiliar area of work can use common themes to assist in understanding a new activity. For example, lineal feet of white or black pipe have the same installation cost. Installation of 3/4" conduit and 3/4" copper pipe in the same situation will have similar installation cost. Using standard units of measure, with records of productivity adjustment due to travel time to the work site and productivity in the work area, can produce quite close approximations of unfamiliar work items.

Material unit costs are determined in a similar manner. Invoices and job records from past projects can be used in times of stable material pricing. (Prompt payment discounts, such as a 2% discount for payment within 10 days, or restocking charges for returned materials, are not included in the unit baseline costs. These cost modifications are caused by good or bad management, which is a future unknown.) Job specific material quotations are necessary in times of material price instability, and always for new or different types of work, or work in unfamiliar regions

For vendor purchased equipment or subcontract items, detailed records broken down into labor, material, and their sub-vendor pricing must be recorded. Occasionally, a subcontractor will perform only a single task on a project, which will show some unit costs. Other times, they will give unit cost information that you can understand, check, and believe. As projects are executed with estimates using these unit costs, monitoring of job site productivity can continue to refine these unit costs and improve the accuracy and the completeness of the subcontractor baseline costs over time.

Making a cost library is not difficult, but it is tedious, slow, hard work. This internally generated cost information is the only method that works for estimating costs, feedback and control, process improvement, and job control. Cost indexes, such as RS Means, can only be used for public relations and discussion purposes with the owner. These cost services have baseline costs that must be adjusted by multipliers for productivity, quality of construction, type of construction, and region of the country—each of which can produce 10%-20% ranges. Such broad ranges with a loose definition of how they are determined do not produce costs anyone can take to the bank. They also do not produce the detailed component counts that are the start of project planning and management.

Burdens Applied to Labor Costs For Your Own Use and the Owner's Acceptance

Costs that are imposed by the government, insurance companies, or your own internal costs that must be added to the raw cost of labor are called burdens. These include government payroll taxes such as Social Security and Medicare; insurance tied to payroll such as worker compensation; a portion of liability insurance tied to payroll; union dues and contributions; health or pension contributions; mandated training costs; vacation and sick pay; and sometimes small tools and supplies. These costs now center in the area of 50% of gross payroll. Safer trades, such as carpet installation, will have a lower burden (maybe 40%) than dangerous trades, such as ironworkers who will have a higher burden (maybe 70–90%).

These burdens must be allocated in a way that is easy to understand, easy to check, compatible with your company's accounting system, and acceptable to the owner. Owners will accept your burden if it is similar to the burden they see in other areas of their lives. For example, a car mechanic will charge an hourly rate, which includes labor and a fee for the maintenance of the shop, tools, and equipment. Lawyer's and accountant's hourly rates include the expense of their time plus expense for administrative support and the maintenance of their office.

At least some actual cost figures are typically presented to the owner at some time for most projects. Even if your methods of allocating burden costs are entirely justifiable and supportable, the owner will take severe exception to certain types of burden allocation, and readily accept the same burden presented in another manner. Know the truth, but tell them what they want to hear, the way they want to hear it.

Checking Your Estimate During Preparation

Estimate the way you build—don't be satisfied until it makes sense

Since estimating is a process of building the project in your head and on paper, count the components in the order they will be installed. For example, estimate clearing the site, digging the hole, installing the foundation, installing the structure, then installing the roof. Estimate plumbing sanitary waste, then vent, then water. The process will be real and make sense. You will not miss anything, and you will realize if something is missed from the instructions you receive from others. When performing a count of components by system in order of installation questions such as, "What holds this up?" "Where does this water drain?" and "How is the equipment powered?" will emerge. Do not be satisfied until the complete project makes sense to you.

Comparing expected results with estimated results—make sure it is reasonable

Earlier, completeness—making sure everything is counted—rather than high precision was emphasized. Very close to right, but imprecise is good—not right but very precise is not. Completeness can be checked for reasonableness. This is done by constantly comparing your expected values with estimated values.

For example, some figures—such as ratios of material to cost of labor by component, component percentage of the total project cost, component cost per square foot, component man-hours per square foot or man-hours as a percentage of the total project cost, and historical value from past project to the estimate for this project—are used to spot unusual patterns or deviations. The figures may help you to discover errors in your estimate, or they may provide the knowledge that some work component has unusually expensive or inexpensive material; unusually high or low labor; or unusually large, heavy or numerous components. This both produces an accurate estimate and gets you to, "know the job as you are estimating."

Summary

Estimating is developing the cost part of the workable approach. An organizational template for your type of project is essential to ensure every component is counted and costed. These components are broken down into labor, material, and sub-vendor components, and then measured and counted. Baseline unit costs for these components from your cost library are applied. Adjustment to the library unit costs for waste, productivity, market and regional variations, and risk are made.

The estimating organization system and the information it produces are the start of project planning and management.

2.11 Estimating to Achieve Target Project Costs

If everyone can count and measure the same, why do prices differ?

"To vanquish a superior force by clever tactics is beyond the comprehension of the masses. They see the victory but cannot understand the tactics that achieved it."—The Art of War

In the previous chapter, we discussed counting, measuring, and costing the components of the permanent building. Although, all bidders can count, measure, and cost the same, their prices differ. Why? The answer is that pricing is not just a collection of calculations, but refining costs to achieve targeted pricing—either the owner's statement of the price that fits his purpose, or the bidders' assumptions of the price needed to get the job. Temporary work is required to build the permanent work. The nature and scale of this temporary work is determined by the approach selected. Assumptions, expectations, market forces, and risk affect the approach both to the permanent and temporary work, and therefore costs. A back and forth process of refining the approach and assumptions and adjusting the costs continues until the target cost is reached.

Temporary Work is Required to Build the Permanent Work

General and special conditions

General and special conditions are the terms customarily used to describe work required to complete the project, but not included in the finished work. These work items are not shown on any blueprints or specifications—you have to know from experience what is required. So, your approach heavily determines the scope of general and special conditions.

Also, the general and special conditions are more affected by time than the permanent parts of the work. Supervision and equipment rental incur costs every day they are on the job, regardless of what is accomplished. Additional expenditure on general conditions, such as more or bigger cranes, hoists, and haul roads can vastly increase productivity and the speed of permanent construction, but at a cost. So, the development of the workable approach continues with an estimate of the general and special conditions, and possible revisions to the productivity and time of the permanent project construction. The permanent and temporary estimating methods are the same: a reusable template is reviewed for each project. All components are measured and costed using the labor, material, and sub-vendor breakdowns—and adjustments for productivity and time are made. Costing temporary work as a percentage of construction should be avoided, or used only for the last few very small items, as described below.

Job site supervision and management

Job site personnel working only on the site, but not directly installing the permanent components of the building, are general construction costs. These include site managers, supervisors, project mangers, superintendents, project engineers, foreman, and safety personnel. These costs are estimated using each of these personnel's unit cost and their estimated duration on the job site.

Temporary structures and facilities

Temporary structures and facilities can include: roads; retention walls; hoisting equipment such as cranes and temporary elevators; storage sheds; job site office break and change rooms; toilets; safety barricades; and utilities such as power, water, light, and heat. These are estimated using the same method as permanent work, not as a percentage of construction.

Equipment, vehicle, and small tools

Equipment costs for large equipment intensive projects, such as road or dam construction, will be a significant portion of the total project cost. Individual pieces of equipment will be costed the same as supervision—unit cost and anticipated time of use, plus the maintenance and servicing costs multiplied by time. In addition, the costs for setup and removal must be added.

Even for work where the equipment costs are small, such as carpet laying, a calculated equipment cost should be made. The common practice of calculating equipment costs as a percentage of work is misleading, inaccurate, and troublesome. A percentage cost can be added to the material or labor portion of each work item, but differences in labor rates or material costs will make these inaccurate. (Cheaper labor doesn't use less equipment. More expensive carpet doesn't take more equipment to install). A percentage could be added to the entire project, or a cost can be included in the project overhead. The last two burdens typically tend to raise owner objections. They see an increase in overhead as an increase in profit. Also, if they see certain tools and equipment that are not in constant use at all times on the job site, they have an emotional reaction that a credit is due for every moment that the tool is not in operation.

Fees and Soft Costs

Permits

Building permits, permits such as for road use, and dump fees vary widely by area, change frequently, and are only limited by the imagination and greed of politicians. These must be specifically calculated by permit type and checked for each project.

Project specific insurance not tied to payroll

Bonds, such as payment and performance, street use, insurance, such as liability insurance and builder's risk that are project specific mandates by the owner or government, have costs obtained using project specific quotations from the insurance agent or carrier.

Office overhead and profit—same as temporary construction but different location

Office overhead and profit must be added to the cost of all work items. Home office overhead includes some components of tools and equipment, home office vehicle expense, and insurance not included in the direct cost of the work as described above. In addition, it includes the office employees such as project engineers, estimators, and clerical support, and shop labor, home office rental, utility expenses, office services, and supplies. Profit is what is left over after all costs are paid. It is the payment the market will bear for the risk of the project.

The project owners, however, emotionally cannot help but view office overhead (a real cost) and profit as the same thing. Further, owners tend to think that their and their designers' instructions for the project are completely self-evident and can be executed by robots on autopilot. Therefore, for most owners it is important to minimize office overhead as a line item. This, unfortunately, results in relocating costs that are legitimate office overhead (for the work the project owners require and demand) to the labor and material direct cost of the work. This clouds the clarity and the use of the estimate information, but may be necessary to sell the job to unsophisticated owners.

Estimating Your Approach

Companies executing large projects well know the size and importance of temporary work. A mine, refinery, or power plant constructed in the wilderness can require marine structures to accommodate ships, haul roads, temporary utility plants and fuel storage, and temporary housing and support structures—which can take years to construct before work on the permanent project can start. The man and material hoists and tower cranes for construction of a high rise can cost 6% of the total project cost, but are the lifeblood of the project as they help in determining pace and productivity.

The facts gained in preparing a detailed component estimate increase your knowledge of the project. At the conclusion of the counting of all the components, the order of magnitude of the project and each of the components are known. Probable range of costs for each component, and the total project, and the range of probable construction times are known.

A minimum amount of temporary work is required for a project. Above the minimum, additional temporary work can be effectively added if the cost of the additional temporary work is exceeded by the decease in cost through increased productivity, or shortened construction times. Although this cost-benefit trade-off is known to large contractors, it also applies to all efforts larger than a repair job where a tradesman can carry all the tools and materials for the job in his hands.

Every firm has one speed, and will visualize only a small range of possible approaches. Large firms may spend more time, effort, and money mobilizing for a small project than a small firm will spend completing the project. A small firm will not grasp the temporary work required for a large project, and will fail to complete the project, or even start it well. Although each firm must work near its normal range, expanding the range even a little can increase productivity, reduce time, reduce cost, and produce continuous improvement.

Big or small, the approach is the same: estimate an approach, cost the temporary work required by the approach, review the cost of the approach vs. the benefit of increased productivity and shortened schedule, and continue to refine until the targeted costs and schedule is obtained. Small firms can expand the possibilities they explore by realizing that there is not just one way. Spending money on temporary work can have a greater cost reduction in productivity and schedule savings. Larger firms can also increase their range of possible approaches by reviewing the cost-benefit trade-offs.

Time and cost

The temporary work determines the range of construction times possible—and time determines much of the cost of the general conditions and temporary construction. So, the approach and time, which determines general conditions and temporary construction, must be adjusted and revised until the owner's targeted cost and time are reached. This cycle of revising approach and time is similar to the cycle of approach and cost.

Everyone and every firm have one speed—and everyone around you will know yours. So, your ability to rapidly change your approach to build projects faster and more efficiently (and therefore get lower subcontractors pricing) will not be believed immediately or without heavy explanation. Either long-term gradual change or immediate selection of alternate vendors, whose only speed is faster, can be sought to achieve the required improvements.

Estimating the costs of the permanent project discussed in the previous chapter, and estimating the costs of the temporary work in this chapter would, in a stable and rational world, produce bids from comparable contractors that are far closer than are achieved in the real world. The world is not stable, and people are not rational, so further modifications to costs occur.

The Irrational Modifies Cost

Assumptions about materials affects grade and cost

Owners seldom tell you what they really want, and architects, engineers and owners seldom completely mean what they say. Specifications for model numbers that do not exist, from companies that have gone out of business, with grading systems that are no longer used are normal. Architects and engineers "borrowing" or buying canned specifications produce these errors. This may mean that no one has seen or knows anything about the specified product.

Further, there are regional conventions that even though clearly stated are assumed to be incorrect. For example, a painting specification for one prime coat and two finish coats is widely accepted to mean one prime and one finish in some regions—"everybody just knows." Each installer will have certain standards. Either they will know code and manufacturer's requirements, or they will have their own standards superior to the specifications—"we do it this way because we want to be proud of our work and we do not want any callbacks."

These assumptions will produce different interpretations of materials to be used. These assumptions can range from, "this is the code conforming, best, accepted way" to "they didn't tell me what they want so I will just give them this" to "they told me what they want, but they do not really mean it." All of these are good faith efforts to do the right thing, but produce different material selections. Out right cheating, "I know what they want, but I will give them something less" also occurs.

Expectation influences reality

Each type of project will be known to have certain acceptable rates of productivity, risk, and cost—and these become self-fulfilling prophecies. For example, an apartment building will be a far less expensive project than a college dormitory, even though the completed results may be similar. The cost difference is greater than the cost of generally increased grade of material that exists in a college dormitory. This is true because everyone knows apartments have to be cheaper if you want to get the job, and this expectation produces a certain level of effort and urgency. This would be similar to the productivity an employee might achieve Monday through Friday at their job, and achieve a much lower productivity for work around the house on the weekends. Same person, different expectation and results.

Risk modifies cost

There is also the risk of unexpected events. These would include government interference, such as restrictions on transportation to the site. For example, use of public highways to and from the site may be completely legal and customary, and have been used for years, but a specific project may produce neighborhood or political objections that make far longer and therefore more expensive haul roads necessary. Weather is an unforeseen only when it is significantly worse than the normal weather for that location at that time of year. (The impact of normal seasonal variation is not unforeseen, and should be included in the estimated costs.) Another risk in this category is nonpayment by the owner. The greatest single risk is unanticipated changes in productivity due to owner activities. Failure to provide correct information when required, frequent changes in the work, or scheduling their vendors to work concurrently with the construction of the building can all cause massive reduction of productivity.

These risks can cause either an increase in the unit labor cost due to lower productivity, and increase in temporary work and office overhead due to extended time, or an increase in the profit for these risk premiums.

Market boom and busts affects cost and prices

Construction continually moves through periods of boom—where the demand for material, skilled labor, and available vendors exceeds the available supply—and bust—where firms will take drastic measures to keep busy. This will affect the costs (expenditures to achieve a result) and prices (the charges to achieve a result, regardless of the cost). Costs and prices, which usually are closely related, can temporarily disconnect in times of boom and bust.

Different regions of the country, and different countries will also have variable or opposite ups and downs. Project types will not move up and down at the same times. Single-family residential housing may boom while electrical power plant construction is nonexistent for years. The type and location of the project will affect the construction types customarily used, which will affect the materials and labor skills required.

In times of boom, the costs will increase because factories and field labor are stretched beyond their limit. Some overtime can be used, for additional cost, or lesser skilled labor can be added, who will produce less. If factories, contractors, and shipping companies are all at their limit, many will raise prices further above their costs than usual to make a quick profit.

These swings in cost and price are sudden, temporary, and the causes are too complex for anyone to understand. (Demand for structural steel in China may outstrip the capacity of the new steel mills in India, so the cost of structural steel in New York rises.) The practical answer is to have a general understanding of the global forces that affect the materials and labor used in your project type so you can know the possibilities for change. Then, specific determination of the cost and availability for all ingredients for your specific project must be made in the project planning stage. These specific costs and delivery times must be included in your estimates for your workable approach.

Summary

Once the work of the permanent project is costed, the necessary temporary work is costed. Estimating the temporary work is similar in approach and method to estimating the permanent work. It differs first because nothing is drawn or written to show you what to do, you must know the possibilities from experience. Also, temporary measures are related more heavily to time—they cause costs by the time they are used, and they can shorten or lengthen the construction time of the permanent project. Further, permanent and temporary costs are modified by irrational assumptions, expectations, risk, and market forces—which requires further revision to approach (cost, grade, and time) to reach the targeted costs.

2.12 Schedule Planning

Can your planned estimated approach be made to work?

Scheduling is a tool using graphs and numbers that shows if your estimated decisions together achieve the workable purpose. Scheduling also takes the activities (and their resources established in the estimate), and specifies their relationships—to produce the estimated project duration.

Scheduling occurs late in project planning because it needs the activities and resources produced by the estimate to start, but it is not an afterthought. Scheduling is not a separate activity occurring late in the project development process where you discuss: "We know what we want to build, now how long will it take?" Also scheduling will not "keep a project on schedule"—people do that—by determining and managing a workable approach. Scheduling identifies resources and a sequence of activities to be altered to achieve your priorities of cost, time, grade of material, and use of limited resources.

Scheduling used to be done by hand (or on a mainframe computer), but such handwork exceeds the patience of most project personnel. So scheduling was given to a specialist—removing the activity from the management mainstream of the project—and thereby losing much of its usefulness. Scheduling tools on personal computer programs now make multiple evaluations of alternate scenarios feasible within the usual time and effort limits, making more widespread participation possible. The discussion below assumes (without specifically discussing) the use of personal computers in scheduling.

Activities—Identify and Show Relationships

What activities to include

All work activities identified in the estimate, including permissions, administrative work, engineering, and material procurement, must be included in the schedule. If a purchase order or a subcontract is issued, even for equipment delivered in a single day, it must be identified in the schedule so nothing is missed, and to answer the question, "Where's my stuff?"

Summarize activities to show relevance to other activities

Because all activities are related to other activities, they must be summarized in a form that has meaning to both the installing party and to others. For example, when pouring a sidewalk the activities consist of:
1. Propose concrete design mix, obtain design mix approval.
2. Fine grade, install forms, install reinforcing mesh, pour concrete, finish concrete.
3. Strip forms, concrete cure, and apply sealer.

These should be summarized to:
1. Concrete Design Mix Determine. (Requires interaction between concrete contractor and engineer.)
2. Sidewalk Install. (Requires prior completion of utility work below sidewalk.)
3. Sidewalk Cure. (Makes area inaccessible to full weight equipment until cure completion.)

The greater detail excluded from the summary is important to the installer, but not to others.

Every activity has a beginning (predecessor) and an end (successor)

Once all activities have been identified, they are set in order by specifying their relationship to other activities. The project has one starting point and one ending point, and every activity has one or more preceding and one or more succeeding activities. There can be no "orphan activities" that do not have both a predecessor and a successor.

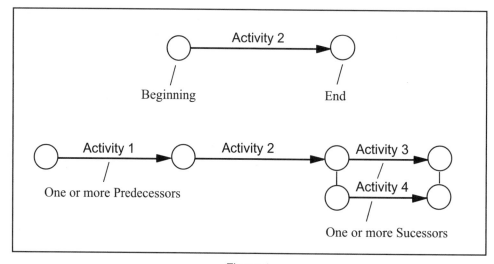

Figure 1
Activities require predecessors and successors

All activities identified in the schedule are necessary for project completion. So, they are broadly related. But "everything is related" does not show the importance of the relationships. The skill and the art of specifying relationships is to show all necessary relationships, by specifying only the most important ones. Nothing can be missed, but the fewest relationships possible will best communicate the meaning and importance of these relationships.

The activities should first be listed in order by system, exactly as the installing contractor will install them. Listing in installation order, but not yet specifying predecessors and successors, will speed the processes and maintain common sense. (This short cut is limited by the number of activities in sequence you can keep straight in your head.)

Then, the relationships between all activities in all systems are specified and connected. For example, in a single story building the earthwork, concrete, steel, and roof installers will dig the hole, install footings, install foundation walls, backfill, install concrete slab, install structural steel, and install roof. The plumbing contractor will install underground rough in, above grade rough in, and later (after finished walls and materials are installed) install fixtures and trim. The relationship between activities in both systems becomes: dig hole, install footing, install foundation walls, back fill, install plumbing rough in below grade, install concrete slab, install structural steel and roof, install above grade rough in, install finished walls and materials, install plumbing fixtures and trim. By showing listed activities by system you are "building the installer's work in your head and on paper." By connecting the activities in all systems you are "building the whole project in your head and on paper." See figure 2 on page 100.

Resources Assigned to Activities add Meaning and Scale

Resources are executers of an activity, usually in the same form as the estimate: labor, material, equipment. These resources and estimated quantities are transferred to the activities in the schedule. For all activities you control, the estimated quantities and the resources assigned determine the activity's duration.

Working calendar

Establishing durations for individual activities must be proceeded by establishing a working calendar for the project—showing the number of hours to be worked for each day of the project. This is an annual calendar for the specific project location that specifies the number of hours to be worked per week (five 8-hour shifts per week, twelve 8-hour shifts per week), and nonworking time due to seasonal weather, holidays, and other nonworking time observed such as hunting, fishing, farm planting and harvesting. See figure 3 on page 101.

Labor

The most common resource is labor of the required skill and capacity. The man-hours for an activity from the estimate and the number of men assigned will determine the duration of the activity. For example, if an activity is estimated to take 40 man-hours to complete and one man is assigned (working 40 hours per week), the task will be completed in one week. If five men are assigned to the same activity, the task will be completed in one day. See figure 4 on page 102.

Equipment

Scarce equipment is another assigned resource. For example, if you have a high cost, specialized paving machine for which no identical machine can be obtained in time for the project, the resource of one paving machine, the hourly production of the machine, and the estimated quantity to be installed determines the activity duration. Small tools and equipment that are not scarce are not assigned as resources.

Material

Material can be, but is not frequently, an assigned resource. Assigning material as a resource makes sense when it is sufficiently large or heavy to make transportation to the work area limited by the available transportation means. For example, if 10,000 cubic yards of a material were required, but the haul road could only handle 1,000 cubic yards per day, material might be assigned as a resource. (Treating material procurement- purchasing, engineering, fabrication, and delivery as an activity, not a resource, is common and used on most projects.)

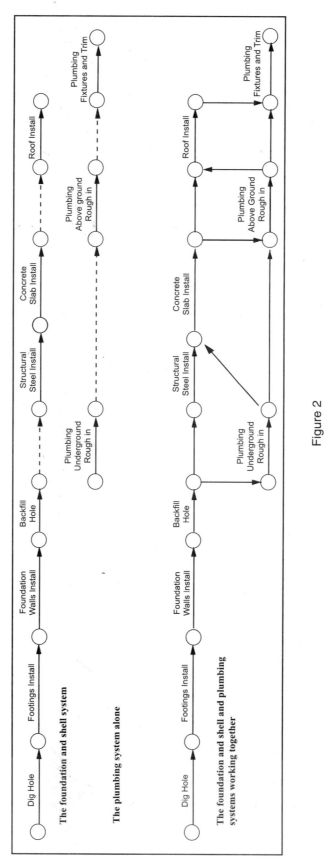

Figure 2

A schedule showing the relationship between the activities in two systems

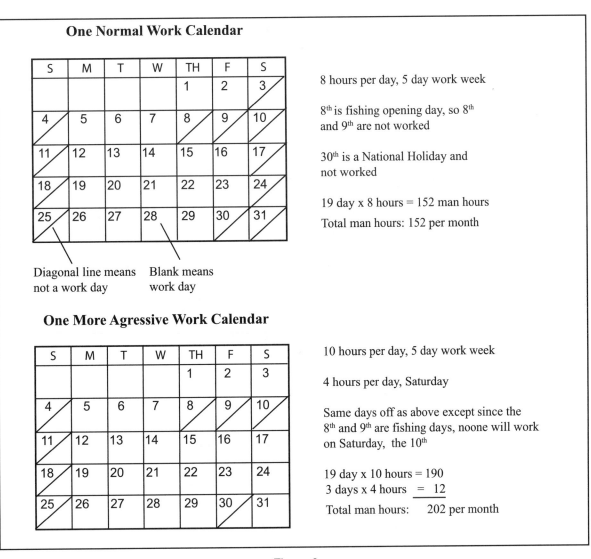

Figure 3
Work calendars differ by project

Many more calendars can be developed for the work hour and nonworking customs for the project, but they must be real. These calendars must show what you and all other project participants will do, not what you wish they would do. The farming, hunting, fishing days and other holidays employees assume are not worked in your project area must be shown as nonworking on the calendar. If your calendar requires overtime or shift differential pay, this additional cost must be in your estimate.

Cost

Cost is another resource that can be, but seldom is, used to determine duration—at least obviously. If the owner's money to pay for a project is only available at certain intervals, the project can be scheduled so that the dollar value of construction completed is always slightly less than the money available. This is very seldom used obviously, but can be used as a management tool if you know the owner has intermittently available funds. Assigning money as a resource is frequently done, not to determine duration but to project cash flow needs.

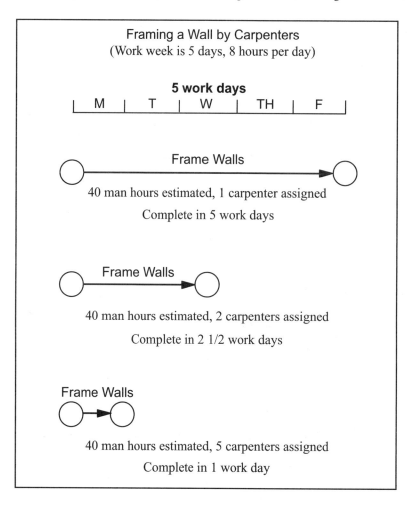

Figure 4
Adding manpower can shorten durations

This example shows how estimated quantities and resources assigned determine the duration for activities you control. In the real world, you would have to check that the job site density would allow five carpenters to be assigned to this activity without severely reducing productivity, and thus increasing duration and cost. Such common sense and practical knowledge must be used at all times. You are building a real project, not just playing with numbers.

Schedules not made from estimating information are useless arts and crafts

It should be noted that resource assignment requires detailed knowledge of the estimated resource for this project at this time. This can only be obtained from the estimate. Schedules made with only intuition, and general historical knowledge of past projects without project specific information cannot predict time, evaluate allocation of resources, or help manage a project. Such schedules, however, are common and useless.

Time–Determined by Resources or Fixed

Time for activities you control

The desired time of each activity and the total project are estimated during the development of the workable approach. However, in scheduling, the real time of the activities and the project are determined as the result of the resources assigned to activities. If this resulting time proves unacceptable for your purpose, it must be altered by changing resources, or predecessors and successors as described later. Arbitrary assignment of durations to activities you control has no basis in fact, and is wishful thinking, but not prediction and management.

Time for activities you do not control

Activities controlled by the owner, outside vendors, chemical cure time, or weather will have specified dates or times. For example, a school remodeling will start after the year's last day of classes, and be completed before the start of the next school year. Some products will have a production date set by the manufacturer. Some excavation and all landscape planting cannot be done in frozen ground. Some of these fixed dates are unavoidable, but when a fixed date is specified, you lose all ability to manage that activity. So, fixed dates should be avoided whenever possible, and this includes most subcontractor/ vendor activities.

Group Activities into Bite-Sized Pieces to Aid Understanding and Monitoring

Job site activities have maximum two-week durations

Every job site activity scheduled must have a duration of a maximum of two weeks or it will not have reality to most people, nor will it permit monitoring during construction sufficiently early to take necessary corrective action. When a longer activity must be subdivided into two-week durations, use readily identifiable breaks, such as: "Pour concrete floor level 2 northwest," not "pour 1/4 of concrete floor." The two-week long maximum duration does not apply to offsite wait times controlled by others. For example, if equipment is to be produced on a specified date three months in the future, the three-month activity need not be broken into two-week segments.

Subprojects and milestones help define activity grouping

Similar to the two-week maximum duration for onsite job activities mentioned above, breaking a longer schedule into bite-sized pieces of grouped activities increases understanding and eases monitoring. Subprojects are grouping of activities that have a natural relationship. Groupings by a team or crew of people, at the same time, at a specific location, or working on a shared task help people recognize, "Oh! There I am and that's my work."

Milestones designate the start and end of a subproject, or other grouping, that have a natural relationship. The milestones for these groupings must be unmissable and should be identified by an event that takes no special knowledge or information; for example, an activity such as permanent power is on, or permanent conditioned air is being delivered.

Four useful subprojects are:
1. Permissions, such as permits, and job specific licenses.
2. Preparation such as finance, job specific insurance, and design completion.
3. Material order, engineering, fabrication, and delivery.
4. Job site construction.

Subprojects for the construction portion of a building construction might be:
1. Site preparation.
2. Foundation and structure.
3. Weather enclosure.
4. Interior construction.
5. Final site work.

In all cases, all activities in the whole project are still related as if no subproject existed, but the grouping will aid in understanding and later monitoring.

Production Limits

Scarce resources available, maximum jobsite density, chemical cure times

All projects have production limits, either absolute production limits determined by scarce resources or chemical cure time of materials, or desirable production limits to achieve maximum job site productivity. The scheduling tool will show the cumulative effect of all the individual decisions you made when determining predecessors and successors and assigning resources to activities so that you can see if these activities together exceed the production limits.

Critical path—the production limit for the project

The critical path is the series of activities from the start to the end of the project that determines the project duration. For each day one of these activities changes, the overall project duration changes by one day also. The critical path, therefore, forms the production limit for the entire project, given the approach you have selected, and the activities, relationships, and resources you have estimated and assigned. This path will be critical only for these predecessors, successors, and resources. If any of these are changed, an entirely new set of activities could form a new critical path.

Does Your Approach Work? If Not, What Can You Do About It?

Reports from the schedule

The schedule tool will produce reports that summarize all of the decisions you made for each resource to show manpower, material, equipment, and money used for all activities for each unit of time—hour, day, week, and month. Although you made the assignments and decisions when assembling this schedule, the cumulative effect of all decisions was not immediately apparent. With these reports, specific over allocations of any resource can be determined so necessary actions can be taken.

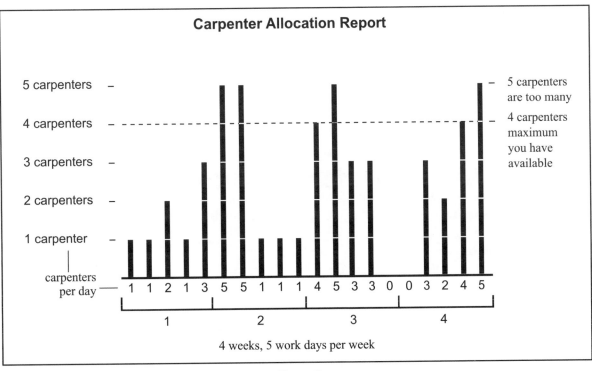

Carpenter Allocation Report

Figure 5
A report that shows the results of your scheduling decisions

Carpenter allocation is produced by the decisions you made about estimated quantities, assigned resources, sequences of activities, and the working calendar. This report shows the cumulative result of all decisions you made for all activities. There is no other way (within the normal limits of time and patience) to show the effect of many decisions made at and for different times.

If you have only four carpenters of the required skill available for work on this project, or four carpenters is the maximum who can fit in the project area without loss of production, changes must be made. If you are trying to maintain a steady crew size, changes are also required. Changes to activity sequences, assignment of activities to other parties, change in resource quantity assignment, or change in working calendars are a few ways to level the carpenter allocation. The scheduling tool allows you to instantly try these adjustments and see the results.

Time of the overall project

Scheduling is usually thought to be about time, "How long will the project take?" But scheduling is not just lines drawn on paper. That is only wishful thinking. As described above, time shows the results of the decisions made when developing the workable approach. It is not, "How long will it take?" but, "With the facts that I know and the assumption that I made—what is the resulting time?" This will either confirm that your workable approach achieves the required time of duration, or it will show the problems and opportunities for correction.

Adjustments for Schedule Improvement

If the resulting schedule does not achieve your required duration, minor modifications can make improvements, while staying within the limits of your estimated approach.

These are:

Overlap activities—lead and lag times

The predecessor and successor relationships were first specified as end-to-end relationships, one cannot start until the other is finished. But, this is not how things work in the real world. Frequently, you can start some of the succeeding activity before all of the preceding activity is completed. For example, you cannot paint a wall until it is built, but you can begin painting some walls before all walls are built. This overlap of predecessors and successors can accelerate the schedule, but you must recognize the real world and project specific production limits. Practical knowledge of how things are done limits the overlap. A minimum of a three-day head start (three days of work available for the succeeding activity) is also a practical management limit.

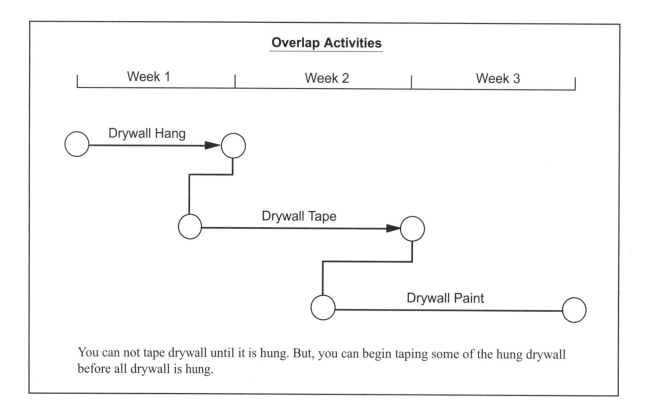

Figure 6
Activity overlap shortens durations

Resources

Additional resources assigned to an activity will shorten the activity duration. Resource assignments up to the maximum you have available, while still within the job site density production limits, can be added without increase in cost. Another possibility is to assign a different resource to the same task (a different trade or an outside vendor).

Predecessor and successors—consider other possibilities

Your assigned predecessor and successor relationships were your best choice, but not always the only choice. For example, for interior construction wall rough in, the plumber (who has larger pipes that must slope to drain) should work before the electrician (who has smaller conduit that does not slope). With coordination and good tradesmen, however, the electrician could work first. Such a change can change the critical path and the whole project duration.

Working calendar

Working calendars can be changed to work more hours per week to shorten the project duration. The ability to achieve this without additional cost is governed first by the work and compensation practices in the project area. Shift pay premiums, and overtime costs, as well as supervision and utility cost for extended work hours all impose additional costs. The work limits per man per week that can be worked without loss of production and increase in errors is another limit (about 50 hours).

Summary

Scheduling is the graphic and mathematical tool to show the time that results from your estimated workable approach. Itemization of activities, relationship between activities, and resource assignment produces a schedule. This chapter describes how to make a schedule that can be made to work. The next chapter describes how to make it work well in the real world.

2.13 Schedule Implementation and Management
Adjusting the workable approach so success is probable, and revisions unusual

Making a schedule that could be made to work was discussed in the last chapter. Here we discuss making the schedule work well so that success, even with normal error and variation, is the normal outcome.

How Scheduling Developed and Changed

The beginning of scheduling systems

Fredrick Taylor and Henry Gantt developed industrial production time and motion studies in the early 1900s in America. They believed that the source for specifying and reducing activity duration was scientific management (upper management, not the production worker). Their graphic tool, the bar chart (also called the Gantt chart), assembled bars representing activities, with lengths representing durations, organized in their proposed order of installation. Bar charts represented their opinion of how things should be done. But they could not be used as a tool for management and control of these activities because they presented the conclusion, but did not show how the conclusion was reached. This was management's conclusion and used no input from production workers.

Scheduling systems that permit management and control

Scheduling systems began after World War II in the United States, about the same time as project management. In 1956, the DuPont companies began developing CPM (Critical Path Method) scheduling for construction projects. In 1957 the U.S. Navy, working on the Polaris submarine project, began developing PERT (Performance Evaluation and Review Technique) scheduling. Unlike the bar chart described above, these scheduling techniques showed the relationship between activities and assigned resources to the activities. This produced an overall project schedule duration based on how facts influence activities, rather than the opinions of upper management. Management and control of the schedule, and therefore the project, was then possible.

These techniques were originally applied to very large projects with 1,000's or 10,000's of activities. Computers were therefore required to process and reprocess this data sufficiently fast to be of any use, and this required engineers. The engineers processed massive amounts of data on mainframe computers to produce workable, supportable solutions—solutions where the logic and information that produced the schedule is still clearly visible in the schedule itself. This engineering mentality and personality is still required and in use for most scheduling efforts. Shoot from the hip—seat of the pants—managers lack the discipline, and willingness, to do the hard work it takes, to make, use, or evaluate a schedule. They are top down managers (who start with a conclusion and then get the facts), while scheduling is a bottom up process (get the facts then build a solution).

Why is this history important? Scheduling is a unique and powerful tool now available to many that can adjust the approach to help make project success normal. Even with these historical improvements, it is still in a form understandable to few. While scheduling was developing, project management knowledge and decisions also became more dispersed to more participants. Scheduling using the knowledge and decisions of many, done by the few, with the benefits then used by many is the result, and is discussed below.

Most People React Poorly to Schedules— Communication Requires More Effort

Few work well with scheduling charts, graphs, and symbols

The schedule is a management tool only for those ready, willing, and able to work with it as a management tool—a very small group. Only management personnel who have over a two-week time horizon can possibly work with the benefits that can be gained by scheduling. Many people do not like to plan, they prefer to operate and react, and many people cannot understand interrelations between activities. Also, few people will do the required tedious detail work.

Further, most people are incapable of using the graphs, mathematical symbols, and tables that are part of scheduling. They just do not think this way naturally, and education helps only a little. Presentation of a schedule to people who do not possess the ability to read it will produce unhelpful reactions such as (if their activities appear too long), "We've got plenty of time, we can take it easy on this one." Or (if their activities appear too short) the reaction is, "The office is wrong, they have no idea how things are really done out here." Many owners with no review or thought will say, "How can we take 10% off of this?" Less than 5% of project participants can positively and effectively use a schedule.

Few can or will make a schedule, yet input and reaction is required from many

This is a paradox—scheduling is a bottom up activity requiring the participation of many, but most can not read or work with a schedule. Yet, there is no other tool that can so rapidly analyze, adjust, and confirm a workable approach that makes success probable. The solution is to obtain the input in words and numbers from many project participants. Valuable information that could not be obtained any other way will be gained. Also, since most people greatly exaggerate the size of their contribution, many will feel ownership, or think they single-handedly created the schedule themselves. Someone in the 5% that can understand schedules, then makes the schedule using this input. Later adjustments and revisions are best done not with the schedule, but with verbal, written instructions, and with technical information the 95% are accustomed to.

Scheduling information is understood by few, job cost reports by many. For example, "completion of schedule items 135 with related coordination is required between work day 65 and 72" would probably be understood only by the scheduler. But, "Pour floor l7 northwest quarter from next Monday until the following Tuesday with a crew of 8 laborers and 6 finishers. Plumbing embeds must be installed, electrical penetration will be cored later" will be understood by those installing the work. The confidence that these instructions are correct was produced by the schedule, but the directions are communicated by other means—words and numbers. The process is: get the input in words and numbers, make the schedule with symbols and graphs, and show the results in words and numbers.

Make a CPM Schedule, show the bar chart, then add word and numbers

The CPM (Critical Path Method) scheduling as described above, takes real activities, assigns resources, and specifies their relationship to predict a real result that can be managed. This can be presented as a graphic showing the relationships between all preceding and succeeding activities, as well as their duration and resources. This permits ready visualization and management of problems and opportunities. It, however, is difficult for most people to grasp. Some say, "It looks like a wiring diagram."

All information contained in the critical path schedule can be condensed into a bar chart that shows only the bars representing the durations of the activities, sometimes accompanied by mathematical notations of predecessors and successors and assigned resources. The activities and durations of the critical path schedule can be contained on the bar chart, but none of the relationships are visually apparent and therefore management of the schedule using a bar chart is unfeasible. The critical path schedule can be condensed into bar chart, but a bar chart cannot be expanded into a critical path schedule. Further, an attempt to begin the scheduling process directly with the bar chart cannot work. Durations and relationships between activities are only a statement of wishful thinking, based on no facts and expressed as arts and crafts. This has no use in a successful project. A CPM diagram is needed for management and control. See figure 7 on page 112.

When you must give the schedule to someone in the other 95%, give them the bar chart, not the critical path version, and accompany the schedule with supplemental information presented in other forms, usually words and numbers. Their reaction will be, "OK, they did their homework, now what are we going to do?" and the words and numbers will give the instructions.

Scheduling Helps Refine and Improve the Approach

The priorities for the project (the workable purpose) should have been set well before the scheduling tools are used, but the confirmation and refinement of priorities and the visualization of their impact can more readily be seen at this point and adjustments made. The project will be scheduled to optimize a particular priority, always at some expense of other priorities. The schedule can be developed to complete the project in the absolute minimum time possible, or it can be developed to optimize productivity and therefore minimize cost, or it can recognize limited resources to work with their limits, or the priority can be the steady use of one resource. For example, if a contractor has a core crew of excellent high production personnel and wants to keep them operating at optimal capacity to achieve optimal production and profit, the schedule can be adjusted to achieve this result (such an approach must usually be disguised from the owner who usually has different priorities).

The most common approach to scheduling is to find the project duration expectation that is normal and customary in the project area and try to work to this time. The cost will go up slightly, and the grade of material may vary somewhat to achieve the expected project duration. Skillful adjustment of resources and relationships can improve productivity and profit, and improve manageability somewhat, but any improvement must be within the requirements of the owner's workable approach and purpose.

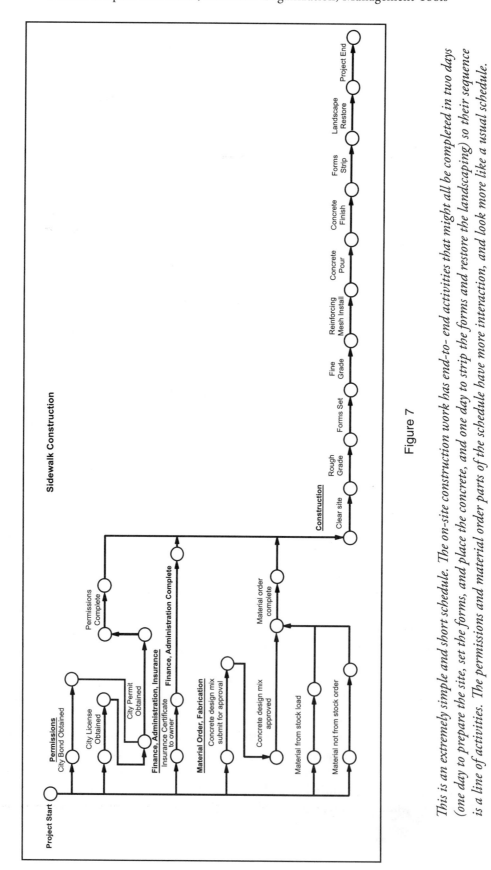

Figure 7

This is an extremely simple and short schedule. The on-site construction work has end-to-end activities that might all be completed in two days (one day to prepare the site, set the forms, and place the concrete, and one day to strip the forms and restore the landscaping) so their sequence is a line of activities. The permissions and material order parts of the schedule have more interaction, and look more like a usual schedule.

The minor revision techniques to achieve the intended results discussed in the previous chapter were: resource allocation changes, predecessor and successor changes, and working calendar revisions. If these minor changes still cannot achieve your intended result, or you seek larger improvements such as huge increases in productivity or profit, more radical scheduling revisions can be explored as discussed below.

More Radical Scheduling Related Changes

Method and location of production

Substituting machine production for hand labor can overcome production limited by scarce skilled labor. Fabrication of components off site can overcome job site density limits. Purchasing site prefabricated components from an outside vendor could also solve this problem. These decisions will usually have an effect on cost, grade, and time so the costs and benefits need to be weighed. Also, they may be executed by different companies (the subcontractors used for hand labor may not have the machines for a mechanized solution), so these decisions must be made before awarding contracts.

Big approach change

A radical change in planned execution will increase some costs in exchange for the possibility of decreasing other costs or time. For example, a sewage treatment plant with many separate concrete structures and much connecting piping is usually constructed by individually excavating and backfilling each structure for each trade, with much duplicated effort. A radical alternate approach could be to excavate the entire multi-acres site to the bottom of all the concrete structures and build them all at once. Large increases in earthwork costs might be overcome by a 300% increase in labor productivity for the concrete structures. This is a big and risky bet with possible big payoffs.

Change systems and components

A change in building system type will affect grade, cost, and time. One common example is the selection of a concrete or steel-framed building. Selection of prepackaged rooftop mechanical units or multi-component site assembled systems in an enclosed mechanical room is another example. The merits of these will vary with the prevailing construction customs, availability of labor, material price, and market forces of each project at each location and time. These decisions affect design of the component and probably related systems such as structural and electrical as well. So, these decisions should or must be made early in the project development process.

Change start, finish, and delivery time

Changing a project start date when one phase of the project is affected by weather can reduce general condition costs, increase productivity (decreasing cost or increasing profit), and in some cases reduce overall project time. For a project in an occupied building, changing the owner's proposed phasing that maintains ongoing operations can change both the delivery time and cost. For example, the cost of constructing temporary facilities for owner operations may be offset by the savings of vastly improved field productivity, with the additional benefit of reduced project delivery time.

Schedule Adjustments Can Help Make Management Success Probable

Build on opportunities and build in problem avoidance

Any pinch points or over allocation in resources must be identified and corrected. This is done after the schedule appears to work. Any activity that is scheduled beyond the available resources, or the production limit of the job site must be adjusted to conform to these limits. Scheduling programs automatically produce multiple reports that show the over allocations and make this effort easy and fast. Once you have made these adjustments, the schedule can be made to work. You then move to making it work well, as described below.

The largest opportunity to ensure success is to make the critical path consist solely of the activities you are best able to control. If you are performing some of the work with your own forces and you are confident of your ability to perform on time, or you have a strong subcontractor with the same characteristics, placing these activities on the critical path will help make success probable. Similarly, any activities that are not completely within your control, such as weak and less than competent subcontractors, or activities that still require approval from outside agencies or the government, should be uncritical.

Next is to choose activities that can lead by example and momentum and make them critical. Then, schedule related tasks by the less aggressive trades slightly earlier than usual. Get them involved early. Many people need to physically see work before they feel urgency. Identifying a series of baby steps for the weaker contractors will build in an early ramp-up of production, and drag them along.

Further, it is best to make the activities surrounding a critical activity supportive of it and with a more tolerant fit. If a critical activity begins to appear incapable of maintaining the required duration, some of the supporting activities around it can be accelerated or slowed to assist the speed of the critical activity. For example, if other activities in the work area can be finished earlier or later, the work area will be less congested—permitting more resources and greater productivity for the critical activity.

The tolerance of the fit surrounding critical activities can be seen by the activity's float. Float is the number of days that actual duration can miss the planned duration without changing the overall schedule. For example, if an activity has a float of 5 days, it can be up to 5 days late without changing the project's critical path. (Activities on the critical path by definition have no float.) The activities surrounding the critical path can be altered in the same manner. The critical path was altered by changing resources, successors and predecessors, and lead and lag times. Increasing the float of the weaker activities surrounding the critical path will increase the tolerant fit. More error will not produce an overall bad effect.

Precision of the estimated quantities and resources for activities is readily achievable, and should have been done in the estimate. This precision is good, get it done right once and leave it alone. Precision of the fit between the activities, in contrast, is not desirable and will not produce a schedule with the give and go to absorb the variation in results that always occurs. (We are dealing with people here, so there will always be variation.) A tolerant fit between activities, with well placed shock absorbers, is the goal.

Adjustments to the critical path made in the planning stage by changing resource allocation, changing responsibility for a task (do yourself, or sub out to one or more parties), or changing relationships between activities to start earlier can be done at some cost, no cost, or sometimes less cost. The cost of getting it right to start with is always less than fixing a problem later.

Getting Started and Finished

Getting out of first gear and overcoming the goal line defense

As all experienced managers know, getting started and up to full production, and getting finally completed (every last detail including documentation) requires focused management attention. The schedule can be organized to assist this management effort. First, more milestones can be added early and late in the project so a sense of urgency and opportunity for management are created—not, "Oh we have lots of time, no need to rush now." Every activity—administrative, engineering, fabrication, and shipping—is a work item. Once people start working, it is easier to get them to work more and in the way you require.

Next, build in completion as part of doing the work. Ideally, all close out documents, adjustments, repairs, and certification should be done before the trade performing the work leaves the job site completely. If they are totally gone, return trips and getting familiar with the job again will drag out completion unnecessarily. Also, in the schedule there should be certain certifications and demonstrations to make completion a debugging and verification process, not just end-of-project paper work. All closeout activities—testing, certifying, and documenting—are work items.

Schedule updates during the project should be rare

The properly constructed schedule as described above will almost never have to be updated. All activities, their relationships, and resulting durations are based on actual estimating data. If you do not make the schedule, you do not make the estimate. Pinch point or over allocations of resources have already been identified and corrected to achieve a tolerant fit. Over 95% of the schedules constructed in this way achieve the original completion date with competent, but not extraordinary, management of the project.

The schedule will identify where management needs to focus attention. The critical path, strong and weak and activities, driving and weak players, probable problems and opportunities are learned and managed when making the schedule. So, even project personnel who have no knowledge of the schedule can know the right priorities. Working on the right problems, the reasonably competent and hard working will probably succeed.

A schedule should only be updated during the course of the project if an extraordinary event occurs that alters the critical dates by more than a week. (Extraordinary events are by definition rare and may not occur in a person's entire career. Normal seasonal weather variation, late decisions by government officials, labor disruptions at time of labor contract renewal, seasonal delivery difficulties for some materials, and troublesome weak subcontractors are normal and should be included in project planning.)

A practice used by some of a two-week schedule revision means that there was no schedule established at all. Every two weeks new descriptions of what fires are being put out at the moment are itemized. The status of the failing project is described, and guesses for the next two weeks of fire fighting are presented.

Scheduling Used for Other Purposes

Scheduling for job costing and management communicates poorly

Scheduling to monitor the productivity of the job can be done with the scheduling tool. Those familiar with and competent in scheduling techniques will see this powerful tool as obvious and natural. However, as described above, these people are few. Everyone else did not understand the original schedule, so they also will not understand the updates. (This failure to understand will also include those in accounting responsible for job cost accounting.) Attempts by the few to manage with the schedule that others cannot understand will sound like, "It is so because I say it is so. Now just do it." This attitude will neither convince nor help cooperation.

Litigation—lawyers wearing hardhats

When a project has failed so badly that the rubble and ashes are being sifted in court, scheduling tools can be used to show the location, cause, and size of the failures. All the decisions above and in the previous chapter are directed towards increasing possibilities for improvement to make success probable. If these improvements were not made, or no planning took place at all, the same tools can be used to measure the resulting failure. The methods are the same, but the numbers for failure are usually much larger.

Summary

Scheduling takes the knowledge of many in word and numbers, makes a schedule by a few with charts and symbols, then provides the results for many in words and numbers. Scheduling shows the time that results from your decisions on approach, grade of materials, and cost, then adjusts these components to get closer to the project purpose. A tolerant fit between activities provides the shock absorbers that make success normal and revisions unusual, even with the unavoidable performance variation and error.

2.14 Choosing to Make Project Success Normal
The right attitude, and type and timing of effort

Choosing project success or accepting failure is a fork in the road at the start of a project. Both attitude and type and timing of effort are involved. The successful approach requires opening your eyes, looking in the right direction, getting the right facts every time, making your decisions, and then getting out of the way and letting others do their work. Success starts with understanding the nature of things (and the facts) and builds an approach bottom up.

With the wrong attitude, success can occur only occasionally—by luck—and failure is normal. Success requires intense effort and hard work early in the project, and less later. Success requires less total project effort than failure.

Successful attitudes and efforts, and their contrasting failures, are discussed below.

Successful Attitudes

1. Define a purpose that can be made to work

Success
Define a purpose that others can execute

Success starts with a workable purpose that only the highest levels of the organization can define. This purpose must define the grade, time, and cost for the project, including priorities and trade-offs. You cannot have it all. Precisely define requirements only when necessary, otherwise provide acceptable ranges. These directions must be right and complete, but the shortest directions are best. (Right and short are the hardest to do well!) The purpose and priorities should state what you want to achieve, *not* how to achieve it. Definition of the priorities and trade-offs of grade, time, and cost form a purpose others can understand and use to develop a workable approach.

Failure
Do not define a purpose, operate blind and wild

It may seem obvious that if you do not say what you want to accomplish, no one can accomplish it for you. Yet, many projects start and are completed with this shortcoming. Making a decision about what you want to do is hard and some never do it. If you do not decide, someone else will decide for you, and you will be disappointed. You will find yourself in mid-project patching and repairing unsatisfactory results. Or worse, find yourself married to the wrong players who cannot possibly achieve the desired results. Unless the boss has the talent, brains, and backbone to make a decision, which others can execute, project failure will be normal.

2. Build an approach that seeks excellence, not perfection

Success
Move ever closer to excellence

Once a workable purpose has been set, execution builds bottom up, starting with the nature of things, then the facts, organizing the facts, and developing an approach that will achieve in excess of 95% of the intended results. This approach is then protected by building in a tolerant fit, so that the normal variation of many small errors will not prevent achievement of the project purpose. Evaluate possible workable approaches for their potential to achieve the workable purpose, not against a standard of perfection.

Failure
Hope for perfection, get what you are given

Seeking perfection and working down to whatever you can get leads to a very low spot. Demanding perfection you know cannot be achieved is fruitless. "Only the best for us" is quickly followed by, "If you can not give me what I want, what can you give me?" You hope that what you will eventually settle for somehow satisfies your needs, but instead you will get what they have a lot of, which is rarely what you need. This approach slides down into mediocrity and failure.

3. Open your eyes and ears and see what is in front of you

Success
See the character and nature of things and situations

People and companies have a character, capacity, nature and tendency. Materials are scarce at one location, price, and time, and abundant at others. There are physical limits such as the weather, cure time of materials, and density limits to work areas. And there are customs for all of these things in each market. Know your materials, equipment, and methods. Know your people and your market. Build on their strengths, and manage their weaknesses.

Failure
Impose arbitrary decisions

Failure involves making arbitrary demands for people, material, and processes without checking to see if they are even normal or customary, let alone possible. Since project success involves executing all of the required work items all of the time, even one slip up can cause significant problems. Arbitrary demands nearly ensure partial or complete project failure.

4. Involve those closest to the work, but with guidance

Success
Make the hard decisions, delegate, get out of the way, and let them do their job

Tell them what you want to achieve, give them the methods so they can determine if they are achieving it, but do not tell them how to execute. This is not a process of giving them the keys to the place and hoping for the best. It is setting a purpose, involving them in the development of the approach to achieve this purpose, and providing specific targets so they can evaluate their progress. When those doing the work are in self control, they know what they are supposed to be doing, they know what they are doing right now, and they have the ability to change the first to the second.

Getting the best out of everyone is slow and hard work, but the results can be and frequently are better than the original request. Management must still ensure that all the pieces fit together and resolve conflicts between players. Although those closest to the work know their work best, they may have difficulty seeing how it fits with other parts of the project, so guidance remains a management task.

Failure
Tell them how to do the work, micromanage everything

In contrast, management decides and directs everything. And everyone else executes their instructions. Management believes that they are the process—everything starts and later flows through them. Usually their failure to define a purpose is, in part, intentional. Thinking that "I know what I want. As long as I am here, it will get done." Micromanagement and firefighting follow. Their instincts and hopes are the high point, and execution is always downhill from there.

Further, there will only be a gravity flow of information. Communication goes down only, not up. Management will tell and others will listen, but not the reverse. This means that all of the knowledge and facts of everyone except the top guys are unused. Further, those executing the work won't really have bought into the solution, so they will not execute with enthusiasm.

Management Systems That Make Failure Normal are Widely Used

If you think that failure is normal, you will get it. Entire management systems have developed to avoid decision making, then assigning blame and managing the resulting failure. The goal is to make your failure look unavoidable, and caused by forces beyond your control so that you do not get fired. This is accompanied by documenting whatever results occur—to make them appear that proper procedures were followed. Failure managers may be called: project manager, program manager, owner's representative, or consultant, or a currently fashionable title.

When charging for their services by the hour, there is an incentive to make failing projects as bureaucratic as possible. A failing project requires more service, and more fees can be charged. For these people, a failing project is a profitable project. Entire companies and even industries have used this pattern for so long that they cannot imagine that success is possible. Managers never decide, and then hire construction bureaucrats to cover their tracks.

Successful Efforts and Management

1. Get the facts—organize the facts

Success
All project components are measured and counted

Everything is counted and measured, and specifically checked for each project. These observations are organized in a framework to have use and meaning. Facts are turned into information, and information into knowledge.

Failure
Assume an approach, get the facts later or not at all

The alternate approach is to start with assumptions about what approach should be used and get the facts as needed, which will be later or not at all. With this approach, no organizational system will occur. So, the facts will be incomplete and have no context or meaning. However, facts are very persistent, and a failure to recognize them will ensure project failure.

2. Check in each particular case

Success
Specifically check everything for each project

Success recognizes that all resources are abundant at one time, location, and price and scarce at another. So, availability must be checked for each particular project in each location. This availability can change by the hour or by events such as: plant shutdowns due to maintenance or catastrophic event, a major supplier who gets an extraordinarily large order that takes all of their capacity, a new project in an area that absorbs much of the available skilled labor, vendor bankruptcy, or new government regulation.

Failure
Assume you can do it now like you did it then

Some with big egos assume they can always do exactly what they want. "If the subs won't give us what we want, get somebody else." or "Just do it like the last time. These are cookie cutter projects." Or "It is a simple job, just do it."

If the scarcities are small, subordinates will attempt to make it look like they are precisely executing the boss's instructions even though they are doing something entirely different, possibly with materials of a different grade and price. If the scarcities are large, the project will fail completely.

A Change in Attitude and Outlook—Thinking Right and Controlling Your Ego

Project success can and should be normal. And the total project effort for success is less than for failure. Egos and attitudes must be focused and managed to take the path of least resistance to success.

Perfection is not of this world. Seek excellence at the 95% level, which appears perfect if you back up a few steps. The emotional reaction to admitting you are not seeking perfection must be overcome.

Success starts with critical thought and hard work from the first day of the project. The work is heaviest in the early part of the project, then diminishes. (Get it right and get it out of the way.) Others hope their grand ideas and magnetic personalities can overcome all facts in the natural world, so hard work can be delayed or avoided. Their heads may be hard, but concrete is harder and the facts will prevail!

Success is ordinary people working hard on the right things, in an organized way, to achieve the extraordinary. Nothing is harder for the management "elite" to accept than ordinary people doing extraordinary things unblessed by fancy theories and big words.

Define a purpose that can be made to work. Build an approach that seeks excellence, not perfection. Open yours eyes and ears and see what is front of you. Involve those closest to the work, but with guidance. Get the facts and organize the facts. Check in each particular case.

Each step is common sense and achievable by all with the right attitude. With the right attitude that controls the ego, involves others, and believes success can and should be normal, project success can and will be normal.

Part III: Facts Are The Building Blocks Of Knowledge And Judgment

Understanding and Using the Parts and Pieces of the Building Well

Introduction

Facts and knowledge must be distributed to many. "We hire good consultants for that" is not an acceptable approach. To delegate all responsibility to a consultant is to forfeit all ability to manage the project.

You must know which consultant to call. And each one will have their own nature and speed—pick them and that is what you will get. And their purpose and values may not match yours. Once selected, you can change their output only a little. They will tell you there are only a few ways, and say that what others are routinely successfully achieving is unfeasible or impossible. And they will ask you questions for which your intelligent answer matters.

Call the subs, vendors, and reps for information and advice? Same problem. If you're in charge you must know something before you can even ask the first question. You cannot know everything but you must know something—enough to manage. Each building work area and task is complex, and includes traditions and ingrained work practices that may not be obvious, rational, or optimal. So no one, no matter how clever and intelligent, can figure this out without some help.

This part of the book provides this help. The chapters are divided into the main parts of the building. A little theory about why things work, a description of how things are done and why, and common misconceptions, problems, and solutions are presented for each work item. No previous knowledge of the subject is required or assumed. Only the minimum amount of technical information is presented. (Some areas may seem to contain a lot of technical information, but wait until you are asked a question. This information may seem barely enough. A second reading for reference may be needed.)

Knowledge of the information in this part of the book will put you in the top couple percent of all those in the building business. You will be able to more effectively hire project personnel (consultants, contractors, subcontractors, and vendors), evaluate their presented alternatives, answer their questions, and review their work in progress.

And one other thing happens. Because they will notice that you have taken the time to really learn about their work (not just learning a few buzzwords to fool them), they will be flattered. And respect you more. Communication improves and you manage faster, easier, and better.

3.1 Water and Building Systems

Water is required for life and useful chemical reactions. It is everywhere and affects all parts of buildings, and must be managed by building contractors, designers, and owners

Introduction

The earth's surface is 71% water, and human adults are 60% water (by weight). Next to air, it is the absence of this substance that will kill us first. We need water to live. But too much will kill us either by drowning, or within the human body, due to high blood pressure and/or imbalances between internal organs. Water balance (humidity) in the air is required for life and for comfort of people. Water also provides the temperature stability that makes life on earth possible.

Water has the capacity to dissolve and hold chemicals for cleaning, cooking, and industrial processes. Water forms a part of chemical reactions, such as concrete, where water chemically combines with cement to form a third unique material—concrete. Water also expands materials, and can produce mold and oxidation, such as rust.

The building "weather envelope," consisting of the roof, walls (including doors and windows), and the foundation waterproofing, must maintain the water balance—keeping liquid water out and moist air in. The transportation of water in the plumbing and heating systems is required, and the balance of the moisture in the air is regulated by HVAC systems.

It is the water location and therefore the movement, form, and balance that matters for people and for buildings. This balance affects all parts of buildings. Water is necessary and unavoidable, but exerts powerful forces that are not consistent at all temperatures and pressures. Worse, water frequently performs in a way that is opposite of common sense.

These properties and their implications for buildings are discussed in this chapter.

Water Weight, Volume, and Form Are Affected By Pressure and Temperature

What is water really?

Pure water is rare—hard to handle—and doesn't stay pure long

Water consists of two parts of hydrogen and one part oxygen. Most people have never seen or touched pure water. Pure water only exists if it is produced by mechanical processes such as distillation, deionization, or reverse osmosis. This pure water instantly absorbs surrounding gases. It also dissolves and absorbs metals and minerals. (Thus, industrial, scientific, and medical systems that use pure water can only use pipes and containers made of glass, special metals, or plastics—normal building materials will be attacked and dissolved.)

Water from streams, lakes, and the tap is not "pure." It contains dissolved gases, minerals, and usually biological material such as bacteria and algae. At room temperature, a volume of liquid water contains an equal volume of dissolved atmospheric gas. When starting to boil water, the small bubbles that first form on the sides of the pan are actually the dissolved atmospheric gas escaping from the liquid before water boils. The actual boiling of the water (converting a liquid to a gas) then follows.

The mineral and biological content of water is always there, but usually ignored until it causes a problem such as unsightly and unhealthy mold, or algae that harms a concrete mixture. Impure water is considered "pure enough" if it does not cause a problem for your purpose.

The Weight of Water Can Be Tremendous
Foundations, roofs, marine structures, and pipes and tanks must withstand water's weight

The weight of "pure" water at room temperature is approximately 62 pounds per cubic foot. When the depth of the water is more than 1 cubic foot, the weight and pressure at the bottom is equal to the sum of all the cubic feet of water stacked above. For example, the bottom of the 36,198 foot-deep Marianas Trench off the eastern coast of the Philippines in the South Pacific produces a weight and pressure of approximately 21,000,000 pounds per square foot. Lesser, but still great pressure, is caused by the weight of the water at the bottom of foundations and under ground pipes, tanks, and tunnels in water-saturated soil.

Pressure Does Not Change Water Volume
Hydraulic systems made possible

The volume of water at a given temperature will not compress by applied pressure. This is well known in hydraulics where the fluid pressure through hoses on cylinders can be used to do useful work, such as operate your car's brakes. But, water does change in volume and density with temperature, as shown below.

Temperature does change volume and density—but not evenly
Keeps lakes from turning into blocks of ice. Hugely important for cooling system and boiler design

	Temperature (degrees F)	Pounds per cubic foot
Ice	32°	57.3
Water turning to ice	32°	62.41
Maximum density	39.1°	62.42
Room temperature	70°	62.30
Hot	100°	61.99

	Temperature (degrees F)	Pounds per cubic foot
Mechanical systems temperatures	200°	60.11
	300°	57.41
	400°	53.62
	500°	48.78
	600°	41.49
	700°	25.38

This shows an important property that is unusual to water. From very high temperatures, such as 700F, the water becomes increasingly dense as it cools until it reaches its maximum density at 39.1F. Then, as it cools further, it becomes less dense again. When it freezes to ice, it becomes even less dense. This means that ice floats on top of water. It also has the additional property that, as water approaches freezing, it sinks. This will invert (surface water goes to the bottom) a lake, to mix the water. Fisherman will know this as the lake "turning over," as the mixing occurs. Lake turnover can also be caused by storms for shallow lakes.

This property of water makes life possible. If water performed like other materials, and became increasingly dense as it cooled and froze, ice would sink to the bottom of the lake and continue to accumulate until the entire lake was a block of ice. With the unique density properties of water, this is avoided by mixing. To a lesser extent, this variable density of water can have a mixing effect as well for parts of mechanical systems.

Pressure decreases water's freezing point
Increases the range and capacity of cooling equipment

Most materials continue to contract when freezing, and their melting point is raised by increased pressure, but not water. Water expands when freezing, and increased pressure on water decreases the freezing point. Skis and ice skates glide over snow or ice. The pressure of skis and skates temporarily melts the ice and forms a thin film of water that provides lubrication. Those hardy enough to attempt to ski or skate at -40°F find that the pressure is no longer enough to melt ice, and the glide stops. The lowering of the freezing point by pressure allows cooling systems to operate more efficiently by making and circulating chilled water at temperatures lower than the normal temperature of ice.

Pressure increases water's boiling point
Makes heating equipment more efficient and effective

The effect of pressure on the boiling point of water is as follows:

Boiling points of water	
No pressure (a vacuum)	32° F
Atmospheric pressure	212° F
95 pounds pressure	324° F
600 pounds pressure	486° F

The increase in boiling point with pressure is useful to the design of boilers, where high temperature water can circulate and heat more effectively.

Relative humidity—how much water can the air hold?
Humidity control is a driving factor in heating, cooling, and ventilation systems design

The relative humidity is the amount of moisture that air can hold at a temperature without condensing. (The moisture holding capacity is relative to the temperature, hence the name relative humidity.) Warm air can hold more moisture and cold air less moisture, without condensing into fog, dew, or droplets of water. The amount of moisture the air can hold varies with temperature, but it does not increase equally for each degree of temperature rise. At the hotter temperatures, the moisture capacity increases far more than for lower temperatures.

Higher temperature and pressure air holds lots more water
This is a critical factor for cooling system design. Also, it affects condensation in walls and insulations as the air is cooled—frequently a problem, and always an important design consideration

	Temperature	Water weight in a cubic yard of air
Freezing	32.0° F	= .1300 oz/cy
Cooling Coil in an Air Conditioning System	53.6° F	= .2848 oz/cy
Normal Room Temperature	68.0° F	= .7904 oz/cy
Temperature of Human Skin	98.6° F	= 1.1268 oz/cy

The relative humidity is also affected by pressure—higher air pressures can hold more water. For example, a tunneling operation can have very high humidity and be in constant fog. But, when blasting is performed, for a few seconds the increase in pressure caused by the blast will temporarily remove all fog, and one can see clearly for great distances. The effects of pressure on relative humidity are not generally discussed for human comfort in habitable spaces up to 2,000 feet above sea level, because the pressure effects are small. But in mechanical systems, the pressure effect on relative humidity is an important consideration. Also, in building systems, small pressure differences that force moist air to move through parts of a building (that have different temperatures such as attics, walls, and windows) are now understood to be a very important source of moisture accumulation to be managed.

Water Is temperature stable

(It takes a lot of energy to change water temperature.)
Water maintains temperatures that permit life on earth, but also increases energy use in heating and cooling systems

Water is the most temperature-stable material that we commonly encounter, and is the benchmark for all others. The specific heat, which compares the quantity of heat required to change the temperature of one unit of weight one degree is as follows:

Specific heats of some common materials (water is the benchmark)

Water	1000 (most temperature stable)
Aluminum	210
Iron	211
Lead	31 (least temperature stable)

And the heat to change the state of water from ice, to liquid, to gas is even greater. The specific heat units are:

Freezing	80,000
Change liquid water 1 degree F	1,000
Vaporize water	539,000

If you are moving from ice to water vapor, you must add heat to the water to achieve this change of state. If you are moving in the opposite direction, from water vapor to a block of ice, you must remove heat in the same quantities to achieve the cooled change of state.

The stable nature of water, and the huge energy to change its state, can be seen by common observations. In some southwestern climates, water is placed in a clay jar, similar to a flowerpot that is very porous. As the water seeps through the jar walls and evaporates, it actually cools the water inside the jar to a lower temperature than the surrounding air (change of state from liquid to gas produces cooling). A mechanical cooling system for a building can freeze a block of ice in the basement in winter using the surrounding cold, and use the change of state from ice to liquid water in the summer months to provide building cooling. The energy of the change of state, not the temperature differential of the colder water, does the work.

In a desert (that has very little water vapor present in the air), as the sun goes down the air is cooled extremely rapidly, from well over 100 degrees to freezing in minutes. Similarly, in a very humid climate such as New Orleans, Louisiana, the heat of the day persists with much less temperature drop into the evening hours. (The increased water vapor in the air provides the temperature stability.)

Movement of Water
Water will move when we do not want it to, and will resist movement when we do want it

Gravity is always at work.

Gravity will move water through building systems—reliably and free. Systems that rely on gravity to shed water, move water, or drain water tend to be a good first choice, but they can be overcome by other forces that also move water.

Water sticks to surfaces with great force
Water sticks to surfaces with great force, and this forces water to travel through building materials in undesirable ways. Also, it restricts and slows water flow through pipes. Water force is one of the largest factors in soil strength, stability, and therefore earthwork and foundation design and construction

Water has a strong attraction to the side of any surface it touches. For example, if you look sideways at a glass of water, the water actually curves up the side of the glass. This is referred to as capillary action. Capillary action is extremely strong, particularly for small spaces. For spaces several thousands of an inch across, the capillary action can actually move the water vertically up 100 feet. Since this small constant dimension between materials is difficult to maintain, and there are usually breaks in the material, a 100-foot rise is seldom achieved. But capillary action moving water up through building materials 4 feet is routine. Hence, a roof leak that drips into the building uphill and sideways from the point of entry through the roofing membrane is known to all who have attempted to diagnose roofing leak problems.

Similarly, clay that has a grain shape that is flat like a thin piece of paper is held together by huge attractions of the water to the grains. When completely dry, clay is a powder that can blow in the wind. When it is moist, it is extremely stiff and can hold a vertical bank without support. When fully saturated, it is a gooey mess that can mire powerful earth-moving equipment. The amount of water in the soil is of huge importance in soil engineering and earthwork.

This same capillary action produces pipe friction, which acts as a thin film that sticks to the walls of all pipes. This thin film reduces the flow of water through pipes, making larger diameter pipes more efficient. And this is important in pipe size calculations.

Dispersion spreads water evenly
Water, and substances in water, will tend to spread evenly, no matter what you would like

Water or chemicals in water will tend to spread themselves evenly, without stirring, throughout the liquid or gas. For example, in a glass of water, if a drop of food coloring is slowly and carefully placed on the top of the water, after a time the food coloring will disperse until the entire glass of water is an even lighter shade of the food coloring. The same occurs with water vapor when introduced in a portion of a space; it will equalize and disperse the water evenly through the entire space, even without any airflow.

Pressure can move water unpredictably
Roofs, exterior walls, doors, and windows must be designed to resist the movement of water in all directions. Every detail in the building weather envelope becomes important

Water can be moved by pressure. Wind pressure, pressure of water, or pressure of other materials, can move water uphill or sideways—contrary to gravity and, frequently, common sense. Mechanical pressure produced by pumps or fans will also move water, but in a controlled and predictable way, as described below.

Expansion—absorbed water expands some materials
Material selection and installation must accommodate this expansion

Water will expand by temperature as described above. Water will also cause other materials to expand when absorbed. The expansion caused by the absorption of the materials can produce forces greater than most building components can withstand. For example, an ancient quarrying technique to produce the limestone blocks used to build the pyramids involved drilling a series of holes at the edge of a block to be quarried. Then, by stuffing plant material, such as straw in the holes, and adding water, the water expanded straw material would break the block loose from the mountain. Damage to buildings caused by expansion of water to ice is familiar to those who live in northern climates. Absorption of water in some soils, such as expansive clays, produces forces that will lift the building off its foundation.

Water's Effect on People and Building Systems

Temperature and humidity vary greatly by location
Building systems for humidity and water control in Houston, Texas, will usually be opposite in purpose and design from those in Minneapolis, Minnesota

The presence of water and temperature vary greatly as shown below.

Hottest	Yearly Average	Coldest	Yearly Average
Miami, FL	75.9° F	International Falls, MN	36.8° F
Brownsville, TX	73.8° F	Caribou, ME	38.8° F
Phoenix, AZ	72.6° F	Fargo, ND	41.0° F

Driest	Yearly Precipitation	Wettest	Yearly Precipitation
Phoenix, AZ	7.66"	Quillayate, WA	105.18"
Bakersfield, CA	5.72"	New Orleans, LA	61.88"
Las Vegas, NV	4.13"	West Palm Beach, FL	60.75"

And, these are the ranges for normally occupied areas. Parts of the Spanish Sahara in Africa have no rain for years, and parts of the island of Kauai in Hawaii receive 450 inches of rain per year.

The building and mechanical systems required to accommodate these variations produce wholly different problems and responses in different parts of the world. For example, Houston's high temperatures increase the water carrying capacity of the air, and high rainfall provides the water to fully saturate this air. The HVAC systems must be designed for much dehumidification, and building materials (walls, roof, and interior finishes) must be designed and selected to withstand high humidity levels that will still exist even after much dehumidification. In Minneapolis, the lower temperature air can carry less water even if the rainfall was similar to Houston. Dehumidification becomes less important and heating more important. Overall, however, a narrow range of temperatures and humidities are acceptable for human use. But, these produce vastly different building types and mechanical systems in different climates.

Temperature and humidity acceptable for human comfort varies little
Mechanical system design must focus on narrow ranges—of a degree or percent or two. Small changes in requirements can produce big changes in equipment and cost

The real world effective temperature (considering both temperature and humidity) that is now considered ideal is 68 degrees F winter and 71 degrees F summer. This is for normal adults with light clothing in conditions of little airflow. Old age, poor health, and airflow will increase these temperatures. Heavy clothing and physical activity will decrease them. But the total extreme range would vary up or down less than 20 degrees. This is small in comparison to the 160 degree range (-40 degrees F to 120 degrees F) of outside temperature. Temperatures or humidity 10–20% above these ranges can severely reduce people's ability to perform normal activities, and can produce a health hazard or even death.

Water Causes Most of the Work of Heating and Cooling

Do not demand an ideal temperature and humidity unless you can and will pay to build and operate it

As stated above, water makes the environment temperature stable. This stability affects the work needed to change the air temperature or the humidity, as shown by the heat units required to change from 0F to 70F at different relative humidities. (Cooling to remove the humidity requires giving up the same amount of heat.)

Temperature Range	Relative Humidity	Heat Units
0–70°F	10% RH	15 Heat units
0–70°F	50% RH	255 Heat units
0–70°F	100% RH	340 Heat units
40–50°F	50% RH	35 Heat units
50–60°F	50% RH	40 Heat units
60–70°F	50% RH	50 Heat units

So, changing from 66°F to 68°F takes less energy than going from 68°F to 70°F. Humidity matters hugely in energy use.

Summary

The weight and resulting pressure of water affects foundations and underground tanks and piping. Water's capillary actions affect earth strength and workability and are a driving factor in soil and foundation design and construction. Volume stability at all pressures is used in hydraulics. The volume variability with temperature mixes water in tanks and pipes. Pressure that decreases water's freezing and increases water's boiling point, as well as water's temperature stability, affects heating and cooling design. Water moves by gravity, capillary action, dispersion, and pressure—and expands some materials when absorbed.

These properties of water (which are different or opposite most other materials) make life possible, govern the limits to the design of the building envelope, affect material selection, and cause much of the energy use and complexity in mechanical heating, cooling, and ventilating systems. Failure to deal with water's properties (which are sometimes the opposite of common sense) causes most of the problems with cracking and leaking foundations, leaky roofs, water-damaged and moldy walls, windows, doors, and uncomfortable HVAC systems. These properties of water, and their effective management, will be revisited in the following chapters.

3.2 Material Properties Best for Strength —with Some Give and Go

Good for structures and exterior walls

Introduction

Construction projects require lots of materials and these materials tend to be heavy, so transportation costs are important. Also, the materials must be handled, fabricated, and assembled using the locally available labor with minimal additional training. Materials must, therefore, be abundant, reasonably priced, and well known in the project area.

Effective use of these few materials requires knowledge by everyone of the materials' nature and the properties. And this means you. For owners and those in finance and insurance: "We have architects and engineers that handle that" is not an adequate defense. They will ask your approval of their work, or suggest new products or systems, and you need to be able to make an informed choice. General contractors must make similar choices when selecting subs and products from vendors. And, all installing tradesmen make choices about materials and assembly methods everyday. Given enough time, all problems become everyone's problems. Knowledge by all helps avoid these problems and makes project success normal.

Materials Can not Be Good at Everything—You Must Choose
Good decisions early minimize problems later

For many purposes, one quality is desired and the opposite quality is avoided. For example, in brick masonry construction, the bricks must be hard and resistant to compression, but the caulk joint between the bricks must be resilient and compressible. For this purpose, the opposite properties are desired and sought.

For other purposes, a property with multiple good characteristics is desirable. For example, steel for the structure must be able to: (1) resist the compression, tension, bending, and shear of the structural load, (2) resist rust and, (3) temporarily withstand the heat of a fire. Wood members must similarly: (1) resist the structural forces, (2) resist weathering, (3) accept coatings such as stain and paint but, (4) may have limited resistance to fire.

Usually, a material with many good qualities costs more. All materials must be evaluated considering both the benefit of their good qualities and their cost. So, the most common approach is to select a material for its most desirable cost effective properties, and construct an assembly of multiple materials, each of which has its own particular benefits. For example, a steel column (for strength) encased in gypsum drywall (for fire resistance) and clad in wood (for appearance, paintability, and weather resistance) might be used in an office building.

Materials are complex and specialized—but we need to know enough to use them well—and know right now
Understanding helps wise choice

Materials are complex and specialized, and experts can spend a lifetime on a few characteristics of a single material. For example, the advances in alloys, and chemical and heat treating of metals have produced materials now in everyday use that would have been considered science fiction 50 years ago—such as strong, corrosion resistant steel that remembers its shape, and also dampens sound. We need experts, but we also need to know enough to determine who to ask, and be able to determine that the answer is probably right. Experts are always in short supply and hard to reach. And, all people in a management or supervisory position in the building industry—owners, lenders, contractors, and material suppliers—must have a good working knowledge about everything. Discussion (below) of the most important characteristics of building materials addresses this need.

Units of measurement can make the simple appear complicated
These ideas aren't that hard—so the presentation shouldn't be either, but it is!

The engineering and scientific study of construction materials accelerated during the industrial revolution, from about 1650 to 1900 AD. Mathematicians, scientists, and engineers developed this knowledge in northern European countries and the United States. Each person worked in their own way, with their own units of measurement. And, they named their measurements after themselves!

For example:
> Amp – (electrical power) Andre Maria Ampere, French mathematician and physicist 1775–1836
> Coulomb – (electrical charge) Charles Augustine Coulomb, French physicist 1736–1806
> Henry – (inductance) Joseph Henry, American physicist 1797–1878
> Hertz – (frequency) Heinrick Hertz, German physicist 1857–1894
> Joule – (energy, work, or heat) James Prescott Joule, English physicist 1818–1889
> Newton – (force) Isaac Newton, English mathematician and physicist 1642–1727
> Ohm – (resistance) George Simon Ohm, German physicist 1787–1854
> Pascal – (pressure) Blaise Pascal, French mathematician 1623–1662
> Tesla – (magnetic flux density) Nikola Tesla, American electrical engineer 1854–1943
> Volt – (electrical potential) Count Alessandro Volta, Italian physicist 1745–1827
> Watt – (power) James Watt, Scottish engineer 1736–1814

The originally developed form of these measurements still exists, but they have been inbred and crossbred so that we have some very peculiar situations. For example, the watt, which was originally developed in Scotland using English units to measure the power of steam engines, is now used as a measure of electrical power—and is frequently mixed with metric units.

These units of measurement were developed for good historical reasons, but if they were trying to make it as confusing as possible they couldn't have done any better. To minimize this confusion, and to show the important relationships and order of magnitudes of properties of materials in the discussions below, we use a single unit of measurement. If one unit of measure is used in all cases, we use that unit. If, however, multiple units in metric and English measures are used for different applications, we only provide a single unit, related to one square inch or foot.

Do the Right Thing—and Do Not Do Stupid Stuff

The purpose of understanding material properties is to do the right thing, know why you are doing it, and avoid making major errors. To focus this discussion, we have grouped the discussion by purpose and use, not by type of material. We discuss the properties for which a material is valued, and for which it is in common use. Or, we discuss a material property for which it is an exceedingly poor selection, and its use should be avoided.

Material Properties for a Good Structure
Must handle tension and compression

Tension

Tension is the ability to resist pulling. The limit of the ability to resist tension is the point at which the material either snaps, or rapidly elongates—thereby decreasing the tension resistance capability.

Compression

Compression is the ability to resist the pushing on a material. The limit of compression is when either a brittle material randomly shatters, or a material, such as concrete, shears on the diagonal. (For example, a crack can go from the upper right to the lower left corner.) Compression describes effects on single pure materials such as concrete. Composite materials, such as concrete reinforced with steel, can fail by buckling, bending, or shearing, and they will be discussed in later chapters.

Strength to weight and strength to cost ratios

The weight of components in small buildings is seldom a major consideration. The minimum commonly available sizes for structural members—and the sizes required for fastening (screws and nails will not split the wood) are larger than the sizes required for strength. For example, a 2 x 4 in the wall of a residential house is 15 times stronger (and also larger and heavier) than required for strength alone. In contrast, for larger, tall, long, or slender structures such as high rises, bridges, antennas, or high voltage power line supports, the strength to weight ratio becomes a large consideration. Strength to cost is a consideration in all cases. Tension-compression strengths for common building materials include the following:

Name of Material	Tension	Compression
Concrete, temporary	Typically 8–12% of compression	1,500 psi
Concrete, usual conditions	Typically 8–12% of compression	3,000–5,000 psi
Concrete, special strengths	Typically 8–12% of compression	3,000–6,000 psi
Clay brick	389 psi	1,500–3,000 psi
Concrete hollow load bearing block	Typically 8–12% of compression	600–1,000 psi
Mortar	15–32 psi	750–2,500 psi
Granite	150 psi	15,000–30,000 psi
Marble	125 psi	1,000–23,000 psi
Limestone	125 psi	4,000–20,000 psi
Grey iron	20,000–60,000 psi	83,000–187,000 psi
Ductile iron	55,000–130,000 psi	About three times tension
Reinforcing steel	40,000–75,000 psi	About three times tension
Douglas fir	1,900 psi	1,450 psi
Oak	1,900 psi	1,375 psi
Pine	2,000 psi	1,400 psi
Aluminum	13,000 psi	9,000 psi
Wire rope	104,000 psi	Flexible
Glass	Not measured	80,000 psi

These values suggest good uses and uses to avoid. Steel can withstand high tension and compression, but high cost is a consideration. The extremely low-tension strengths of stone make it unsuitable for any application where tension is present. Wood's medium strength, both in tension and compression, makes it a versatile material—tolerant of installation mistakes!

Material Properties for a Good Building Envelope
Walls, roofs, windows, and doors need special material properties

Expansion
Expansion is everywhere—accommodating expansion makes a problem-free building

Heat expands components

Materials will expand with heat and contract with cold, but not equally. The range of temperatures that materials may be subjected to is approximately -20°F to 160°F in some climates. Some warmer climates will never reach the colder temperature, but the higher temperature is caused by the sun, and will be obtained in all climates and can be reached on -20°F days, if sheltered from the wind.

The expansions caused by this 180°F range in temperatures (the expansion from -20°F to 160°F) for 10-foot lengths of common materials are as follows:

Material	Expansion in 10 feet
Aluminum	.52"
Concrete	.26"
Steel	.23"
Glass	.19"

For large structures, such as concrete parking garages measuring several hundred feet on a side, 2–5" of expansion needs to be accommodated. For assemblies such as walls and windows, variable expansions for different materials must be accommodated. For example, an aluminum window with glass, in a concrete structure, must accommodate the very large differences in rates of expansion—.19" for glass up to .52" for aluminum. Further, internal fastening devices such as bolts and screws may be steel, but tightly fasten aluminum—further adding to the complexity of the variable expansions. These variable rates of expansion require careful attention to joints throughout the structure, and to flexibility in weather proofing membranes and caulks that touch these materials. Failure to properly consider these variable expansions will immediately lead to a leaky, cracking building.

Water Expands Components Too

Many building materials absorb water and increase in dimension, but not at an equal rate or an equal amount. For example, dimensional lumber can take months or years to fully saturate (almost all woods typically float, but will eventually sink when saturated). A brick wall, in contrast, can become fully saturated and leak in less than a minute.

Irreversible movement caused by water

These materials will expand and contract as water is added or removed. However, some materials, such as marble, brick, and engineered wood products—such as OSB (oriented strand board)—will increase in dimension when wetted, but remember this larger size, and will never fully return to the original size even if all water is removed. (This new larger size will expand and contract with further wetting and drying.) Brick is driest, and therefore it's smallest, when it leaves the kiln. But it may be attached to materials that do not permanently expand with water. So, masonry expansion joints must be included in the plan to accommodate the permanent expansion of brick, as well as temporary expansions and contractions.

This permanent expansion can produce minor cosmetic problems in residential construction where the OSB swells and telegraphs through to the finished surfaces. Or, it can cause major problems for marble building cladding, such as the Standard Oil Building in Chicago, Illinois. This building was originally clad with a thin white marble. As this expanded and buckled, complete removal and re-cladding of the building at a cost of hundreds of millions of dollars was required. This cost was many times the original building construction cost. So watch out that this doesn't happen to you!

Some guides to the order of magnitude for expansion are listed below.

Reversible movement caused by water

Material	Change in a 10 foot length from dry to wet	
Clay brick	.012"	Small change
Concrete brick	.048"	
Concrete	.096"	
Drywall	.120"	
Plywood	.150"	Large change

Although these numbers seem small, the forces of expansion are great—capable of breaking concrete and bending steel. When expansion is likely, tight joints that frequently are seen as a sign of "good workmanship" will fail. Joining materials with different irreversible and reversible movements requires joints with give and go. Once this is recognized, and these joints installed, many of the common building problems will disappear.

Conductivity
Heat, light, electricity, sound, and water move through all building materials, but at variable rates. Control theses movements and increase the life of the building

Heat transmission

HVAC applications, such as a heat exchanger that transfers the heat from the source (electrical coil or flame) to the air or the water to be heated in the building, require minimum transfer resistance in the material. On the other extreme, insulation for a structure makes the maximum resistance desirable. The resistance for 1" of thickness for common building materials is as follows:

Material	Heat resistance	
Aluminum	7	Low
Steel	32	
Granite, marble	50	
Limestone, concrete	80	
Face brick	110	
Common brick	200	
Float glass	910	
Pine	1,250	
1" insulating glass	2,000	
Fiberglass batt	4,000	High

Light transmission

Light transmission—through a material that is intended to be clear—is measured in percent transmitted. For example, float glass has 84%, and acrylic sheet has 90% transmission. Similar measures are also used for light reflection. Raw aluminum material reflects 87% of light, and painted or coated materials can be engineered to reflect from over 90% to nearly 0% (no reflection at all, looks completely black).

Electrical conductivity
Good for electrical work—bad for everything else

Electrical conductivity is desirable for electrical wiring intended to carry current. It is, however, undesirable when the current travels through dissimilar materials, each of which can be degraded by the electrical action at variable rates. Electric current accelerates most chemical reactions, but not equally. And, there are very mild electrical currents in all materials—the earth, buildings, and our bodies. Resistance to electrical conductivity in common materials are:

Material	Resistance	
Copper	2	Low
Aluminum	3	
Steel low carbon	10	
Cast iron	66	
Stainless steel	75	High

Failure to separate materials with different electrical resistance and conductivity can disintegrate materials within a year. With separation, these same materials can last decades—well beyond the useful life of the building.

Summary

These are the material properties that are most important for a successful, trouble-free building structure and envelope. These material properties are universal, and useful for many other purposes besides the building structure and building envelope. For example, electrical conductivity for electrical work is well known, and well addressed by the electrical industry. However, electrical conductivity is not always well-known or used for the building structure and envelope—so it was discussed here.

For all of these materials and for the entire building, everything is moving and changing. Heat, water, and electricity are always moving through materials. And, this makes materials expand, contract, and chemically change. Once you understand that all materials are constantly moving at different rates, design of assemblies to accommodate these movements becomes common sense. Building problems are then minimized, and success becomes normal.

3.3 Good Materials (Best) for Managing Motion and Impact—and Resisting the Environment

Abrasion resistance, hardness, friction, brittleness and elasticity. Moisture and sound control—biological, fire and chemical resistance

The previous chapter discussed the strength properties most useful for structures and building envelopes. This chapter discusses properties that are most useful for finishes (interior walls, ceilings, and floors), membranes (roofing, waterproofing, flexible expansion joints), and supports for things that move (doors, elevators, and mechanical or electrical equipment).

Resistance to Abrasion and Movement

Friction
Each material has its own natural friction—use materials to fit your purpose

There are natural frictions between materials, even with no lubrication. Addition of lubrication can reduce the friction, but not equally for all materials. Natural friction (force necessary to move one material across another) of some materials are shown below:

Material	No Lubrication	Lubrication
Teflon to teflon	4	4
Brass to steel	35	19
Wood on wood	25–50	Not measured
Wood on metal	20–60	Not measured
Polystyrene to polystyrene	50	50
Brick to wood	60	Not measured
Glass to metal	50–70	20–30
Plexiglass to plexiglass	80	80
Steel to steel	80	16

Glass to glass	90–100	10–60
Iron to iron	100	15–20
Copper to copper	100	8
Aluminum to aluminum	135	30
Solid on rubber	100–400	Not measured

The low friction between brass to steel indicates why (in addition to the corrosion resistance, relative abundance, and easy machine-ability) the combination of brass and steel is typically used in locks, and in sleeve bearings. It also explains why rubber-bearing pads, having high friction with most materials, are effective for the bases of machinery where resistance to motion is desired.

Hardness
Essential for impact or abrasion resistance

Hardness is the ability to resist indentation when pressure is applied at a point. Hardness of some common building materials are:

Material	*Hardness*	
Cast iron	180	Hard
Stainless steel	165	↑
Muntz metal (commonly used in windows)	130	
Steel low carbon steel	80	
Copper	42	
Aluminum	20	↓
Lead	4	Soft

Improved alloys, heat treating, and fabrication techniques for these metals can increase hardness by 500% for common applications—more for non-construction applications, such as machine tools.

Brittleness
A strange property that limits trouble free uses of many materials

Brittleness is a strange property that limits trouble-free uses of many materials. Brittleness is the ability to resist shattering when subjected to sudden stress or impact. All materials will shatter if hit hard and fast enough, but these forces and speeds are not reached under normal building conditions. So, some materials are labeled as brittle, as follows:

Material	Force to Shatter	
Pure ductile steel	10,000–100,000	Not brittle
High strength steel	1,500–12,000	
Polyethylene	600–800	
Reinforced concrete	20–400	
Common timbers	50–200	
Concrete (un-reinforced)	3	
Glass	1	Brittle

Decades ago, explanations of why materials are brittle were offered. But, these have been found to be inaccurate—so we now have no accepted explanation. However, we do know from experience that brittle materials tend to break easily and soon when formed into inside corners. Inside corners should be avoided for glass—and concrete inside corners must be reinforced. Isolation of brittle materials from vibration and sudden impacts must also be considered in material use planning.

Elasticity
A shock absorber for expansion

Elasticity is the ability to accommodate expansion and contraction, while still returning to the original shape. Examples of elastic materials are caulk, resilient membranes such as roofing, and some, but not all rubbers and plastics. The elasticity of the material is expressed in the percentage it can elongate, while still acceptably returning to its original shape. For example, a 1" caulk joint that can stretch to 2", then return to 1" without damage, is 100% elastic. Some plastics are 200–400% elastic (such as nylon rope). Caulks are now at most 100% elastic. Caulk elasticities have doubled in the last 20 years—and continue to improve. Elastic membranes (roofing, expansion joint materials) are usually less than 30% elastic. The rest of construction materials—concrete, brick, steel, wood—are less than 1% elastic.

Note: elasticity is not the same as bending—a brittle, inelastic material can still bend well. For example, glass is brittle and inelastic, but fiberglass batt insulation is flexible. Also, flexible and springy diving boards for swimming pools can be made of reinforced concrete.

All Building Components Must Resist the Surrounding Environment
Common materials have poor resistance—so choose materials carefully

Water transmission
Managing water movement in building materials is one of the most important ingredients for a trouble-free building and avoids damaging material expansions, and mold and rot

All material will transmit water, although the transmission of some materials is so slow and small it is considered zero for construction purposes. The vapor transmission of common building materials and the thickness in which they are commonly manufactured are as follows:

Material	Transmission (perms)*	
Tyvek (house wrap air barrier)	75.0	High transmission
Gypsum drywall	50.0	
Paint—3 coats	30.0–85.0	
Plaster	15.0	
Felt #15	5.0–20.0	
Plywood	.2–10.0	
Polystyrene bead board	2.0–6.0	
OSB	.3–6.0	
Concrete	3.0	
Concrete block	2.0	
Clay brick	.8–1.1	
Polystyrene board extruded (Blue board)	1.2	
	1.0	Vapor barrier defined
Polyethylene 4 mil (poly)	.08	
Polyethylene 8 mil (poly)	.04	
Aluminum foil	0	
Asphalt adhesive	0	No transmission

* Measured in perms—(1 perm is 1 grain (1/7000 of a pound) per square foot of material one inch thick in one hour).

Saturation of a material can speed transmission for some materials, and slow it for others. For example, plywood transmits water faster when wet, and OSB transmits water slower when wet—so mixing of these materials when water transmission is a consideration can cause problems. Water can be forced to move to and build up in some parts of the building, deteriorating insulation, and causing mold and rot.

Sound Conductivity
Reduction and control are usually desired—but you must decide

Sound conductivity is concerned with compression waves traveling through a material. The more dense the material, the faster the sound moves, as illustrated by:

Material	Sound Conductivity Feet per Second
Vacuum (no material)	0
Air	1,088
Water	4,760
Copper	11,513
Steel	16,447
Glass	18,092

Those working on a concrete or steel structure, where the sound of hammering or drilling can be transmitted six stories away, are familiar with the conduction of sound in dense materials. Yet in most building applications, you do not want sound to conduct. You want the opposite—to reduce sound between different rooms or parts of the building. To accomplish this, a combination of high-density materials alternated with air spaces is used to reduce the sound transmission between rooms. The sound scale is illustrated below:

Source	*Decibels (db)*
Jet engine within 500 feet	130 decibels
Elevated train	120 decibels
Lawnmower	100 decibels
Heavy city traffic	70 decibels
Quiet residential neighborhood	30 decibels
Still night in the country	10 decibels

Controlling Sound Traveling Through Heavy Material and Through Air are Two Different Problems Requiring Two Different Solutions.

Stopping sound traveling through heavy materials (concrete or steel) or between rooms requires air or resilient material gaps between the heavy materials

Stopping sound within a room requires absorbing materials to reduce the number of sound bounces

The reduction *between* rooms that can be obtained is:

Wall Construction	*Decibels (db) (Reduction)*
Framed wall with 1/2" gypsum on each side	28 decibels
Framed wall with 5/8" gypsum on each side	29 decibels
Framed wall with two layers of 1/2" gypsum each side	31 decibels
4" brick	40 decibels
8" concrete block	48 decibels
6" concrete	52 decibels

These are the sound reduction limits in common wall types. If greater sound reduction is required, multiple walls of similar construction must be constructed.

Reduction of sound *between* rooms by massive materials separated by air spaces or resilient materials is a different problem and solution than reduction of sound *within* a room. Sound will move through the air in a room until it hits a wall, ceiling, or floor. Then, a portion of the sound (2% for polished marble, 40–50% for wood, and over 90% for some fabrics or premium acoustical tiles) will be absorbed, and the rest reflected. Here, the material's sound-absorbing capacity, not the mass of the material, does the work. This continues until all the sound is absorbed.

Large spaces (the cathedrals of Europe, an indoor sports stadium, or a 500,000 square-foot warehouse before the merchandise arrives) which can have reverberation time of up to 10 seconds—you can actually feel the sound power on your body. Smaller spaces will have reverberation times of .5–2 seconds.

The design of buildings usually builds in sound control in walls and ceilings. Understanding sound conductivity and absorption explains why multiple layers of gypsum drywall reduce sound transmission between rooms, but poorly absorb sound within a room.

Design of buildings frequently gives little or no attention to reduction of sound transmission through materials. This is left to the installing trades. Understanding that dense material transmits sound well and air gaps or resilient materials reduces or stops this transmission aids correct installation of the required materials. Spring isolators and inertia bases (slabs of concrete) on resilient materials for vibrating equipment supports, "canvas" (now other fabrics) connections in HVAC duct work, isolation membranes for hard surface floors all reduce sound transmission.

Attacks on Materials

Chemicals
Materials have weak resistance—choose carefully and protect

Common building materials have poor resistance to chemical attack. Long-term, most common materials can only tolerate chemicals, which are very close to neutral. For example, on the scale of 1 (alkaline) to 7 (neutral) to 14 (acidic), a variation of about 1-1/2 from the neutral will deteriorate most construction materials.

The ability of concrete to resist common chemicals is varied:

Material	Rate of Disintegration	
Molasses, corn syrup, and glucose	Slight attack	Slow
Vegetable oils		
Milk		
Carbonic acid in water		
Acetic acids		
Hot distilled water	Rapid disintegration	Rapid

Salts will also rapidly deteriorate concrete. Calcium chloride (common table salt) is used in northern climates as a deicing agent in winter, and this, along with highly alkaline soils found in the southwest United States, and salts from the sea will rapidly attack concrete. Similar attacks will take place on other common materials such as wood, aluminum, and steel. Only special coatings or specialized construction methods will prevent these attacks.

Heat and electricity speed up these attacks

Further, chemical attacks are accelerated by heat and electricity. This chemical disintegration is assisted by the flow of electricity—called "galvanic action." One example of galvanic action is on the battery posts on your car, where an accumulation of white chalky substance indicates an attack on these materials. Similar attacks take place on the plumbing pipes in a building, since they ultimately contact earth (which has electrical current) at the water service entrance. There will be a slight electrical flow through these pipes, and materials such as plastic must separate them from any steel building structure.

Similarly, attack on elevators and underground steel piping is assisted by electrical flow. This can be handled by connecting pieces of magnesium that are intended to be sacrificial. That is, the electrical current will flow to the magnesium and dissolve it more rapidly and leave the steel temporarily alone. These magnesium blocks must be replaced periodically.

Similar concerns are important when installing curtain walls where you may have steel, aluminum, rubber, and glass components attached to a steel or concrete steel structure. Isolation between the components is essential to avoid galvanic action and chemical attack.

Sun
Constant radiation attack every day

The sun is a hydrogen nuclear reactor 93,000,000 miles away. The sun's radiation will attack and degrade plastics, wood, fabrics, and coating on materials, as well as any petroleum-related products such as roofing, asphalt, and rubber. The effects of the sun's attack on material can range from drying out, to complete change in the chemical composition, resulting in deterioration—turning membranes into flaky dust. The rate of deterioration is expressed in the time of direct sun exposure before a certain percentage of deterioration occurs.

Freeze Thaw
Unavoidable. Choose materials that can take it

Effects of heat and cold have been previously discussed in expansion, chemical reaction, and the effects of water. But, one other specialized measure is the change from freezing to thawing on certain materials, such as asphalt, concrete, masonry, stone, and roofing membranes. The results are shown as the number of freeze-thaw cycles that the material can sustain before suffering a specified amount of deterioration. It should be noted that the freeze-thaw cycle does not occur once in the fall and once in the spring, or even several times in the winter. But rather, every time the sun goes behind a cloud material can experience a freeze-thaw cycle. So, cycles of 10,000–500,000 (before deteriorating) are the common relevant measures. Cycles of up to 5,000,000 are encountered in some cases.

Biologicals
Annoying and destructive—but easy to avoid, if you plan ahead

Mold and rot
Get moisture low enough and the problem will go away

Mold (which is unsightly or a health irritant) will grow on any (former) plant or wood product—paper (including paper on gypsum), particle board, OSB, flake board, dimensional lumber, and straw or grass products—when the water saturation of these materials is over 16% by weight. These materials begin to decay when the water saturation is over 20% by weight. (Decay is bacteria eating parts or all of these wood or plant materials.) Once started, higher temperatures will accelerate the growth of mold or the rot. Once below about 15% moisture, biological action stops.

Insects
Chemical warfare is usually the answer

Insects, such as termites, and some beetles on land in warmer climates, eat wood. Other beetles on land, and wood boring insects in the oceans create hollow tunnels in wood for their eggs and house larvae. These tunnels can weaken or destroy the wood. These insects can be controlled by chemicals or barriers—steel plates to reduce entry, and then chemicals to kill the insects once entry has started. Electrical shock has also been tried.

Fire. No Fire is Best—a Slow, Well Behaved Fire is also Manageable
Burning materials should behave acceptably until the fire department or fire suppression systems can put out the fire

It would be ideal for fire safety if the building components did not burn at all. However, the building components that do not burn, such as concrete, have no sound or thermal insulating values—making them unsuitable for some applications. Therefore, selecting the right materials for fire safety involves two steps:

1.   Select materials that tend not to burn, or will burn slowly.

2.   If you must select materials that burn, pick ones that behave acceptably, so occupants can safely exit and firefighters or fire suppression systems can control the fire. The goal should be that the building will not be structurally damaged before the fire is extinguished.

Materials that Tend not to Burn Very Much

Flame spread
The speed a flame travels across a surface

The first measure of likeliness to burn is flame spread. This is the speed a fire will move across the surface of a material. The speed of flame travel changes with the material, and its area and thickness. So, the flame spread is a comparison (including these multiple factors) to red oak. Zero is no flame spread and red oak is flame spread 100. The flame spread ratings for common materials are:

Material	Flame Spread	
Gypsum drywall	15	Low flame spread
Cedar	70	
Plywood	95	
Douglas fir	70–100	
Red Oak	100	
Particle board	118–178	
Pine	130–230	
Popular	170–185	High flame spread

Self-extinguishing materials
Heat from an outside source required to maintain the fire

Some engineered finish materials, such as carpet, fabrics, and plastics used as a finish material are self-extinguishing. They will start to burn only when sufficient heat from another source is applied, and they will stop burning when this heat stops. The amount of heat required to continue the fire is called the Critical Radiant Flux. Since the self-extinguishing materials are manufactured, the manufacturers perform the tests and publish the results for their materials.

Smoke developed
Smoke blocks light and hinders evaluation

The first measure, both for the evacuation of the occupants and the safety of the firefighters, is "smoke developed"—the amount of smoke that an individual material will contribute while burning. The smoke developed measures the portion of light the smoke blocks—no blockage is 0 and complete blockage is 500. Smoke developed of common materials is as follows:

Material	Smoke Developed	
EIFS (synthetic stucco—Synergy, Dryvit)	450	High smoke
Western red cedar	213	
Styrofoam board (extruded)	165	
Maple	157	
Pine	122	
Solid surface counters—polyester (Corian)	100	
House wrap (Tyvek)	10	Low smoke

Smoke developed only measures light blockage, but smoke from different materials can also be sticky or toxic. So, although smoke developed is the only commonly used measurement, it is not the whole story. Common sense and judgment are required.

It should be noted that flame retardant coatings or chemical additives to some materials can reduce the initial ignition of the material, but then once ignited will subsequently produce more smoke than an untreated material. In this case, you have to pick your poison—smoke or fire.

Fire resistance (to deformation)
Get the occupant out, the firefighters in, and save the building if possible

The next consideration is that if the materials are on fire, the heat of this fire should not weaken the material sufficiently so that it deforms and either becomes unstable or collapses entirely. This is measured by the fire rating of the material—in number of hours of resistance to a temperature rise of 1200–1500°F—that would occur in a fire. Fire ratings of common materials are:

Material	Resistance
1" gypsum	1-hour
8" concrete block (depending upon amount of fill of the cores)	Max 3-hours
Sprayed fireproofing of structural steel	Max 3-hours

Assemblies of multiple materials rated at four hours are possible. Ratings over four hours can be required for industrial or military uses, but not in the normal building industry.

Summary

All building materials have structural properties such as tension and compression—building envelope properties such as heat and water expansion, and conductivity—and resistance to the environment including abrasion, chemicals, biologicals, fire, sun, and freeze-thaw cycles.

Materials can be selected for cost effective superiority for one purpose. However, all of these building materials must work together for all purposes. And, particular attention has to be paid to the different chemical reactions, expansions, and conductivity of each of the materials in a combined assembly. Understanding these properties helps make clear why good building assemblies work, and why the stupid stuff (totally unsuitable material selection) is stupid and will fail. Avoiding mistakes will put you on a very good level. Some understanding—even if not expert—of why the good stuff works, can move you to the excellent level. This knowledge can make project success normal.

3.4 Soil—A Slow Moving Liquid

The largest source of surprise variation in construction cost and time

Looking and Common Sense Alone cannot Produce Understanding

If one is tackled hard in football, the ground does seem hard and unyielding. Also, if one is gardening in a clay soil and cannot penetrate the soil with the shovel and has to dig with a pick, the earth does indeed seem hard, immovable, and fixed. But, this is not the case. To understand the behavior of earthwork, one must think on a geological scale, with large loads, long time frames, and big areas.

The crust of the earth is a thin layer floating on liquid layers beneath. The earth in this floating crust is also changed and moved by water. Although the earth is composed of solid matter, it appears to behave like a slow-moving liquid. One can see some of the symptoms of water, such as dampness, or feel the symptoms such as consistency. But, water also changes the strength and rate of flow of the earth, and this is invisible. Also, water is continually moving and flowing, so the strength and other properties of earth are always changing. If you "get it," "it" will change the next time it rains.

Theoretical knowledge is needed to understand the invisible characteristics of earth, the time effect of water flow—and to manage these factors effectively. The history of soil engineering is not long. Our knowledge is still incomplete, and on some subjects completely absent.

In the 1700s, the French noticed that some of their earthwork military fortifications collapsed for no reasons that they understood. Some scientific and engineering exploration was done at that time to improve this deficiency.

The next major advances took place around 1930–1933. Formerly, construction of railroads that had to follow very shallow grades had used bridges to span any steep grades. As we began constructing roads for higher speed automobiles, the need to understand earthwork embankments and support structures increased. Automobile roads hug the side of steep embankments, and therefore we needed engineering knowledge to permanently construct these slopes. Much of our soil engineering knowledge is based on knowledge gained by 1933—and remains unchanged to this day. There are, however, properties of soil for which we have some idea of what happens, but little or no idea about why.

Around World War II, the need to accommodate the increased loads required for landing strips for heavy planes advanced our knowledge somewhat. The introduction of geotextile fabrics (large sheets of specialized plastics) introduced in the last quarter of the twentieth century was another advance.

Soil Particle Size and Weight

What Is Soil?

Soil is composed of three components:

1. Small particles of broken down minerals or rocks
2. Water
3. Air

The spectrum of soil materials and materials surrounding soils are:

1. Solid rock
    Igneous, sedimentary, and metamorphic rock in the same solid form originally made hundreds of millions of years ago—sometimes called bedrock. These are a parent material for soils, but are not a soil themselves.

2. Gravel
    Gravel is formed from high silica content rocks, such as quartz or granite. It is granular, acidic, and is usually light in color.

3. Soils
    a. Sand has the same origin as gravel, but has smaller particle sizes.

    b. Silt is formed from small particles of rocks that are high in iron, magnesium, calcium, and sodium, but little silica. It is fine particled, basic (alkaline), and usually dark in color.

    c. Clays are fine particles originally formed from rocks high in silica, alumina, iron, and magnesium. But, clay is not just little pieces of these materials—it is chemically changed to form another material that is unique and different in chemical properties. We do not yet fully understand the chemical nature or behavior of clay.

4. Organics
    Organic soils are formed from plant materials that are still in the process of decomposing. They are not technically soils, since they are not formed from mineral components. However, they can be deposited immediately next to or mixed in with soil types, and so they must be considered when evaluating soils for construction.

Water is in all soil types. Gas is also in soil, usually in the form of air. However, radon (decay of uranium), polonium, and radioactive wastes, methane, carbon dioxide, ammonia, hydrogen sulfide, and nitrous oxide can also occur in some soil types. Presence of these gases, which cause humans to lose consciousness and die, must be managed in deeper or more confined excavations.

Particle size

Particle sizes from large to small include the following:

Material	Sieve Size (openings per inch)	Familiar example
Boulder	12 inches	Larger than basketball
Cobbles	3 inches	Grapefruit
Coarse gravel	3 inch-3/4 inch	Orange
Fine gravel	3/4 inch-no.-4 sieve	Grape or pea
Coarse sand	No. 4-no. 10 sieve	Rock salt
Medium sand	No. 10-no. 40 sieve	Table salt
Fine sand	No. 40-no. 200 sieve	Powdered sugar
Fines	Less than no. 200 sieve	Dust

Fine sand is the smallest particle than can be seen with the naked eye.

The increased roughness of the coarse particle's surface will increase friction and therefore strength. Although we know this to be true, it is usually overlooked in soil engineering—"sand is sand." But, more careful analysis can increase the allowable soil capacity, which can permit a more economical foundation.

Another characteristic of soil is the distribution of the particle sizes in the soil mix. A "well graded" soil will have an even mixture of different particle sizes, so the smaller particles can fill up the spaces between the larger particles. The coarse grain particles have no electrical or chemical attraction between particles. (Excluding the attraction water can produce between particles.)

Fine grain particles such as clay or silt, in contrast, are composed of tiny flat particles, resembling sheets of paper, sometimes with lengths hundreds of times the thickness. The angularity and roughness of the particle does not matter. But, the extremely small size produces electrical attraction between the particles themselves. This electrical attraction is increased by the presence of water.

Weight of soil

Soils for construction—sand, silt, and clay—all normally weigh about 70–110 pounds per cubic foot dry and 110–145 pounds per cubic foot fully saturated. Solid rock weighs 155- 180 pounds per cubic foot, and organic topsoil (black dirt) weighs less at 65–90 pounds per cubic foot. Clay retains water for years while sand will drain in minutes, so clay used in earthwork operations is usually heavier than sand.

Soil Particle Workability

Compression

Described above, soil consists of particles of weathered rock, air, and water. The soil grains and water are not compressible. Air or gases are compressible, but if all the soil grains are touching, air compression is not feasible. Compression of soil, therefore, can only occur for cohesionless soil, such as gravel and sand, by rearranging the particles to a denser configuration. Or, for all soil types squeezing out, or otherwise removing, water.

For cohesive soils such as clays, the particles are already small and touching, and are attracted by their own electrical forces. So undisturbed virgin cohesive clays can be compressed, not by pressure, but by extraction of the water in the soil.

Density

The relative density is defined for cohesionless granular and sand soils as the percentage of the maximum possible compression and consolidation achieved. Loose has a relative density of 50% or less, firm 50–70%, dense 70–90%, and very dense 90–100%. These are measured by the Proctor Test (named after the man who developed the test). The standard Proctor Test developed in about 1933, applies 25 blows of a 5-1/2 pound weight falling 12" on each of three layers in a 4-inch diameter mold. And, the modified Proctor Test developed around 1940, of 25 blows with a 10 pound weight falling 18" on each of five layers. The densities of these compacted samples are compared to a theoretical maximum. The usual maximum value is 95% of Proctor density. Theoretical maximum soils densities (100%) can occur rarely in undisturbed soil, but are not practically achievable or sought in relocated soil in construction.

Although the Proctor Test is frequently stated as the standard to be achieved, it is a laboratory test—and field operations usually cannot wait for lab results. So, the sand cone, balloon, and nuclear test methods can be used to determine densities in the field. Requiring performance determined by one test, but checking achievement by a different test lowers certainty of success—yet this is what is done every day. Further, the Proctor Test is a laboratory test, but job site conditions are more variable and less controlled—adding further variability. Both more tolerance in the design, and best care on the job are required.

Permeability
How fast does the water travel through the soil?

Rates water will travel through soil are:

Soil Type	Permeability	Feet per Year
Course Gravel	Very Permeable	105,120
Fine Sand	Medium Permeability	1,051
Silty Sand/Dirty Sand	Low Permeability	10.5
Silt/Fine Sand Stone	Very Low Permeability	1
Clay/Mud Stone without Joints	Impervious	Less than 1

Highly impermeable soils will resist water transmission from other areas. This slows groundwater seepage into an excavation, and makes a dry soil slow to take on moisture—producing beneficial embankment stability. Once wetted, however, impermeable soils shed moisture slowly. If oversaturated, removal of the excess water is slow (months or years) or expensive (dewatering or removal and replacement with drier material). High permeability soils will have the opposite strengths and weaknesses.

Plasticity

The term plasticity describes the soils' ability to hold together and support its own weight. The common descriptions are:

Term	Dry Strength	Field Test
Non plastic	Very low	Falls apart easily
Slightly plastic	Slight	Easily crushed with fingers
Medium plastic	Medium	Difficult to crush
Highly plastic	High	Impossible to crush with fingers

These casual sounding descriptions are defined in the Unified Soil Classification system as rolling a piece of the soil into a 2–6 mm roll (making clay snakes), standing this roll on end, and observing the stability of this roll. These characteristics are important because higher plasticity soils tend to have higher strength, and also the capability to maintain a steep embankment, reducing the amount of earth that must be excavated.

Color

Although color in soil in itself is not an important characteristic, it is an indication of what has happened to the soil before. As discussed above, it can indicate the source of the soil's parent rock. Further, it can indicate the process that the soil has undergone, or some of the chemical content. For example, yellow- and red-colored soils typically indicate severe weathering. Dark green color can indicate organic matter.

Soil's Properties for Construction

Soil has a memory

Soil is altered by the physical weights and chemical forces it has been subjected to in the geological past. For example, if a soil has been heavily loaded and compacted—by glaciers or by a previous overburden that has since eroded away—it will remember its previous load and compact less than a soil that has never experienced such a load. Knowledge of this difference can make estimates of required earthwork quantities more accurate and placement more effective.

Also, if the soil was previously submerged under salt water, it is permanently changed chemically. For example, some soils along the St. Lawrence Seaway—between Canada and the United States—liquefy when vibrated by earth moving equipment. We do not yet understand how or why this change happens.

Strength of soil

The grain type, size, proportions, orientations, water content, density, and previous geological loading affect the strength of soil. To get an approximate idea of soil-bearing capacity, the typical presumed bearing capacities for virgin soils used in some building codes are:

Soil type	Presumed bearing capacities (pounds per square foot)
Very loose sand, dry	1,000–3,000
Firm sand, dry	3,000–6,000
Dense sand, dry	6,000–12,000
Soft clay	0–1,500
Firm clay	1,500–2,500
Stiff clay	2,500–5,000
Hard clay	5,000–10,000
Layered, laminated fractured rock	10,000–30,000
Massive rock, occasional seam	30,000–80,000
Sound massive rock	80,000–200,000

These can be increased up to 300% for optimal conditions of preloading, density, and moisture. But, for soils within 30 feet of grade, most bearing capacities will usually be between 2,500–8,000 pounds per square foot.

It should be noted that organic soils are not listed here because organic soils are still in the process of decomposing and consolidating. They cannot be used in or around any structure that requires minimal settlement. Where construction in organic soils, such as when a road across a peat bog is unavoidable, settlements on the order of 2–4 feet plus complete disintegration of the road within 30–40 years must be anticipated.

Soil mixtures

Pure soil types do exist. But, a mixture of multiple soil types is more common. When soils are mixed, they tend to be a combination and compromise of the soil characteristics of the individual soil types, with a few exceptions. When the clay content of the soil is 50% or more, it behaves as a clay. The other sand and silt grains essentially are floating particles in the clay and have little engineering effect.

For organic soils, such as peat, an organic content of less than 5% has little effect. Between 5%-25% peat content, it will still behave like a mineral soil. But, over 25% the mineral soil properties will disappear, and it will behave like an organic soil.

A further complexity is when there are stacked layers of different soil types, each with different characteristics. This is addressed further in the soil classification systems below.

Soil Classification Systems

There are three soil classification systems.

1. The USDA (United States Department of Agriculture) System, which focuses on the needs of growing crops and erosion control.
2. The AASHO (American Association of State Highway Officials) System, which is used by some highway departments.

3. The Unified Soil Classification System, which is used throughout private industry and by the United States Federal Government. It is by far the predominate soil classification system.

This system structures the ideas described above—soil type (sand, gravel, silt), particle size, plasticity, and color. And it also has a heavy emphasis on the probable geological history of that soil—how it was placed by erosion, by wind, by water, or by volcanic activity—and forces to which it was previously subjected, such as glaciers or heavy overburden—so the soil's memory can be known.

The need to classify soil during excavation is immediate. You need to know it right there, right now, with little testing equipment, and no laboratory available. The machines are waiting, and time is money. Soil classifications are, therefore, heavily structured as visual assessments, with verbal description. Although the descriptions seem causal, such as "silty sand, brown, firm," each of these terms has a specific scientific definition. As an example, the proportions of the silt in some sand could be defined as "50–80% retained on no. 200 sieve (.003in) greater than 50% coarse fraction passes no. 4 sieve (3/16"), the colors are defined with a Munsell color chart, and the stiffness could be defined as 5–8 blows of a standard penetration test (after Terzaghi and Peck)." So, it is not as simple as it looks—casual sounding terms describe precise scientific values that can be used for engineering calculations. An earthwork contractor working in a single local area would be capable of readily understanding the usual soil types. However, identification of all soil types and formations does require a trained soil engineer.

Water Changes Soil's Nature
Water movement and effects are usually invisible

Water flows through soil

Most of the unfrozen water in the world lies and flows beneath the ground. All surface rivers, lakes, and streams contain approximately 30,000 cubic miles of fresh water. The ground up to one-half mile deep contains about 960,000 cubic miles of fresh water, and ground water deeper than one-half mile contains about 1,200,000 cubic miles of fresh water. 99% of the unfrozen fresh water on earth is in the soil. We know some of this water has been in the same location for tens of thousand years—and that some of this water flows. But we do not know well enough to predict how, where, and when the global subterranean water will affect a particular site. (If soil and water conditions of a site are all well known, an engineer can calculate the rates of water flow at that location at that time.)

The water is restricted by the permeability, as described above, but pressure is also important. The flow is the permeability of the soil multiplied by the pressure. Anytime you dig a hole or add soil on top of existing soil, the water pressure of that area and the surrounding area will be altered. So, the water flowing through the soil will also be altered. All earthwork will affect the speed and location of the flows of these underground rivers.

Capillary action

Capillary action is the force caused by the interaction of solids, water, and air that moves the water up, down, or sideways—unrelated to the forces of gravity. This capillary action can be seen in a glass of water as water moves up the side of the glass to form a curved surface. Capillary action is influenced by the void sizes, moisture content, and temperature in the soil. The heights that water can rise in soils are:

Soil Type	Height (in feet)
Small gravel	.4
Course sand	.5
Fine sand	3
Silt	30
Clay	90

This capillary action can also temporarily make uncohesive soil, such as sand, more cohesive. A walk on the beach where the sand closest to the water is firm—or the knowledge that you need wet sand to build sand castles—demonstrates this capillary action.

Water determines soil's strength

Water is part of the soil's strength. The soil strength equals the intergranular strength plus "pore" water strength. If the water strength increases while the intergranular strength stays the same, the soil strength must decrease. There is a direct and opposite relationship between water pressure and soil strength. This relationship has extreme importance for construction, as a couple of examples will show:

In one example, if you are digging a hole near a lake, the deeper you go, the higher the water pressure on the soil at the bottom of the excavation will become. When the water pressure exactly equals the intergranular strength of the soil, the soil strength will be zero, the soil will liquefy, and the excavation will collapse.

In another example, if a huge force, such as an explosion or an earthquake applies force too fast to let the water move and escape, the water pressure increases by the force of the explosion and the intergranular strength again goes to zero, and the earth liquefies.

In another example, involving vibration from pile driving or vibratory compaction, the water may have time to escape, the water comes to the top, and the sand densifies. Here the water has time to migrate out of the soil and not build up pressure, so the soil densifies and increases in strength.

A more common example involves the bank of an excavation. If rain increases the water in the soil of the embankment, at some point the water pressure will overcome the intergranular stress, and the strength of the soil can no longer support its own weight, and the bank collapses.

The relationship between the water and intergranular strength is one of the most important drivers of stability and strength in earthwork operations. It is similarly important for the completed building, since a post construction change in the ground water conditions could produce a similar decrease in soil-bearing capacity—and adverse settlement, or collapse.

There are types of soil that are unusually moved by the action of moisture. First is expansive clay, which occurs in many areas of the United States, and was formerly submerged under oceans (but not in the upper Midwest). These clays can move unacceptably large amounts when wetted. Even traces anywhere in the substructure can lift the building off the foundation.

Another type is soil that collapses when in contact with water. Certain types of clay will shrink and dissolve when wetted. This has caused problems when veins of these clays are near a dam. Disintegration of these veins acts as a pipe to transmit water around the dam, undermining it, producing collapse, or requiring significant repairs. Finally, very loose or saturated sands, and silts in earthquake zones, will become liquefied during earthquakes.

Some of these examples are for very specific soil types and situations. But, water will affect all soils at all sites all the time.

Water can increase soil's weight

Air has no measurable weight in soil, water weighs about 62 pounds per cubic foot, and soil weighs a little over 100 pounds per cubic foot. If water displaces air, the soil will be heavier. If water displaces soil particles, the soil will become lighter. Rates of water saturation change (and weight) will be seconds for course granular materials, but years for clay.

Freezing water expands soil

Water expands about 9% in volume when freezing and soil will expand 3–4% when freezing. In most northern heavily occupied climates, the practical frost heave is 1–2" per year under normal circumstances. This will occur every fall and reverse every spring. This movement must be accommodated in any construction design.

Under some circumstances, significant frost heave, up to 12", can occur. This occurs when trapped pockets of solid water within the soil expand the full 9% of the water, not the 3–4% of the soil. This can also occur because of capillary action. As portions of the soil begin to freeze, the unfrozen part becomes smaller, and capillary action increases—pumping water up from the ground water below. This pumping will produce a higher water volume in the then freezing soils than existed before freezing started. If the 12" heave wasn't bad enough, in the springtime the heaved area will thaw top down, thus saturating the upper soils to the point where the soil liquefies and loses all strength.

Summary

Soils are small particles of rock and mineral. The particle size, roughness, shape, density, plasticity, cohesion, and permeability influence strength and stability. The Unified Classification System organizes these many factors to aid understanding. Soil-bearing capacities of 2,500–8,000 pounds per square foot are most common, but can vary up to 300%.

Water is the largest cause of variation in soil strength and stability. Water produces strength through interparticle attraction and capillary action, and reduces strength by water pressure. The soil's strength equals the interparticle strength plus the "pore" pressure of the water. High water pressure means low soil strength. When the water pressure exceeds the intergranular strength the soil strength, is zero and it liquefies.

Because water in soil is continually changing, time matters hugely for earthwork. Timing the work around the timing of water changes is one of the largest drivers in planning earthwork operations.

3.5 Soils in Construction

Managing movement, pressure, water, time, and cost

Soil Movement

Settlement

The causes of settlement are:

1. Loads imposed—both structure and additional soil
2. Changes of water in the soil
3. Soil consolidation due to vibrations

The uniform even settlement for an entire structure that is considered tolerable is 3–4" for brick buildings, and up to 24" for drainage or access structures, not immediately aligned with other construction. However, differential settlements within a structure have lower tolerance. Differential settlement can make the structure crack or tilt. Generally, settlements of 1 unit of settlement in 250 units of length (of the entire structure or any portion of the structure) are acceptable. Brittle finishes can increase the 250 to 360. And housing precision machinery in the structure can require even less settlement. Normal settlement in normal soils will occur for up to four years after the start of imposition of the load. However, most of the settlement takes place in the earliest periods. So, most settlement has occurred before the final grades and structures are installed. However, some accommodation for the settlement over the later periods must be considered in the design and construction or cracks, back sloping, and ponding of water will occur.

Shear strength reduces usable strength

Shear is one part of an object sliding by another part of the object. This condition exists for the edge of any structure foundation, where there is load at the edge of the foundation and no load immediately outside of the foundation. The building foundation will move downward, and shear the adjacent soil. It is this action that causes the differential settlement between the building and the adjacent areas to be unacceptable. Therefore, the shear strength, which is typically about half of the compressive strength, governs the calculation of the allowable strength of the soil.

But, the allowable strength is not simply half the strength of the soil. The forces of the building pressing downward go out in a 2:1 slope (for every 2' you go down the forces go out 1') thereby forming a

161

triangle of force underneath the structure. Since the area of support is larger the farther down you go, the total soil-bearing capacity under the structure is greater. This will continue for about 10–20' below the structure. The actual calculations of this force triangle are done by engineers, but it is important to understand the principles at work so the soil's strength of this triangle will not be compromised by construction in this area—such as removing part of this support triangle.

Managing Earth Pressure

Earth pressures are huge

Vertical earth pressure is the sum of all the earth stacked above. In addition to this vertical pressure, since soil is a slow-moving liquid, there will be horizontal pressures as well. The more liquid the soil is, either by its particle nature, or by the presence of water, the more pressure it will exert to the side.

The horizontal pressure is equal to the weight of the earth stacked above that point multiplied by a factor for the type and condition of the soil—that will range from about .4 for loose sedimentary soil, to about 3 for heavy pre-consolidated soil.

For example, for a 10' high wall, with earth weighing 100 pounds per cubic foot, the total earth vertical pressure would be 1,000 pounds. Multiplying the vertical pressure by a factor of .4 to 3 produces a load per square foot at the bottom of the wall of 400–3,000 pounds per square foot. Every square foot of the perimeter of the foundation would be subjected to this same load, and each square foot above would be subjected to a similar, but lesser, load corresponding to the decrease in earth at that point.

If this 10-foot high wall was the basement of a 1,500 square-foot house measuring 30 by 50 feet, the total earth pressure on the foundation wall would be 2,208,000 pounds. For a larger commercial structure measuring 300 by 250 feet with a 30-foot basement, the total earth pressure would be 11,600,000 pounds. Planned, not emergency, measures are required to manage these loads.

These forces are modified by the restraint of the adjacent surfaces. If the adjacent wall is allowed to deflect slightly, the earth forces are reduced significantly. These forces are also affected by the presence of water in the soil—the more liquid the soil, the higher the forces. The liquid nature will change throughout the construction process by either drying out during dry periods, or increasing density during wet periods, making the pressures on both the permanent structure and the temporary embankments continuously variable—and thus should be "managed" as discussed below.

Construction precautions for earth pressures

Earth is a slow-moving liquid exerting huge pressures as described above. These pressures must be managed during the construction operations. This is necessary to maintain efficient construction operations and for safety of the workers. If earth weighs 100 pounds per cubic foot, and a man's surface area is about 8 square feet, even a one-foot thickness of earth on top of a man's body prevents him from self-rescue —leading to death by crushing and suffocation. For a small excavation, the general rule is to have no excavation unprotected that is more than 5' deep. The most common methods are to slope back the excavation. With granular materials this can be as gradual as a 1:1 slope. For cohesive clays, it is typical to stair-step the excavation sides. Even with these precautions, the changes in the moisture must be watched very carefully since it can produce huge changes in the strength and pressure of the soil.

The next precaution, typically used in long skinny excavations such as pipelines or water and sewer service entrances, is shields. Here, two parallel steel, aluminum, or wood plates are held apart either by fixed metal bars or by hydraulic cylinders. Here the slopes aren't necessary, and a long skinny excavation with nearly vertical banks can be controlled safely.

For sites deeper than about one story or sites where no slopes or steps are physically possible, such as a zero lot line building, or sites with high ground water transmission, temporary earth retention structures must be installed.

Temporary Retention Structures

Sheeting

Sheeting is a corrugated steel panel with interlocking edges. These sheets are driven vertically into the ground by a pile driver. It should be noted that pile drivers were originally steam, can occasionally be mechanical (a cable lifts the weight and then drops it), but most frequently, now they are driven by compressed air. Therefore, when driving sheeting you will require a pile driving crane, a tender crane (to put the pieces of sheeting into place), a compressor, and trucks or a storage method for the sheeting. Space for this equipment needs to be considered in planning and design of the retention system on what is often a tight site.

Sheeting can be used for shallow excavations of less than 10 feet deep. The sheeting can sometimes be driven in with a backhoe for these depths. Depths of up to 100 feet deep are possible. Here, one length of sheeting is driven to near the ground level, and then an additional length is welded to the first and then driven. The lowest part of the sheeting is called the "toe." Toe is what holds the bottom of the sheeting in place, and is usually 10–20 feet below the lowest level to be excavated. The required depth is governed by the soil type and water content, and is specified by a soil/structural engineer—not guesswork and rules of thumb!

The temporary sheeting can be removed if the design and site conditions permit. Or it may have to be permanently left in place—at a significant cost.

Soldier beams and lagging

A similar system is soldier beam and lagging, where wide flanged (H shaped beams) are driven vertically into the ground and square timbers are inserted horizontally into the centers of the H. This forms a continuous wall of alternating vertical beams and horizontally stacked timbers. Sheeting and soldier beams can be installed in most soil types.

Slurry walls

A slurry wall is a concrete retaining wall around the site. This wall is constructed by a very skinny (less than 2' wide), crane-mounted, clam bucket excavating the area to receive this retaining wall. As this excavation is taking place, a slurry of a material such as bentonite clay with the consistency of heavy cream is pumped into the excavation to exert a balancing pressure against the walls of the earth to prevent collapse. When the desired bottom elevation is reached, a steel tube is inserted vertically on each side of this just excavated area, and a long vertical tremmie (temporary pipe) is inserted to the bottom and concrete is poured bottom up, displacing the slurry mixture.

Upon setting of the concrete, the two tubes are removed and the adjacent excavation takes place in a similar manner. The purpose of the tubes is to permit excavation right up to the adjacent slurry wall segment without having to clean off the earth at the edge of the previous excavation. Similar to sheeting, this requires a crane for the clam bucket and a tender crane to free up and move the pipe. It also requires a retaining pond to hold the slurry, earth moving equipment to load the removed soils, trucks to remove them, and maybe a concrete pump. The slurry wall operation can monopolize an entire site, and the sticky slurry can cause cleaning problems on the surrounding streets.

Slurry walls can be used in cohesive, but not granular, soils. The "temporary" slurry wall is not removed, and becomes part of the permanent structure.

Bracing of temporary retention walls is also required

Any of these systems—sheeting, soldier beams, or slurry walls may be quite deep—50' to 100'. However, they cannot be cantilevered for this full height without additional support against horizontal earth pressure. If there is solid rock near the retaining wall, holes can be drilled into this rock, and tensioned cables or rods can horizontally brace the retaining structure. If there is not rock in the vicinity, soil nailing can be used. Here, holes are drilled through the retaining structure into the earth downward at a 60° angle. And, at the end of the hole, cement materials are injected to increase the dimension around the cable and to provide anchoring. When set, the cable is tensioned.

Another method is to place horizontal members such as pipes or wide-flanged beams into the face of the retaining wall interior to the site. These can either go to temporary concrete structures on the bottom of the excavation, or horizontally across the site to other temporary walls. The layout of the cross members must be carefully considered so the structure can be constructed, and also with minimal interference from these temporary members. Also, since these braces are installed and the excavation done top down, room for earth-moving equipment, trucks, and haul roads must be allowed.

In all of these systems, some time during the construction the earth pressure is finally supported by the building structure itself. Permanent structural members—walls, floors, and beams—take the place of the temporary retention structure. So, the timing of the transfer of the loads from the temporary retention structure to the permanent building structure requires knowledge of how the building structure itself works, including curing of concrete, and tensioning of bolts and cables. Once transferred, these loads are forever. So, subsequent remodeling operations that might consider removing parts of the structure, must have temporary means to support the tremendous earth forces that this removal would impose.

Freeze the surrounding soil

One last, less commonly used earth retention method is freezing. In some very specialized soil types and situations, the area surrounding the site can have refrigeration pipes drilled in and placed into the ground. The entire perimeter of the site can be frozen to permit excavation within the frozen retention ring. This technique requires a specific combination of soil type, moisture content, type of construction effort, and skilled personnel, so it is used infrequently.

Dewatering

Keep it dry

The best form of dewatering is always to avoid the problem entirely, by starting in a relatively dry season, and possibly protecting the embankment with sheets of plastic to maintain stability throughout the construction operation.

Next best is gravity draining of the water from the entire construction-site. Maintaining the low water level both increases workability on the site, but also maintains soil strength in the surrounding embankment areas.

Pump it out

Next is mechanical pumping—with a mobile pump—of the surface water from the excavation areas. After that is to drill and sink well points (perforated pipes) 3–10' apart surrounding the entire perimeter of the site, then connecting these points to pipes and sucking the water out—in effect, building a dewatering wall around the whole construction area. The depth of the well points is limited to 18–20' due to the lifting capacities of a pump. Greater depths require concentric rings of well points, which step down (sometimes called benching) to lower elevations.

If still deeper dewatering is required, holes approximately 2' in diameter, surrounded by a filter fabric that lets water enter but keeps soil out, can be used. The wellhead and pumping structure is dropped to the bottom of each of these drilled pits to increase the vertical lifting height.

Remove the water with electricity

The process of electro-osmosis can also be used in low permeability soils. Here, a positive anode hole is sunk into the ground, and a negative anode hole, also functioning as a well point, is sunk into the ground some distance away. An electrical charge is placed on the anodes, and the water migrates to the negative anode, and is pumped out.

These water management measures were listed above in ascending order from free (avoid the problem) to most expensive. The most expensive can cost over 10% of project cost for a building structure—even more for tunneling operations. Such dewatering methods can only be successfully introduced in the planning stage. Mid-project emergency measures will produce cost over-runs or complete project failure.

Foundation Types

Footings and pads

Spread footings are used for shallow foundations, usually less than 20' deep. This requires soil of satisfactory bearing capacity at this location. The footing spreads out the load and helps bridge over soils of variable capacity. A strip, usually 18" to about 36" wide x 12" to 24" deep, of concrete with reinforcing steel is poured underneath the foundation walls. These strips are supplemented by similar square footings (pads) underneath column locations.

In some cases, one gigantic footing (matt) can be poured underneath the entire footprint of the site. This can be several acres in area and 10'-20' thick, and include heavy reinforcing steel. This requires significant planning since, in a medium-sized town, all of the city's available concrete pumping equipment, and the capacity of more than one ready mix concrete supply company may be needed—and the pour may last between 8 and about 20 hours of continuous pumping.

Piles

Piles are a long, skinny tapered piece of wood, steel, or concrete driven into the earth. The installed system is similar to driving sheeting as described above. The strength of the pile is calculated by the distance the pile moves with each blow of a dropped hammer. The pile will achieve its design strength when it either refuses to go further, increased penetration for each blow becomes acceptably small, or it is calculated to have sufficient friction against the side of the earth. Each of these values, as well as the weight of the hammer and height of the drop, is specified by an engineer before installation.

It should be noted that vibration, and therefore soil consolidation and liquefaction are a factor in pile driving both for the pile beam driven, and for the adjacent piles. Liquefied or consolidating soil around a pile will sink and drag the pile down with it—thus producing negative bearing capacity. This can occur during the pile driving operation, or at a latter time due to a large vibrating machine housed in the structure, or other vibration on adjacent sites.

Caissons

A caisson is a drilled column in the earth that is then filled with concrete, and in the upper part, also reinforcing steel. In some areas, caissons are used even on very small structures, such as homes, and require more like a fence post auger, than a large crane. These are used to suspend the structure over expansive clays, and sometimes have horizontal ridges carved on the side of the caisson to resist the uplift of the clay.

On larger commercial projects, the caissons can be drilled to over 100' below grade. The bottom size is increased by using a device that hollows out like a cone at the bottom of the caisson shaft. Loose soil from the drilling operation must be cleaned out by lowering men to the bottom. Deeper caissons can have out-gassing from the soil, and this must be monitored with instruments to ensure that dangerous gasses do not accumulate.

Also, caissons can have temporary steel liners (cylinders) installed near the top of the caisson to restrain loose soil. But, caissons cannot be installed in the most granular soil types—some soil cohesion is required. Caissons require a drill crane, a tender crane, earth moving equipment to remove the spoils, trucks to haul the spoils, concrete placing equipment, and space for drill bits and liners.

Piles and caissons are capped with reinforced concrete

Piles and caissons, once installed, have a cap—a reinforced concrete structure. Piles will usually combine together multiple piles in one cap. Caissons have one cap per caisson. The purpose of this is to spread out the load and for placement of further foundation structures. For these, and also in some cases for footings, a grade beam—concrete beams beneath the earth level—are then constructed to span between footings, pile caps, and caisson caps. The grade beams, footings, and foundation walls complete the foundation system.

Improving the Strength of Soil

Compaction by vibration, tamping, and kneading

Normal compaction of a typical structure utilizes soils with particle size less than 4", no organic material, and is placed in 8–12" lifts. Water content of about 15% will produce the optimum practical achievable density, which is far less than the theoretical maximum.

The compaction equipment for granular soils can be a vibratory, or a tamping type, to rearrange the granular configuration. For clay soils, the vibratory compactors do not work, and you need either applied force such as tamping, or kneading type equipment.

Practically, granular materials are used for backfilling around structures because clay is far more difficult to place in the required lift heights in confined spaces, and is more difficult to compact. In addition, clay materials will impose a greater lateral load on the foundation, and will inhibit drainage around the structure.

Preloading

Preloading places a temporary load in excess of the final permanent load to accelerate the consolidation of the soil. Drains through the area to be compacted can more rapidly remove the moisture and increase the rate of settlement. At the end of the consolidation, which can take up to four years, the temporary load is removed, and construction can begin on the consolidated earth. Transportation cost is a limiting factor. The required quantity of the temporary earth must be "loaned" from the site, or another source of economical supply and disposal found. The preloading can also be done by placing the permanent structure, such as an oil tank, at a temporarily higher elevation, and connecting it to surrounding structures with temporary flexible connections. Permanent connections are installed after settlement is complete.

Dynamic loading

Earth can be consolidated by dropping a heavy weight, up to 50 tons from a height of about 150', typically about 5 times per location. This can consolidate the soil up to about 300 feet deep. A similar imposed force can be achieved by explosive blasting. Another consolidating technique is to drill and insert a vibrating machine into the soil. This consolidation is more appropriate to granular materials. All of these techniques require neighbors that do not mind, or no neighbors at all.

Soil mixing

The soil to be consolidated can be injected with cement and fly ash and water and then mixed to form a type of low-grade concrete. This mixing is done with a crane-mounted rotary eggbeater type mixer, and can mix to 90 feet deep.

Raising and lowering the water table

Where a site will permit such an activity, repeatedly lowering and raising the water table will consolidate the soil. Each time the water table is lowered, the soil will consolidate. This can be repeated for up to 4–5 times, and then no further consolidation takes place.

Geotextiles

Geotextiles are woven or spun sheet plastic placed in layers—usually less than 2 feet thick—to improve the soil characteristics. This is similar in concept to using reinforcing steel (strong in tension) in concrete (strong in compression, but weak in tension) to form a composite material that has both desirable characteristics.

Geotextiles have different pore sizes, permeability, and strength characteristics that must be selected appropriately for each application.

The Cost of Moving Earth

Transportation

The cost of transporting earth is the cost of transportation labor and equipment, minus payment for selling unneeded earth, plus the payments made to dump unwanted earth on someone else's property.

Earthwork cost will be lowest if you do not move any earth off site—balancing the earth. That is, any earth removed from an excavation has another place on the site where it can be used as fill. No off-site transportation costs are incurred, and you pay no one for dump fees, and purchase no earth from outside vendors. This can only be fully achieved if this balance is designed in at the beginning of the project.

If earth must be transported on or off the site, the larger the transporting equipment, the lower the unit transportation cost. An approximate order of transportation cost, lowest to highest, is:

> Ship
> Barge
> Rail
> Mine car
> Off road equipment
> Conveyor
> On road trucks
> Hand transportation

When considering method of transportation, the proximity of the transportation method, such as ships and barges requiring close waterways, is relevant. So is the cost of moving and assembling the transportation equipment on-site, such as rail lines, haul roads, and conveyers. The cost of the transportation method, combined with the cost of setups and adjusted by the limitations of the site, govern the optimal cost and time solution for a site.

Off road equipment or rail may require haul roads, extension of rail lines, and temporary foundations for some of the required structures. So, most medium or smaller sites are limited to on road trucks. In the United States, the most common capacity of a semi-truck is a 40,000 pounds load limit. In some locations, multiple trailers on a semi-truck are allowed, increasing the per vehicle weight limit.

With heavier cohesive dense soils, such as clay, the load limit will be reached far before the trailer is loaded to volume capacity, thus giving the appearance of leaving the trailer half empty. You are not being cheated. The driver is just observing the legal load limits.

For highly granular soils, the soils are "fluffed up"—increased in volume—when loading into a truck. This increases the volume about one-third. Here, you can reach the volume limit of the truck before you reach the weight load limit. In either case, you have to calculate the actual hauling capacity of the soil in vehicle measure, not the measure excavated from the earth.

Getting paid for soil

Removed topsoil, frequently called black dirt—and clean granular material—can be stock piled and sold. However, it frequently cannot be sold immediately because seldom is the cost of transporting it to an alternate stockpile economically desirable. So you might have to inventory it for years on-site if your project site will permit. Some processing is frequently required, such as sifting and grading the granular soil, and pulverizing the black dirt, which has some additional cost as well.

Frequently, good clean fill of an uneven graded nature is sought. But, you may be able to dispose of it for only the transportation cost.

Paying for soil

Importing granular fill that has been processed, as described above, has to be purchased. Also, if you have unsuitable soil on site that cannot be used in back fill, or even in landscaping operations, no one else is going to want it either, and you are going to have to pay to dispose of it. Increasingly, in some urban areas, in addition to paying the owner of the dump for disposal, the government imposes additional environmental type taxes, further escalating the cost of disposal.

The combination of these factors can produce massive differences in costs. For example, for 100 cubic yards by ship, barge, or off-road equipment, the transportation costs could equal the wages of a tradesman for 2 hours. If, however, the soil was unsuitable and had to be disposed of—including transportation, disposal, and environmental fees—and imported granular material had to be purchased and transported to the site, the same 100 cy would cost the equivalent of 500 man-hours. Recognizing these huge cost swings in the design process can minimize earthwork transportation costs and avoid huge surprises mid-project.

Time Is Crucial

Earthwork involves expensive machines and equipment, and time is money. Any delay or uncertainty during the operation has huge additional costs. But the even bigger costs are caused by changes in moisture. Soil that gets wet may completely collapse banks and have to be re-excavated. If the cohesive soils become wet and disturbed, such as by earth moving equipment or by trucks, it can take months or even years to completely dry out, and during this time it is unusable. So, practically, if you get a clay disturbed and wet, you throw it out and put some new soil in its place.

Also, changes in water pressure, due to the excavation, will continue to occur over time. As pressures can slowly equalize during the construction process, things change. The conditions you had on Friday afternoon might not exist on Monday morning. Further, changes on adjacent new construction sites can drop or raise the water table. And, changes in the regional ground water table over time can also change pressures, and weaken or strengthen the soil and cause unexpected settlement. Even something as small as a 1-1/2" overlay on an adjacent road can change the ground water pressure, and cause a previously acceptable, well-performing structure to begin to heave and crack.

The most common approach for successful earthwork operations is: (1) plan well, (2) hit it hard, (3) move fast, (4) ask few questions, and (5) do not stop until you are done. While this is second nature to earthwork contractors, the principles described above may communicate the urgency to general contractors, building owners, and managers in understanding the extreme costs of poor planning and any delays—and the importance of time in earthwork construction.

Reducing Uncertainty, Making Success Normal
Testing provides required information

The variables of soil type, layers, structure, and ground water can produce a bewildering array of possible outcomes. To reduce this uncertainty, testing and exploration can be done on the site to get a far greater knowledge of the specific conditions and to make more informed judgments. The most common soil exploration tests for soils uses a split spoon auger. For this test, a truck-mounted drop hammer mechanism drives a two-piece tube about 2" in diameter into the earth. The number of blows per foot of the drop hammer is recorded, and then the tube is extracted and the soil type, and water content (both moisture content and solid water) recorded for each elevation. Detailed diagrams of each of the boring logs on the site are presented and the soil is described with the Unified Classification System. The soil engineer will than make a recommendation for the foundation and retention types, and any special procedures for temporary dewatering or permanent draining of the site.

These recommendations are helpful, but since the descriptions are uniform, with experience one can understand the probable excavation procedures, slopes of banks, and speed of excavation required in different parts of the country, including ones with which you have had no previous familiarity. So a test doesn't just say, "It's all clear to build," it is an aid to designing the building and planning the excavation process.

Other exploration techniques involve inserting an explosion in the ground and timing the travel of the shock waves to remote locations to calculate the probable soil types. This is a technique borrowed from geological and oil exploration. In another method, an electrical charge is inserted in the soil, and the resistance to another location can be used to help determine the subsurface conditions. These are used less frequently, and usually on much larger sites.

Other soil-testing methods such as penetration tests (to determine soil penetration resistance), tests to determine permeability (that involve the timing of draining water from a hole), and shear strength tests (such as the vane shear apparatus, torvane method, and pocket pentrometer) can be used to assess soil conditions once the excavation has started, and are useful for that purpose, but are less useful for planning.

Once good information is obtained, optimal value and minimal surprises will be achieved by including this information in building planning. If your position does not permit inclusion in the building planning, at least in the project construction planning stage, it can still achieve large, although lesser benefits. Many times, selecting something that everyone knows will work, even if it has a more expensive initial cost, avoids the risk of huge losses in time, embankment collapse, or other problem excavations. Small initial costs can avoid huge surprise costs later. And, without planning, the surprises will come—it is just a question of how big and when.

Finally, communicating the possibilities and the approaches to the owner can reduce uncertainty, so that the risk can be shared, and the optimal solution sought. In some European cultures, the attitude is, "Whatever is down there, it is the contractors problem." In American cultures, frequently a more cooperative approach is possible. With the problems and opportunities, optimal solutions are discussed in the planning stage so uncertainties are minimized, and everyone can win.

Summary

Earth is a slow-moving liquid. It was formed in geological time and has a memory, both in compaction, and the effect of salt water on its chemical structure. This nature of the earth will not change for your project. Water and time are the major sources of variation of earth characteristics, and since the effect of water in the chemical interaction is invisible, common sense alone is not a good guide. Some understanding of principles is also required.

The distance and method of haul, and economic value of earth, has one of the largest impacts on the overall project costs of any line item. Only by including the consideration of the earthwork cost, and managing the uncertainty of earthwork—due to variations of moisture and other subsurface unknowns—can the earthwork process be effectively managed, uncertainty reduced, and project success made normal.

3.6 Concrete—A Workhorse Material for Foundations, Structures, and Floors

An on-site chemical reaction requiring local knowledge and management

Concrete is an ancient, durable, and low cost material

Concrete has been used in construction for about 4,000 years. Strong compressive strength, good resistance to water, adequate resistance to everyday chemicals, and low cost due to use of local materials make use of concrete common. The ancient Romans, approximately 2,400 years ago, refined and used concrete extensively in their buildings. For example, the Pantheon built in 100–124 AD in Rome, Italy, is a concrete building with the walls and roof constructed of concrete. And it is still standing—in remarkably good shape. If they could do it then, we should be able to do it now—and better.

Concrete's low cost requires use of local materials

A cubic yard of concrete typically has the same cost as two hour's wages of the installing tradesman—if the materials are trucked from within 15–30 miles of the project. Usually, materials are available within this distance. If ship, barge, or rail lines are available, these economical distances can be greater. There are, of course, projects at greater distances from material sources that still use concrete. For these projects, costs skyrocket and transportation methods become hugely important. They require focused management attention.

Four of the five ingredients of concrete—water, air, fine aggregate, and coarse aggregate—are available on all occupied continents, and frequently not far from a building site. Many, although not all, rocks are suitable ingredients for concrete. The fifth ingredient, cement, is produced from many different rocks, so it is also widely available, though it is not produced as close to all job sites as the aggregates.

Local production requires local knowledge

The benefits of local production cause another dimension: the "factory" is local, so the "factory workers" must know concrete. Everyone involved with the construction process must maintain the quality of the concrete produced, and any single person anywhere in the production chain can completely ruin the concrete. Also, managers and owners—lacking knowledge—can demand speedy construction, and starts in disadvantageous seasons, thus radically reducing the quality of the finished concrete product.

What Is Concrete?

Concrete is a solid hard mass formed from two or more materials. This concrete mass is different in nature and properties than the components. Some rocks are natural concretions—assemblies of unique rocks into one new rock. Blacktop paving, an assembly of rocks and bituminous material, is an example of a building material like "concrete."

However, in construction the word "concrete" is usually used to define a mass made up of specific ingredients in specific proportions. Pure concrete is made of big rock (coarse aggregate), small rock or sand (called fine aggregate), cement (baked stone of particular types ground to a powder), water, and air. Other ingredients are frequently added as discussed below, but these five ingredients form pure concrete.

What Goes In? The Ingredients of Concrete

Water

Water as a liquid, or for hot weather, ice, of a reasonably pure form, is required. Salts, minerals, or biological materials—such as algae or decaying plant matter—must be minimal. City tap water usually fits these requirements and is acceptable. Water from rivers, lakes, or streams must be laboratory tested to verify that the content of unacceptable materials is low enough. Similarly, well water—if the wells are shallow, or close to oceans where salt-water infiltration can enter the well—must be similarly checked. Salt water from oceans is never acceptable.

Coarse aggregate

Rock of uniform structure and compressive strength—well in excess of the concrete strength—may be used. Quartz rock and limestone are two commonly used types. Others are also possible. Stone of layered structure, such as laminated sandstone or shale—where layers can later break apart—cannot be used. Rocks that are either soft or contain organic material such as soft sandstone, lignite, limonite, and clay are also unacceptable. Rocks that will expand when wetted, such as cherts (silica combined with micro-silicates), and iron—that will produce rust that will expand and spall (shatter and pop out surface pieces) from the concrete, are also unacceptable.

The most commonly used diameter sizes of coarse aggregate are 3/8" for toppings on structural floors and structural infills of confined spaces, 3/4" for slab and walls of 4"–8" thickness, and 1-1/2" diameter for footings and thicker walls and columns. Larger diameters of 3"-8" can be used for mass civil engineering projects, such as large dams.

Fine aggregate

Fine aggregates use the same acceptable—and avoid the same unacceptable—rocks as coarse aggregates. The sizes of the fine aggregates are measured by sieve numbers from 4 to 100. The sieve is a screen material, similar to a window screen, and the number is the openings per linear inch. The fine aggregate can be no larger or smaller than these sizes, and tend to concentrate in the center (16, 30, and 50 sieves) and taper off on the largest and smallest (4, 8, and 100). A typical example in percentages might be:

Sieve Number	Percentage by Weight
# 4	2%
# 8	13%
# 16	20%
# 30	20%
# 50	24%
# 100	18%
Greater than 100	3%
Total	100%

A smaller particle size will increase workability. A uniform grading can reduce the cement content (and therefore cost). Aggregates in the number 30 to 100 range will retain the most air in the concrete mixture. So, the proportions of each fine aggregate particle size affect the workability and cost of the concrete mixture—and the appearance of the cured concrete.

Once these considerations are well known for a project area, and the particle sizes of the available fine aggregates are recognized, a few mix designs become standardized. Then, fine aggregate size will no longer be of much concern to those placing the concrete. However, if the project is in a different area, entirely different proportions, workability, and placing considerations must be learned again. Or, if the proposed use (structural to decorative), placing method (pump to wheel barrows), or environment (caustic chemicals or salt water) change, an entirely different fine aggregate grade may be required.

Cement

Cement is formed by taking rocks that contain lime, iron, silica, alumina, gypsum, and magnesia, baking them to approximately 2,700°F, and then grinding them to a fine powder (#200 sieve). These are found in: Aragonite, Limestone, Marl, Shale, Iron-clay, Iron mill scale, Silica-clay, Sand-shale, Alumina, Clay, Fly ash, Gypsum, Calcium sulfate, and Cement rock (and in other rocks as well). Cement is almost always the most expensive ingredient in pure concrete.

These materials can be blended in different proportions for many alternate cement materials. Joseph Aspdin, an English mason, invented the commonly used blend in construction, called Portland cement, in 1824. Portland cement was named for the color of natural limestone quarried on the Isle of Portland, a peninsula in the English Channel.

For concrete construction, the customary types of Portland cement are:

Type I.	Normal
Type Ia.	Normal, air entrained
Type II.	Moderate sulfate resistance
Type IIa.	Moderate sulfate resistance, air entrained
Type III.	High early strength
Type IIIa.	High early strength, air entrained
Type IV.	Low heat of hydration
Type V.	High sulfate resistance

The close cousins used for masonry mortar construction are:

Type N	Lowest strength
Type S	Medium strength
Type M	Highest strength

Less commonly used are expansive cements:

Type E-1 (K)
Type E-1 (M)
Type E-1 (S)

These can be used to slightly expand to either (1) counteract the natural shrinkage of concrete or (2) impart tension on the reinforcing steel.

Other cement relatives are used for sealing oil wells—classes A, H, and J. And plastic cements are used for making plaster and stucco.

The type I cement is used in the vast majority of concrete building cases. And, air entrainment (trapping tiny bubbles in the concrete that act as shock absorbers to prevent freeze-thaw damage to the concrete) can be achieved by using either type Ia or by using the type I cement and adding additional chemicals at the time of concrete mixing.

It is possible to work an entire career encountering only a few types of cement. However, it should be noted that these other possibilities are available with costs and benefits for specific situations. It should also be noted that the related cements, such as masonry cement, are completely unsuitable for concrete construction, and cannot be substituted. You must know what you are doing and/or have knowledgeable contractors!

Air

Air is entrained in the normal concrete naturally—to some extent—about 1-1/2% of volume. For air-entrained concrete, the air volume will increase to about 6%. Small (.0004-.004 inch diameter) uniformly spaced air bubbles have no strength, but are beneficial to the stability of the finished concrete. This will be discussed in the section below on air-entrainment additives and agents. Larger uneven sized or spaced air bubbles, caused by improper mixing or placing, reduce the strength and serviceability of the finished concrete and are to be avoided. The good small bubbles are too small to be seen with the naked eye. So, if you can see it, it is an undesirable void—not a bubble!

The mix of the five ingredients

One typical cubic yard of concrete would contain:

Cement	564 pounds (6 sacks)
Water	300 pounds (36 gallons)
Sand	1,235 pounds
Gravel	1,878 pounds
Air	1%
Total batch weight per cubic yard	3,977 pounds

Tens of thousands of mix designs that vary these quantities are used, but this is the typical mid point. The nominal weight of normal concrete is 140–150 pounds per cubic foot.

What Comes Out—How Cement, Water, and Aggregate Becomes Concrete

Cement chemically combines with water to form a third unique material—in an irreversible chemical reaction. This chemical reaction happens once and only once. If you were to grind up the set concrete to a fine powder and add water a second time, you would only have gray mud, not concrete. The water chemically combines with the cement, it does not evaporate, soak into the surrounding earth, or concrete forms (although excess water in a concrete mixture can behave in this way).

Concrete will set under water. If a mass of concrete is placed under water, as would occur with the construction of piers for a bridge, it will become concrete just as if it were placed above water on land. Also, once the liquid concrete mixture is in the process of setting, adding additional water, to make the mixture more workable and easily placed, will not reverse or slow the chemical reaction. But it will weaken the concrete.

Concrete for buildings typically achieves compressive strength of 3,000–6,000 psi in 28 days, depending on the mix design. Strengths of 1,500–2,000 psi can be used for temporary construction, such as "mud slabs" (temporary floors to assist construction of the permanent floors). Higher strengths are also possible. Starting in about 1980, concrete strengths of 20,000, then 30,000, then 50,000 psi concrete were announced. Good uses for these high strengths are few, but the capability is there if needed.

The chemical reaction of cement and water produces heat as the concrete is setting. This heat, and how to handle it, will be discussed in more detail below. Starting immediately after the concrete has set, the solid concrete shrinks irreversibly. This shrinkage is small in dimension, but huge in force, and must be managed as discussed further below.

Good Concrete Must Be Installed Well

Water-cement ratio–low is good
A large variable and the most common error in quality control

Water-cement ratio is the single largest variable in quality control. The concrete will have between four and seven pounds of water for every ten pounds of cement, depending on the specifications of the mix design and the strength required. The mixes that have the lowest water-cement ratio (that will produce the hydration of the cement) will produce the highest strength concrete. For example, a water-cement ratio of four pounds water to ten pounds of cement could produce a 5,000 psi concrete, whereas a water-cement ratio of seven pounds water to ten pounds of concrete in the same mix, will produce 2,400 psi compressive strength concrete.

Increasing the water beyond these limits means the water cannot chemically combine with the cement, and therefore must bleed out of the surface, soak into the soil, or soak into the forms. As this water migrates to the other areas, it leaves voids in the concrete that weaken the concrete further, in unpredictable locations. Every batch plant and every concrete mixing truck has a water tank, and anyone from the original mixing at the concrete plant to the final placing at the job site can add water. This could be disastrous!

Slump—how "liquid" is the wet concrete
The best (low) slumps are difficult to place well

"Slump" defines how liquid or solid concrete is, and is measured by a slump test. The slump test is the accepted technical test used as a visual guide to the probable water-cement ratio and degree of set. The test is performed using a 12" high tapered cylinder with a 4" diameter opening at the top and an 8" diameter opening at the bottom. The large side is placed down, the cylinder is filled with concrete, consolidated with a smooth rod moved up and down in the concrete, and tapped on the exterior a specific number of times to further consolidation. The cylinder is then removed, and the distance (in inches) the top of the concrete settles (slumps) defines the slump of the concrete mixture.

Zero slump concrete is possible for civil engineering applications where the concrete must be placed with earth moving equipment, but cannot be finished to provide an acceptable visual appearance. For structural concrete such as columns, beams, and large retaining walls, a 2"–3" slump is typically specified. For flat work, thin floors, and sidewalks a slump of 3"–5" is specified. Greater slumps, achieved by adding more water, will rapidly degrade the strength and water permeability resistance of the concrete, and must be avoided.

Mixing concrete
A specified number of rotations within 1-1/2 hours

Concrete is mixed in a rotating drum with internal mixing blades. The concrete is considered mixed with 70–100 revolutions of the drum at mixing speeds of 6–18 revolutions per minute. It then will be reduced to an agitating speed of 2–6 revolutions per minute. Total revolutions of mixing and agitating must not exceed 300, and must be completed within 1-1/2 hours. More mixing, or mixing for longer periods, or at higher speeds will result in strength loss, temperature rise, excessive loss of entrained air, and accelerated slump loss.

Placing concrete
Minimize freefall, then consolidate

When placing the concrete from the drum to its final location, freefall of the concrete must be minimized to a few feet. This is necessary because the coarse aggregate is the heaviest, the fine aggregate is the medium heaviest, and the cement paste mixture the least heaviest. If freefall is permitted, the heavier materials will have greater force and end up on the bottom of the placement, and the cement paste will be segregated to the upper parts of the placement, thereby not producing concrete at all, but layers of the individual ingredients.

Concrete must be "consolidated"—moved around obstructions such as rebar and pipes, and into the small corners of the forms. For thin slabs, this can be done by an up and down motion of a shovel. Larger concrete masses require a vibrator—a vibrating head on a flexible extension. The goal and result is uniform mixture of all concrete ingredients in all areas of the poured concrete.

Freefall is reduced by shoots, tremmies (gravity tubes), pumping concrete through tubes and hoses, conveyors, and using buckets suspended from cranes for placement. Proper placement with minimal freefall is essential for sound concrete. This placement activity is substantially in the control of the field personnel placing the concrete, so this principle must be understood and proper procedures followed.

But, owners and managers must know that demands for out of sequence work can have large and costly implications for the placing operation. Demands that exceed the capabilities of the equipment, or people on the project, frequently cause poor placement and poor concrete.

Time of mixing, setting, and curing
Mix 1-1/2 hours, set in about 8 hours, working strength in 28 days, full cure years later

Concrete will continue to strengthen and become more dense and impermeable to water as long as the relative humidity of the concrete is 80% or greater. Some indications of improvement for 100 years have been seen. More extensive studies have been done indicating improvement for 50 years. Analysis for the period of 5 years is far more common. Most of the time discussions, however, focus on the very brief time during mixing, placing, and initial curing. The time sequence of concrete placing and setting is:

Mixing	1-1/2 hours
Initial set	2–4 hours after mixing, depending on temperature
Completion of initial set	1–3 hours after start of set
Three days	45% of strength
Seven days	75% of strength
Twenty-eight days	95% of strength
Five years	100+% of strength

Warmer temperatures will accelerate and cooler temperatures will retard all of these times. The curing is also affected by moisture—the wetter the better. Concrete entirely submerged in water will have the highest strengths and least shrinkage. Moist or steam-cured concrete wrapped in impermeable material, such as plastic, will be next best. Concrete with applied chemical sealers to entrap the water is next best. Unprotected exposure to the atmosphere is least effective in prolonging hydration, increasing strength and permeability, and reducing shrinkage.

Temperature Control for Mixing, Setting and Curing is Crucial

Temperature of the mixing, curing, and setting concrete

The temperature of the concrete at time of placement must be well above freezing and not much warmer than room temperature.

The combination of cement and water is a chemical reaction (hydration) that gives off heat—producing an increase in temperature of 30°–40°F. No heat rise takes place in the mixing phase (first 1-1/2 hour), then heat production peaks at about ten hours after the start of mix. It then declines, and then has another smaller peak in heat 2–3 days after hydration has started.

Excessive heat can cause the concrete to completely disintegrate and crumble into its components. This heat is seldom a consideration in concrete placements less than 3' thick. In more massive structures such as dams, this heat must be considered.

The possible solutions are:
1. Select a design mix that has less cement, with the same strength
2. Reduce the water to cement ratio

3. Cool the ingredients e.g., add ice to the water, or cool the forms
4. Install cooling pipes and circulate cooling fluid through the newly installed concrete

Hot weather placement
Cool the mix and place during the cool times of day

Placing under 3' thick concrete structures in hot weather has similar considerations, but is complicated by the heat of the atmosphere, earth, and the forms added to the heat of hydration of the concrete.

The counter measures that can be taken are:
1. Cool the water (use ice, not liquid water)
2. Slightly reduce the temperatures of the aggregate by wetting, and allowing the temperature reductions caused by evaporation to cool the aggregates
3. Wet the surfaces where the concrete is to be placed
4. Move the placement operation to another time of day, usually part of the night, or early morning
5. Schedule the concrete operations for a cooler time of year

Cold weather placement
Heat the mix, then insulate and heat the completed work

Hydration slows hugely at 32°F and stops completely at about 8°F. The heat of hydration of the concrete is a benefit when placing concrete at these cold temperatures—allowing successful placement in temperatures well below freezing.

The measures that can be taken in the cold weather are:
1. Heat the water
2. Heat the aggregates
3. Create enclosures around the area to receive concrete and heat this work area
4. Insulate the newly placed concrete with blankets designed for the purpose

With these measures, mass concrete can be placed when air temperatures are near 0°F. However, concrete can seldom be placed successfully on frozen ground.

Movement is Unavoidable and Must be Managed

Shrinkage during and after curing
Concrete will continue to move and change dimension indefinitely, but changes are largest close to the time of placement.

The types of changes in dimension and their sizes are:
1. Irreversible movement.
    a. Concrete shrinkage shortly after placement
        Concrete will shrink shortly after it is set and as it is curing. This shrinkage process will continue for approximately 2 years. It will result in shrinkage of properly

designed and placed low water-cement ratio concrete of .12" in 10 feet. However, increasing the amount of water in the same mix will radically increase the shrinkage by approximately 700%.

b. Creep due to applied load

When a concrete structure is subjected to the load it is intended to bear, it will creep (shrink). If the load it is intended to bear is applied within 120 days of placement of the concrete, an irreversible shrinkage of about .02" in 10 feet will occur.

2. Reversible Movement

a. Changes in temperature and moisture of cured concrete can cause the concrete to shrink or grow .26" in ten feet. These will continue forever—whenever moisture or temperature changes.

b. Creep due to applied load

If the load to the structure is applied 1,000 days or more after placement of the concrete, shrinkage of .02" occurs, but is reversible (will spring back) when the load is removed.

The movements in the concrete, though small in 10 feet, can become quite large in a larger structure, and the forces in all cases are large and irresistible by any normal building system.

How to Accommodate Concrete Movement

Using a low water-cement ratio and allowing proper curing time of the structure before loading can minimize movements. For building construction, the movement vertically, such as columns, and horizontally, in beams, have no special movement provisions. As the concrete structure comes closer to the sky, or a little wider, and is not restrained, nothing bad happens to the concrete itself. However, definite measures must be taken to allow for this expansion and contraction of the exterior curtain wall and vertical conveying systems attached to concrete, such as elevators and piping.

For a longer structure, such as longer retaining walls or guardrails, breaks in the concrete with infills and expansion joint materials must be specifically engineered and installed. For flat work (floors, sidewalks, paving surfaces) the movement of the concrete is addressed by control joints. The control joint does not stop or lessen the shrinkage, but rather manages the place the shrinkage will occur, so cracking is in a more acceptable location.

Typically, joints are cut 1/4 of the depth of the slab with spacing 15'–30' apart. Cracks occur within these depressions and can be manageably infilled later with finish materials and leveling compounds. Very large slabs or slabs between two different structures must include an expansion joint that is resilient, similar to guardrails as discussed above.

Common Additions to Concrete to Improve Performance

Reinforcing to add strength in tension

Concrete is strong in compression (5,000 psi) but weak in tension (500 psi). This is a drawback both for structural concrete and for controlling the movement of concrete. To improve the tensile performance of concrete, reinforcing steel, commonly called rebar, is installed. Rebar is a steel bar made for this purpose with a yield strength of about 40,000–60,000 pounds per square inch in tension, and includes bumps and ridges (deformations) of specific size and spacing to grip the concrete. (Smooth bars without deformations are useless for this purpose.) The reinforcing steel (strong in tension) combines with the concrete (strong in compression) to form a structural member that is strong in both characteristics.

Reinforcing also reduces concrete movement

Concrete has reversible and irreversible movements as described above. Steel changes dimension slightly less than concrete for temperature, and it does not change at all in dimension when subjected to moisture. Therefore, installing grid work of steel wires in the concrete controls and reduces the movement. These are typically 6" x 6" grids with wire sizes of 4–10 gauge. These grid are called welded wire fabric, or wire mesh. Also, they are sometimes called temperature steel, because they help reduce movement caused by temperature change.

An alternate ingredient that can be used to control the same movement is mixing short (3/4"–1-1/2") plastic fibers such as polypropylene in the concrete mix. These plastic fibers will also limit movement of the concrete, and is sometimes called fiber mesh concrete.

Other aggregates

As an alternate to the coarse stone aggregates described above, lightweight aggregates formed by heating blast furnace slag (to expand) can be used. This is typically found in floor toppings where the underlying normal weight concrete structure provides the strength, but the light weight is desirable to decrease the overall weight of the structure. On the other extreme, if very high weight is required, the stone aggregate can be deleted and steel aggregate can be added. This is used in applications such as bridge counter weights—where the highest weight in the smallest volume is desired.

Cement Related Products to Improve Performance

Fly ash
Cement's Hamburger Helper®

Fly ash is the ash produced by burning coal. This waste product is cheaper than cement, and can replace portions of the cement in the mix. It has a similar gray appearance to cement, but has a finer particle size, and provides the following benefits:

1. Reduces cost
2. Produces a higher strength concrete than can be obtained by Portland cement alone
3. Increases finishability (producing smooth uniform appearance)
4. Reduces bleeding of water
5. Easy pumping
6. Reduces the heat of hydration
7. Is more resistant to some alkaloids
8. Usually more resistant to sulfate attack

Decreased cost and improved performance makes fly ash a common ingredient in concrete.

Air entrainment chemicals
Manages freezing and thawing

Air entrainment is desirable to produce evenly spaced air bubbles of a uniform small size. These bubbles act as a shock absorber for freeze-thaw conditions, permitting concrete to remain undamaged indefinitely—whereas, concrete without these bubbles would deteriorate significantly within a couple of years. So, air entrainment is used for exterior application in climates subject to freezing and thawing.

Air entrainment can be achieved by using either Type Ia air entrained cement as described above or by adding air-entraining chemicals to Type I cement during the mixing process. The standard benchmark air-entraining material is a neutralized Vinsol resin made from pine wood stumps. Other air-entraining chemicals are also made from byproducts of the paper industry, petroleum refining, and animal and hide processing.

Water reducers
Increasing slump and workability without adding water

A low water-cement ratio is desirable for the ultimate strength and permeability characteristics of the finish concrete, but low water-cement ratio cements are difficult to place or to finish acceptably. So, water-reducing mixtures can be added to reduce the water used by up to 20%, while retaining all of the other strength characteristics of the concrete mix. Water-reducing chemicals are lignosulfonates, hydroxylated carboxylic acids, and carbohydrates made from natural sugars.

Retarders and accelerators
Manage the concrete set time to suit the temperature

Manufactured chemicals can be added to the mix to retard the setting of concrete during hot weather. Accelerating chemicals are used in cold weather to accelerate the set. The most common accelerant is calcium chloride. However, this chemical has severe drawbacks. It becomes corrosive to imbedded reinforcing steel, and should be avoided. It is strictly prohibited for some projects.

Things that look like concrete—but are not

Just because it is gray and is found on a job site, it isn't necessarily concrete. The following may seem similar in look and feel, but they are completely different and cannot be substituted for concrete:

1. Mortar used in masonry
2. Grout used in masonry
3. Chemical grout (a name for materials used to infill between structural steel base plates)
4. Concrete block
5. Floor leveling compounds
6. Concrete patch materials

Making the Complex Local and Simple, and Success Routine

Concrete possibilities are vast and complex

Concrete is a site-manufactured product heavily influenced by the water-cement ratio, temperature, and time. The combination of variations in course aggregate rock types, fine aggregate types and gradings, performance improving chemicals, and reinforcing, makes for tens of thousands of different mix designs— and each detail is important. Project types, local construction materials and customs, and daily and seasonal weather variation add further complexity. Engineers can spend an entire career on just one aspect of concrete, and continue to produce valuable improvements.

Owners and site personnel need simplicity

Building owners and installing tradesmen can and will spend far less time in study than these engineers, but still need to get it right. The discussions above explain how and why concrete works. This knowledge can guide informed decisions when changing type of work, location, or considering new concrete-related products. The discussions below show how to digest this complexity, and make success local, simple, and routine.

Concrete design mixes—choose only a few then learn them well

The performance of cement, water, fine aggregate, coarse aggregate, admixtures, water-cement ratios, temperature, and time are all interactive. Mix designs prepared by an engineering specialist exactly for your type of work and your method of placement will usually be provided free of charge from the concrete supplier, but you have to ask, and ask for exactly what you want.

For example, a builder of single family homes placing the concrete by wheel barrow or chute might only need three mix designs: one for the interior flat work (basement floor), a second for the basement walls, and a third for the exterior flat work (walks and drives). Work in a very cold or hot climate, or placement by pump or conveyor would require additional mix designs. Once the few designs are selected, learn them well—how they place, consolidate, finish, and cure. You can then forget all the complexity of concrete chemical reactions—this knowledge is embedded in the mix design. (Different types of work, or work in different locations require repetition of this process and learning again.)

Water control produces quality—place dry, cure wet

The lowest feasible water-cement ratio produces the strongest, most water impervious, and dimensionally stable finished concrete. Adding water to make the wet concrete easier to place is the single most common and largest mistake, and can degrade the finished product up to 700%.

Selection of a mix design that is suitable both for the finished product, and feasible to place is usually done by owners, architects, or engineers. These specifiers must include ingredients (such as fine aggregate of smaller size, fly ash, water-reducing admixtures, and plasticizers) that increase flow and help placement while maintaining low water-cement ratio. It is then the responsibility of the site personnel placing the concrete to maintain this ratio, even though placement of the stiffer concrete will be harder work. Hard work is possible, but if the mix design makes the site personnel's job impossible, they will have no choice—water will be added. It is everyone's responsibility to maintain the low water-cement ratio that high quality concrete requires.

Once placed well, a slow moist cure is best—with the best conditions under water. Concrete will continue to become stronger and denser for 50 to 100 years—as long as enough water is present. Timing of form removal, covering with sheet plastic, or coating with sealers can help proper cure. But, project owners must allow the time for these activities.

Time—concrete is a chemical reaction that you can manage but not control

The times of mixing, placing, finishing, and curing are fixed by chemical reaction. And these chemicals do not know or care about your wants or needs. The site personnel must understand each hour at the time of concrete placement and initial set requires a specific activity. And, that each activity (keeping the concrete moist, and timing of form removal) in the first days and weeks of the curing process affects the concrete's permanent strength, resistance to water, and shrinkage and cracking. And, the owners must temper their demands for schedule acceleration to realize these benefits of a slow moist cure.

Temperature—place concrete that is at room temperature

The temperature of the concrete must be within the prescribed limits. Measures described above can be employed to maintain these limits by the site personnel placing the concrete. However, the owners of the project should be aware that their decisions about time of project start and aggressiveness of the schedule can bump up against the technical limits the site personnel can achieve. If the owners push too hard in these areas, substandard work will be the result. The knowledge described above—and project planning by owners, managers, and site personnel—will make this mistake easy to avoid.

Placing concrete—limit freefall and consolidate

Freefall of the wet concrete must be limited to a couple of feet. Although this is primarily the responsibility of the site personnel placing the concrete, owner's demands for out of sequence work that makes use of available placement equipment difficult or unfeasible can force unacceptable placement. Listen to the site personnel when they are explaining how and why they want to sequence the work. Also, use equipment to consolidate, so uniform concrete makes its way to all intended locations.

Knowledge is local

Your knowledge is not portable—and can become incorrect even 30 miles away. Work in a very different climate, or substantially different in character (move from building construction to construction of a lock and dam) can mean entirely different applications of the same general rules.

The knowledge of others—including experts from afar—is not portable either. New materials, methods, chemical additives that "have worked for years" elsewhere need to be carefully evaluated for your location. This evaluation takes knowledge, time, and money. If you do not have all three, let someone else be the early adopter.

Summary

The discussion above does not describe how to execute all these rules for all locations. But it does describe the principles that are involved, so you can determine which local answer is right. Simplify this knowledge to a few local mix designs, and learn to use them well. Routinely using these successful materials and procedures, concrete that continues to become stronger, denser, more impervious to water for 50–100 years can be yours.

3.7 Masonry—The Pieces and Ingredients

An assembly of earthen pieces constantly moved by moisture and temperature

What is Masonry?

An ancient material assembled locally requiring local knowledge

Masonry is an assembly of earthen pieces constantly moved by moisture and temperature. Masonry is the on-site assembly, usually by hand, of small, uniformly-sized stone and earth pieces. It is most commonly used to construct walls and sometimes roofs. So, keeping the weather out is an important requirement. It can also be used for heating vessels such as ovens, boilers, incinerators, and smoke stacks. So, fireproofing capabilities are significant. Alternate heating technologies have substituted metal for masonry construction for many of these heating devices. But, the capability is still there, and some of the terminology and thought processes from the older technology are still in use for fire-resistant wall construction.

Masonry is an ancient material, over 6,000 years old, using earth materials found near the job site. Use of unbaked mud bricks in a dry climate with a crew as small as one, was, and in some parts of the world, is still used. Skilled installation using sophisticated materials and larger crew sizes of about 5–12 is more common in the developed world. In all cases, the materials are local, the assembly is local, and so the knowledge of owners, managers, and site personnel must also be local.

Masonry is strong in compression, otherwise weak
Use the strength, manage the weakness

Masonry materials are strong in compression, but weak in bending, shear, and tension. Much of masonry assembly has traditionally been orienting the pieces so they are placed in compression. Arches and domes place all pieces in compression. Older masonry construction increased compression with massive loads of very thick wall construction. More recently, since about 1940, steel has been added to the masonry assembly to provide tensile strength and reduce necessary wall thickness.

Water is important in the manufacturing, installation, and function of masonry
Expansion and contraction, and conduit for water flow

Masonry materials are made wet, shipped wet, installed wet, and will gradually dry out and change in size. Masonry mortars rely on water-cement chemical reaction. Mortar and the masonry pieces require proper humidity in the brick or block for suction and bonding of the mortar. Once the masonry construction is completed, the absorption and movement of water through the wall must be managed, and expansion accommodated. The impact of water is discussed below—with the discussion of each component.

Masonry is perceived to be more solid and permanent
An interesting bias

Many in the western world feel that masonry is a more solid and substantial material (than wood or metal) with great longevity—suitable for more "important" buildings. The children's story of the three little pigs—the first one built a house of straw, the second sticks, and the third (and the best pig) building it of bricks, so the wolf couldn't blow it down—illustrates this prejudice. Although masonry is a good material, it is not always superior. Cultures who have a tradition of building well in wood, such as Japan and Norway, have built all wood buildings that are still functional 1,000–1,500 years after construction.

The Pieces: Bricks, Blocks, Others

Bricks

What is Brick?
Brick is a baked piece of clay

Clays are compounds of silica and alumina made from weathered rock—feldspar, granite, and gneiss. The clay particles, when dry, appear as a fine dust. Their structure is flat, like sheets of paper, so that once wetted they have great suction between the particles—and are dense and cohesive.

Clay usually contains impurities. These impurities frequently include aluminum, iron, shale, and calcium carbonate. Occasionally, other materials, such as sawdust or coal dust, are added to the mix to make fired bricks more porous. These additional materials, as well as the heat of firing, discussed later, will influence the bricks' appearance, density, and resistance to water.

How are bricks made?
Clay is quarried, dried, pulverized, filtered, rewet, formed, and baked

Clay—occurring in natural ground deposits—is quarried, dried out, ground to a powder, filtered for large impurities, and then rewet. In ancient times, bricks were formed by hand or pressed by hand into wooden forms. In some areas of the world, this is still done. So, some imported bricks can have a crude finish and irregular dimensions.

Now, the moist clay is pressed by machine into molds. Holes in the center of the brick or depressions, sometimes called frogs, are cast in the brick. Another process extrudes a long, continuous rectangular shape (including the holes) from a die, then slices off brick size pieces with a wire. These are sometimes called "wire cut" brick. This extrusion process can only install holes, not depressions. The surface texture of the brick can be changed by dragging the still wet face of the brick over a flat surface. Sand or water on this surface will produce other different textures.

The purpose of the holes or depressions is to reduce the weight of the brick without appreciably decreasing its strength. It also makes all parts of the brick about the same distance from the surface, for even and complete firing—using less fuel. Bricks, even with these depressions and holes, are considered "solid" masonry materials if more than 75% of the brick is clay (25% of the volume is holes).

Firing of the bricks
Drying, oxidizing, vitrifying (turning to glass)

Firing of the brick is a process that gradually increases, then decreases the heat over a period of 40–150 hours. The steps are:

1. Drying or dewatering, sometimes called smoking
2. Dehydrating from about 400°-1,650°F
3. Oxidation from about 950°-1,850°F, sometimes called sintering
4. Vitrifying from about 1,650°-2,800°F, turning to glass
5. Then gradually cooling to room temperature in steps

Some brick types will be oxidized only, and not heated to the point of vitrification. Sometimes waste gases can be injected into the kiln during the hot stages of the process to permanently alter the surface color of the brick. This can be done by injecting natural gas or reducing oxygen in the firing chamber. Over or under cooking the bricks will both affect the color and resistance to water.

When a brick leaves a kiln, it will be the driest, and smallest that it will ever be. Moisture of the brick will be about 25–30% when wet and extruded or pressed, about 10–15% when dry, and very close to zero when exiting the kiln. Dimensional shrinkage through the complete drying and firing process can be up to 20%, and this must be allowed for in determining the sizes of the form or extruding die, so the finished piece is the desired size.

The common grades for brick are:

1. SW—(severe weathering). Good for frost resistance. Nominal compressive strength 3,000 psi.
2. MW—(moderate weathering). For dry locations only or locations not subject to frost. Nominal compressive strength 2,500 psi.
3. NW—(no weathering). Suitable only for interior work, never subjected to weathering. Nominal compressive strength 1,500 psi.

Strength of the brick varies with the direction it is laid and stressed
It is not just about appearance

Brick's compressive strengths will range tremendously from about 1,500 psi to about 20,000 psi (in compression only). In bending, the strength reduces to 120–2,900 psi. And when withstanding tension, the strength is negligible—approximately 400 psi.

Bricks are usually placed with the largest faces parallel to the ground (on the mortar bed) to maximize strength. Bricks laid in any other orientation will be weaker. For example, if laid the largest face parallel to the ground the strength is 100 %, on the edge may range from 29%-92%, and on end from 11%-65%. So, rotating brick may have a decorative effect that is acceptable for non-load bearing walls only.

Concrete Blocks
Concrete cast in forms to make shapes

Concrete blocks are a mixture of Portland cement and very small, course aggregate that is either poured into a mold, or—for a dryer mixture—pressed by a machine into a mold. The concrete blocks gain in strength in the same manner as concrete—a chemical reaction between Portland cement and water, taking 28 days.

In contrast to brick, when the block leaves the mold, it is as wet and large as it is ever going to be. It will shrink a lot for the first 28 days, and less thereafter. Concrete blocks are sometimes "autoclaved" in an oven with a moist steam cure. This process, which was popularized in the Scandinavian countries, accelerates the set of the block and increases the dimensional stability. The product will be superior in quality, but the process is unheard of in many parts of the United States and the world.

Other Pieces

Brick and concrete block are by far the most common building pieces, and so were discussed in detail above. But, other types of pieces were or are used—and require some knowledge about their pros and cons.

Hollow clay tile was formerly used as a back-up material for facing masonry or plaster. It was dimensionally inaccurate—maybe 3/4" out of line in one piece—so it could only be used if covered by plaster or other masonry. The material is no longer installed in new construction. Care must be taken when remodeling this type of wall. It is weak and brittle, and a new small penetration may cause the entire wall to disintegrate. This is a definite problem for renovation!

Glazed clay tile is still used for decorative water-resistant applications, such as toilets and animal containment rooms. It is also dimensionally inaccurate. Since it has one finished exposed face, the dimensional inaccuracy must be accommodated by laying two back-to-back walls with the good faces out. Further, the wall is usually laid with the rough mortar joint recessed from the face. Later, a finer "pointing" mortar is used to finish the same joint. This additional effort increases cost 3–5 times more than expected.

Precast concrete, *cast stone*, and *cultured stone* are all forms of solid concrete block—with a decorative intent. The appearance is changed by substituting other types of stone aggregate, pigments, and casting the blocks in unusual molds. As long as the piece weight is similar to a normal block, installation is also similar. Larger pieces (maybe 2–4 times larger than normal) will require temporary support wedges until the mortar is set. Very large pieces will usually be supported by steel, not the surrounding masonry.

Glass block and *quarried and cut stone* may also be used. If the material is absorbent—such as limestone and sandstone—the installation is the same as precast described above. If the material is not absorbent—such as glass block or granite—the pieces will move during installation like a piece of butter in a hot frying pan. Final bond will also be poor. Use of setting wedges, followed by a finer "pointing" mortar to finish the same joint (just as with glazed tile described above) will probably be required. Steel anchoring ties, and adhesion-improving mortar additives are also used. This additional labor and material significantly increases cost.

Mortar and Grout
Fills the voids and bonds the pieces

Aggregate for mortar and grout
Sand and "pea" gravel

Sand, the aggregate for mortar and grout, is typically quarried out of the ground. Quarried sand will usually have more rounded edges. Sand can also be manufactured by crushing and grading stones, and will have sharper edges. Mortars made with sharp edge aggregates can have high compression strength, low permeability, and good bond, but poor workability. In contrast, a finer, rounder sand will have good workability, but less of the other good characteristics. Gradation of sand for mortar:

Sieve size	Natural sand	Manufactured sand
4	100	100
8	95–100	95–100
16	70–100	70–100
30	40–75	40–75
50	10–35	20–40
100	2–15	10–25
200	-	0–10

This "mason sand" has more of the finer particle size than the sand used for concrete.
Coarser gradations are used for grout (the structural infill of the hollow portions of masonry). If the least dimension of the hollow space to be filled is, free and clear exclusive of reinforcing, less than 3", sand aggregate will be used. For grouted spaces greater than 3", 3/8"-1/2" diameter aggregate (sometimes called pea gravel) may be used. In extremely large spaces (rare in masonry construction) up to 3/4" aggregate size is sometimes permitted.

Portland cement and masonry cement

Portland cement, sometimes called hydraulic cement, has high compressive strength, is dense, impervious to water, durable, and bonds well. However, it also has high drying shrinkage and rigidity, and is likely to cause shrinkage cracks and offer little resilience. Masonry cement is a blend of Portland cement, fillers, plasticizer chemicals, and air-entrainment agents that improve some of these deficiencies.

Portland cement sets by a chemical reaction between cement and water that begins an hour and a half after the initial mix of the mortar or grout, sets hard to the touch over the next six hours, and continues to harden and gain strength over 28 days, and continues more slowly for years.

Lime—a stabilizer
Limestone baked, crushed to powder, then soaked in water

Quicklime is heated limestone that is ground to a powder, and then soaked in water. Formerly, the soaking process was done on site with tubs of lime soaking for weeks. Now, pre-hydrated lime (soaking is done at the factory) eliminates this process on the job site. The setting process for lime is different than Portland cement. The lime initially dries out, but does not set. It then converts to calcium carbonate crystals over months and years. This can provide a self-healing effect for cracks as the Portland cement dries and cracks slightly, the crystalline structure of the calcium carbonate can grow into these cracks.

Mortars made with lime are more ductile, shrink less, and are tolerant of movement. Further, lime has a greater tendency to retain its water, which is a benefit if used with highly absorbent brick. Lime can facilitate the laying process and provide enough time for the cement hydration. Lime does, however, reduce compressive strength.

Mortar—Fills the Voids and Bonds the Pieces
Cement, lime, aggregate, water, and air

Mortar consists of Portland cement (and/or masonry cement), lime, sand, water, and air. The higher the portion of lime in the mortar mixture, the lower the strength, but the greater the resilience and ease of laying. The common designations of mortar consists of every other letter of the two words "mason work," in declining strength from highest to lowest.

Type M	1 part Portland cement, 1/4 part lime, 3-3/4 parts sand Usually used for below grade applications such as foundations 2,500 psi at 28 days
Type S	1 part Portland cement, 1/2 part lime, 4-1/2 parts sand Used for above grade applications requiring high tensile bond 1,800 psi at 28 days
Type N	1 part Portland cement, 1 part lime, 6 parts sand Suitable for exterior above grade applications, with severe weather exposure, that requires extreme workability of the mortar, and loads that are not excessive. 750 psi at 28 days
Type O	1 part Portland cement, 2 parts lime, 3 parts sand. For non-load bearing interior walls with low compressive strength requirements. 350 psi at 28 days
Type K	1 part Portland cement, 2-1/4 to 4 parts lime, sand parts 2-1/4 to 3 times the sum of Portland cement and lime. Used for tuck pointing, but not new construction mortar.
Grouts	1 part Portland cement, 1/10 part lime, 2-1/4 to 3 parts sand. Grout is used only for the infilling of the hollow portions of the masonry, not for mortar.

(All parts by volume, not weight.)

Air

Air will be entrained in the mortar naturally to some extent, and provides some frost resistance. Air should be maintained at less than 12% or excessive water retention and reduction in the tensile bond will result.

Pigment
Decorative but weakening

Pigment—sometimes used in mortars for decorative purposes—will weaken the mortar and should be limited to 3–10% of the volume.

Slump—how "liquid" is the wet mortar
Water content affects strength, workability, bond

Mortar must contain more water than a concrete mixture. This is required first because of the greater need for workability in the small dimension mortar joints. Also, the bricks or blocks will absorb some of the water in the mortar mixture, and sufficient water must remain in the mortar mixture so that the Portland cement can hydrate and set. Concrete mixtures have a maximum slump for the wettest conditions of about 5", but mortar will typically have a 5"-8" slump. Grout (because consolidation, which is an important part of the placement of concrete, cannot be effectively accomplished in the very small voids that exist in masonry) will require a slump of 8"-11". This added water does lower the strength of the grout.

The Weakest Mortar for the Purpose Is Best

As described above, the mortar must have adequate compressive strength, but also good adhesion and some resiliency. Portland cement will be strongest in compression, but weaker in the other two characteristics. Lime is the opposite. Therefore, mortar is a material where the weakest mortar that is structurally adequate will be the best mortar for the job. This is opposite common sense, but true.

Reinforcing Steel
Adding pieces strong in tension

Since brick and mortar are strong in compression and weaker at resisting other forces, the usual approach is to orient the pieces so that they are subjected mostly to compression loads. An additional strategy to supplement this approach is to add steel pieces that are strong in tension to create an assembly that is both strong in tension and compression.

This is a relatively recent improvement in masonry design. Up until about the mid 1800s in the United States, iron or steel pieces of any kind—nails, wire, steel angles, and beams—were partially hand-fabricated and a rare luxury good. In the following 50–75 years, steel fabrications became mass-produced, reasonably priced, and widely available. Introduction of steel into standard masonry construction followed, but lagged about 25 years. By about 1950 it became a widely accepted practice, and thereafter became normal operating procedure.

Summary

Masonry is an assembly of earthen pieces strong in compression but weak in tension. Using this strength and managing this weakness is the focus of much of masonry design and installation. This involves orienting the pieces effectively, adding reinforcing steel, and using the adhesion and resiliency of mortar.

Masonry pieces expand and contract when drying and curing, when later wetted, and with temperature change—but not at the same time or rate. Bricks are their smallest and concrete blocks largest when made. These different movements must be accommodated in design and installation. These few principles will help ensure successful masonry work:

1. Select pieces—bricks and block—that are appropriate to the weathering characteristics—expansion, contraction, and moisture absorption—for your purpose.

2. Pick the weakest suitable mortar. Two of the ingredients of mortar—Portland cement and lime set in different ways and at different times. Portland cement sets by a chemical reaction with water beginning 1-1/2 hours after mixing, is set within 4–6 hours, and fully cured in 28 days. This mixture is strong in compression but brittle. Lime dries out in hours, then changes in crystal structure for years. Lime is weak in compression, but has good adhesion and is resilient and self-healing. Mix the mortar ingredients to optimize the good qualities, and minimize the bad. This means selecting the mortar with the weakest compressive strength that the structure will allow—to maximize adhesion, resilience, and provide some self-healing properties.

3. Manage water and time. The moisture content of the pieces will govern adhesion during installation to the mortar—and their expansion and contraction forever. Mortar is a chemical reaction between cement, lime, and water where the water-cement ratios and time of mixing, setting, and curing must be managed carefully. Water transmission in and through the completed masonry work will continue forever. This is the real world governed by the laws of physics and chemistry—and will not change for the ignorant, wishful thinkers, or egotists. Owners, project managers, and installing contractors must understand these laws, and include the time restraints in the planning of their work.

Use of these principles will be put to work in the next chapter on masonry construction.

3.8 Masonry—Assembling the Pieces and Ingredients into a Building

Working with the components as they are—to build a structure
that manages movement, water, fire, and sound

Masonry Works with the Entire Building Structure
Not just a stack of bricks

Using compression and managing all other forces
Design improvements require increased knowledge

For most of the history of masonry construction, the thickness and heights of masonry walls were done by rules—based on experience. This made for a very tall, skinny triangle. A common rule went, "the top story is two bricks wide, the next story down three, and adding a brick-width per story down to the basement." This would produce walls up to twenty feet thick. Since this rule, in many cases, produced significantly overbuilt walls, not a lot of knowledge was necessary. However, starting in about 1950, acceptance of engineering advances, and the introduction of steel into masonry construction produced entirely different ways of calculating the "right" wall height and reinforcing—and made comparatively thin wall assemblies the norm. This, however, does require some understanding of the structure of a wall so that you know how to build it and how to brace it in a temporary mode until the building is finally completed.

Wall strength varies with direction of stress

As stated in a number of places previously, masonry walls are very strong in compression. For example, if a wall is intended to support a floor above, it will be very strong if the floor is placed entirely over the top of the wall. However, typically, the floor structure favors the interior side of the building. This is called "eccentric loading" and tends to make the outboard face of the wall bow out slightly—causing tension at the bulged-out part of this bow. This means the wall must be vertically reinforced and its reinforcing grout cured, before it can take this eccentric load.

Wind and earth loads—timing matters

Other loads imposed on a wall are wind above ground, and earth below grade. Walls are weakest against horizontal forces that produce tension and bending (it is easier to push the top over, or the middle out) than the vertical direction—(pushing down on the top to hold up the structure). Further, if there is face brick in addition to the block, it makes a minor contribution to the structure of the wall. Although it is common to place the face brick at the same time as the wall, it is not always done. It should be recognized that you will have an incomplete structure until the face brick is installed, tied together, and cured. These considerations have sequencing and scheduling implications for the installing trades people and the owners and managers of the project.

Another consideration for the site personnel is wind loading during construction. As described above, a masonry wall is not strong in the horizontal direction. An un-reinforced masonry wall (an uncommon occurrence) can only be constructed 8' high before temporary or permanent bracing is installed—generally called wind bracing. Reinforcing in the wall may increase this height to about 12'. This can be weakened slightly by flashing at the bottom of the wall, which interrupts the bond of the mortar joint.

It is critical to install the wind bracing as the wall is being constructed to prevent the wall from blowing in or being sucked out by a negative pressure. Either bracing both sides of the wall with scaffold planks does this, or bracing one side of the wall with pipe columns bolted to the wall and to a concrete dead-man (a temporary concrete mass poured in or on the ground).

Assembling the Pieces
Using each component's best qualities to form a superior assembly

Piece sizes have standardized
Standard piece size influences design possibilities and work flow

There are many brick sizes, and they were historically used in an area their name implies: Roman, Saxon (from Germany), Norman (from northern France), and Flemish (from Holland). These brick sizes were used in many parts of Europe and the United States. It was common at one time also to have what was called full-dimension brick. So, for example, the brick would be 8" long. However, when you added a 3/8" mortar joint, the assembled wall with the 8" plus the 3/8" could have some very peculiar dimensions that made the insertion of standard-sized doors and windows troublesome.

Although these different sizes of brick still exist—and are used in the United States, we have tended towards two sizes of bricks. One size is the modular standard brick, which is 2-1/4" high x 3-5/8" wide x 7-5/8" long. With a 3/8" mortar joint, the length is exactly 8". Three thicknesses, equals two widths, equals one length is the reason for the name "modular." This module also lines up with the face of the modular concrete blocks, which have block face sizes of 15-5/8" x 7-5/8". The common block widths of 4", 6", 8", 10", and 12" do not all line up as well. A larger jumbo or economy brick measures 3-5/8" x 3-5/8" x 11-5/8" and matches the concrete block vertical coursing.

Other brick sizes are still available and used when a unique look is desired. Selection of these unusual bricks will bring back all the dimensional problems modular bricks were intended to avoid. Overcoming these problems requires management skill, installation capabilities, and more cost—so careful evaluation is appropriate before selection.

Deformation of fired pieces affects dimensions of the finished work

As described above, masonry is usually the hand assembly of small pieces to form a larger assembly. Pieces are generally limited to what a man can lift, usually with one hand. But there is another limitation on the size of masonry pieces. The larger the piece the more it will deform during the casting and firing process. Further, to reduce weight, larger pieces are more hollow, which will further increase the deformation. The addition of glazing on a face of the masonry can further increase this deformation.

If a piece is bowed or warped, and a minimum sized mortar joint is maintained on one side, the joint will be larger on the other side. Dimensions of the assembly will unavoidably grow larger than the intended and expected modular dimension. Since interior wall framing materials, and doors and windows, are made to the modular dimensions (metal studs are made 9-0 long but not 9-2), the results can be disastrous—with wasted material, small infills, and patch and repair. This problem is greatest for large hollow bricks, and least for concrete blocks.

Further, the blocks must be laid out so that the hollow cores line up, so that vertical reinforcing and grout can be continuous for the height of the wall. Finally, masonry uses mostly full pieces, or same size cut pieces to look like you "meant it." Small fractional pieces of varied sizes surrounding windows, doors, terminations, or building edges will have the appearance of using scraps. Therefore, the sizes of the building, windows, doors, and openings of any kind must be laid out with the dimensions of the brick in mind.

The assembly's strength is different than the strength of the parts

The alignment of the joints also affects the strength of the assembly. The bricks are 3–20 times stronger in compression than the mortar. If the mortar joints are offset half the length of the block (vertical joints between the blocks do not align)—what is called a "running bond" will distribute the load through the stronger brick or block, thereby making a stronger assembly than if the mortar joints are stacked vertically.

For running bond, the strength of laboratory tested samples of an assembly tested wall can be up to three times the compressive strength of the mortar. The confinement of the mortar, and the distribution of the loads through the bricks, help overcome the weakness of the mortar. However, in the real world, the masonry is stressed also in tension and bending—for which resistance is poor. This deceases the "allowable load"—the real world usable figure—to about 10–20% of the laboratory value. For example, a brick with 4,500 psi compressive strength, and a type N mortar with a 750 psi compressive strength, has a confined laboratory test strength of 1,800 psi, but an allowable strength of 250 psi.

This radical drop in allowable strength, at first seems puzzling, but recall the tensile strength of mortar is only about 400 psi. Also, this reduced value—about 4,000 pounds allowable load for one brick—is sufficient for most purposes. Note that this reduction of assembly strength, caused by the weakness of mortar, wastes the extra strength of High strength bricks. So, do not seek them out or pay a premium hoping to make a stronger assembled wall.

Masonry piece orientation used to be fancy, and structurally important

For most of the history of masonry construction, before steel was readily available, the walls were constructed extremely thick—feet to tens of feet. Much of the additional strength was obtained by bonding the bricks—crisscrossing the bricks like a basket weave so that the walls were tied together and the loads transferred to the strongest part of the brick. This was a good part of the mason's skill. It is discussed in older books about masonry, and is historically interesting. However, it is not used in modern masonry, because the needed tensile strength can be obtained with reinforcing steel in a thin wall.

Reinforcing Steel to Add Tensile Strength

Reinforcing in the hollows of the pieces

The principle is to install reinforcing wire assemblies in the mortar bed and grouted rebar in the brick or block hollow spaces to form horizontal and vertical reinforcing grids. The horizontal reinforcing is accomplished by using what is called a "bond beam" block, which resembles the capital letter "U"—open at the top. In this "U" are usually placed between one and four rebars (reinforcing steel) number 3 through number 6 (3/8" through 6/8" (3/4") diameter). These are filled with grout. For the vertical reinforcing, similar reinforcing steel is placed in the hollow core of the brick or block and filled with grout.

Reinforcing placed in the mortar bed

In the horizontal mortar joints between the blocks and bricks, a wire grid assembly—sometimes called "Durawall" or as ladder or truss reinforcing—is used. The wire, typically about 9 gauge, is slightly less than the width of the block and/or combined block and brick, and is commonly laid in every other course (in every other horizontal mortar joint).

When face brick does not have the ladder or truss reinforcing, it can also be tied to other portions of the adjacent wall—back-up block, framed wood, or concrete—with corrugated or wire ties. For a block wall, these corrugated or wire ties can be laid in the concrete block mortar joints as it is installed. For other assemblies, such as wood or poured concrete walls, it can be mechanically fastened with a powder actuated fastener, screwed in place, or in some cases, have inserts cast into the concrete.

Physics and Chemistry Influence Job Flow and Timing

Structural requirements restrict installation sequences

The spacing described above is descriptive and is sometimes done by common practice or designed by a structural engineer. The purpose is to form a larger assembly (on the order of 30 feet long) that acts as a unit—strong in tension and moderately strong in shear and bending. Constructing larger assemblies that function as a unit has implications for installing personnel and managers. You are not just stacking up pieces, you are building part of a system that works with other components. Therefore, you must understand how the structure works so that you start, stop, and brace the work in a way consistent with the design of the entire building. This has scheduling and phasing implications.

You can not do whatever you want; you have to do something that works within the design and structural limitations of the building. If you need to leave portions of the wall out, for example, for access for very large mechanical equipment, you must give particular attention to the bracing and the structural considerations in the temporary mode—or the results can be disastrous.

Portland cement set and cure time influences crew size, work flow, and scheduling

Initial mortar set starts about an hour and a half after mixing, and hard set is completed 4–8 hours later. So, only about a two-foot height—(three 8" concrete blocks) or 9 bricks high—can be placed at one time in a full production mode. There are definite densities of manpower, and scheduling limits caused by the mortar set time limitations. Once these two feet have been placed in a work area, another work area must be available, or there will be significant reductions in productivity while the trades people wait for the set to take place. So you either need an appropriately sized crew or a larger work area.

An additional scheduling implication is that until the mortar has properly cured in approximately 28 days, the wall will be incapable of bearing its intended weight. So placing of full structural loads, such as floors, and beams on the wall, before that time is forbidden. Owners and managers must schedule within these limits, or pay a premium for reduced productivity and/or quality output.

Performance Improving Chemicals
Help in cold and hot weather—improve adhesion and water resistance

Cold and hot weather

Chemicals can help with extremely cold or hot weather installation. Accelerator chemicals can be added to the mortar mix in cold weather to speed the chemical reaction of the Portland cement, which has been slowed by cold. Retarders can be used in extremely hot weather to slow the chemical reaction to suit the speed capabilities of the installing tradesman. It can also have another use that is less common—where the mortar is actually batched at a central plant, similar to concrete, and is dispatched on trucks rather than being mixed close to the point of installation. This can extend the mortar initial set time by 4–8 hours.

Water resistance

The second type of improving chemicals is waterproofing add mixtures. Chemicals can be added both to the concrete block as it is being cast and to the mortar during mixing to increase the water repellency of the assembly. Chemicals that are in the silicone family—such as silane and siloxane—can be added both at the plant when casting the blocks, and in the field when mixing the mortar. Another approach to waterproofing that is used more extensively in extremely humid and warmer climates is to apply a petroleum mastic on the outboard face of the concrete block. This is trowel or spray applied after block installation and then some types of facing material, face brick, or other materials are added on the outboard side.

Adhesion

Finally, additives to increase the adhesion of the mortar can be added. This must be done where extremely high tensile strength is required, such as when trying to make factory prefabricated brick walls, and then hoisting them in place with a crane. The demands of transportation require this additional tensile strength. Multiple other chemicals for highly specialized applications are available: for example, additives to withstand animal-related products such as blood and urine. Use of these chemicals has a cost and acceptance is not widespread.

Masonry Constantly Moves—Manage and Accommodate This Movement
Bricks feel hard and solid—but water and temperature force movement

A masonry wall will move as long as it is standing. It will move a lot near the time of initial installation, due to the final curing and moisture-related changes of the materials. But it will continue to move forever, whenever there are changes in temperature and/or moisture. Irreversible movement occurs close to the time of installation. As described above, a clay brick will be its smallest when it leaves the kiln. As it absorbs moisture during storage, transit, and installation, it will irreversibly grow in size (irreversible growth of .02-.10%). In contrast, a concrete block will be largest when it is initially cast, and as it cures it will irreversibly shrink (irreversible shrinkage of .02-.09 %). Mortar will be largest at the time of installation and shrink as it cures and dries (irreversible shrinkage of .04-.1%). These differential movements between the components of the masonry will continue for the first few years of installation, and then continue further, but taper off significantly over the life of the masonry wall.

Temperature or moisture changes will expand and contract the materials. A dark sun-baked brick can rise to 160°F, then plummet to -20°F (and change in dimension of 1/4" in ten feet), while the interior face of the wall stays at 70°F. The exterior face may be saturated by rain (an increase in dimension of 1/32" in ten feet), while the interior face remains dry. All masonry materials will expand, but different materials will expand at different rates in response to the same temperature or moisture changes. Further, the walls may be multiple widths, having an interior and exterior face which will have different temperature and humidity conditions, so each component and each face will move differently. These movements must be accommodated.

Fully cured pieces and forgiving mortar

An always, good response is to have the materials, bricks, and blocks fully cured before installation. This is always desirable, always specified, and frequently violated. In times of boom, concrete blocks can frequently be viewed leaving the production plant destined for a job site still steaming from the initial casting moisture. Another response is to choose a mortar that has more resiliency—give and go.

Control joints—gaps in the masonry for give and go

The last method to accommodate movement is to install control joints—gaps in the block, brick, and mortar that are infilled with some resilient material, such as caulk. These gaps are typically approximately the size of a mortar joint and go continuously through all widths of the wall. These are typically installed vertically at about 30' on center of the wall. They are also installed at points of stress.

Masonry is a brittle material and brittle materials crack at inside corners. Therefore, an inside corner—such as the edge of a window, or door—gets a control joint. A change in building height, such as the change from a one-story to a two-story building, requires a vertical control joint at the inside corner of this intersection. These additional inside corner control joints are usually in addition to the 30'-on-center control joint, but some judgment must be used.

For buildings of a few stories in height, generally under 50', the masonry can go vertically without a horizontal control joint. For higher buildings, where the building structure holds up the masonry facing (the masonry is not load bearing), control joints are typically installed at the floor line, continuously around the building—thereby producing a grid work of both horizontal and vertical control joints.

Managing Water in the Finished Masonry Wall
Water moves in and through the wall

Masonry is an extremely porous material that will rapidly transmit water. A driving rain can penetrate a face brick wall and have solid water dripping down the inside in less than one minute. There are three approaches to address water transmission through masonry.

Three Water Management Approaches:

1. Water storage

The first approach was used extensively in older buildings—water storage in the masonry. When masonry walls were extremely thick, sometimes several feet up to twenty- feet thick, the driving rain could begin to saturate the brick, but it would generally stop raining before the wall became fully saturated. After the rain stops, the stored water in the wall would then migrate out again. This is a perfectly acceptable approach. However, it has less use in the thinner masonry walls being constructed today, although it still works to a lesser extent.

2. Water proofing

The second approach is to waterproof the masonry. Chemicals can be added to the block and mortar material. Or, waterproofing chemicals, designed for this purpose, can be applied after completion of the masonry wall. Extreme care and comprehensive knowledge of the entire building system must be used when applying these chemicals—so that you do not develop an exterior vapor barrier in the weather side of the wall that traps interior moisture within the wall, causing undesirable results such as mold and efflorescence.

3. Water shedding-(nothing works perfectly—use two lines of defense)

The next approach is an interior face that is water-shedding. That is, water will enter, contact the barrier, and then be drained out to the exterior in an acceptable manner. This can be done by applying building paper (a paper-like product impregnated with petroleum products). For face brick on a wood-framed building, plastic or petroleum mastics (fluid or trowel applied) on the outboard-concealed face of a multi-width masonry wall can be used.

No matter what the approach, it will not be perfect—there will still be some leakage. Therefore, sound masonry construction always requires two lines of defense. The second line of defense is typically a flashing and weeping detail. A flashing will be an impervious material, such as sheet plastic, copper, or stainless steel that is placed inside the wall. Any water that penetrates the other barrier drips down the center of the wall where it contacts this flashing. On the exterior weather side, there are weeps, which are voids in the mortar joints produced by cotton sash cord or plastic fabrications designed for this purpose. These flashing systems are installed at the bottom of the wall, at the top of the door heads, or window heads, or other penetrations—wherever there is an obstruction to the vertical water flow. And for multi-story buildings, they are used where there is a control joint at the floor line.

The strategy is to make a reasonably waterproof wall and then put in a second line of defense because when it fails—and it will fail to some extent—the moisture can find another way out, and thus preserve the water integrity of the wall.

Mortar joints usually must shed water

Masonry walls are usually required to shed water. So, the joints must be shaped accordingly. Concave round or V, sloping, or flush joints are used. Any unsloped ledge that can allow water to accumulate must be avoided. For interior masonry, or exterior masonry in climates with little or no rain, these restrictions do not apply, and other joint types can be used.

Efflorescence
That annoying white residue telling you water management needs improvement

Efflorescence is a water-pressure-caused migration of dissolved minerals and salt in a masonry assembly. This efflorescence usually appears as a white powder or crusty nodules, and will appear on any surface where drying occurs. It is typically the exterior face of the wall, but can be the interior face of basement walls, or can migrate up several feet from the earth at a foundation location. When the efflorescence comes from the brick or block itself, it can represent a leaching out of impurities that were inappropriately cast in these materials. When the efflorescence appears at the mortar joint, it is typically lime staining caused by the calcium hydroxide leaching from the mortar and causing calcium carbonate crystals on the surface. This is the same process that forms stalactites in caves. Salts from unwashed sand used in the mortar can also cause the whitish deposits.

Use of properly washed sands, bricks, and blocks without unacceptably high levels of impurities will eliminate a significant portion of the problem. However, the most common reason for efflorescence is a continuous one-way migration of water. This usually indicates improper construction details or barriers. A "round trip" of the water—the blocks become wet and then dry out—will not cause the efflorescence. But, if you have a condition such as a foundation wall that is always wet on the outside, and the water is always migrating through, the efflorescence will appear on the interior. On a parapet condition (a wall that projects above the main building roof area), if one side of the more porous concrete block is unprotected from the weather, water can migrate through to the more protected face brick side and can cause efflorescence. Pure materials and managing the path of migration of the water will substantially eliminate efflorescence—or at least reduce it to an easily maintained problem.

Masonry is a Good Fire Barrier
Masonry does not burn, and resists temperature rise

Some, but not all, masonry walls are constructed as a fire barrier—to make compartments in a building that help manage the spread of an accidental fire. Masonry is a desirable fire barrier because it has zero flammability and zero surface spread of the flame. It also can maintain its strength and stability up to 1,850°C. It has a relatively slow thermal conductivity for the masses typically used in construction.

If it is a fire or smoke barrier, it must be completely continuous for its entire height and width. This means particular attention must be given by the mason to install tightly to all penetrations, structures, and pipes. And, following trades who make holes must pack voids with materials such as mineral wool, Fire-resistant caulk, or sealant that bears a UL fire rating appropriate for the masonry fire assembly.

A 4" ungrouted wall can have a 1-hour fire rating. Thicker grout walls can have fire ratings of 3-hours. (A fire rating is the length of time a wall can withstand a fire of a specified heat while specifically limiting the temperature rise on the other side of the wall.) Companies such as Underwriters Laboratories (UL) do physical tests of wall assemblies. If you need a fire rating, you must exactly duplicate in every respect—block size and type, mortar type, and reinforcing type and spacing—a tested assembly with published results. Reasoning and common sense have no place here—use a tested assembly.

Masonry Reduces Sound Between and Within Spaces

Sound reduction between spaces

Masonry is a material with a high mass that functions well in reducing sound between two spaces. The more mass separated by some resilient hollows, the better the sound reduction between spaces. If it is designed to act as a noise barrier, seal all penetrations, and stagger openings through the wall, such as electrical outlet boxes, HVAC, grilles, and pipe penetrations, so there is no clear path of sound through the wall. A single width of hollow concrete block has an STC (Standard Transmission Class—a measure of a material's sound transmission reduction capacity) rating of about 48. (About equivalent to a good party wall between apartments.)

Sound reduction within spaces

Sound reduction or management within a room is a different problem. This occurs in auditoriums and churches where noise reduction by the masonry is required. Typically, a porous brick with a rougher face is sought. The selection of the brick can increase the noise reduction of the masonry by about 50%—the more porous, the more sound reduction. Concrete block has about three times the sound absorption of brick. Note that subsequent painting of this masonry ruins the sound absorption. The first coat will destroy approximately 55% of the sound reduction capability, and the second coat 90%.

Unpainted masonry will absorb 7–35% of sound. Improvement can be obtained with hollow masonry with slots in the face, or staggered pieces open to the cavity behind. An acoustical engineer usually designs these applications—with specific acoustic performance requirements.

Summary

Masonry is a strong durable material good for fire resistance and sound reduction, and its use is widespread. However, the nature of the chemical processes in the brick, block, and mortar, as well as the customary dimensional constraints of the masonry, limit the possibilities for design, sequencing, and scheduling. It is important for both the site personnel to know how to effectively execute their work, and for owners to understand that there are limitations that must be observed for excellent masonry construction. The following must be observed:

1. Work within the dimensional limits of the masonry pieces. Piece sizes and dimensional variations must match the design dimensions. The hollows of the pieces must line up so reinforcing can be installed.

2. Select pieces—bricks and block—that are appropriate to the weathering characteristics—expansion, contraction, and moisture absorption—for your purpose.

3. Select the mortar with the weakest compressive strength that the structure will allow to maximize adhesion, resilience, and provide some self-healing properties.

4. Recall that masonry is strong in compression, weak in bending, and weakest in tension. Design with these limitations in mind. Understand the purpose and correctly install reinforcing and ties to make an assembly that is both strong in compression and tension.

5. Accommodate expansion and contraction. Install properly cured materials. And install vertical control joints at about 30' on center, and at intersections of inside corners—and for high buildings, at the floor lines.

6. Manage the path of water. A combination of water storage, waterproofing, and water-shedding can be used. When that does not completely work (which is always), have a second line of defense that allows the moisture that does get through to weep acceptably out to the exterior.

    Understanding of these principles and application of these rules by owners, designers, and contractors will make successful masonry construction normal.

3.9 The Building Structure: Managing Loads and Motion

Loads are not uniform and continuous. And structures are not rock solid and unyielding. Partially predictable loads are managed by the elasticity of materials

The Loads to Be Managed

Dead loads—the weight of the structure itself
They can be precisely calculated—but are frequently estimated

The dead load is the weight of the structure and permanently attached equipment. These loads can either be calculated precisely—by measuring each component of the building—or estimated based on past experience such as "40 pounds per square foot."

Live loads—the weight of the people and moveable contents
Vary over time and can only be estimated

These loads can range from vacant and unloaded, heavily loaded on one side, to fully loaded evenly. Because of this uncertainty, live loads are assumed from past experience. Common ranges may be: *roofs* 10–30 pounds per square foot, *private residential floors* 40–60 pounds per square foot, *office floors* 125 pounds per square foot, *assembly and light industrial floors* 250 pounds per square foot, and *heavier industrial* 450 pounds per square foot. These assumptions are built into the structure. So, changing from a residential to commercial use after the building is built may be impractical.

These loads assume even distribution and relatively light objects—something you can get up in an elevator with furniture movers. Over about 2,000 to 5,000 pounds, certainly 10,000 pounds, reinforcing must be added to the floors, beams, and sometimes columns at and around the load location.

Live loads—the weight and forces of wind, water, and earth
Are both estimated and calculated

Wind—a horizontal load

Wind is everywhere, but speed varies by area of the country and increases with distance from the ground. Wind pressure at grade level can vary from 10 to 30 pounds per square foot—increasing to 250 pounds per square foot at the top of a high-rise building. And this is for normal weather, not a storm.

These loads add up to large numbers. For example, a skyscraper 125 feet wide by 800 feet high could have wind load pushing on one face only of 125 million pounds. And this is just one face. As the wind moves around the building, a greater negative pressure pulls on the other side (similar to the lift on an airplane wing). Walls fail more frequently by being sucked out than pushed in.

Water—snow and rain—a vertical load

In northern climates an even snow load of 10 to 30 pounds per square foot is possible. To this must be added a "drift" load where snow may drift higher and increase loads. For all areas, a roof water load may have to be added for water that may be temporarily ponded on the roof during a heavy rain. The regional differences in rainfall and snow produce large differences in the structure's requirements that must be recognized when moving from one area of the country to another.

Earth and water below grade—another horizontal load

Soil exerts horizontal pressure on a foundation or retention structure. The amount of the pressure will vary with the soil type. And it will increase significantly as the water content in the soil increases.

Fire and water resistance—not a load, but a factor in structural design

Although fire is not itself a load, heat reduces the load bearing capacity of a structural member, so it is mentioned here. Wood is combustible and has no fire resistance (older heavy timber buildings are an exception). Steel will soften and weaken long before it actually melts, so it has limited fire resistance. And concrete and masonry have the highest fire resistance. Addition of fireproofing materials—such as spray-on fireproofing, layers of gypsum drywall or plaster or masonry—can increase resistance. Three-four hours of resistance is the practical maximum for a single assembly.

We Make Structures That Probably, (but Not Certainly) Won't Fail
Not a comforting thought—but true

Up until the middle of the 20th century, most structural design was done by rules of thumb. Walls were short thick pyramids—"increase the bottom wall width one brick for each story in height." Beams were short and windows were few. And structural failure and building collapse was considered normal. Traces of this thinking remain in people's attitudes—and in some building codes.

We now calculate or estimate different types of loads for different portions of the structure. We then estimate probabilities that these different events will not all occur at the same time, and design for these assumed reduced loads. This is a vast improvement over the former approach, and produces far safer and more economical and varied structures. But it still only says that it probably, but not certainly, won't fall down!

Not covered at all

First, there are certain occurrences we do not even attempt to resist: tornado, lava or mud flows, flood, sink holes or earthquakes opening ground under the building itself. Although we know these things occur, and where they are more likely to occur, they are called "acts of God." We make no attempt to design for them—and the loss is usually excluded from most insurance coverage.

Only covered to an assumed "normal" maximum

For other natural disasters—wind, rain, hurricane, and earthquake—we only design to a specified "normal" maximum. A common maximum is the worst-case for the last 100 years. Occasionally, the worst-case for the last 500 years is used. Above these limits the occurrences again are called "acts of God." Failure from these causes may be partially or completely uncovered by insurance.

And even these limits are not certain

Even with these restricted limits, we do not say it won't fail, we only say it probably won't fail. A 95% probability of non failure is most common, 98% and 99% are rarer.

Safety factors help but don't solve the problem

Because of the uncertainties mentioned above, and because there is natural variation in the quality of all materials, safety factors are added to structural calculations. "Make everything stronger to make up for the things we do not know for sure." A safety factor of 1.5 is marginal for low-quality temporary buildings. 2.5 is a standard workhorse figure for much commercial construction. And 5 is used where there's greater uncertainty, or the consequences of failure are unusually high.

Many components of a structure will have a far higher safety factor due to the use of standard shapes. But the safety factor applies to all components, including the weakest link in the chain. And the safety factor is not a cushion or slush fund that can be used to justify cutting corners or improper workmanship in the field. "We can leave a few of these out because there is probably some safety factor somewhere" is never an attitude that can be tolerated. Do not jump onto the pile; it is high enough already!

Managing the Load with Elasticity—Springiness Produces Strength

How does a material resist a load?

You are now sitting in a chair and have not crashed down to the floor or floated up into space. The force of the chair pushing up exactly balances the load of your weight pulled down by gravity. The chair is able to push back because of elasticity.

Every material—stone, concrete, steel, wood, and rubber bands—has elasticity. The elasticity varies greatly but every material has it. When a load is applied, the material deforms slightly and stores energy like a spring. This stored energy exists for the whole material itself—its crystal or cellular structure, and its atomic structure. All this energy forms lines of force moving away from the direction of the applied load. And similar forces in another direction can redirect these force lines. For example, in the famous old stone cathedrals, the sloped roof structure forced horizontally outward on the exterior supporting walls. Large weights on top of these walls, such as the statues and decorative objects, redirected the force lines vertically downward. The statues, which appear to be decorations only, are really part of the structure.

This loading and unloading can continue indefinitely without changing the shape of the material as long as the change of shape remains within the material's elastic limit—and the limits of time. If these limits are exceeded, two things can happen: first the material can fatigue and eventually break, after millions of cycles. Failure by fatigue is common in machinery, is sometimes checked by inspection in structures such as bridges, but is not a concern or something we even look for in building structures. Second is creep. The material changes shape slightly in the direction of the load when heavily loaded for a long time—maybe 1 to 8 years. The dimensional changes are small but the forces are great. And creep does occur and must be accommodated in buildings. A slightly beneficial effect can be obtained when a beam bears on a slightly bumpy concrete surface. Creep can force down the bumps and level the surface.

When building an entire structure, creep must be accommodated. If a high-rise building structure could be erected in one day, creep between 8 and 24 inches, depending on the materials, would shorten it. Since buildings are constructed more gradually, creep on the lower floors is taking place as the upper floors are being completed, so creep doesn't happen all at once.

But it still happens and must be accommodated in any of the elements that rise vertically through the entire structure—exterior curtain wall mullions, elevator rails, and pipe and conduit risers. Expansion joints must be included in these elements. And if an element is installed early in construction—before the creep has taken place—a larger expansion joint must be included. Failure to accommodate the creep will produce disastrous results that can only be partially solved by patch and repair.

Compression, Tension, Shear, and Torsion
Resisting loads, managing motion

Materials contain uneven capabilities—they are strong in one characteristic but weak in another. So materials can be selected for their strongest qualities, but it is nearly impossible to ensure that they are only subjected to the loads to which they are best suited.

Compression—pushing down

Compression is the ability to resist a load pushing down on a material. Since two objects cannot occupy the same space at the same time, compressive strengths are high for many materials. For example, 5,000 psi concrete weighing 150 pounds per cubic foot can support its own weight in a column 4,800 feet high—far higher than we ever need or use. Failure in compression is usually a shear crack, usually on the diagonal. More ductile materials such as steel will bulge. Fibrous material, such as wood, will buckle, usually at 90 degrees. Fiberglass or carbon fiber materials will crease along the diagonal.

Tension—pulling out

Tension is the ability to resist a load pulling out on the material. Materials fail in tension first by elongating and narrowing, usually in a three to one ratio. Then they elongate rapidly with a rapid decrease in strength followed by breaking. The common working structural capacities for common materials are as follows:

Material	Compression	Tension
Concrete	4,000–6,000 psi	Negligible
Reinforcing Steel for Concrete	Not usually measured	60,000 psi
Masonry Walls Including Mortar	5,000 psi	Negligible
Wood	1,450 psi	1,100 psi
Structural Steel	3 times tension	36,000 psi

These are the midpoints of the common ranges. Concrete and structural steel can have up to three times these strengths. And wood can have about 50% more or 300% less depending on the species and grade—and whether the load is parallel or perpendicular to the grain.

Shear—sliding past

Shear is one part of a material sliding past the other. Very little motion—usually less than 1 degree—takes place before breaking.

Torsion—twisting

Torsion is twisting of a material. Although this is a large structural consideration for things that move, such as airplanes, it is not given great attention in building construction. Buildings usually consist of square boxes, so accommodating compression, tension, and shear is the focus—hoping to eliminate considerations of twisting in the process. This usually works. But torsion occasionally causes a problem, such as the Copley Square office building in Boston, where twisting of the structure from wind caused the windows to pop out and fall to the street below. Larger, more unusually shaped or constructed structures must be specifically engineered to resist torsion.

Motion everywhere—but some rigidity required to minimize cracking of finish materials

The structural elements are constantly moving under load, as discussed above. In addition, beams continually bend and unbend. Materials will change size when heated or cooled. All this produces greater motion than most interior finishes can accommodate so increased rigidity is sought. A traditional standard was that a beam could deflect at midpoint 1 inch for every 360 inches of length—this was thought to be the maximum deflection plaster could accommodate. These ratios can change from 360 to 180 for drywall. And although drywall is far more common than plaster, the 1 in 360 standard for plaster is frequently still used. 1 in 240 is a frequently used compromise.

To achieve this rigidity, structures are strengthened. So, rigidity, rather than the ability to resist loads and not fall down, is the highest governing design criterion. If a building will receive no interior finishes—such as an industrial or warehouse building expecting maybe 3–6 inches of deflection—a lighter, more economical structure can be chosen. But this building cannot successfully be converted to an office use.

Beams, Columns, and Diaphragms—Basic Building Blocks

Beams
Simple (single) spans with unrestrained supports.

A beam is a horizontal structural member. The simplest beam supports but does not restrain at each end—like a board resting on two concrete blocks. One-half the load is supported by each end. So the exact midpoint of the beam supports no load, and the ends have maximum shear. This is the opposite of common sense, since the midpoint of the beam bends the most, but it is true. This is why—when extreme lightness of structural members is required—such as airplanes and racecars, the material near the center of the span will be cut out.

As a beam bends, the bottom stretches producing tension, and the top compresses producing compression. The exact center of the beam will be in neither tension nor compression. The capacity of the beam increases with depth, but must also resist buckling. So when economies of material or lightweight are sought, the beam shape tends towards the shape of a capital I. Steel wide flange beams, wood trust joists, and precast concrete beams are some examples. (Steel shapes are developed for buildings. Different shapes are used for railroads, ships, and machinery. These other shapes may look similar but are not the same—and can not be used for structural construction.)

Cantilevers and multiple spans produce complexity

If a beam is supported at one end (cantilevered), the tension and compression reverse. The top is in tension and the bottom is in compression. And if a single beam is supported in more than two places, the top of the beam will alternate between compression at mid-span and tension at the supports. And the bottom will alternate, but opposite.

This location of supports is hugely important—loads that are the opposite of what is intended, and different in size, can result from addition of more supports. Adding supports to make a beam "stronger" seems like it could only help, but it is a disastrous, but common, mistake.

Columns

A column is a vertical structural member. If a column remained extremely short and thick with the ratio of column width to height of 1 to 5–10, high compressive strengths described above would make column sizes small and economical. Except, almost all building columns exceed this ratio (a 6" wide column could only be 60" high) so these taller columns begin to buckle at a load far smaller than the compressive strength limit.

Diaphragms

A diaphragm is a flat plate that can be used to transfer a load and produce lateral (horizontal) stability. Lateral stability could be produced by an interwoven system of columns and beams, but this would require precise design and installation and lots of labor. Instead, an entire flat plate, which contains the equivalent of all these beams and columns plus a lot of infill material, can be used. And this diaphragm frequently serves other purposes as well. Examples include foundation walls that hold back the earth, sub grade floors that hold back the foundation walls, and above grade interior walls (shear walls) that resist the wind pressure on a building.

Connections Both Hold Pieces Together and Transfer Loads

How rigidly is it connected?
Rigidity increases strength in one place but causes problems in others

The discussions of beams and columns above assume that these members do not have a hard rigid connection—the surrounding members are free to move. When they are free to move, they behave just as described. For this reason, some beams are installed to rest on a rocker or a cylinder and are not tied down or supported any other way. This method can be seen supporting the steel beams over interstate highways. The connection is visible as you drive by.

Columns similarly can be greatly increased in strength (4–5 times) if they are rigidly attached to the structure above and below. But this creates other problems and considerations as well—force lines are redirected in unintended ways and areas designed for tension become compressed. And when either beams or columns have multiple spans as they do in a larger building, the structure becomes more complex. The decision to move from an unrestrained connection to a rigid connection (sometimes called a moment connection) changes the forces on and behavior of all surrounding members. The natural inclination to "make it tight, make it strong" can be seriously wrong.

How Beams and Columns Are Connected
Flexibility is sometimes, but not always good

Connections resist the same forces as beams and columns—tension, compression, and shear—but they are also subjected to pull out and bending. The type, number, and location of connections must satisfy the overall structural purpose. Failure to understand connections (or their purpose) is one of the most common and disastrous construction mistakes.

Rivets—an old system to join steel

A rivet is a shaft with a head on one end. It is heated by one person, placed in a hole in the materials to be joined by a second person, then the shaft hammered into a second head by a third person—to complete the connection. This connection has some limited flexibility. It, however, is labor intensive, so when high strength bolts and welding began to be trusted, rivets were phased out—in about 1960. You may not install new rivets, but you may work with them on renovations.

High strength bolts—one current method to fasten steel

High strength bolts are used for structural steel connections. The threads resist pullout so a specified number of threads must project past the bolt to ensure the required strength. When fully tightened, the threads permanently deform slightly. So if the bolt must be later removed, it must be discarded and a new bolt used. (Failure to recognize this fact has produced great loss of profit for many. Removal of installed materials to permit access of large equipment required repurchase of the bolts—an unbudgeted expense.) Fully tightened bolts have virtually no flexibility. The bolts are sometimes designed to be "finger tight only"—to introduce needed flexibility. Here again stronger isn't better, it's wrong.

Welding—another current method to fasten steel

Welding occurs when two materials—in buildings usually structural steel, occasionally aluminum or brass—become atomically close. This is usually done with arc welding. The weld is as strong as the surrounding material and it has no flexibility.

Nails, screws, bolts—usually unengineered fastening devices

These types of connections are usually not specifically strength engineered. They are far stronger than necessary in shear, and weaker in bending and pullout. Anyone who has driven a nail has also bent a nail—and then pulled it out. But this same nail can support several tons in shear.

Pull out can be resisted by making the fastening device more elastic than the surface into which is driven—for the same reason a bird has difficulty removing an elastic worm from the ground. For most applications—wood framing or drywall—the strength is not critical. If it is in, it will be strong enough. But where strength is critical, these devices have an upper limit—simple ones between 5–10,000 psi, more complex ones between 10–20,000 psi. Above these capacities the connections tend to be engineered. Installing one of these unengineered devices where higher strength is required, "it's a bolt, and it's here, and fits" can produce disastrous failure.

Drywall, wood sheeting, or finish carpentry fasteners are not engineered. Wood and metal framing may or may not be engineered. Structural connections are always engineered. And this engineering is done partially by the designing structural engineer, and partially by the steel fabricator hired by the contractor. So, many parties must understand connections to get the job done correctly.

Cast in anchorage devices—increases strength, decreases cost, but requires planning

Higher strength (and economical installation of anchorage devices in masonry and concrete) can be installed when concrete or grout is still wet. High-capacity structural inserts can only be installed in this way. Casting in anchorage devices does require someone to have figured out where they go (coordinated with all following trades), someone to tell the installing tradesman where to put them, and tradesmen willing and able to listen. All these conditions do not always occur. Further, installation of projecting anchorage devices in concrete forms requires cutting a hole in the form, which can reduce its reuse value.

Adhesives—long trusted for wood, increasingly trusted for anchor bolts

Adhesives with strength greater than the materials being bonded are available. At present they are increasingly being used to install anchor bolts in concrete and masonry when a specified strength must be achieved. They do, however, require dry surfaces, which are not always available. And they are temperature sensitive. They cannot be installed below freezing and the setting time can range from 1/2 hour to 14 hours, depending on the temperature. In addition to these restrictions, they are more expensive than alternate anchorage devices. Adhesives between wood products such as plywood and glue-laminated wood beams has been well established and accepted since the mid 20th century.

Location of joints is important

For all methods of attachment the location is also important—sometimes you have no choice, such as with a beam to column connection. When you do have a choice, such as a splice, the third point (1/3 of the way from one beam support to the other) is usually chosen to avoid the shear forces near the support, and is a compromise between the compression forces on the top of the beam and the tension forces on the bottom. This common 1/3-point splice can again be seen on the steel beams on the bridges over interstate highways. (These connections are also used in buildings, but are concealed and harder to see.)

Common Structures and Their Advantages and Disadvantages

Single family residential in the United States

In the United States, we typically have an abundance of low cost wood and a shortage of skilled labor, so the wood framed house is the usual structure type. The conventional single-family platform framed house (less than 3,000 square feet) has the following structural characteristics:

1. The floors are framed with dimensional lumber (with a safety factor of about 2.5) covered by some sheeting plywood, OSB, and/or particle board, with diagonal or solid bridging between the floor members. This assembly also forms a diaphragm to resist earth loads imposed on the basement, and wind loads on the above grade walls. This is a scheduling consideration, since the first floor usually must be installed before the basement walls can be back filled.

2. The walls consist of 2 x 4 framing with a safety factor of about 15 (framing size is governed by resistance to splitting from nails or screws, not structural requirements). Plywood or engineered wood sheeting is applied to the exterior. Sometimes, dimensional lumber or metal strap diagonal corner framing is added. The sheeting on the exterior walls forms a diaphragm to resist wind loading.

3. The roof consists either of dimensional lumber framing forming a triangle (2 roof surfaces and the ceiling support below) or engineered roof trusses also forming a triangle both with exterior sheeting. This assembly will resist snow and wind load—and support the highest ceiling.

Larger fancier houses complicate the structure

This conventional house has simple structural elements—beams supported only at the ends, walls aligned vertically so one supports the other, fully self-bracing roof structures, and a conventional number of exterior windows and doors. When the conventional house grows and becomes fancier, the following changes can occur. As the building grows larger and taller, additional shear walls may be required. If more or larger windows and doors are added, the deleted diaphragm area will require replacement elsewhere. High, open cathedral ceilings with no bottom bracing will require additional means to redirect or resist the thrust of the roof members. Cantilever projections of windows and balconies so that the wall framing members no longer vertically stack can change simple span beams into complex supported beams, including cantilevers.

This changes the structure from one that can be executed with common sense and rules of thumb to one that requires specific knowledge and engineering. If this is not supplied, floors will buckle, walls will crack, doors will misalign, and the building will creak and groan. And usually the mistakes are so fundamental that they cannot be fully corrected economically. Patch it up and live with it, or move is the solution.

Steel framing instead of wood requires different knowledge

There's one other emerging complexity in residential single-family construction—the change from wood framing to light gauge metal. There is one significant change with this development. The connection's screws used and their torquing requirements now become an engineered connection. Close enough is no longer good enough as it was in wood framing. Specific screws and specific screw guns must be used by people who know how to use them—or the structure will be deficient. And this mistake will be difficult or impossible to catch and fix later.

Commercial Structures

Commercial structures can mix and match different wall systems and floor and roof systems, so each of these components is discussed separately below.

Vertical Support

Masonry walls

Exterior load-bearing masonry walls are typically used for buildings up to about three stories. Higher is possible, but less common. The advantage is that masonry is strong in compression, Fire-resistant, and requires no off-site fabrication. So, engineering is minimized, quick mobilization is possible, minor variations in the previously installed structural work is easy to accommodate, and masonry can be installed even on very tight sites.

The disadvantages are that masonry is very weak in tension—so resistance to high lateral load such as wind is limited, installation in cold and wet conditions is restricted or impossible, and an abundance of skilled labor is required in the project area—and this is not always available.

Steel framing

Structural steel framing (10 gauge or more) can be used from single story commercial buildings to the highest skyscraper (over 1,500 feet in height). Its advantages are that it is both strong in tension and compression, can be rapidly erected in any weather conditions, and is more flexible in shape and possible spans.

The disadvantages are that it is not Fire-resistant, will move, and deflect more than other structures. Although it can be erected in any weather, following cladding and interior shear walls cannot. Significant cranes and hoisting capacity are required, and trucking larger members through congested areas can be a logistics problem.

Poured-in-place concrete

Poured-in-place concrete structures can be used from a single story building to skyscrapers—usually just under 1,000 feet in height. The advantages are the same as masonry described above except that with the addition of reinforcing steel, the concrete can also be adequate in tension. The internal reinforcing steel consists of a larger (#6-9) reinforcing steel run continuously for the height of the building. These bars are usually not connected but rather lapped, frequently about 18 bar diameters. These larger bars in a column are wrapped horizontally by a square box of smaller (#3-4) bars called ties or stirrups. Beams are similarly constructed.

Precast concrete

Precast concrete wall panels are frequently used for warehouses. Precast columns and beams are less frequently used in mid-rise construction. A combination of the two can be used for car parking garages. The advantages are that the materials are Fire-resistant, can be rapidly erected, can form the exterior skin of the building, are resistant to the weather, and can be erected in any weather (although final grouting of the base plates and caulking cannot be done in wet or freezing conditions).

The disadvantages are off-site engineering and fabrication requires competent personnel and equipment available at the desired time, which is frequently a problem—and always a consideration. The logistics of getting large pieces to the site can be troublesome. Sufficient room around the site must be available to permit hoisting and erection. The site personnel must have completed the foundation extremely accurately or the precast will not fit. Cranes, trucks, and ironworkers standing idly by waiting for the problem to be fixed can produce sky-high change orders and schedule delays.

Horizontal Supports—Floors and Ceilings

Many of the considerations, advantages, and disadvantages are the same for the vertical and horizontal so they will not be repeated. Only unique features of the horizontal system will be mentioned.

Wood structures

Wood dimensional lumber, wood engineered joists, and wood trusses can be used for floor and roof structures. The advantages are that they are light and easy to erect—even on a tight site—and are resilient, which is a necessary feature in earthquake areas. (Wood wall and roof structures are used for light commercial and seismic areas for this reason.)

The disadvantages are limited spans for off-the-shelf material: dimensional lumber about 20 feet, truss joists about 30 feet, roof trusses about 40 feet. Also higher deflection, and they are not Fire-resistant.

Metal joists and deck

Metal joists are engineered fabrications with top and bottom chords (the horizontal parts) and triangular braces in the web (between the horizontal parts). Steel bridging is connected to the trusses perpendicular to span to resist twisting, and diagonal bracing is added between the truss ends and the wall structure. The deck is a range of corrugated steel decks. The truss, the bridging, and the deck all work together—the structure is not complete until all parts are in place and finally connected.

This assembly can be used either as a floor structure, with the addition of concrete topping, or as a roof structure with or without the addition of concrete topping. It is one of the most common workhorses for light commercial construction. The advantages are quick availability in off-the-shelf configurations—speeding delivery and minimizing engineering, light enough to be easily erected even on fairly tight sites, and workhorse spans of up to 40 to 50 feet. (Longer spans are readily available also, but truss height, camber, and deflections increase inconveniently for longer spans.)

Disadvantages include that it is not Fire-resistant, and can have inconveniently high camber. Although this is usually not a disadvantage for roof structures, for floor structure it can produce an undulation that becomes visibly noticeable when the furniture does not align.

Precast hollow core concrete

These hollow core concrete planks about two feet wide by the length of the span are supported by steel beams or load-bearing masonry walls. Use for apartments, motels, and industrial mezzanines is common. It has the advantage of requiring limited engineering, is Fire-resistant and resistant to airborne noise, and can be erected on a fairly tight site. The disadvantages are limited spans in the 30-foot range and questionable timely supply from a limited number of local vendors. Further, impact noise, such as people walking on the floors must be managed.

These planks will appear identical. However, the internal reinforcing is custom engineered for each location in the building (changed by extra heavy point loadings or holes such as stairwells, duct shafts, and mechanical risers) and will differ. Each has a piece mark and must be installed in its intended location. And the entire assembly is not complete and structurally adequate until all specified grouting and toppings are installed.

Precast beams and T shapes

Precast concrete is roughly shaped like a steel "I" beam or an "I" beam with the bottom cut off—(T shapes). These are used for parking structures and warehouse and industrial buildings, particularly where moisture resistance is required. Precast is Fire-resistant and is capable of longer spans—2 to 3 times hollow core spans.

The disadvantages are: off-site engineering is required, and supplies may be limited as described above. Logistics of getting the longer materials to the site can be a challenge. Also, hoisting and erection room must be available on site.

Poured-in-place concrete flat slabs—with reinforcing steel bars

Flat plate concrete with dropped capitals (thickened slab areas) around the columns (to resist the high shear in this location) is a workhorse of high-rise residential construction. The advantages are: fire resistance, rapid erection with significant reuse of forms, and much of the mechanical electrical piping and conduit can be embedded in the structure, producing significant cost savings for these trades. With the addition of a textured coating, the underside of the slab is considered finished ceiling—producing further economies. The only disadvantage is impact noise. It will readily transmit through the concrete floor.

Reinforcing steel is installed in the slab, but unlike the columns described above, it is frequently not continuous. The steel, which is being installed for tensile strength, may be omitted entirely where no tensile strength is required, such as in mid-span. Installation of the reinforcing steel where and only where it is intended is required. Again, stronger is not necessarily better, it may be wrong.

In addition to the reinforcing steel bars, welded wire mesh is frequently installed. It can have both the structural function of reinforcing steel and also can be "temperature steel"—meaning it helps reduce the expansion and contraction of the concrete due to changes in temperature.

Cast-in-place concrete with beams, columns, and coffers

Cast-in-place concrete can be used for a range of commercial, institutional, and industrial buildings. Unusual shapes, variable appearance, and loadings and elevation changes can all be accommodated. Institutional buildings, such as universities and museums, use concrete exposed ceilings for dramatic effect.

Many architects believe that visible expression of structure is desirable. Fewer occupants of such buildings share this view. Cast-in-place concrete can also be used when extremely high loading is required.

Poured-in-place concrete flat slabs—with post tensioning

Concrete is strong in compression but weak in tension. This deficiency can be overcome by installing steel cables in the concrete and then tensioning the cables after the concrete has set. This has the advantage of increasing the between column spans to about 40 feet, which can produce desirable column free areas for office construction. The only disadvantage is that later cutting of holes through this floor is extremely restricted.

How to Choose a Structure for Your Purpose

Desirable clear spans and floor-to-floor heights

First, define the requirements for your purpose. Required floor loading capacity, and desired spans between columns and floors will rule out some possibilities. Focus on only a few. For example, in a multi-story commercial office the requirement for 125 pounds per square foot loading and the desire to have the interior and exterior offices with landscaped office areas in between, defines the column spans and narrows the economic choices to flat plate concrete and structural steel with metal decking and concrete topping.

The flat plate concrete structure is far thinner, permitting approximately two feet less vertical rise per floor while still maintaining the same ceiling heights and accompanying the same mechanical and electrical construction. A 50-story office building can be a hundred feet shorter while still providing the same rentable area—a compelling cost advantage.

Time of construction

Speed of construction, including weather implications in the project area, is another consideration. The concrete building will usually be slower to erect. The faster structural steel building can decrease construction loan interest during construction. Or you may have a requirement for an early completion date.

Availability of skilled labor and low-cost material

The construction environment in the project area is also a cost and time consideration. Adequate availability of skilled labor for each type of construction may be limited—making construction slower, more costly, and of poor quality. Also, the cost of materials can vary hugely by location. Availability of sand, gravel, or wood at or near the project site can make concrete and wood a low-cost material in one location. In another, the requirement to truck the same materials long distances can prohibitively increase their cost.

Each correct decision is project specific and local

Extremely high humidity, high winds, earthquakes, and hurricanes can influence the selection of structural types and make some economically unattractive or impossible. The combination of all these considerations makes the best choice of structure project specific. The structure that is right in one location can be unworkable in another.

Unusual Structures

Most building structures have square corners and four of them. This minimizes material waste. And it makes joints that fit using off-the-shelf materials, so installation labor is far more efficient. Curves and continually varying angles makes joints custom fit and removes this economy. And since furniture and equipment also usually come with square corners, getting the square pegs into round holes can produce lots of wasted space. Yet where there is a purpose, building unusual structures may be justified.

Fabric structures

For example, pneumatically supported fabric structures are frequently used over tennis courts where no furniture is installed and economical clear spans are desired. Fabric roof structure supported from either concrete or steel columns can be used to enclose large spaces. The Denver airport is one example.

Arched structures

Curved and arched concrete shapes can effectively cantilever over portions of sports stadiums such as the stands of racetracks. The curves assist in structural support and to provide a dramatic structure with no supports to obstruct the view. Arches are not new. Masonry arch construction was the workhorse for most of history. Before steel (which is strong tension) was produced in large quantities, arched masonry was one of the only systems available for large buildings. And some magnificent and ingenious structures were built and still stand today.

Light structures made with struts

Space frames (structures made of a latticework of many small struts) are used for large open areas, such as toll plazas and service areas at amusement parks. Geodesic domes (struts to form a circular shape) are extremely strong and can be used for light enclosures that house radar and microwave equipment in harsh wind environments such as the Arctic.

Each of these unusual structures has one big advantage and many disadvantages. Limited suppliers and skilled installation labor, both for the initial construction and future maintenance, are large concerns. Finally, since the structures are unusual, there is frequently an irrational emotional resistance from building officials, lenders, owners, and occupants. If the requirements of your project make the big advantage compelling, be prepared to fight all the battles on these fronts.

Structures During Construction Require More Engineering and Temporary Bracing
The structure needs to be strong right now, but it won't be all the way strong until it is complete

Above, we saw that structural design only attempts to make it probable, not certain, that the fully completed building will not fail. But during construction only portions of the structural design are complete, so the uncertainty is temporarily even greater. All this is too much for the design engineer and they pretend the problem doesn't exist. "We have no responsibility for construction means and methods" is commonly found in the engineer's specifications. This leaves the responsibility with the contractor. Critical considerations and common methods follow.

Foundation construction must manage lateral bracing

The below grade foundation structure must be braced during construction using a combination of temporary supports and the permanent structure. For multiple-story foundations, a separate structural engineer specializing in retention systems (not the engineer who designed the building itself) designs this combination of temporary and permanent structural members. Sheeting, shoring, soldier beams and lagging, slurry walls, soil nailing, soil grouting, and temporary internal steel supports are used until the permanent diaphragm floors are in place. Placing of the final soil on the exterior of the structure must be coordinated with these operations. And since the amount of water in the soil hugely affects the soil pressure on the foundation, dewatering must be considered as well. Failure to perform the required operations in the required sequence can completely or partially destroy the foundation structure, collapse the surrounding streets, and cause injury and death.

Concrete cures in 28 days—temporary shores required until then

The concrete in a poured-in-place concrete structure will not achieve full required design strength for 28 days—or slightly longer in very cold temperatures—making the newly installed concrete useless or weaker than required and a dead load as well. Up to two floors per week can be installed, but only one full set of forms is usually on the job site. So, forms must be removed immediately. Temporary posts called "reshores" provide the required support. Reshores will extend from about two to eight floors below the floor under construction. Removal should only be done when testing of the concrete proves the desired strength has been achieved.

Structural steel erection is a three-step process

Structural steel beams and columns will be loosely erected for multiple stories with hand-tightened bolts only. This frame will then be adjusted to square and plumb with steel cables. The bolts are then tightened as specified. If the connections are welded, many weeks of installation labor will still follow. Do not be fooled when it looks like it's installed—much time will still be required before the next trades can begin work.

Shear walls must be in place as well

For both a structural steel and a concrete building, concrete or masonry shear walls and floor diaphragms may resist lateral forces. The race to get the structure up must be closely followed by the race to get the shear walls and floors in place. In high-rise construction, the shear walls usually form part of the entire center core containing the elevators, stairs, toilets, duct shafts, and electrical and phone closets. So coordination with these trades for holes, openings, and embedded anchorage devices is required at this early phase of construction. For high-rise construction, these shear wall cores are sometimes erected several floors ahead of the structural steel.

Temporary structure design, installation, and maintenance are critical

Other temporary structures such as tower cranes, temporary elevators, and scaffolding are also engineered, again not by the building structural engineer. The engineering of the tower crane foundations and supports is by a structural engineer, frequently the same firm who does the foundation engineering. The temporary elevators and scaffolding each have the engineering performed by the supplying firm. This critical engineering requires management attention to design and install it correctly in the first place, and particular management attention to keep it in place. Loose bolts or removed structural members, because they were inconveniently located, can have disastrous results.

It should be noted that the structural engineers capable of designing these temporary measures are exceedingly rare—probably less than one percent of the entire population of structural engineers. And you want years of experience, not someone trying something new. Plan to acquire his engineering early in the project planning process.

Common Problems, Solutions, and Misunderstandings

Holes in structural members—small details have large consequences

Holes in structural members are required for ductwork, pipes, and conduit. A hole will cause the energy lines of stress to move around the hole, thereby increasing stress at the edges. So holes are important. A small round hole will triple the stress at the edge of the hole. And square corners and notches cut across the lines of force and this will further increase concentrations of force. The number, size, and location of the allowable holes is determined when selecting and designing the structural member. For wood, structural steel, and conventionally poured concrete beams, the allowable areas will be in the mid-span, and usually prohibited near the ends. Penetration through columns are seldom required and usually completely prohibited. Precast concrete members are each specifically engineered. Although they may look the same, the internal reinforcing can be completely different. The possible hole locations range from certain specific locations, as described above, to complete prohibition of any holes at all!

When larger holes are desired, such as for a new stairwell in an existing slab, reinforcing may have to be added. Structural steel support can be added around the opening, or carbon fiber reinforcing can be added at the areas of high tension.

But this isn't just strengthening up the area surrounding the hole. Strong in one area affects the structural behavior of the surrounding areas. For example, for multiple structural steel bays, the original structural design would have the top of each beam at mid-span in compression and the top of every beam at the column in tension—a wave alternating tension and compression. If an entire bay was cut out and the surrounding area reinforced, the wave would be interrupted and the top of the beam at the column will change from tension to compression. Or if a portion of a bay were heavily reinforced to support a new load, the alternating wave would again be interrupted—affecting the adjacent bays. This produces a result opposite of common sense. If you make one beam too strong it has an adverse effect on the surrounding beams. Again, stronger is not necessarily better.

How to later reinforce for a heavier load

If the building has been designed and constructed and a heavy piece of equipment must be added, the allowable floor loading may be exceeded. One solution is to spread out the load using a flat piece of steel somewhat larger than the size of the machine. The steel plate is typically between one-half and one-inch thick and must be fully grouted in place so there is full and continuous contact. A similar effect can be obtained by adding carbon fiber reinforcing in tension areas of the beam or floor slab.

Finally, if further reinforcing is still required, additional beams can be installed as support from below and span from column to column. These again must be fully grouted in place to maintain continuous contact. If additional reinforcing is required for the structural steel beam itself, additional plate steel can be welded to the top or bottom of the wide flange—not in the web as you might expect.

Hurricanes and Earthquakes Require Special Measures

Hurricanes

Hurricanes increase the wind loading on a building, and can be accommodated by increasing the structural capacity against this load. The weak point for a wood building, however, is not the wood itself but the pullout of connections in tension. Wood is strong in tension, but nailed joints are weak in pullout. So metal straps, which are strong in tension, are added to add tensile strength to these joints.

Earthquakes

Earthquakes are shock waves moving horizontally through the earth that accelerate the lower parts of the building with the upper parts to follow—similar to someone pulling the rug out from under you. There are a couple ways to resist this load. The first is to make the entire structure extremely rigid. This approach can work on smaller portions of the structure or on very small structures, or structures where cost, appearance, and the building's ability to have windows and doors takes backseat to the structural considerations. The second approach is to make the entire structure resilient and flexible so that it moves back and forth without damage, like a tree in the wind. This is one of the more common approaches—smaller commercial buildings may be built of wood for this reason. The third approach is to make the floors act like a stack of greased dinner plates—each will slide past the other temporarily and then slide back in place. The final approach is an active damping system where weights and forces are mechanically applied to counterbalance the force of the earthquake. Unfamiliarity with this system and fear of the disastrous consequences of mechanical failure make this approach rare.

A seismic retrofit of a building that was constructed before knowledge of these techniques existed or was damaged in an earthquake can involve a number of these methods. Encasing the columns in steel to increase their tensile strength, and installing slip connections between columns and beams are common.

Summary

We would like to think of structures as predictable, definite, and unyielding, but reality is closer to the opposite. Although some loads can be definitely known, most loads such as wind, water, snow, or people and their possessions are variable and can only be estimated. So, we have a range of probabilities that failure will not occur and include safety factors to compensate for this uncertainty. Management of the small but powerful motions in a structure is the critical task that requires management attention by many on every project. (Avoiding structural collapse is also critical, but is easier to manage.)

And materials resist these loads not by being immobile and unyielding, but rather by being elastic and storing or redirecting the received energy. Many materials are strong in compression—concrete, stone, masonry, steel, and wood—and a few are also strong in tension—wood and steel. Usually these members are not sized only for structural requirements. Sizing will be increased to minimize deflection so that plaster or drywall does not crack, and avoid nails or screws splitting wood, allow enough space for bolts for structural steel connections, allow space for reinforcing steel within concrete columns and beams, and use off-the-shelf sizes. So only a small number of the structural members will actually be designed "just strong enough."

Connections are the portion of the structure that can be the most critical and cause most of the engineering and field installation problems. The connections themselves have the same consideration as the structural members—compression, tension, and shear but also add pullout and bending. These connections form part of the entire structural system and therefore the entire structural system must be understood before these connections can be properly installed. Stronger is not always better, and it's frequently wrong.

Similarly, holes in structural members affect the structural capacity of these members. Usually holes are restricted in size and number and are usually located where forces on the member are least. And adding reinforcing around these holes doesn't make this problem go away, but simply redirects the force lines and can further concentrate the forces in undesirable locations. Cutting holes in the wrong locations is one of the most common ways to damage a structure. It can be done by anyone in minutes and later detection may be difficult or impossible. Field personnel who have this knowledge are the only defense against this all too common damage.

Selection of a structural system for your project involves consideration of: columns spans, floor-to-floor heights required, along with mechanical and electrical to be attached to or embedded in the structure, space restriction of the site, available skilled labor, plant, equipment, and suppliers in the project area, and environmental considerations such as snow, hurricane, or earthquake. The combination of all these considerations will probably restrict the appropriate structural type to one or two for a project. But it should be recognized that what seems like the only solution, "I've been building here for 30 years and we've always done it that way" may be the right answer for a given set of circumstances at a given time. But if any of these things change, skilled labor becomes unavailable, a precast manufacturer goes out of business, or a particular structural material greatly increases in price, the best choice may have to be considered again. And if you move to a different area of the country or a different type of use for the building, the best choice again may be entirely different.

Engineering knowledge and responsibility is distributed to many. The traditional design structural engineer performs only a small part of structural engineering. The structural engineering of some permanent structural components (trusses, precast concrete, structural steel connections, and light gauge steel structures) of the temporary facilities, and the installation means and methods (such as foundation walls, temporary elevators, and cranes as well as all temporary support measures while the building is under construction) are left to the contractor. And anyone with a saw or drill can cut holes that alter the structure. The knowledge described above can assist owners, lenders, insurers, and project personnel to install the structure as intended, avoid the all too common mistakes, and best ensure project success.

3.10 The Building's Water Envelope

The movement of water and the materials to manage it

Water is everywhere always. In the wrong place at the wrong time water causes big problems—staining, corroding, mold, rot, and destruction of materials. Water problems are a major source of complaints about buildings. If the wrong approach is built into a project, correction is so difficult and expensive that it is seldom completed. Select the right approach and the problems never happen at all—as described below.

Managing the direction of water flow for the benefit of people

The building envelope (the lowest floor, the four walls, and the roof) directs liquid water and ice away from people and peoples' property. It also controls the humidity in the building's air—for human comfort and proper functioning of machines, such as electronics. The movement and change of form of water (ice, liquid, or vapor) is constant. You can only control the direction and speed of the flow, but never stop it. The behavior of water, and the materials used to control this behavior are discussed below.

How Water Moves

Gravity always works—make it work for you

Several hundred years ago, an apple fell on Isaac Newton and gravity was discovered. Gravity should now be obvious to all, but is ignored everyday. The failures caused by this ignorance—such as roof flashing details that can only work if water flows up hill—can be seen during a short walk from where you now sit.

Gravity will move water downward unless overcome by stronger forces. Gravity is continuous, but these other stronger forces come and go. So, gravity is your friend and is usually the first force built into all water direction systems followed by ways to manage the other forces.

Capillary action moves water up hill

Capillary action is the force that moves water upward—where a solid material, water, and air all meet. A common example is the small curved surface of water that moves up the side of a glass of water. Smaller spaces between solids produce greater capillary forces, which move the water greater distances. In the smallest of materials, such as fine clays, the capillary action can move water against the force of gravity up 90 feet. Vertical rises of 1–5 feet occur everywhere, every day.

Absorption sucks water in and saturates materials

Some materials, such as metals, will not absorb any measurable water within the time that matters for construction. However, most materials—soils, concrete, masonry, wood, and many plastics—will absorb moisture, but at vastly different rates. For example, brick masonry can experience full water penetration through a wall in less than a minute, but full saturation of solid wood may take several years. This absorption will occur. So selecting materials with absorption times suitable for the purpose is critical.

Diffusion spreads water evenly

All water vapor seeks to spread evenly throughout the entire volume of a space. Water molecules bumping into each other and pushing each other apart cause this. For example, when a puff of steam is released in one corner of a room, the water molecules will continue to bump into each other until they are spread evenly throughout the room. So every cubic foot of air contains the same number of molecules. This is an unstoppable force caused by the natural behavior of water, and occurs at all places at all times.

Air and Water Pressure Moves Water

Water pressure tries to equalize on both sides of a barrier

Water pressure seeks to equalize on both sides of a barrier, so water moves in all directions to achieve this equalization. Water pressure exists on entirely flooded above-grade structures, such as a roof after heavy rains, or on sub-grade structures, such as a foundation, when the surrounding soil is saturated. Since water weighs around 63 pounds per cubic foot, and water pressure at a point is the sum of the weight of all water stacked above, pressures can be huge. For example, the water pressure at the bottom of a 10-foot high basement wall is 630 pounds per square foot—enough to force water through each and every crack.

Wind pressure and load—a water mover and structural load

Wind pressure on the exterior of a building also causes water to move in all directions. And it will also force both moist air and water to move between building components. These pressures come and go and vary in strength. (The wind doesn't always blow or blow with the same force. And it becomes stronger higher above the ground.) For example, if a wind force is 20 psf at grade level, it increases to 140 psf at 130 feet off the ground. Those who have constructed high-rise buildings know that a stack of plywood must be strapped or weighted down, or the wind can toss the sheets to the street below like a deck of cards.

Further, similar to the negative pressure on the top of an airplane wing that produces lift, the negative wind forces on the downwind side of a building—or building components—is stronger than the forces on the upwind side. The downwind forces on a soffit overhang are the strongest of all—up to 250 psf. These strong forces must be managed by the building structure.

Air pressure within the building—even small forces have big effects

Mechanically ventilated buildings are designed to produce a very slight positive pressure on the interior of these buildings. This continually forces air out through any leaks in the envelope, so there are not hot and cold spots in the building caused by inward leaking. This is also done so that exterior doors can be opened by the strength of average people. Even the slightest negative pressure in a building can exert sufficient force so the doors simply cannot be opened.

This useful outward pressure, however, does cause a continuous movement of moist air out from the interior to the exterior of the building—through walls, siding, ceilings, and roofs that have different temperatures and pressures. Condensation will occur at these locations.

Within the building, this unintended and undesirable condensation also is caused by the HVAC system. Here, the supply system moves either heated or cooled moist air under pressure throughout the building and later returns this air at a lower temperature and pressure through the return ducts. If this airflow crosses multiple building components, changes in temperature and pressure can cause significant condensation problems.

Both Temperature and Pressure Changes Water's Form

Ice, liquid, and vapor are forms of water

Water can occur in the form of solid (ice), liquid, or gas (vapor). Although it is well known that this change is caused by temperature, it is also caused by pressure. It is the combination of temperature and pressure that determines the exact point when water will change form. Pressure decreases water's freezing point and increases water's boiling point. Some common pressures and boiling points are: no pressure (a vacuum)—boiling 32 degrees F; atmospheric pressure—boiling 212 degrees F; and 95 psi pressure—boiling 324 degrees F. So, a pressure drop will cause water at a constant temperature to condense.

Further, higher temperature air can hold more water. For example, the temperature and maximum water capacity of one cubic yard of air are: Freezing (32 degrees F)—.1300 oz/cy; normal room temperature (68 degrees F)—.79604 oz/cy; human skin (98.6 degrees F)—1.1268 oz/cy.

Finally, a drop in pressure causes a drop in temperature. An example is a direct expansion air conditioning system (common for single family residences) where the drop in pressure at the coil produces cooling in the air stream. Water behaves in a similar way.

This complicated combination of temperature and pressure is inconvenient. We want stable and predictable performance—temperature and humidity should be what we want it to be when and where we want it. The answer is to seal building compartments from each other to minimize the effect of pressure. Dealing only with the change in temperature is a more understandable and manageable problem. Practical ways to achieve this are discussed in the next chapter.

Requirements of Materials Used to Direct and Control Water Flow

Controlling water transmission with membranes

Water vapor transmission is measured by the perm (1 perm is 1 grain (1/7000 of a pound) per square foot of material one inch thick in one hour). Perm ratings for some common materials are: house wrap (such as "Tyvek") 75, paint (2 coats) 30–85, 15 pound felts 5–20, polystyrene extruded insulation (blue board) 1.2, Polyethylene sheet (poly) 4 mil 1, aluminum foil 0, asphalt adhesive 0. Something on the order of .1 is considered a solid water barrier, and 1 is considered a vapor barrier—but no one told the water. These are but arbitrary points, and the partial water transmission capabilities of materials that are close must be considered as well. Further, water transmission capabilities of all materials in a building assembly must be considered together. Multiple layers of a vapor barrier will begin to act like a water barrier—so looking at the bigger picture is required.

Resisting fire
Chose fire-resistant materials or add fireproofing chemicals

For most of human history, roofs were built of flammable materials—thatch, wood shingles, and petroleum products, such as pitch and tar. Fire-retardant chemical additives or surface treatments are now well established and widely used. But, discussion of the Fire-resistant properties of roofing is still presented in all technical data to confirm that these fire management capabilities are present in the materials you intend to use.

Resisting attack from the sun
Good materials slow, but do not stop this attack

Sunlight's radiation attack is relentless. The sun is a nuclear reactor 93 million miles away producing ultraviolet and infrared light that can reduce elasticity, discolor, increase brittleness, and disintegrate the surface of materials. This destruction is measured by the percentage loss of elasticity, surface cracking, or surface discoloration over a time period—usually 5 to 10 years.

Stone and masonry materials are unaffected by sunlight. Some structures are still in satisfactory condition after 2,000 years—so the materials are not tested. Untreated wood is deteriorated by sunlight, so it is almost always coated. The performance of the coating, not the effect on the wood itself, is stated (stain resists 95% of ultraviolet light). Periodic re-staining or painting is expected. Useful lives in the range of 10–15 years are common.

Roofing materials for flat roofs (plastics and rubbers) are tested by the manufacturer and describe the loss of elasticity and surface cracking. Useful lives in the 10–25 year range are common. Fiberglass shingles formerly rated by weight are now rated by the manufacturer's estimate, with little supporting information, of the useful life. One example is "25 year shingles." While the manufacturer estimates a useful life of 25 years, 50–75% of that stated useful life might be more realistic in the real world.

Proprietary coatings on metals (used for roofing, siding, and curtain walls) will both state the tests performed, and the results achieved (similar to flat roofing materials). They can provide a factory material warrantee of up to 50 years.

Controlling chemical and biological attack
Choose materials wisely, then keep them dry

The chemical ozone naturally occurring in the air deteriorates some plastics and rubbers. This deterioration is measured, tested, and presented in the same way as the flat roof materials described above—percent surface deterioration after 5–10 years. Other attacks from chemicals discharged from the processes in the building must be considered. For example, the grease discharged from the exhaust hoods in restaurants will deteriorate rubber roofs—so other roofing materials must be selected. Industrial operations can have multiple chemical discharges that also require specifically engineered roofing systems.

Biological attack in the form of mold or rot must be considered too. These will occur when plant materials—including wood and the paper products found in many building materials—remain saturated at

20% or more humidity. Chemical treatment of the materials is possible, but removal of the water is more effective. This provides other benefits, such as dimensional stability from less absorption and swelling.

Managing Expansion

Temperature change causes expansion

All materials will expand and contract with temperature, but not equally. Expansion of a 10-foot length of some common materials from -20 degrees F to 160 degrees F are: aluminum .52", concrete .26", steel .23", glass .19", wood .1". When these materials touch, joints that accommodate the differential expansion must be installed.

Water absorption causes long and short-term expansion and contraction

Materials will also expand because of water. There are two types of expansion: one is the long-term permanent expansion or contraction that occurs once and only once—and is irreversible. The most common example of this is clay masonry, which will expand irreversibly after firing—as it absorbs water. In contrast, concrete block will contract irreversibly as it shrinks and gives up the moisture it received during casting. Other materials, such as marble, will permanently and irreversibly expand when saturated with water for the first time after being quarried. Granite does not permanently and irreversibly expand after being quarried.

After the irreversible movement occurs, materials will continue to expand and contract each time they are wetted and dried, but again, usually at different rates. The reversible movement from wet to dry of a 10-foot length of common materials are: clay brick .012", concrete brick .048", concrete .096", drywall .12", plywood .15".

Temperature caused movements will vary by type of material and location of the material in the building (exterior or interior). Moisture caused movements will vary with material type and time. All materials will behave differently at different times, but must work together. Careful selection of materials, and correct placement of joints to accommodate expansion are required.

Speed of Water Flow

Centuries, years, seasons, days, minutes

Water continuously moves, but not always at the same rates. Some absorption in materials can take place in seconds, and some changes in water tables can take centuries. It is well known that most areas have a wet and a dry, and a hot and a cold season. There are also yearly seasonal changes in all factors affecting the water flow in and around a building—temperature, humidity of the air, and wind pressure. Similar but lesser variation occurs between night and day and from unpredictable changes in the weather.

Man made changes cause unexpected water problems

Man can also cause long-term and permanent changes in water location and movement. Construction of structures, cutting new roads, or changing the grades in the vicinity of a previously completed construction project can alter the water flow over and through the earth—and below grade water pressure. Also, extensive use of deep wells for agricultural irrigation can permanently lower the water table over decades to centuries.

Equilibrium is sought—achievement is temporary and conditional

When the water moving forces balance, equilibrium is reached and no water flows. An illustration of this equilibrium occurred in the VAT (Vinyl Asbestos Tile) floors used in the mid part of the 20th century. When it was recognized that asbestos was an undesirable material, much of it was removed. For some slab on grade VAT floors that had been in successful use for decades, upon removal of the floor tile, water moved rapidly through the concrete floor—wetting the entire floor surface. Here, equilibrium of water forces had been reached and maintained, and once removing one portion of the vapor retarding materials from the assembly upset the equilibrium, the equilibrium was destroyed. Some floors took months to dry.

All factors—temperature, pressure, and humidity—must be considered for all building components when making any changes. And the known seasonal variations must be built into the design. High humidity levels and wetting occur in the wet season, but later dry in the dry season. A design, which is successful in one climate, may fail completely in another with different seasonal changes. Practical management of this inconvenient variability is discussed in the next chapter.

Materials to Redirect Water Flow

For floors (slabs on grade—touching the earth)
Plastic under the slab, sealers on top of the slab

Only a few materials are used to slow water transmission through concrete slab on grade floors. Sheet plastic (usually polyethylene of 4–6 mil thickness) placed beneath the concrete slab before installation is most common. The perm rating is .2. The plastic is not susceptible to either fire (in this below grade location) or biological attack, and it is resistant to most chemical attack. Some slightly more advanced sheet plastics can be used for slightly increased performance.

If a slab on grade is to meet a moisture sensitive material—such as wood, welded sheet plastic, or resinous poured floors (where moisture can delaminate or destroy the floor)—a liquid-applied chemical sealer can be applied on the interior surface of the concrete. Although this does violate the rule of placing the vapor barrier in one and only one place, it does not appear to create a problem since concrete can be continuously saturated with moisture with no detrimental effect.

For Walls

Sub-grade walls (application on the exterior of the wall) can be wet all the time

Foundation waterproofing almost always involves petroleum products. Spray-applied liquid asphalt, sometimes followed by asphalt-impregnated sheets, or application of plastic sheets all on the exterior of the foundation wall are used. Similar to a slab on grade, waterproofing, fire, crushing, and biological attack are not factors.

The one alternate system that is not petroleum is bentonite clay, which is highly resistant to water transmission. Bentonite clay is inserted into the interior corrugations of cardboard, and the cardboard sheets are applied to the exterior of the wall.

Above-grade walls, windows, and doors are wet sometimes

Exterior walls should contain an abrasion and impact-resistant outer surface—a water barrier. Exterior cladding materials consist of masonry (brick, block, or stone), glass, metal (usually steel or aluminum, or less commonly copper, brass, or bronze, and formerly zinc, tin and lead), wood, and plastic.

Masonry is impact resistant

Masonry nicely resists mechanical impact, such as hail. Brick, block, and to a lesser extent marble, sandstone, and limestone are absorbent materials, but granite is not. They are all not susceptible to biological attack or fire attack, but some bricks, marbles, and limestones will be deteriorated by sulfuric acid, sometimes produced from acid rain, or by the acidic discharge from the combustion of natural gas.

Glass is not very impact resistant

Glass resists continuous pressure well, but impacts pressure poorly. Tempering (heat treating) and laminating (placing a sheet of resilient plastic between two sheets of glass—similar to automobile glass) improves impact resistance. Resistance to normal abrasion is good, but resistance to purposeful scratching, such as vandalism, is poor. Glass will not transmit or absorb water. It will not melt or deform by fire (in any conditions except a catastrophic full building fire), but can shatter when heated by fire, then rapidly cooled—such as by a fire hose. (Heat-treated, wire glass, or chemically altered glass can improve fire related shatter resistance—but at an additional cost and a reduction in transparency.) Biological attack and attack by most non-industrial chemicals is not a factor.

Metals can be strong

Metal less than 1/8 inch thick is susceptible to mechanical damage, but thicker metals are not. Metals are impervious to water (and are a vapor barrier). They are not flammable, have un-measurable effect from biological attack, but will readily react both with oxygen in the air or water and will oxidize and rust. Metals used on the exterior of the building are now frequently coated at the factory to prevent oxidation.

Wood is practical

Wood has satisfactory resistance to mechanical impact. Wood is slow to absorb and discharge water. But, without treatment, it is flammable. And with the right moisture conditions, it is susceptible to biological attack.

Plastics are engineered

Plastics are engineered for a purpose, so they can be made to resist impact and biological attack. Plastics are made of petroleum, so they tend to melt and burn. They can be engineered to have adequate, but not excellent resistance to fire. But once ignited they can produce toxic smoke. Plastic sheets will not absorb water, but most foams will. Water in foam will first reduce the insulating capacity, then turn the foam to useless dust. Plastic foams' insulating value are now stated with their "thermal" drift. They deteriorate with age—drift downward—so, the insulating values are published not as the best values at the factory, but as the lower values after about 5 years of real world use. Both sheets and foams are vapor barriers.

Vapor Barriers Should Be Planned

Three products are intentionally used as vapor barriers:

1. Polyethylene sheet plastic can be installed near the interior of a space, typically behind the wall facing, such as drywall.
2. Aluminum foil can be installed in this location as well, or behind the exterior facing, such as brick or stone.
3. For warm or humid regions (where the water barrier is applied on the exterior of the building) petroleum products similar to sub-grade waterproofing described above are used.

These are the intentional vapor barriers. However, other materials typically used in wall assemblies also have very low vapor transmission capabilities. One example is rigid insulation frequently used on commercial buildings, that in itself is an additional vapor barrier. Factory-applied foil facing of this insulation adds yet another vapor barrier.

Other unintended vapor barriers are interior vinyl wall covering, very heavy impervious paint coatings, or fluid-applied resinous coatings (usually industrial applications). The impact of the vapor transmission of each component of the entire assembly must be considered, not just the intended and designed water vapor barriers. The materials Do not know what you intended; they will behave the way they always do.

Roofs Must Be Planned Too

Plant materials were common

Grasses, thatch, and leaves of plants have been some of the more common roofing materials used throughout history. They are still used in many developing countries. They are highly flammable, and subject to biological attack. They have no compensating advantage that suggests their use for modern building systems.

Wood shingles have similarly been used throughout history—and have similar defects. However, now they can be suitably fireproofed to form an acceptable modern roof. They should be selected if such an appearance is desired. But, for waterproofing, they are not the optimal choice.

Another plant-related roofing product is a wood product impregnated with asphalt. Some of these products are 15-pound felts, 30-pound felts, rolled roofing, and asphalt shingles. Here, a piece of paper (made from wood) is coated with asphalt materials. Starting in the 1950s, fiberglass replaced the paper in theses products to improve the biological and flame resistance.

Petroleum-based membranes were more fireproof

Most roofs are made of petroleum-based products. One of the most common materials for single family, detached residences are shingles, which are fiberglass or paper coated with asphalt, and covered with granules for wear and ultraviolet light resistance. These can be used only on slopped roofs.

For flat roofs, an older approach was a layered system of felts and liquid asphalt, usually covered by some type of stone, such as gravel. These were developed in the mid 1800s but suffered from severe flammability—and also deterioration due to sunlight. The response was to attempt to throw in everything but the kitchen sink to remedy these defects. Layers of copper, slate, and clay tile were imbedded between and on the roofing membranes. However, this vastly increased roof weight—up to 30–50 pounds per square foot (modern roofing will typically be less that 3 pounds per square foot)—and it still only partially remedied the defects.

"Built up" roofs were then used again. These consisted of layers of hot fluid-applied asphalt and 15 or 30 pound felts. Two to four layers were common with gravel placed on the final top layer. These were flammable, and when a large building fire started, the liquid-dripping asphalt added fuel to the fire—burning some buildings to the ground.

In 1972, the price of oil temporarily skyrocketed so roofing systems that used less oil were sought. Thin sheet rubber and plastic products, and engineered sheet petroleum products, such as modified bitumens, were developed to optimize the performance and resistance to flame, sunlight, and chemicals.

Sheet plastics that are now commonly used consist of thermoset plastics, which are formed in the factory and can be joined only by the use of adhesives in the field (for example, EPDM is a compound of ethylene, propylene, and diene monomer). Thermoplastic products can be joined by heat in the field (for example, Modified Bitumens consisting of chemicals and reinforcing sheets added to bitumens, and TPO, a blend of polypropylene and ethylene-propylene polymers—frequently, with added reinforcing).

These materials are engineered and frequently patented. The patent holder and manufacturer specify all installation components and details necessary for a satisfactory installation that can be warranted. You are no longer just buying materials from a supply house. If you choose a patented material, you are also choosing their system. (This shifts most design of roofs from the traditional architect or engineer to the manufacturer and installer.)

Metal materials are even more fireproof

Metal materials can only be used on sloped—not flat—roofs. Bronze, copper, and zinc have been used for hundreds of years for sloped roofs. Steel, with factory-applied protective coatings, is now more common. These materials resist fire and biological attack, and with engineered coatings, are also resistant to ultraviolet light, oxidation, and most commonly occurring chemicals.

Masonry type materials are similar to metal surfaces

Stone, such as slate, clay tiles, and concrete tiles, can be used, but only on sloped roofs. They have all the similar resistances as the metal roof materials described above, except they are absorbent and tend to be damaged by freeze-thaw conditions. They, therefore, are more suitable for warm climates.

Safety Backups—Common Second Lines of Defense

Flashings

There are joints between even the best of materials. And there should be joints between dissimilar materials. The water flow is directed around these gaps by flashing. Flashing is a sheet metal material that covers the gap. For roofing, there are "U" shaped caps over the top of the wall. For wall systems, the flashing goes from the most interior part of the wall that solid water can reach, to the exterior of the entire assembly. Flashing is typically made of copper, stainless steel, coated steels, and/or plastics.

Caulking

Caulking is also used as a second line of defense. Caulking with expansion and contraction capacity of up to 100% is now available with 30-plus years' resistance to ultraviolet and biological attack. Urethane materials are most common, followed by silicone. (Acrylic materials are usually unsuitable for any exterior use.) Urethane material has become more popular because it is made in more colors, and is more compatible with other following materials, such as paint. Caulking is the barrier of last resort and cannot be considered as the first line of defense in any system that is intended to succeed and perform well for decades.

Weeps

For flashing and caulks, a weep—a small hole that allows moisture to exit—must be installed intermittently (2 to 4 foot on center) at any location that water will try to exit. Weep materials are cotton sash cord, or a manufactured plastic or metal product that maintains a hole or can be fabricated as a system, such as a curtain wall.

Summary

Water is moved by gravity, capillary action, absorption, diffusion, and water and wind pressure. Water changes form—ice, liquid, and vapor—by both temperature and pressure. Further, materials can resist water transmission, fire, sunlight, chemical and biological attack, and expansion and contraction, but not in the same amounts or at the same rates. There is too much motion and variability when stable predictable performance is desired.

The practical approach to increase stability is to know the materials, select wisely, and seal the building components into compartments that provide selective relief. Various ways to achieve this stability are discussed in the next chapter.

3.11 Water—Slowing or Redirecting Movement for Human Comfort

How to make it work—building a water resistant six-sided box

The six-sided box consists of the roof, four walls, and the floor touching the earth. All six are related. Water off the roof can cascade down the walls to the foundation walls and then seep under the lowest floor. Although this is obvious and common sense, each surface is frequently treated as a separate and unrelated task—each designed by different people and installed by different contractors. None of these contractors may know or be involved with the other contractors' work. The roofer seldom knows what type of windows or under slab vapor barrier were installed, but these all function as one assembly.

One and only one strong and continuous water barrier is best

A single continuous water barrier will cause water on both sides of this barrier to bounce back and seek another place to discharge. So, this barrier must be placed carefully, and multiple continuous barriers cannot be installed or water will be trapped between these two barriers with no means of escape. But note, building components—roofs, walls, foundation walls, and slabs on grade—each have different usual and optimal surrounding temperatures, pressures, and humidities. And these must work together or else there will be trouble.

Two lines of defense manage imperfection
Nothing is perfect or perfectly installed—accept it and deal with it

All approaches redirect, but do not stop the flow of water. They select the direction the water will move, the form (water or ice), and where it will accumulate. Even materials termed "waterproof" have small amounts of water transmission that can accumulate over long time periods. The usual problem is that materials used to manage water come in pieces measuring 2', 4', 8' and 10', but building structures are far larger. Joints and gaps are everywhere, and leakage is constant. So, a second line of defense is installed. When the leakage gets through one line, it is redirected by the second line to an acceptable location. The first line redirects most water, and the second line redirects most of the rest of the water.

Liquid Water Direction Management—Three Solutions

Waterproofing

Waterproofing membranes catch and redirect liquid water to a suitable location. However, if the membrane is waterproof, it is also usually a vapor barrier. This must be taken into consideration. The interior moisture trying to get out will bounce back to the interior.

Water shedding

Water-shedding materials are only partially waterproof, and have many gaps. The gravity flow of water off these less than perfect materials redirects the water to a suitable location. Some, but not all, water-shedding roofs can be designed not to also function as a vapor barrier if certain materials—and the right arrangement of these materials—are selected. This can allow the building structure to breath and dry out.

Water storage

Absorbent materials can temporarily store water and then later discharge it. As long as the water does a round trip—goes in and comes out the same location—and does not penetrate to the interior of the space—it will be acceptable to the occupants. And, undesirable leaching of minerals from the materials will not occur. This round-trip water storage is typically found in masonry and concrete structures (also in soil)—whether intended or unintended.

Water Vapor Direction Management—One Barrier Only

A vapor barrier is designed to slow the rate of transmission. It is typically installed on the usually warm side of the structure. The barrier must be located wisely when the warm side changes seasonally. And, the barrier location is different in different climates—typically on the interior in predominately cold climates, and the exterior in predominately warm climates.

One and only one barrier in an assembly is the goal. Where multiple vapor barriers are installed, the failures are well known. For example, in the Gulf States of the United States, where EIFS (synthetic stucco) was installed on the exterior and vinyl wall covering on the interior of the building, mold grew in the wall behind the wall covering. Correction required—at a minimum—complete gutting and remodeling and—at a maximum—demolition of the entire building!

Build Sealed Compartments—but Allow For and Direct Relief

HVAC, wind, and other pressures must be segregated by building components—roofs, walls, sub-grade foundation, and attic spaces. To properly engineer a single assembly, such as a wall, for the variations between seasons, time of day, and unusual events is hard enough. It is beyond our capabilities to engineer all building systems to work together when they behave differently in reaction to these forces. Design each one well, keep them separated, and then choose the desired location of relief from each compartment.

Sloped roofs are a compartment to be separated

Venting of attics seeks to make the roof a uniform temperature—different from the building below. If this is not done in cold climates, ice dams can cause deterioration and even structural failure on the edges of the roof (the warm water on the top of the roof flows down to the colder roof edge and freezes). Venting at one time was thought to improve the performance of attic insulation, but now it is doubtful.

One Task and No Moving Parts for a Compartment Works Best
Components that move or do more than one function are more complicated, expensive, and prone to failure

Whenever a building system is required to perform multiple functions, it will become more complicated and expensive. For example, one type of skyscraper curtain wall construction uses a gasket to hold the window glass in place. The gasket is both structural to hold the glass in place, and also redirects water. Demanding two critical functions of this one material greatly increases the initial gasket cost. And, when the gasket has deteriorated and requires replacement, the replacement cost will be a significant portion of the total cost of the entire building. An alternate system that uses a metal to hold the glass and uses gaskets only for water redirection does not have this drawback.

Very common examples of materials that perform multiple functions are windows and doors. Here, all of the considerations of redirecting the water away from the top of the window or door (such as the top flashing and drip), and sealing the opening against both solid water and infiltration of moisture vapor must be addressed. Further, internal weeping must be provided for all window or door components. This, in effect, makes the window or door assembly a small version of the entire building—with accommodations for all of the considerations of moisture, temperature, and pressure. This complexity makes windows and doors at least four times as expensive per square foot as the surrounding wall. (Windows are necessary, but fewer larger ones will be more economical than more smaller ones.)

All systems are related—waters flows from one to another

Roofs, attics, walls, foundations, and slabs on grade are all related parts of a six-sided weather envelope, and they must be seen as such. The water from one system is discharged onto the other systems. Expansion of one bumps into the expansion of the other. This is common sense and is necessary to ensure a successful six-sided weather envelope. It is, however, a radical departure from common construction practice, where the components are designed and installed by different people who communicate infrequently or not at all.

Necessary Additional Details
Joints cause the most troublesome leakage; special attention and costs are required

Expansion must be accommodated

Materials expand at different rates due to the influence of temperature, applied stress such as a heavy load, and the absorption of water. Wherever different materials meet or where a single material has a long continuous run (and the expansion exceeds the elasticity of the material), expansion capabilities (joints) must be built into the system.

Isolate with gaps

Absorption and capillary action can be contained by purposely putting breaks (small gaps—even as small as 1/8") between materials so water movement stops where you want it. These gaps also control temperature transmission from the interior to exterior. This is very simple, but contrary to trades peoples' instincts—that tight joints or no visible joints are "good workmanship." But, understanding the reason for these gaps—segregation of compartments to control water flow—makes these intentional gaps acceptable. A gap is usually covered and concealed by another material for appearance.

Slip joints are reliable

A slip joint, where one material laps over the other, will last and perform reliably for the life of the building. With slip joints, gravity directs the path of water downward over solid materials. Exterior covering is not usually added.

Flexible membranes add flexibility

Flexible membranes (rubber or plastic) are used for vertical joints or as a supplement to slip joints. These membranes are flexible and can be installed with some slack to accommodate movement. Modern engineered materials can have a useful life of 10–40 years. But, even with these long lives, this is not permanent. And replacement can be extraordinarily complicated, troublesome, and expensive—and may be delayed when the leakage starts.

Weeps let water out

A weep is a purposely-installed drainage way to ensure that trapped moisture is directed to a suitable point of exit. This can be a drilled hole. Or, it could be inserted manufactured products, such as small metal or plastic piping systems, or common cotton sash cord. The weep material itself is not of critical importance. But proper placement is and requires thought about the entire building system.

Caulk may slow leakage and redirect water flow

Caulking can be used in an attempt to seal all joints. Caulking materials can now be obtained with a 10–30 year nominal life. However, since even one small failure anywhere in the caulk joint will start leakage, the actual useful life in the real world will be a fraction of the stated life at the factory. If all you have is a caulk joint with no other backup means to direct moisture, you really Do not have much.

A caulk joint must be installed to use all of the elasticity (now around 100%) of the caulk material. Caulk at rest will be a rectangle between the two wall surfaces. When stretched it will have an hourglass shape. And when compressed, it will bulge in and out. To allow the interior of the caulk to move this way, the caulk can only touch the wall at two, not three places. A backer rod (a foam "rope") is placed in the joint prior to caulking to prevent contact with the third surface. (Tapes, and chemical bond breakers can also be used.) Caulking the joint full without the backer will bind the caulk, preventing expansion and contraction—and the joint will fail.

It should also be noted that the gaps at intersections of assemblies or materials are where the internally trapped water can escape. Therefore, the temptation to caulk every opening must be resisted. The purpose is to redirect the flow of water to acceptable locations. Stopping it entirely is never possible or desirable.

Making It Work—Building the Six-Sided Box

The Site
Direct water away from the site

Stable, predictable water pressures and water flows never occur in the real world; change is constant. The first step to increasing water stability is to direct water away from the building. Roof water will drain down internal roof drains or external gutters and downspouts into horizontal storm sewers and then into the municipal water treatment system—or to a lake or river. Similarly, site surface water will drain away from the building. Water that seeps into the ground is collected in drain tile near the bottom of the foundation and drained or pumped to the sewers. If the topography of the site permits, it is best to drain this water by gravity to the outside.

These measures—to make the earth "as dry as possible"—are still imperfect and variable, but that is the best we have. And, these measures are a necessary part of building an entire six-sided box. (Some of these measures can be reduced for extremely dry climates, steep slopes, or construction on bedrock.)

Building Below-Grade Floors and Walls

Floors on grade

Slab on-grade floors offer limited choices to manage moisture. The first option is to minimize water pressure beneath the slab, as described above. Floors typically use a plastic sheet, such as 4 or 6 mil polyethylene, underneath the floor. Other manufactured systems are also possible. For critical floor applications, such as wood flooring, continuous welded sheet flooring, and fluid applied resinous floorings, a sealer is applied on top of the concrete before installation of these materials. Early removal of the moisture in the air and construction materials is required prior to installation of any sealers or floor finish materials. Removal of the moisture through ventilation, heating, or cooling can take weeks or months, and must be included in the project planning process.

Below-grade walls similar to floors

Most of the concerns about pressure and relief discussed for slab on-grade floors (above) apply to the walls as well. More choices of waterproofing membranes—petroleum type membranes—either fluid applied, applied in sheets such as modified bituminous material, plastic sheets, and on occasion clay products can be used on the exterior of walls below grade.

Above-Grade Walls

Masonry walls

Untreated masonry is an extremely porous and absorptive material that permits solid water transmission through a wall in minutes. Single width walls are typically used in structures, such as warehouses, where the exterior appearance of concrete block is acceptable. They should have additives cast into the concrete block, such as silane and siloxane, which are relatives of the silicone family. These chemicals also must be added to the mortar in the mixing process. These similar chemicals can be surface applied after completion.

However, this is typically done with an extremely heavy flood coat application, where the heavily applied material will run down the face of the building. This can be a concern if it is applied after the installation of windows, doors, or finish materials. Planning this application before the installation of doors and windows is best.

For double-width masonry walls, such as block backup with face brick exterior, the water management systems will vary by the humidity and predominant temperature of the project location. In high humidity warm areas, such as the Gulf Coast of the United States, typically an asphaltic membrane is applied to the outboard face of the concrete block. This creates a water barrier between the exterior of the concrete block and the interior of the face brick. This is both waterproofing and the one and only vapor barrier in the entire wall assembly, including interior finish materials. For northern climates, with seasonal variability (and extremely dry winters), this waterproofing is frequently omitted. Vapor barriers are installed, with the finish materials, on the inside of the wall.

In all masonry systems, both single and double width, a flashing material (plastic, stainless steel, or asphalt-coated copper) must be installed at all heads of windows and doors, structural penetrations through the masonry, and at the bottom of walls. Any place the vertical path of water hits an obstruction, flashing must be installed to direct the water around this obstruction.

Masonry walls can also be installed as a water storage system. However, with the reduction in widths used in modern masonry, this is seldom intentionally used in new construction.

Wood siding

Wood is a material that absorbs water and dries out very slowly—on the order of months to years. Wood pieces used for the exterior siding of the building typically come in 4" to 12" widths—so there are many gaps. Therefore, wood is used as a water-shedding system, not a waterproofing system. The wood siding must be supplemented by installing an additional water-shedding material, such as asphalt paper, underneath—to drain to the bottom behind the wood siding. The surface-applied coatings (sealers, stain, and paint) on wood siding retard the absorption of moisture and also limit the deterioration of wood due to ultraviolet light.

Metal siding

Metal siding (typically steel, occasionally aluminum) coated with sophisticated materials with up to a 50-year factory warranty is used for siding residential, commercial, agricultural and industrial buildings. The siding is not absorptive, and is also a vapor barrier. Therefore, it is installed in a similar manner to wood siding (see above). Some plastics, such as vinyl, can sometimes be substituted for portions of the metal siding assembly.

Synthetic stucco cladding

Synthetic stuccos emerged in about 1980 as an economical exterior cladding capable of many colors and shapes at a low cost. It consists of an exterior membrane (made of a plastic reinforcing mesh with a troweled on—acrylic enhanced—cement coating), a bead foam Styrofoam insulation board, and a troweled interior mastic drainage layer over a sprayed waterproof membrane. The exterior membrane retards the solid infiltration of the water, but is not a vapor barrier. The interior mastic performs a water resistant and a vapor barrier function.

This combination of vapor and water barriers causes complications wherever there is a penetration—a window, a door, a conduit for an exterior light, or a hose bib. If any of these are not properly installed, with the required flashings, water will build up between the stucco and the waterproofing membrane and disintegrate the foam. Removal and replacement of the entire system is required if leaks occur. If every detail of the entire system is understood and correctly installed, these problems will be avoided. In the absence of such perfection, problems are frequent.

Openings With Many Purposes—Open, Let in Air, and Keep Out Water

Doors and windows

Exterior wood doors are solid and resist water and water vapor when stained, sealed, varnished, or painted. Metal doors, such as steel, aluminum, or bronze are hollow and have internal weeping systems that allow any trapped water to discharge by gravity through the bottom of the door.

Similarly, a wood exterior doorframe will have lapped solid members, which accommodate a very small amount of expansion and contraction. Metal doorframes typically allow weeping to the bottom of the door and accommodate the expansion and contraction with a resilient joint between the doorframe and the surrounding wall.

For all door and frame materials, there must be a gap of about 1/8" between the door and frame to permit the differential expansion due to temperature, and wood door swelling caused by seasonal humidity. (The doorframes will touch the walls, but will not change in dimension as quickly as the doors.) Fitting a door too tightly can cause expansion when heated by the sun, or swollen by wetting, that temporarily binds the door shut.

Curtain walls and storefront walls—look similar but work differently

Curtain walls and storefront systems (an aluminum-framed wall and window system) appear similar in appearance but are entirely different in internal construction and function. Storefront construction consists of four-sided windows mounted to a surrounding wall. These are designed to resist the wind load by bracing to the adjacent construction—and to weep moisture at the bottom of each four-sided frame. Wind loading restricts the storefront height to about 12 feet. The surrounding caulk joint accommodates the thermal expansion of the aluminum, so stacking of storefronts is not possible.

Design of storefront walls uses tables and rules of thumb. Materials are pre-engineered. Manufactured components are economical and permit fast (days or weeks) fabrication from stock components. The aluminum framing can be "thermally broken." A thermal break consists of an interior extrusion (like a box tube) and an exterior extrusion connected by a resilient material, such as vinyl. This provides a gap in heat transmission so condensation or frost does not occur on the interior of the window. Storefront construction is typically used throughout single story commercial applications, such as retail stores and shopping centers.

Curtain walls are also an aluminum-framed glass and metal panel system used on the exterior of commercial structures. They appear similar to storefront, but function and are designed completely differently. They are custom engineered for the specific project by specialists in this type of system. They plan wind loads, water barriers, weeping systems, and structural attachment to the building. The components are semi-custom or fully-custom extrusions. The components of the framing system are structural and can span multiple stories. Thermal expansion is engineered into the system. Further, they have multiple story water weeping capability within the components.

The time of engineering and fabrication—and the cost—is significantly greater for curtain walls than for storefront systems. Design and fabrication can take months to years. Full-custom extruded pieces, and mockups to investigate "artistic appearance" can extend time further. However, for multi-story applications, storefront construction is unfeasible (although it has been installed and failed) and curtain wall must be used.

Roofs

Sloped roofs

Sloped roofs have a minimum of 3" of rise for 12" of run. They may be made of either waterproofing or water-shedding material. Water-shedding roofs use a layer of asphalt-impregnated paper or fiberglass installed in lapped horizontal rows—as a backup line of defense. Where ice on a roof is usual, a heavier layer of asphalt or rubberized product is added at the bottom edge of the roof near the eves or gutters to resist the damaging effects of swelling ice.

A second line of defense, consisting of shingles (asphalt-impregnated fiberglass, wood, slate, clay tile, or steel), is fastened by nails, hooks, or screws. The asphalt-impregnated shingles also have self-sealing tabs, which are dabs of asphalt, which fuse with the shingle it touches when heated by the sun the first time. Ventilation for drying out the area and materials between these two layers is desirable. In construction before the 1900s, furring strips were typically installed on the roof under the roofing materials. This permitted significant drying.

In modern wood shingle roofs, a breather layer (plastic mesh) can be installed on top of felts and underneath the wood shingles to simulate, on a smaller scale, this previous very good ventilation. The rest of the sloped water-shedding systems ignore this ventilation and shorten the life of the roof. This is universal standard practice.

Sloped roof venting minimizes ice dams

For climates with freezing winters, it is desirable to maintain the entire roof—top to edge—at the same temperature. This is done by significant venting. (Allowing the colder atmospheric air to flow from the lower edge of the vent to the ridge on through to the other side.) When this is done successfully, no ice build-up occurs at the roof edge. If this is not built into the original design, only remedial solutions such as heat tracing and mechanically chopping ice off the edge of the roof every winter is possible. The life of the roof and surrounding structure will be reduced if this is necessary.

Flat roofs

Flat roofs are usually defined as being optically flat, but frequently have a pitch of about 1/4" in 1'. The components are sometimes a protection board (1/2–3/4" wood sheet product) on the bottom, always rigid insulation board in the middle, sometimes a protection board on the top, and then always a roofing membrane.

All flat roofs are by necessity waterproof, not water-shedding. The membrane is waterproof, but the rigid insulation boards are also a significant water barrier. If the roof structure is concrete, no downward relief of this water is possible. If it is a steel decking system, attempts at perforating this deck to relieve the moisture have produced poor results. If the roof deck is wood, as frequently occurs in churches, trapped water can be a problem.

Attempts at ventilating the roofing membrane from the top have not proved successful, since the horizontal moisture transmission needed to get the water to the vent is extremely slow. Further, a huge number of mechanical vents will themselves tend to introduce leakage to the roof. So, the consequence in modern day roofing is moisture is trapped within the roofing assembly and this degrades the insulation materials. Even with the best plastic insulations, this will occur. The solution we have now accepted is to accept "thermal drift" as normal. Thermal drift means insulation gets worse and becomes a poorer insulator with time. An insulation value in the midpoint of the insulation's life is the accepted design value.

When a flat roof intersects a vertical member, such as a roof curb for a mechanical unit, plumbing vent pipe penetration, or an adjacent wall, the roofing membrane material should be turned up and over the top of this penetration—and this can be as high as 4–5' above the flat roof. Where the intersecting wall is greater than about five feet, a reglet (slot) should be cut horizontally in the adjacent wall as described below.

Modern roofs are mechanically fastened to the structure below. Membranes are glued or heat welded. (Older built-up roofs used some mechanical fasteners, but mostly hot asphalt to hold things together. The roof membrane is now left exposed to the weather. Built-up systems used to place gravel on the membrane for ballast.) The light reflective color of modern roofing membranes can significantly reduce the sun's heating of the building through the roof—and reduce air conditioning costs.

Covering the Gaps—Flashings, Copings, and Penetrations
The critical second line of defense that prevents most roof leak problems

Flashings and copings are metal or plastic sheets used as a second line of defense. Flashing and copings must be used wherever roofing materials end or have an exposed joint or gap. A flashing is installed at the intersection of horizontal and vertical surfaces, and a coping is installed on top of a vertical surface.

Flashings and copings first resist the gravity flow of water—the strongest and most persistent force. Lapping the flashing materials bottom up so the water flows over the flashing materials and their joints does this. The joints in the flashing materials are not sealed.

For sloped, water-shedding roofs, a "baby flashing" is placed under each shingle or tile, and then turns vertically up the wall and under the siding. A second flashing is installed on the vertical wall to cover the baby flashing. For flat roofs, a single flashing or coping is installed on the vertical wall at the top of the roof membrane.

These flashings work best—all water-flow is downhill over waterproof materials—and should be used wherever possible. Where not possible, such as a single-story addition to a multi-story building, a reglet (a U-shaped metal or plastic shape 3/8–3/4" square) should be installed in the vertical wall and the flashing inserted in this reglet. Omitting this reglet and surface applying a metal termination bar in caulk is a poor alternative. (Although allowed by many roofing manufacturers and frequently used, it is one of the first places the roof will leak.)

Flashing to flashing joints are not caulked. (Flashings to other material joints are sometimes, but not usually caulked.) Caulking cannot be installed because the flashing materials will expand and contract from the heat of the sun. This expansion exceeds the elasticity of the caulk, and will break the bond. Also, the joints in the flashing are the intended relief for trapped water.

Flashings must also resist the vertical flow of water upward—driven by wind. A four-inch high flashing will resist the flow of consistent high winds of 40–50 mph. Four inches will also cover the joint between the wall and the nominal two-inch high (1-1/2" actual) lumber blocking frequently installed on top of the wall. Two-inch high copings and flashings are allowed by many roofing manufacturers, and preferred because of their trim appearance—but will frequently leak.

Mechanical electrical roof penetrations require these same installation procedures, but they are usually an afterthought, or missed entirely. Pipes installed late in the project are frequently punched through the roof and sealed with whatever "goo" the tradesman has a lot of in his truck at the time. A caulk joint alone is not a good seal. Roof and flashing details for pipe penetrations must be included in the project planning—just like the joint between it and other dissimilar materials, as described above.

Summary

The laws of physics will not be suspended for your project—so build to accommodate

Gravity will not be repealed. Freeze-thaw cycles, capillary action, and absorption will exist on all projects, as well as the effects of temperature and pressure on the states of water. Recognize these physical laws and build tolerant systems that accommodate these movements and changes of state. Select groups of materials that work well together.

Materials move and act differently—select carefully, accommodate differences

Expansion, contraction, and absorption of materials are significantly different. It is at the intersection of these materials where most leakage occurs. Select materials—as much as possible—that are compatible. Then, make slip joints and resilient joints that allow for the movement that will inevitably occur. Increasingly, proprietary engineered systems (roofs and curtain walls) have all components previously designed. These must be chosen carefully since the other nonproprietary systems that surround, touch, and are affected by these proprietary systems must accommodate, catch up for, and make up for any deficiencies in the proprietary system. Just because a reputable company has carefully engineered it does not necessarily mean that it is going to work well with all the other components in your project.

Seal compartments—but direct relief to a good location, and use two lines of defense

Many moisture problems are caused by moist air moving from one component of the building to another through different temperatures. Movement of moist air to colder temperatures produces condensation that can condense to the point where it appears that solid water is discharging from this component. Isolate the components to reduce the rate of this pressure-caused flow. Note that the pressure can be caused by mechanical systems from the inside or wind from the outside.

You can slow it, but you cannot stop water. Therefore, do not seal everything. Separate the components as much as possible, but allow a controlled relief so what does get through is suitably discharged in a location of your choosing. It will leak, so give it a way to get out.

Two lines of defense are always desirable for any system. For all wall systems, including windows and doors, two lines of defense are mandatory. Gravity is your friend and capillary action that absorbs moisture must be minimized by providing breaks in the material.

Design for the real world and real people

Water will always flow, everything will leak somewhat, and real people will install this stuff. Allow for the give and go that will inevitably occur. Attempting perfection guarantees failure. You can manage the location and direction and speed of the flow of water, but not stop it. Select materials that work well together and use forgiving, robust engineering so many small failures still will permit overall success. Using these principles will make project success normal.

3.12 Plumbing—Providing Water and Removing Wastes

Plumbing provides and removes water, related liquids, and solids for human use, health, and comfort

What Is in water?

Lots- and solids settled, living matter decays, and bacteria grows

All water has been transported through the hydraulic cycle. Water evaporates from surface lakes and streams into clouds that rain, and is then moved across and through the earth. During this movement, the water will pick up and retain dissolved minerals, salts, solids, other surface liquids, and biological matter, such as decaying plants and bacteria. Every drop of water has been someplace else before and contains traces of the trip.

Providing water to the site—municipal and private water service

Water comes from wells or surface water, such as lakes and streams. For small private buildings, well water is used with no further processing. For government or large commercial water processing and delivery systems, frequently the solids are filtered—usually by allowing settling in basins. The chemical chlorine is added to kill some of the bacteria. And, frequently, fluorine is added as a health measure to prevent tooth decay.

Control of the Water Service for Maintenance, Billing, and Purity

Municipal and private shutoff valves

For municipal systems, there is typically a valve for shut off of the water service. This valve is located on city, not private property, and it is frequently called a "buffalo box." The valve stem is at grade level, but the valve is 3' or more below grade. The city water department closes the valve if the site is vacated or the water bills are not paid.

In addition to city shutoff valves, on the interior of the structure there is typically at least one—sometimes multiple—shutoff valves to permit maintenance within the building.

Water meters—measuring water use

A water meter is typically sold or rented by the city to a property owner. It is installed either by the city or installing plumbing contractor—to measure and bill for water use. Meters can also be used on entirely private water services for managing landlord charge- back of tenant usage. It is typical, though not universal, for the water meter to be downsized one size from the water service pipe dimension. For example, if the incoming water service is 1-1/2" the meter may be 1". This is done because the greater velocity and a lesser pressure produced by the downsized meter provide a more accurate reading.

Back flow prevention—keeps water in the city mains pure

Back flow prevention valves such as check valves and RPZ's (RPZ valving described below) are added for many commercial buildings. These prevent contaminated water within the building from siphoning back and contaminating the municipal water main (if pressure drops in this main). For no good reason, this safety measure is eliminated on many smaller commercial and residential buildings.

Pressure moves water and makes fixtures function

The pressure from a city main or well provides the required flow and pressure to all parts of the building—to make the plumbing devices and valves work. Typically, a minimum pressure of 8 to 12 pounds per square inch at the last point of discharge is required. City mains may be stated as 80 psi at the take off from the main, but frequently are much lower—35 psi is found in many cases.

Some municipalities that have deteriorated water systems or have experienced large growth in the number of buildings (and demand for water)—unaccompanied by increases in the municipal water supply—will reduce the pressure delivered. In this case, each building must install a booster pump and tank to upgrade the pressure.

Water service size—a little bigger is a lot more expensive

Residential services are typically 1". Small commercial services are typically up to about 2-1/2". Medium-sized commercial services are up to about 6". Larger water sizes—over 6"—are used for large commercial and industrial projects.

The municipal fee to install water service escalates rapidly with the size of the service. For example, a residential service main has a fee of 1 to 2 days' wages, small commercial 2 weeks' wages, and large commercial and industrial 1 year's wages. This is simply a tax in addition to the actual cost of the work. Frequently, the plumbing contractor must purchase the meter, install the tap, and perform all material and labor to accomplish a full water service installation, while the city employees stay in the office and cash the check!

Electrical grounding through the water service
The water service entrance is frequently used as the electrical service ground

Except in nonfreezing climates or where there is extensive bedrock, water mains are usually buried in the earth. This large underground piping system provides a good electrical ground, and is frequently used for the ground of a building's electrical service. When this is done, a grounding jumper must bridge over the valving and meters of the water service. This consists of an appropriately sized copper cable or braided wire connected from the incoming service to the piping downstream from the entire meter and valving assembly. This is required since materials such as gaskets or piping compound in the assembly may prevent continuous reliable electrical transmission. This must be remembered since any plumbing maintenance repair activities could inadvertently remove the entire electrical grounding system for the building.

Moving Water in Pipes

Pressure and speed are opposite, friction is constant

When water is not moving, the pressure is easy to understand. The pressure is simply the weight of all the water stacked above that point. For example, water weighs (at sea level and room temperature) about 63 pounds per cubic foot. For water 10 feet deep, the pressure at the bottom of the 1-foot square stack is 630 pounds per square foot.

When this static water starts to move, different principles apply. The father and son team of Johann and Daniel Bernoulli first discovered these principles in 1738. They stated that the speed and pressure together are a constant value. So, if the speed is very high, the pressure is very low and vice versa. Although this at first appears to be opposite common sense, it is true. This principle governs the flow of water through pipes.

The flow of water through pipes is also governed by gravity. Water accelerates downward in free fall at about 33' per second. Water also loses .434 psi for every 1' of vertical rise.

Finally, the interior of all piping produces friction between the water and the surface of the pipe. Since the friction is near constant for all pipe sizes, the water restrained by friction will be a far greater portion of the pipe diameter in a small pipe than a larger pipe. Finally, there is friction in any fitting, valve, device, or joint that changes direction, this will be discussed more below.

Gravity and pumps moves water in piping systems

Gravity can provide constant water flow and pressure. Small pumps—with small and variable delivery—can fill an elevated reservoir. The static liquid head of this reservoir then provides a steady flow of water at a constant pressure. Familiar examples of this are municipal water towers and a tank type toilet. A less familiar example is the mechanical rooms in a high-rise building, which are commonly located about every 20 floors (or 250 feet of vertical rise). Water is pumped to the mechanical floor and then moves down by gravity to the point of use.

If these reservoirs do not exist or the point of use is above the top of the reservoir, additional pumping systems must be added to provide the required pressure—but delivery can be uneven.

Gravity drainage—a narrow range of slopes work well

Gravity drains wastewater well, but the slope must be within a very narrow range. Minimum slopes for piping 3" and less are 1/4" per foot, piping 3" to 6" are 1/8" per foot, and piping 8" and over are 1/16" per foot. Maximum pipe slopes for sanitary lines can only be about 1/4" per foot or the water may be transported so rapidly that solids are left behind in the pipe. For storm water drains that contain few solids, pitches up to 1/2" per foot may be possible.

The pitch of the piping greatly affects the carrying capacity of the pipe—by almost 100%. For example, the capacities in drainage fixture units (described more below) of 8" pipe is 1/16" per foot slope 1,400 fixture units, 1/8" per foot slope 1,600 fixture units, 1/4" per foot slope 1,920 fixture units, and 1/2" per foot slope 2,300 fixture units. For these reasons, the most common pitch is thought to be 1/4" per foot, but settling (because of height restrictions or obstruction) on not less than 1/8" per foot.

Pipe Size and Capacity—Bigger Is Much Better
2 + 2 does not equal 4

The carrying capacity of a pipe is determined first by subtracting the friction loss of the side of the pipe, and then multiplying the radius times the radius. (A 2" pipe has a radius of 1", so the flow is related to 1 x 1 = 1. A 4" pipe has a radius of 2", so the flow is related to 2 x 2 = 4. When the pipe size increase 200%, the pipe flow increases 400%.) So larger pipes will carry a far greater amount of water than their diameter suggests.

The number of 1" pipes required to equal the carrying capacity of a larger pipe are:

Pipe size (inches)	Number of 1" pipes for the same capacity
1	1
2	5.5
3	15
4	29
6	80
12	434

And the pressure loss in small pipes is also greater. At 30 gallons per minute, the pressure losses of different pipe sizes are:

Pipe size	Pressure loss (psi) per 100' copper pipe
1	17.0
2	.8
3	.1

So the capacity increases greatly with pipe diameter size. However, the cost increases in a similar way. For example, 1/2" valve may cost from 5–15 minutes of wages whereas a 5' diameter valve used in large water delivery systems may cost 3–5 years' wages.

Sizing of pipes—minimums for the practical world

Because of the principles described above and practical tolerances of pipe installation in the field, there are minimum piping sizes. Water supply 1/4" pipe can be used only for limited applications, such as filling of coffee machines, icemakers, and some humidifiers. A 1/2" pipe can only be used for very short connections to the fixtures, usually under 20'.

For drainage piping, the free flow of solids requires minimum 1-1/2" drain lines from fixtures with few solids, such as sinks, and 4" drain lines from fixtures discharging large amounts of solids, such as toilets.

For small projects, usually under three stories, the "fixture unit" is used to calculate the piping sizes that work in the real world. The fixture unit assigns a simple number that approximates the amount of water required and drainage discharged from each fixture. For example, one sample table would be:

Fixture Type	Drainage	Water
China Lavatory	1	1
Kitchen Sink	2	2
Bathtub	2	2
Floor Drain	4	0
Toilet (tank)	6	3
Toilet (flush valve)	6	10

So a one-bedroom apartment would add up to the following units:

Fixture Type	Drainage	Water
China Lavatory	1	1
Kitchen Sink	2	2
Bathtub	2	2
Toilet (tank)	6	3
Total	11	8

(Fixture unit number will be included in many state or municipal codes, and will be similar but not identical).

A 4" sanitary pipe can carry 200 fixture units, which will be the equivalent of 21 such apartments. Since the most back-to-back apartments that can be installed on one soil stack—in a three-story building—is 6, the minimum pipe size is far greater than would be required by the fixture units.

Fixture unit calculations and minimum pipe sizes work well for small projects

Similar calculations are done for water-service piping. Pipe sizing by fixture unit calculation attempts to take into account the effects of pressure, velocity, liquid head, pipe friction, and practical considerations of the field. But this common sense approach no longer works for larger projects over three stories—or where extremely high water use is required.

This has two important implications for those involved in project delivery. First, for smaller projects, the minimum pipe size specified by practical considerations and code will be far larger than the pipe size determined by the fixture unit method—also required by code. Detailed pipe size calculations are usually pointless. It is, therefore, extremely difficult to get a mechanical engineer to design smaller projects competently, since his skill and knowledge are wasted.

Engineering calculations required for larger projects—usually over three stories

The second implication is that the common sense rules of thumb and practical knowledge of personnel experienced in smaller projects must be learned anew when they move to larger projects. Here, the mathematical calculations and the work of a competent engineer are required and produce results somewhat different than the common sense results that worked well on smaller projects. Precise calculations can reduce pipe sizes but can also require different configurations and devices. Knowing the limits of your knowledge, and when to get help achieve these economies and avoids disastrous mistakes.

Resisting the force of moving water—serious measures required for larger projects

The lineal force of moving water must be managed when water is stopped by a valve or is redirected by a pipefitting. The first accommodation uses air as a shock absorber in air chambers and expansion tanks. Here, some of the air dissolved in the water comes out of the solution and is trapped in an air chamber at a fixture. It can simply be an upturned piece of pipe about 12" to 18" above the point of valve connection. When the valve is shut, the shock temporarily compresses the air trapped in this pipe and avoids the "water hammer" that can shake the pipes. For larger installations, an actual expansion tank filled with air (sometime with a spring-actuated diaphragm to depress the water) can be used. For still larger valves or higher water pressures or velocities, or very long runs (such as a pipeline), a gradual throttling down of the valve must be planned.

Fittings for moving water can best manage the force of water with a longer (more gradual and sweeping) radius. This is sought where dimensionally feasible, but a longer radius means greater space and heights required to install the pipe—which is not always available.

When pipes over 4 inches must turn a sharp 90° corner, restraint at the turn must be provided or the force of water can blow pipes apart. This can be accomplished with thrust blocks, which are large concrete structures anchored at the pipe turn to resist the force of the moving water.

Finally, for extremely fast moving water, which would occur in storm water drainage piping, the piping materials must resist the scouring of the fast moving water and suspended solids. This requires both proper sweep on the piping or drainage structures and careful selection of the materials. The turns in the concrete pipe can begin to show wear after several years directly through the concrete—exposing the interior aggregate due to the force of the water.

Maintaining Water Purity in the Piping Loop
Travel to all locations outside a domestic water system is a one-way trip

One of the functions and responsibilities of a plumber is to maintain the purity, health, and safety of the domestic water supply—both within the building and back to the main source of supply. The Department of Public Health accordingly regulates plumbing contractors, just as it does doctors and nurses.

Backflow prevention keeps the trip one-way

The purpose of back flow prevention is to make sure that once water is discharged from a plumbing fixture it cannot back siphon, due to loss of pressure in the water lines. This would inject contaminated water into the pure water system.

Air gaps—gravity works well

The best and surest way to ensure no back siphoning occurs is air gaps. Here, the point of discharge of the water is higher than the flood rim of the receiving body. For example, the faucet of the sink will be higher than the sink itself. Another example is the fill spout for swimming pools.

Vacuum breakers—used when the point of water discharge may become submerged

Where an air gap is not possible, such as a flexible hose sprayer for dishwashing, a vacuum breaker is inserted in the water supply line. If a loss of pressure occurs in the main, the vacuum breaker valve opens and shuts down the water supply, so that reverse suction is not possible.

Checks and double checks

Check valves use a hinged flapper that will typically be blown open by the movement of water. But if the water moves in the opposite direction, it is slammed shut—preventing reverse flow. A double check is two such devices in series.

RPZ valves can be adjusted for precise performance

Reduce pressure valve (RPZ) is a type of check valve that has multiple calibration ports along the stream of flow. This permits attaching a calibrated gauge at the ports to check and adjust the valve to close at a specified pressure. About 6 pounds per square inch is the normal pressure loss across a valve. And, the valve may be calibrated to slam shut at a pound or two over this value. RPZs are used where it is essential to ensure backflow prevention. Examples are the water service entrance in commercial structures and delivery to fixtures in a patient dental operatory.

Achieving Health and Purity of Water in Pipes

Piping dead ends produce stagnant water—eliminate or keep them short

Since water contains plant, animal, and bacterial material, it is in a constant state of decay and bacteria growth. One of the soundest principles to avoid this growth is to ensure a continual water flow to all points of the piping. This requires minimization of dead ends—piping that goes nowhere or is not used for long periods of time. The goal is to have a dead end no more than 6' long.

Sanitization—kill the bacteria in the water pipe

Sanitization of the entire plumbing system can occur and frequently does occur at the end of construction of a building. This simply means injecting a sanitization solution, usually bleach, into the piping system, letting it sit for a couple of days, and then flushing it out. If contamination of a system occurs, the piping system can be re-sanitized.

Heating Water for Sanitation and Comfort

Warmer water is more comfortable for human use in washing—and more effectively activates soap to remove oils. Water heating of 120°F is considered to be the scalding comfortable limit for human contact, and 140°F and 160°F are considered to be the temperatures for sanitization—such as restaurant dishwashing and commercial laundries.

High temperatures make high pressures—protection and relief required

To achieve these temperatures at the point of use, the water in the tank must be at a slightly higher temperature, which can produce dangerously high pressures. If these pressures are not managed correctly, the tank can explode and rocket through the floors and roof of a multi-story building—destroying that portion of the building and killing all in its path. To manage these pressures, a thermostatic valve within the tank shuts off the heating source when the specified temperature is reached. In addition, a thermostatic relief and a pressure relief should be installed. When the specified pressure is reached, a valve will open and discharge a portion of the tank water. (This does require pans and/or drains around the hot water heater.) These safety measures must all be maintained and kept in operation.

For water services not protected by backflow prevention, pushing water back into the city main can relieve some of the pressure. If the water service is protected by an RPZ—so that the pressure cannot be pushed back into the city main—an expansion tank must be added to the hot water heater. This allows further shock absorption of pressure variations.

Hot water storage—reduces the size of the heating plant

The specific heat of water is 1—meaning raising the temperature of water requires the most heat of any common material. This can tax the heating capacity of the mechanical equipment—particularly in electrically-heated buildings.

Small hot water heaters have a storage tank integral with the fixture. The storage tank, heating element, control and relief valves are all packaged in one fixture. However, if hot water demand is very high, such as in a commercial restaurant or laundry, and the only source for the heat is electric, the available electric service may not be able to provide the required heated water capacity. In this case, additional insulated storage tanks must be installed outside—and in tandem with the hot water heater. For yet higher hot water capacity, a boiler remote from the storage tank or a heat exchanger (a radiator type device) that is immersed in a storage tank can be used. Since the boiler is a closed system re-circulating its own water, sediment control in the boiler can be minimized and its life extended.

In-line heating elements with no storage tanks are occasionally used. These typically have lesser or even nonexistent thermostatic and pressure relief control. They also have limited or no capacity for removing mineral sediments. Although these devices continue to improve, they are prohibited in many areas.

Removing Minerals By Softening to Reduce Buildup in Pipes and Valves

Hard water contains magnesium and calcium, frequently from water that has percolated through limestone. It is called hard because its mineral contents make it hard to make soaps work well. These minerals are removed by water softeners. They consist of zenolite granules pre-charged with negative sodium ions. The hard water flows over the granules and the positively charged minerals stick until the granules are saturated. The water is then shut off. The tank is filled with a salt solution, and the salty solution strips the minerals off the granules and the dissolved minerals in the salt solution are washed down the drain. Then the softening process starts again.

Remove Solids and Non-Water Liquids on Site
Good flow to the sewer and a pure a discharge as is practical

Where possible, wastes are removed from the piping system on site and disposed of in the solid waste rubbish—to avoid clogging the site and the municipal piping systems.

Removing solids before the sewer—for smooth flow in the sewer

Strainers, which consist of a mesh material similar in appearance to window screen, can be used to remove solids in the water or waste stream. Strainers accompany many types of valves to protect the valve from minerals or other solids that could compromise its function. Solids in storm water can sometimes be removed on site with sediment traps. Here, a pipe discharges its flow over a larger basin, reducing the speed of the flow and the suspended solids fall to the bottom and are later removed.

Strainers can also be used to remove specialized types of solids. Examples include a lint trap, which is simply a box with a window screen type material installed as the barrier. The water flows through, and the lint is trapped on the screen, and is then periodically removed and discarded. Lint traps are used in commercial laundries. Hair traps are a similar device that are used for beauty shops or dog grooming locations.

Removing the non-water liquids before the sewer—to promote purity of discharge

Grease trap and oil separators are also used to remove these undesirable liquids so the pipes do not become clogged. A grease trap is typically used in restaurants. This works on the principle that grease is lighter and will float on water. A box is installed in the piping stream with the inlet higher than the outlet. The grease floats to the top and is periodically removed and recycled off site.

A triple basin oil separator traps the oil and gas leakage that drips off a car and is washed down the drain. This is required for car parking garages or vehicle maintenance facilities. It works on the same principle as the restaurant grease trap except three separate basins in series are used. These basins will always be located at the lowest point—possibly below the city storm sewer—and therefore frequently must be emptied by ejector pumps. This need may cause significant rework and cost if not caught early in the design process.

Finally, highly acidic or alkaline solutions may be neutralized before discharge into the sewer. For acidic discharge, this can be as simple as filtering the liquid through alkaline limestone. Chemical additives can also be used. These dilution methods are used for x-ray film processors and many industrial applications.

Managing Waste Line Air Pressure and Sewer Gas

Traps keep gas in the sewer pipes and out of the building

Wastewater in sanitary sewer systems is constantly decomposing and producing a gas that can be both flammable and have an objectionable odor. A plumbing trap prevents the travel of sewer gas through the fixtures into the building. Every fixture waste line will have a trap, which is simply a u-turn in the waste piping that is filled with water, preventing the transmission of gas. The following can break the trap seal:

1. Evaporation. This will occur at fixtures that infrequently receive water—such as a floor drain. This can be overcome in residential applications by periodically pouring water into the drain. In commercial applications, a trap primer (a small water line feeding the trap) that injects a small amount of water in the trap each time a fixture (such as a faucet) is opened can be used.
2. Wind pressure down the vent stack could blow out the trap water. This is resisted by correct design of the vent piping, including an increaser (piping that gets larger after the vent pipe goes through the roof). This increaser will reduce the wind pressure in the vent system. In an incorrectly designed system, pressure from discharge from other fixtures could also blow out the trap.
3. Capillary action. If stringy material is left in the waste system, the capillary action along this material could wick the water out of the trap. Cleaning out the trap is the answer for this problem.

Vents relieve pressure that can restrict sewage flow

In addition, water discharging through the sewer system must have a free flow of air from the upstream side so the water can flow continually without resistance from a vacuum. Vents—relief pipes—are used for this purpose. The vent must go from the lowest point of sanitary waste in the building up through the roof and discharge to the air. Vents must also slope up from the waste, so they will always stay dry and never become filled with water, which prevents the required airflow. To function correctly, the vent must be quite close to the fixture trap—generally 3' to 10'. This must be considered in the original design and is a restriction on remodeling possibilities.

Public sewers and waste treatment systems process waste off site

For smaller buildings, the sewage is simply discharged into the municipal system. For more complicated structures, or ones with special health requirements such as restaurants, sampling ports can be installed in the sewer to ensure that the grease traps and triple basin separators are removing the grease and oil as intended. Health Department officials will periodically sample discharge to monitor conformance. Processing of the wastewater takes place at an off-site plant using filtering, settling of solids, chemical treatment, and biological decomposition of organic material.

Septic systems process waste on-site

If municipal systems are not available, a septic system on the property can be used. This consists of a receiving basin to settle the solids and then a drain field—where the liquids are discharged. The drain field works by biological action on the sewage materials—bacteria eating up the sewage materials and rendering the waste products acceptable. This process requires that the water stays suspended in the soil for several days for this biological action to take place. Extremely sandy soils may be unsuitable for a drain field—the contaminated sewage leaves the soil and percolates down to the ground water before the biological action is complete. A septic field is not possible here. If the field is extremely impermeable, such as a clay soil, the biological action can take place in the clay drain field basin and the water will evaporate upward. This will require a larger area for the drain field.

A percolation test is used to check that the soil will hold the sewage for the right amount of time. A hole is drilled and filled with water, and the time of discharge is observed. About eight hours is desirable. More elaborate laboratory tests can also be used.

Septic fields require additional unpaved land area on the site. Performance monitoring is light or nonexistent, so partially treated wastes may be discharged into the ground water. Further, septic systems may be completely unworkable for some types of occupancies that either discharge many cleaning agents or antibiotic materials such as a human or veterinary hospital. These materials can completely defeat the biological action of the septic field and raw sewage will percolate down to the water table. For these reasons, private septic systems continue to decline, and may be prohibited in developing areas.

Plumbing Materials and Devices

Piping Materials
Piping materials are chosen for speed of predictable assembly and resistance to chemicals, heat, and pressure

Lead—a good old standby but soft and toxic

Lead was successfully used as a water supply material for over 2,000 years. The word plumber comes from the Latin word for lead. Some plumbing union titles are "plumber and lead burners union," and claim lead works such as lining of tanks for acid operations and even some lead roofing work.

Lead pipe is easily joined and the interior of the piping seems to be impervious to mineral buildup. Lead piping removed after 100 years of use is as clean and smooth as it was the day it was installed. However, it is soft and easily crushed and increasing concern about leaching of the lead materials into the drinking water has eliminated it from use in the last half of the 20th century.

Copper—an above ground workhorse for waste, vent, and water piping

Copper has all the benefits of lead but is harder and does not leach objectionable metal materials into the drinking water. It is joined by sweat soldering and is the most common domestic water piping material used. It also can be used in above-grade waste piping and vents. It, however, has poor resistance to acidic or alkaline solutions—so it cannot be used below grade or where chemical wastes are placed in the sanitary piping system.

Plastic—chemically resistant and easy to install below and above grade

Plastic piping has all the benefits of copper but also has good resistance to alkaline and acid fluids. It can be solvent welded for water, waste, and vent, or joined with compression or compression-gasketed fittings for below-grade waste piping. It is widely used as waste piping and vent piping, and in limited locations water piping and even gas piping.

Steel piping—resistant to impact but clogs, then leaks

Steel piping has good resistance to impact and crushing, however mineral buildup readily occurs on the interior of the piping. In areas of high mineral content, the piping can be entirely obstructed within 20 years of installation. It can be joined by threaded connections, or to speed installations, no-hub piping uses straight, unthreaded, unflared pieces of pipe connected with a clamped coupling. Because of the mineral buildup and the increased labor to install steel piping over other piping materials, it is seldom chosen for new installations.

Clay tile pipe—weak below-grade drain pipe

Clay tile can be used only as sanitary or storm sewer pipe under earth only, not under building slabs, or paved roadways. It can be readily damaged by tree root growth and its use continues to decline.

Cast iron—strong, medium chemical resistance, used below and above grade

Cast iron can be used for both below- and above-grade waste and venting piping. It has good resistance to impact and compression. It is usually joined with oakum (fibrous filler material) and poured molten lead. It can also be joined with a no-hub coupling as described in steel pipe above.

Glass—high chemical resistance for industry and laboratories, but brittle

Glass piping is used where high acidic or alkaline fluid solutions are discharged, such as laboratory or industrial applications. It is used in above grade only and is highly resistant to chemicals but has a very limited resistance to impact. It is joined by a compression fitting with or without a gasket.

Many grades and specifications for each material—each with a purpose

All of the materials described above have many grades and specifications—both for the pipe materials and their joining system. These specification variations accommodate the different chemicals, temperatures, and pressures in pipes. Forces on the outside of the pipe must be considered as well. Suspended above-grade pipes, pipes subject to mechanical impact, pipes buried in the earth, and pipes buried under roads or structures will all have different specifications. Home remodeling supply houses may say, "there's only one kind of plastic or copper pipe." The commercial and industrial supply houses will know the range and purpose of more specialized materials.

Valves Control Flow and Pressure

The choice of valves is governed by the amount of flow control required and the acceptable pressure loss through the valve

Flow control

Gate valve—on and off only, low pressure loss

The gate valve functions as a descending wedge that either fully obstructs or fully opens the entire pipe width. It requires multiple valve stem turns to open or close the wedge and is best for infrequent operations—such as water or sewage shutoff only. It is not used for modulating flow control.

Globe valve—good flow control, high pressure loss

It is called a globe valve because the outside of the body has a round shape like a globe. The valve works by multiple turns of the operating lever compressing a disk on an open ring. It can modulate or shut off the flow. However, since the water changes direction a couple of times as it flows through the valve, the turbulence and pressure drop are large. These types of valves are typically used for faucet fittings, such as with a lavatory.

Ball valve or cock valve—for stops and infrequent flow control

A ball valve has a ball with a hole in the water stream. The operating stem turns up to 90° to shut off or modulate the flow. It can be used as a stop or—with lesser success as a modulating valve. A cock valve is similar, except instead of a ball with a hole it is a cylinder with a hole. These types of valves are typically used for on/off operations, such as a shutoff valve to a fixture, or as a balancing valve with infrequent operation to modulate the flow in a line.

Butterfly valve—for tight spots

Butterfly valves have a flat round disk in the center of the piping stream that can be closed with a 90° turn of the operating stem. It can act as a stop or for modulation with low-pressure loss. Its primary benefit is that it is very thin and can fit in very tight spots—where no other valves will work.

Pressure control

Pressure-reducing valve

A pressure-reducing valve is a regulator that reduces and controls the pressure through the valve. It works as a valve stem screw actuator and is usually accompanied with a strainer so that small solid material deposits do not affect the accuracy of the operation and the quality of the seal.

Pressure or temperature relief valves

Relief valves are as described in the hot water heater section above—basically to relieve excess pressure in a line or tank by discharging to outside air.

Meters Measure Water Use

Disk (displacement) meter—for low variable flow

An off-kilter disk in a chamber rotates to displace water from one side of the meter to the other. The rotation of this disk drives a shaft that registers the water flow—similar to a car odometer. It reads accurately for small and variable flows of water with pipe sizes up to about 2".

Turbine meter—for high constant flow

A turbine meter—as the name suggests—uses an in-line turbine in lieu of an off-kilter disk and rotates to record the water flow. It accurately reads high constant volumes of water for larger pipe sizes.

Compound meter—for either type of flow

A compound meter includes the disk and a turbine meter in series to accurately read both the low and variable, and high and constant water flows.

Supporting Pipes and Managing Pipe Movement
Pipe support becomes increasingly important as project size increases

Pipe is heavy and support is an important consideration. A 4" piece of schedule 40 steel pipe filled with water with the normal amount of hangers and insulation will weigh approximately 17 pounds per lineal foot. The loop around the single story of a 10,000 sf office building might have 800 LF of piping with a total weight of 17,600 pounds. A riser of the same pipe in an eight-story office building will have a weight of about 1,800 pounds.

   Support of the pipe must be considered carefully. Every vertical riser must be clamped at each floor line, and supports for the horizontal piping must be considered during the planning stages. For very small projects, such as residential construction, this is seldom a large concern. But as the project size grows, considerations of piping support require attention in the planning stage. For larger industrial projects with racks of pipe banks, additional structural modifications for the entire building must be planned.

Pipe expansion caused by heat
Safely ignored on small projects, but an engineering task on large projects

Expansion of the piping caused by heat must also be considered. The expansion at a 100°F temperature rise for 100 LF of pipe will be:

Steel .968"
Wrought Iron 1.007"
Copper 1.449"
Cast Iron .845"

For installations where piping runs can be hundreds of feet long, expansion loops must be installed in the piping system. An expansion loop is a detour from the straight line of pipe that uses three pieces of pipe and four 90° turns. This U-shaped detour is sprung at half of the distance of the anticipated expansion. Each leg of the piping expansion loop would be 1" pipe – 32" leg, 4" pipe – 56" leg, and 6" pipe – 68" leg.

Those graduating from smaller projects where piping runs over 50' are uncommon, must realize that in larger work these expansion loops and supports must be installed and included in the planning phase of the pipe layout. Frequently detailed shop drawings are engineered and coordinated with the other major mechanical electrical trades before a single tradesman comes to the job.

Spring isolators and rollers accommodate pipe movement

For larger and longer pipe runs, the thermal expansion, movement, and pipe loading must be accommodated by spring isolators—in the hangers and rollers supporting the pipes. This accommodates the small movements of the pipes that occur with huge force.

Dielectric unions stop electrical transmission to minimize corrosion

All materials have a different electrical current carrying capacity and expansion and contraction characteristics. Whenever two dissimilar materials, such as steel and copper, are joined, a dielectric union fitting must be installed to accommodate these differences. This consists of a fitting with electrical insulation of a somewhat resilient material, such as plastic or rubber, to prevent physical contact of the different metals. If these are not installed, efflorescent and deterioration of the dissimilar piping will occur at the union. These joints tend to leak and require maintenance, so they must be located in an accessible location.

Dielectric separation must also be installed between the water supply piping and the structure. This is required because the water piping is frequently used as an electrical ground for the entire electrical system and does carry current. This current will cause efflorescent that will deteriorate both the structural material and the plumbing piping. Plastic separators are commonly used now to prevent this electrical transmission.

Other Devices and Procedures

Stops and strainers

Strainers are a device that removes solid material from the plumbing fixture waste line before discharge to the sewer, such as the strainer in a sink or bathtub. The stops are the local shutoff valves that permit the servicing of the fixture. In small residential and commercial projects these are seldom of great concern. However, in more complex public projects the importance expands greatly. The ability to prevent vandalism, inadvertent shutting off of valves to critical fixtures, or control by maintenance personnel, and restriction on removal and the loss of strainers makes this consideration important with dozens of choices.

Cleanouts—for rodding (cleaning out) sewer lines

Cleanouts are required for maintenance and servicing of sanitary lines. They occur where every major transition or change in direction or type of pipe occurs—also every 50' for 3" and smaller pipe, and 100' for 3" and over pipe. These are code-required devices and are essential for maintenance of the installed work—to allow rodding out of clogged sewers. They must be considered carefully in the planning stages so they Do not occur in inconvenient locations, such as underneath cabinets or in areas where appearance is an important consideration.

Checks and vacuum breakers for a single fixture

Back flow prevention devices were discussed above, but additional back flow devices may be required at specialized equipment. This will occur in industrial machines that require water for process or cooling, and in many medical and dental machines as well. Provisions must be included in the planning stage since they do require an open drain for discharge of the wastewater when the valve is operated.

Taps of the city water mains—for new water service installation

A tap is a device that permits penetration of the city water mains to connect new water service. The tap consists of a stainless steel, sheet metal band that wraps the city main. On one portion of the band is a valve and drilling device. The sleeve is installed, the hole is drilled, and the drilled slug falls into the water main and stays there forever. The valve is then inserted and the water is connected to the building. Many municipalities require that they perform the tap, other ones have designated service providers, and others permit the plumber to do it with his own personnel.

Re-circulating lines—for fast hot water response time

A hot water re-circulating line, a continuous pumped loop that continually moves the hot water around the building and back to the hot water tank, is frequently installed in commercial applications. This is done to improve delivery response time of the hot water when a valve is opened. Re-circulating lines are seldom installed in residential construction or smaller commercial locations where the hot water heater may be close to those requiring hot water.

Insulation—increases energy efficiency on hot lines and prevents sweating on cold lines

Both cold- and hot-water piping should be wrapped with insulation. For hot water, this is required for energy efficiency and maintaining the heat of the water for prompt delivery. For cold-water lines, it prevents sweating due to condensation in humid environments. (Installation may be omitted when the pipes are concealed in a wall cavity that prevents air circulation.) This must be included in the project-planning phase, both for the additional space required for the insulation and the sequencing of the installation. If the insulation installation is delayed too long, the pipes might become inaccessible and the insulation might be omitted.

Balancing—making water flow evenly throughout the loop

Where a supply and return line exists, such as the hot water re-circulating line described above, the water can be balanced so the supply delivery equals the return. This requires installation of balancing valves throughout the system so that the flow can be adjusted and the water supply and return quantities are made equal. This does require consideration in the planning stage.

Pressure tests—checking for leaks

Domestic water piping is commonly, though not always, pressure tested. This is done by capping any open piping, closing the valves, filling the system with water, and pumping up the pressure to specified pressure, usually around 120 psi. This pressure is then observed and must be maintained for a specified period, such as 8 hours. Sanitary waste piping can be, but is usually not, pressure tested. Here, balloon plugs are inserted at the discharge and a temporary vertical pipe stack of about 10' is installed at one opening, and the entire system is filled with water. The water in the temporary column is observed to see that it does not drop more than a specified distance over a period of time, such as 8 hours.

Plumbing Fixtures

Plumbing fixtures are an assembly that uses the principles of water supply and drainage described above. A fixture will contain a water supply with flow, pressure, and back flow control—a receiving and holding bowl or pan—and a drainage assembly with traps and vents. Understanding the differences, fine points, and comparative benefits of fixtures is a specialty that can consume an entire career. But knowledge of the individual components described above can greatly increase your understanding and use of plumbing fixtures.

Summary

Plumbing is a small part of the hydraulic cycle. Every drop of water has been somewhere before and will go somewhere again. Plumbing protects the purity of water coming to the site for use and consumption. It also minimizes the solids and non-water liquids discharged.

The laws of physics govern water supply flow where pressure and speed total a constant value. So, when pressure is high, speed is low, and vice versa. The friction between water and the side of the pipe is approximately constant, so it has a much bigger subtraction from the flow of the smaller pipe than a large pipe; 2 + 2 does not always equal 4. Bigger is much better—bigger pipes have much larger capacity than their pipe size suggests.

Wastewater discharge must move both liquids and suspended solids. So, only a narrow range of slopes works well—centering around 1/4" per foot. Solids and non-water liquids are removed, where possible, using sediment basins, lint and hair traps, grease traps, and oil separation basins.

Trapping and venting of waste lines prevents sewer gas from entering the building, and free flow of liquids out. The vent stacks must be located close to each fixture and must travel from the lowest point in the building to above the roof. This restricts design, layout, maintenance, and future remodeling possibilities.

Projects up to about three stories can work well with minimum pipe sizes and pipe sizes calculated using fixture units. Larger projects require detailed engineering calculations. Larger projects also require great attention to pipe support and accommodation of pipe expansion. This requires the transition from tradesman knowledge only to engineering that is understood by the tradesmen. This is a big and important jump, but it is easy to accommodate if you know when you have crossed this line from small to large.

Understanding these principles makes installation of the correct components at the correct time probable and project success normal.

3.13 Life (Fire) Safety, Fire Prevention, and Fire Protection

Keep fires infrequent and small. Help the occupants get out, the firemen get in, and save the structure

No one can be against fire safety. But, fire safety is not just adding fire protection sprinklers, fire alarms, and fire extinguishers. These desirable and beneficial devices must work with the walls, doors, windows, building structure, HVAC, and electrical components to form a system of fire prevention. Since these components serve other functions as well, their role in the fire prevention system cannot be known by looking alone. The identical material can be part of a fire prevention system in one application but not in another. And materials that look the same may have completely different fire prevention qualities. Relevant information is needed and is discussed below.

The Purpose of Life Safety Measures

Fewer fires, smaller fires, limited smoke

The purpose of life safety measures is to minimize the fire and smoke that can injure people or damage a structure. This is accomplished first by controlling combustion devices, such as furnaces and hot water heaters, so fire from these sources is extraordinarily rare. (Reduction in open flame space heaters over the second half of the twentieth century was one of the largest contributors to decrease in residential fires.) The second approach is to use materials that ideally Do not burn, or if they do burn, burn slowly and make an acceptable amount of noxious smoke. Finally, fire suppression systems keep the fire small, and extinguish it quickly.

Get the occupants out, the firemen in, and save the structure

The overall goals are:

1. To notify and get the occupants out of the structure safely (except where impossible, such as hospitals and prisons—as discussed below)
2. To get the firemen in as safely as possible
3. To provide the firemen adequate direction about the location and nature of the fire.

These goals require Fire-resistant construction for fire and smoke containment, and safe exit ways and notification systems, such as fire alarms.

Occupancy Types, Building and Hazard Fire Ratings
How difficult is the "fire problem"

Occupancy types—the occupants' capacity for self preservation and rescue

The "occupancy type" describes the probable speed and complexity of self-rescue measures that the intended occupants can be expected to take in a fire. The first consideration is mobility. Occupants who can walk normally are best. Occupants who are partially or completely incapable, such as infants, nursing home occupants, and those temporarily incapacitated in healthcare structures, are worst.

The second consideration is whether occupants can and will respond predictably when a fire is identified. This response will vary with mental capacity, and may vary significantly even among normally functioning people. For example, schools are generally considered to require frequent regimented fire drills to achieve the level of awareness that might be considered normal in an office building, which uses few or no fire drills.

The final consideration is the familiarity of the occupants with their surroundings. It is best if all occupants, except the occasional visitor, are completely familiar with all parts of the structure through long-term daily use, as would occur in offices and factories. The other extreme is auditoriums and sports arenas where familiarly with more than a few parts of the structure is unlikely.

Building structure fire ratings
How long can the building withstand a fire before being unsafely damaged?

The fire rating of a structure defines the time materials can resist a fire before deformation is close. (This is well before collapse.) Wood will deform by charring until the reduced size compromises strength. Steel will deform with softening by heat (not melting). And, concrete and masonry will deform by crumbling. Wood will have around a 1/2 hour rating, steel around 1-hour, and concrete up to a 3-hour rating. Addition of fireproofing materials can improve these ratings.

But "around 1-hour" is not information you can take to the bank. The materials, thicknesses, and heights of the entire assembly determine the fire ratings. The components must be UL (Underwriters Laboratories) tested, and the assembly size must be calculated in accordance with building codes. The sizes of the assemblies are determined by long, multi-step calculations by architects and engineers. Common sense alone cannot safely second guess this process. But, the knowledge that these are specifically constructed assemblies where everything has a purpose, aids correct installation and avoids problems in maintenance and renovation.

Hazard types—how flammable are the contents and operations?

The "hazard type" describes the likelihood that the contents and operations will produce a fire. Office, residential, and retail occupancies (uses) strive to have as little hazard as possible, by careful control of combustion devices and selection of less flammable materials. Warehouse hazards can vary by the contents of the warehouse. Less flammable products, such as steel, carry a lower hazard rating than more flammable products, such as wood products or carpet. The highest hazard is in industrial operations that use flammable, corrosive, toxic, or explosive materials.

There can be multiple hazard types for each occupancy type. Precise determination of the combination of occupancy and hazard types takes knowledge, experience, and calculation. The result makes sense, but cannot be determined by common sense alone.

The physical responses—fire walls, fireproofing, and fire protection systems—required by occupancy and hazard types are specified by building code. These codes are hundreds of pages long and written in language only a lawyer could love. Understanding and applying these rules must be left to the architectural design professional. However, the common sense ideas behind the rules are discussed here to give an understanding of what is being done and why.

For example, a hotel convention center would contain the assembly areas of the convention center, public areas such as the lobby, small meeting rooms, a commercial kitchen, and the residential hotel rooms above—many of which are different occupancies and hazards. Realization of why different construction will be required for each room is helpful. When originally constructing the building, the dividing line between these parts of the building and the fireproofing, fire protection, mechanical, and electrical requirements must be known. These requirements must be considered with even the smallest remodeling project—where moving a single wall or moving or removing a single mechanical or electrical device from one occupancy to another could destroy the continuity of a fire compartment—rendering it useless—with possible disastrous results.

Occupancy type, building and hazard ratings are interactive

All three work together to make a safe building. The occupancy type will limit the choice and specify the dimensions of possible structures. And changes in hazard rating can require changes in building structure or restrict possible occupancies. So all parts of the life safety system must be specified for each project. Common sense, intuition, and rules of thumb alone are not enough.

Fire Control By Limiting the Fire's Fuel and Air

Build with less flammable materials

Use of less flammable materials—steel, concrete, and masonry—has long been normal in industrial structures. Commercial structures, where a more decorative "softer" feel of fabrics and wood is desired, have used more flammable materials. But, improvement in these materials over the last half of the twentieth century has been huge. Fire retarding additives have improved engineered wood products (plywood, particle board, and OSB), and are now stocked in commercial supply houses. Surface-applied flame retarding chemicals can be added to fabrics and solid woods. Improvement in all aspects of synthetic fabrics has made them more Fire-resistant. This reduction in flammability without compromise of material choice or significant cost increase is now the norm in building construction—as well as interior furnishings and window treatments. These improvements lag in residential construction.

Shut off the fuel supply

Wherever a significant volume of pressurized flammable gas or liquid is delivered, this supply is stopped when a fire is sensed. The usual method is to have a fire alarm signal close a powered valve in the fuel supply line. This method is used in industrial fuel handling systems, commercial kitchens, and very large commercial buildings. Few small commercial buildings and fewer residential buildings use this method.

Shut off the air supply

Most commercial structures over about 2,000 sf (with about 2,000 cfm air supply) will automatically shut down the mechanical ventilation blower when fire is sensed. In small commercial buildings without a central fire alarm, this is done by a stand-alone smoke detector in the return air duct. In larger buildings, the central fire alarm system is used. The blower and the combustion source for heating are interlocked—so shutting down the blower also shuts down the flame source. This has a similar effect, but is a poor cousin, to the fuel shutoff described above.

Pressurize compartments to contain smoke

A further measure included in high-rise buildings and similar types of structures to control fire is to mechanically pressurize the space surrounding a fire compartment. This consists of completely shutting off all mechanically supplied air to the space, and mechanically pressuring the air on the other side of the fire compartment. This prevents smoke infiltration into the corridors and adjacent compartments, or the floor above and below, and directs the smoke to the exterior.

Building Compartments—Keeping Fire and Smoke in a Small Box

Compartments to contain fire and smoke

The normal structure is compartmentalized into areas that will contain the fire and smoke originating in an area. The size of the compartment allowed is precisely calculated by a combination of the occupancy and the hazard types as described above. An example of the possible size ranges of the compartments is: warehouses 100,000 sf, retail space in a single-story shopping center 30,000 sf, healthcare occupancy 4,000 sf.

For the highest hazards, where large quantities of highly flammable or explosive materials are contained, a reinforced fire-proof room restrains the blast with heavy reinforcing on all six sides except one small location designed as a point of blast relief. A smoke hatch on the roof, or a wall panel (usually measuring about 3 by 5 feet) that has a weaker connection and will fly out of the wall relieves and directs the smoke or pressure of the explosion to an acceptable location.

Compartments for safe occupant exit and fireman entrance

These compartments are constructed by using fire-rated walls, ceilings, and floors to build a six-sided box around the compartment. The materials used are typically noncombustible concrete, steel, masonry, and gypsum drywall. Using Underwriters Laboratories (UL) tested assemblies when building these assemblies, you must use exactly the components specified in the test. For example, if the test specifies 1/2" drywall, then using 5/8" drywall, even though it would seem to be better, is a failure. Floor, ceiling, and wall assemblies will commonly have fire ratings of one to three hours. Four hours is possible, in some cases, from a single assembly.

The fire rating describes the time it will take for a fire of a specified temperature (about 1,200–1,500°F) burning on one side of the wall to increase the temperature on the other a specified amount, or cause the wall to distort by a specified dimension, or collapse. If the fire-rated walls perform within these limits, the corridor formed by these walls will permit safe travel—by the occupants going out and the firemen coming in.

Fireproofing (ratings) to maximize the structure's resistance time

All of the structural components of a building—floors, columns, beams, walls, and roofs—can be, but are not always, fireproofed to maintain their necessary strength. Fire will damage wood by surface charring and then burning, steel by heating until the structure bends and buckles, and concrete will crumble. In all cases, structural failure occurs long before complete combustion or melting.

Fireproofing includes surrounding the structural component with Fire-resistant construction, such as masonry, concrete, drywall, or a sprayed-on insulating material. Less common are intumescent materials that expand when heated to provide a thicker insulating layer. Again, 1–3 hour fire ratings are common, and a 4-hour rating is possible with a single layer of fireproofing material.

The fire compartments for exit and the fireproofing for the basic structure are made of the same materials. They may even be close and touch, or may even occasionally be the same. They are both working for fire safety, but in different ways—and this distinction must always be remembered. For example, if a column is enclosed in a fire-rated wall, this wall is also serving as the fire rating for the column structure. If the wall is later removed, separate fireproofing must be added to the column. Or, if the occupancy of an existing building is changed, fireproofing of the entire structure may have to be upgraded. This is a complete system, not just a stack of bricks!

Making Fire Barriers Complete and Continuous

Fire stopping the penetrations—seal all small holes

The fire and smoke compartments must be continuous—without gaps, breaks, or penetrations. So, when multiple penetrations occur, such as pipes, conduit, and ducts, each and every one must be sealed so that the hole surrounding the penetration achieves the same fire rating as the overall wall. This is done by fire stopping caulks, putties, insulations, and related sheet metal assemblies. These again are all UL-tested assemblies that must be installed in accordance with the directions. Common sense and intuition does not preclude knowledge here—if it isn't tested and labeled Do not use it.

Fire stopping is not a small task. For occupancies such as a healthcare facility with huge amounts of piping and conduit, the cost of the fire stopping can exceed the cost of the wall. Scheduling the fire stopping construction early, when accessibility is greatest, is the best opportunity for cost reduction.

Fire dampers in HVAC ductwork—seal these large holes too

For HVAC ductwork penetrations, the interior of the ductwork area must also be considered. Usually, for one-hour walls, the exterior of the ductwork is considered sufficient fire barrier, and no additional measures are needed on the interior. For fire ratings greater than one hour, a fire damper must be installed inside the duct where it penetrates the wall. A fire damper is a piece of sheet metal that closes to make the wall barrier continuous. This damper can be activated by a fusible link (melted by fire) or a motor activated by a fire alarm signal. (Note: This damper then becomes a mechanically serviceable part and access panels must be installed in the area of the fire damper for service. Include this space in design and layout.)

Doors—close, latch, and stop the smoke and fire

Doors and frames in a fire-rated wall must have a similar fire rating as the surrounding wall. Usually the fire rating is just a little less than the wall—a one-hour wall may require 45-minute doors, a two-hour wall may require 90-minute doors. The exact requirements are specified by code and must be tested and labeled. The doors must also be self-closing and latching (so they cannot be pushed open by air, fire or smoke pressures). If these self-closing doors must usually be held open for convenience, the hold-open device must be connected to a fire alarm activated release device that closes the door automatically in a fire.

Interior windows are part of the fire barrier too

Windows in a fire-rated wall must similarly be fire rated. The frames are fire rated in the same way as doorframes described above, but the size of a glass is usually limited to about 3 feet square. The glass can be wire glass—where small wires are embedded in the center of the glass. Wire glass is intended to withstand moderate heat, then shatter when cooled by the stream of a fire hose, but still remain in place. (Wire glass is not security glass.)

Specially formulated heat-resistant glass can be used. But, it is slightly discolored, wavy, and not completely clear, and about 20 times the cost of wire glass. Finally, larger fire-rated wire glass openings are possible with a "water curtain." Here, fire alarm-activated sprinklers located on both sides of the glass saturate and cool the glass. This solution is usually found where cost is of little concern.

Fire Exit Corridors From and Between Compartments

Get the occupants out, or suitably contain them in "safe compartments"

Upon notification of a fire, if the occupants are physically able and mentally alert as occurs in most situations, the occupants will exit through the fire corridors down the fire stairs to the exterior of the building and to safety.

However, if all of these conditions are not met, such as in a hospital, nursing home, institution for the mentally ill, or a prison, it is physically impossible to have the staff evacuate the immobile residents fast enough, or to have some undesirable residents on the streets. In these cases, the fire and smoke compartments serve to make safe that part of the building. The staff and the residents stay in the event of a fire, and the fire corridors are not used for immediate evacuation of the occupants.

The second case requires more fireproof materials and more fire prevention systems. However, if one were to attempt to remodel this more hazardous type of occupancy into a less hazardous office occupancy, these fire corridors would have to be added—which might be unfeasible. More demanding occupancy and hazard requirements mean different, but not necessarily universally better, measures are needed.

The basic understanding described above is necessary to understand wet fire protection systems, sprinklers, and fire alarm systems. The building of compartments, fire protection sprinklers, and fire alarms are all using the same theories—to achieve the same goals—and you cannot understand the purpose of one, without understanding the purpose and use of the others.

Get the firemen in

Fire-rated corridors between fire-rated compartments permit the firemen to gain safe access to evacuate occupants, and fight the fire. The corridors exist for these reasons in all occupancies. Proper fire rating of the structure is critical for the safety of the firemen during fire fighting operations.

Fire Protection Sprinklers

Fire protection sprinklers keep fires small and short

The purpose of fire protection sprinklers is to sense fire and spray water on it so it stays small, local, and is quickly extinguished. (In industrial applications, where water cannot extinguish chemical fires, foam and other chemicals can be used.)

Where the water comes from—water service of the required volume and pressure

It is feasible to mechanically pump the water from surface water such as lakes or rivers, but the most common source is the city water mains. The size of the water line required for fire protection is far larger than the size of the water line typically required for domestic plumbing. For example, if a 1" water line is adequate for plumbing, a 4" water line might be required for fire protection. The number of fire protection sprinkler heads (which are related to the area of the building, plus the pressure required to reach the highest point) and their probability of discharge determine the size of the line.

The pressure that is available at the water main is determined by placing pressure meters on the closest and the adjacent fire hydrants near the point of connection. Then the fire hydrants are opened and fully discharged, and the initial pressure and flow and the drop over a period of about 10 minutes is measured. These tests are witnessed by the fire department and then recorded as the accepted pressure available at the main at that point. It is common that the city pressure will be adequate for a single story, and sometimes up to a three-story-building.

If greater pressure is required, a fire pump must be added. This fire pump boosts the water pressure and must be powered by a separate electrical service independent from the building electrical service. The entire service entrance conduit is concrete encased, and typically dyed red. The separate service is required, because in a fire, a fireman will first shut off electrical power to the building, to allow safe fighting of the fire—but the fire pump must continue working.

Separate fire protection sprinkler water to protect the potable water purity

The water in the fire protection piping may stand stagnant for years. Some rust from the interior of the pipes, the oil from the pipe cutting thread, and bacteria will foul this water. When draining down an existing fire protection system, 6"-8" of drain water in a bucket will obscure the bottom. Although this is of little concern if sprayed on a fire, it is of great concern if mixed with water intended for plumbing use inside the building.

A very common approach is to use the large fire protection line from the city main to the building for domestic water. This ensures continuous water flow through the fire protection line to prevent stagnation. The water going to domestic plumbing and the fire protection are then separated in the building by double back-check valves that prevent the fire protection water from siphoning back into the domestic systems if pressure drops at the main. The goal, although difficult to achieve, is to have no more than 6' of dead end piping for any domestic water system. Although this is the most common arrangement, some city water and fire departments require separate fire and domestic water mains from the street to building.

Two other supervisory components are added to this service entrance to signal system shutdown or water flow caused by sprinkler activation. One is a tamper switch, which sends an electrical signal to the fire alarm system if any valve is closed that prevents water flow to the fire protection system. The second is a flow switch that is a small flat piece of metal inserted into the piping which is pushed aside by water flow and sends an electrical signal to the fire alarm system. These signals must be sent back to the fire department, as described in fire alarm systems below.

The final component is the fire department connection, which is an exterior male connection onto which the fire department can attach a hose and mechanically pressurize the system from the pumps on the fire trucks. This is used in the event that the fire pump fails, or the pressure in the building fire lines is inadequate to supply the fire protection sprinklers. These are typically called Siamese connections and are two-headed fixtures on the exterior of the building located conveniently for fire truck access.

Distribution of the Fire Protection Sprinkler Water

Risers (vertical)

The sprinkler water distribution rises vertically through the building in pipe risers. These are vertical pipes located in an area most useful to the firemen, typically the stairwells. Fire hose connections, and sometimes fire hoses, are located on each floor so the firemen can fight the fire in that location. The firemen are assumed to have a maximum of 150' of hose, so if the fire risers are more than 150' apart, additional fire hose cabinets must be added. And, the 150' distance is actually physically measured by rolling out the fire hose and seeing if it reaches the most remote point. So corridors and obstructions must be taken into consideration. Some small remodeling projects can require large fire protection changes to maintain the maximum 150' distance.

Mains and branches (horizontal)

From the risers, a grid work of mains (larger pipes) and branches (smaller pipes) cover each floor area. This grid work may be, but is not always, zoned with 2–4 zones per floor, somewhat corresponding to fire compartments. But there will be more fire compartments then fire protection zones.

The purpose of the zoning is first to send a signal that identifies the location of the sprinkler discharge and fire. The other purpose is to limit the time of maintenance or renovation operations, to minimize cost and maximize safety. When a sprinkler head must be replaced, all water must be drained from the system. Draining and refilling an entire multi-story building can take 8–16 hours. And, no fire protection for the building will be working during this time.

Activating Fire Protection Sprinkler Heads
Fusible links and fire alarms are used

Wet pipe systems—common for most occupancies

With a wet system, all pipes are continuously filled with pressurized water. Each head consists of a diffuser to spread out water spray, a fusible link, and a restraining disk that holds the water back. When a fire melts the fusible link, the disk falls away, and water sprays on the diffuser (typically a star-shaped piece of metal on the bottom of the fire protection head) and spreads an even pattern of water droplets below. Only the activated heads will spray water, so water damage from a single head discharge may not be great. This is the most common type of system, and will be used unless low temperature or high hazards require other systems.

Dry pipe systems—when pipes must be protected from freezing

Dry pipe systems work similarly as the wet systems with one exception. In areas subject to freezing, the piping cannot be continuously filled with water. It is instead filled with pressurized air or nitrogen. When a sprinkler head opens, the pressure drops and a valve near the service entrance fills all the pipes with water and the activated sprinkler heads discharge. Dry systems are usually used in the attic spaces of sloped roof structures in cold climates (e.g. nursing homes, banquet halls, and country clubs). A dry pipe system in the attic is in addition to the wet system in the floor below, so cost and maintenance complexity increases.

Preaction systems—a dry pipe system with faster response

The preaction system is similar to the dry system except the signal to fill the pipe with water is provided by an electrical device, such as a smoke or fire detector rather than a drop in pressure at the head. (The system acts faster—before a sprinkler head is opened.) This system is used where higher hazards exist.

Deluge systems—fast response and complete saturation

In contrast to the three systems described above, there are no fusible links or restraining disks with a deluge system. All heads in a deluge system are always open. And the piping is not pressurized with air or nitrogen nor filled with water. When a signal is sent from a device such as a fire or smoke detector, the entire system is pressurized with water and all sprinkler heads in the system discharge at once. This is typically used where highly flammable materials are stored. The water damage to contents is large.

Halon—when you can not or won't use water

Water is partially or completely ineffective in fighting some chemical fires. The most common application is the exhaust hood over the fryer and stove in a commercial kitchen. Here the chemical Halon is used, which is a gas that can suppress fire, but can be breathed by people in small quantities and for the short times needed to suppress the fire. A small canister (about 10" wide and about 1'-3' high) is located next to the hood. Heads are placed over the hood and can either be activated by a fire alarm signal, or manually by hitting the panic switch near the canister.

Water must be avoided for electronics, such as computer rooms or phone switches, where even a little water will completely destroy the equipment. The activating devices can be far more sensitive—using smoke, heat, and light sensing. The contents are not water damaged, but at a cost. A Halon refill charge for a 20-foot by 30-foot room can equal five weeks' wages.

Chemical suppression systems for flammable or explosive contents

For some chemical fires, water has no effect and can even make a fire worse. In this case, pressurized foam discharge suppression systems are used. The cost and clean up are considerable.

Multiple systems in one structure

A single structure may include multiple types of wet fire protection systems. The most common example is an unheated roof structure above a single-story building, which would require both a wet and a dry system. Further, very early response systems, such as "a water curtain" (fire protection sprinklers sprayed on glass areas to increase their fire rating) may be needed. And rack storage in a warehouse can require a sprinkler grid on each rack. Further, fast response sprinklers for flammable liquid storage may also be needed.

Location of Fire Protection Sprinkler Heads

What must be protected—where main lines must be located

Every horizontal level in the building where a fire can originate or spread—including crawl spaces, floors above ceiling spaces, attics, or roof structures—may require a fire protection system. If the vertical heights between horizontal assemblies are small and all materials are noncombustible, such as a drop ceiling in a commercial office building, sprinklers may not be required in the above ceiling space. Reducing the size of fire compartments and using fire-proof materials can also remove the requirement for attic fire protection sprinklers in sloped roof structures.

These few examples show typical ways fire protection rules are applied—to show these rules are founded on sound principles. The specific determination of where fire protection sprinklers are required, is determined by calculations in the building codes determined by occupancy type, hazard type, size of the building, and materials of the building, and can be further altered by local fire department regulations. (These calculations are about as interesting as filling out income tax forms, and unfortunately, just as necessary.)

But realization that the entire system of fire compartments and protection systems are related is useful. Raising a roofline "just a little" can more than double the cost of a fire protection system. Moving a fire compartment "just a few feet" can make the whole system fail. The need for design by competent architects and engineers, and installation by educated construction personnel is obvious.

Warehouse shelves can greatly increase requirements

One special case that is frequently encountered and deserves mention is rack storage in a warehouse. Here, the spacing of the racks and the combustibility of the materials to be stored can require that each and every level of every rack have a separate branch line with heads. This should be noted because changing racks or changing the hazard of stored material in an existing building can trigger this more burdensome requirement. Since racks are generally installed after completion of the building, and fire protection sprinklers are contractor designed after contract award, they can be missed in the original building design. Missing such a large quantity of fire protection heads can mean the entire service entrance mains and distribution for the system are undersized, and will have to be torn out and completely replaced!

Spacing of fire protection sprinkler heads
Maximum and minimum head spacings and clearances

Spacing of fire protection heads for a light hazard occupancy should be no more that 15' on center with no head more than 7'6" from a wall. The heads can also be no closer than 4' apart and no closer than 4" from the wall. The minimum dimension is required because closer spacing can cause one head to discharge onto an adjacent head—keeping it cool and preventing it from activating when it really should. Personal property, cabinets, millwork, furniture, and equipment cannot be placed any closer than 18" from a sprinkler head (obstructing the water flow from an activated sprinkler head would prevent the needed coverage).

These rules are specified in NFPA13 (National Fire Protection Association) and are meant for construction personnel, so are written in plain language. (The building codes, which are not in plain language, determine if fire protection sprinklers are required, and the NFPA codes describe how to install them.) These are the basic rules of thumb for spacing. For more hazardous occupancies, the 15' spacing can decrease to 10', with a corresponding reduction in some of the other dimensions. For special cases, such as step decorative ceilings (atriums), there are further rules about minimum and maximum spacing. The exceptions are about 100 pages long. Careful engineering is required for each project, but knowing minimums, maximums, and clearances helps you to understand what can and should be done and why.

The fire protection sprinkler bonus—requirements eased, problems solved

The addition of fire protection sprinklers allows a reduction in other requirements. Fire compartment size can be increased, dead end exit corridors lengthened, and lower fire ratings used. Older buildings or a changed occupancy can have so many life safety deficiencies that a complete gut is the apparent economical way to achieve conformance. But addition of fire protection sprinklers can erase many deficiencies and make corrections minimal or nonexistent.

Fire Alarm Systems—Early Warning for Prompt Action

Fire alarm systems detect the presence of smoke and fire and transmit a signal to a responsible person for necessary action. They do not themselves suppress the fire. But, they can send a signal to devices that aid in suppressing the fire.

Sensing Devices in Commercial Applications

Smoke detectors

A smoke detector is typically installed at a ceiling location and can also be installed at above ceiling locations. In addition, a smoke detector can be installed in the return air stream near a mechanical unit for most mechanicals supplying over 2,000 cfm. (These duct detectors can be used to shut down the unit itself—even if no fire alarm system exists in the building.)

Heat detectors

Heat detectors can be installed on the ceiling, or above ceiling locations, and signal in the same way as a smoke detector. A smoke detector can sense smoke from even a very small fire that is not yet producing much heat. A heat detector can sense conditions that will soon produce a fire, even if a fire has not yet started.

Light, gas, and liquid detectors

Chemical sensors in the air, or systems that sense the presence of a liquid by differential electrical current at a floor line, or light sensitive devices that detect rapid variation in light produced by a fire, can be used in industrial applications—but are not typically residential or commercial applications. These devices have faster, more sensitive responses, but higher costs, and more false alarms.

Pull stations (switches people can activate)

Pull stations are a manual switch device typically located near an exit way or stairwell. An occupant, upon sensing a fire, can pull the switch and send a signal.

Tamper, flow, and trouble alarms

As discussed above in wet fire protection sprinkler systems, a tamper or flow switch can send a signal to the fire control panel. Another signal can be sent if a system is in "trouble," meaning that there is a mechanical or electrical malfunction in the system that requires attention—similar to the warning lights on the dashboard of a car. A tamper-and- flow signal can signal an alarm or activate a device, but a trouble light will not.

Fire Alarm Zoning and Notification

Locate the fire for faster response

The building fire alarm zones will be similar to the fire compartments discussed above, though less complete and less detailed. The fire department can be sent an alarm in two ways:

1. The fire control panel located near the entrance of the building will identify the location and nature of the device that sent the signal. This information helps the firemen fight the fire faster and safely.
2. A signal is also sent via telephone lines—either to an emergency response network or directly to the fire department, depending on the municipality. This will typically identify that there is a problem, but will not provide as much detail as the fire control panel.

Hard-wired "point to point" vs. addressable systems— both lower cost and increase precision

Before computers, the fire alarm devices had wires from the sensing device to a central collecting system down to the fire control panel, then back to actuate a device. Every device that sent a signal had a continuous wire to the device it activated—lots of wires. This made extensive zoning technically difficult, and made the diagnosis of any trouble in the system a time-consuming process of tracing wires.

Fire alarm systems are now "addressable" systems—essentially a computer. Each sensing or activating device, such as smoke detectors and heat detectors, contains a chip with a serial number. The fire control panel is a computer. When a device activates, it sends a signal to the computer, the computer sends directions as required—such as turn on lights and bells and close fire dampers. Because the computer understands the location of all the chips from the serial numbers, a more compact wiring system with fewer wires—a "back bone" carrying multiple signals on one wire—can be used. Individual wires from each device to the fire control panel are no longer necessary.

This makes the system far more economical to install, easier to maintain, and provides precise information on the location of a fire. The fire control panel can know the exact location of the smoke or heat detector that went off. Further, if a device must be replaced or relocated, the computer can be temporarily told that the particular device no longer exists. The maintenance procedure can be performed on this device and even if the procedures send a signal to the fire control panel, the signal will be ignored. The rest of the fire alarm systems will stay in operation throughout this procedure.

Devices activate to seal compartments

As described above, the fire alarm signal can activate the preaction and deluge fire protection systems, as well as the Halon systems for computer or electronics rooms. The system can also activate shutdowns of all mechanical blowers and pumps, closing of fire dampers, and closing of any doors held open by magnetic hold-opens. With these actions, the fire compartments are ensured and the mechanical system correctly evacuates air or pressurizes the surrounding compartments.

Monitoring of the fire alarm system—get fast help from afar

Fire alarm systems are electrically powered and work on electronic components. Therefore, continuous acceptable power is required, but this will be absent in a fire. Therefore, fire alarm systems must be powered—in the case of most commercial applications—by battery backup systems. These are typically calculated for the worst case occurring—the building must maintain the system in full operation for from 24- 72 hours depending on the occupancy type and municipality. For some applications, such as hospitals that have a second critical source of power, (an independent source of power from an entirely different power company grid) this critical power can also be used.

Fire Extinguishers—Local Use to Assist Exit, Not Fight a Fire

The function of fire extinguishers is for an occupant to temporarily suppress a fire in his local area, so he can exit to the outside. It is not intended as a fire-fighting tool. A typical fire extinguisher can be fully discharged in seconds and has limited capacity.

Fire extinguishers are typically rated by the source of the combustible material on fire as A, B, and C. These typically use a dry chemical, which discharges under pressure. They cover everything with a white powder that can take some effort to clean up. The alternative is a Halon fire extinguisher, which does not suffer from the same defect, but it is more expensive to use.

The required spacing of fire extinguishers in light-hazard occupancy requires that an occupant be no more the 75' from a fire extinguisher. So, in a long corridor fire extinguishers could be placed at 150' on center. In addition, there is also a requirement that the occupant can readily see the fire extinguishers. This will decrease the spacing, because of bends and corners, so that this requirement can be met.

At one time A, B, and C fire extinguishers were installed in different locations with the C type typically being a water-based system. This practice has faded. Now, except for the locations requiring Halon fire extinguishers, ABC fire extinguishers are at all locations so the possibility of error by misplacement is eliminated.

Summary

The goal of fire prevention is to keep a fire from starting at all. If it starts, make sure it burns slowly and in a controlled fashion, and keep it within manageable compartments. This way the people either get out, or if that is not possible, are suitably contained within safe compartments. Finally, the firemen come in to evacuate the residents and fight the fire.

Use of less flammable materials and minimizing flame sources is the first step in preventing fires. Stopping the supply of fuel and air to the fire is next.

Construction of building compartments keeps the fire and smoke local and assists occupant exit, and firemen entrance. Protecting the building structure with fireproofing materials makes the building safer for the firemen and minimizes permanent damage. Fire protection sprinkler systems and fire alarms all work together using the same principles to achieve the same goal. Understanding that all of these components, which are usually thought of separately, are part of a system makes correct installation of the components more understandable and likely.

In addition, understanding the relationship of components such as fire walls, fire stopping, and fire dampers gets all parts of the fire barrier installed at the same time, which increases productivity and decreases cost. This simultaneous increase in safety, productivity, and reduction in cost enhances project success.

3.14 Heating, Cooling, and Ventilation— Production and Movement

Making and moving heat and managing water as a coordinated system to produce a controlled environment

Heating is older than human history

Most people live in areas with an outside temperature range of about -20°F to 110°F. This 130°F range must be reduced to about a 40° range—centering around 70°F—for effective performance of tasks and comfortable living. Most objects have a greater normal temperature range—from -460°F to about 1,500°F. Adjusting these broad ranges to the narrower acceptable ranges for people is the purpose of heating, cooling, humidity control, and ventilation.

Caveman produced heat by burning wood, peat, coal, or by sitting in the sun. Cooling was not produced. But, the feeling of cooling was accomplished by shielding from the sun, airflow, and large stone buildings that tended towards the average daily (lower) temperatures—so the building would be cooler during the day. (Some low grade evaporative cooling was used in buildings for the very wealthy in ancient Egypt.) When these measures did not produce enough cooling, we suffered.

Cooling Production Started about 1900— Ventilation and Humidity Control Started about 1920

The cooling of things started in about 1900. Cooling for human comfort was phased in from about 1920 to 1950. Mechanical ventilation and humidity control in buildings followed the adoption of mechanical refrigeration. Before this time, operable windows or the natural leakage of poorly sealed buildings provided ventilation, or there was none at all. (Some very large public buildings use huge rooms and a stack effect of higher floors that act as a chimney and draw ventilating air through the building.) Once heating, cooling, humidity control, and ventilation were all introduced, they had to work as one coordinated system—and desired performance standards could be sought. Ideal temperature for human comfort is about 67°F to 79°F in winter and 74°F to 83°F in summer—with a relative humidity of 25% to 60%.

Heating Production—Easy to Achieve When 1,000º F Temperature Rise is Common
Usually a change of form produces the heat

Heating by burning fuel

Burning things most commonly produces heat. Common sources of fuel are:

Wood	3,500–7,000 Btu/pound
Fossil Fuels	
Coal	7,000–14,000 Btu/pound
Oil	140,000–150,000 Btu/gallon
Natural Gas	1,000 Btu/cubic foot
Propane or Butane	2,300 Btu/cubic foot
Electricity	3,413 Btu/kilowatt

When fuels are burned, they chemically combine with oxygen and produce the waste products of carbon monoxide or carbon dioxide, water, acids—and for solid fuel—ashes and soot. And there is an added bonus. The laws of physics state that whenever materials change form, energy is lost—usually in the form of heat, with lesser light and force. This bonus heat is added to the heat of combustion.

Heating—using electrical resistance, solar, and geothermal heat

The resistance of electric current running through a wire or heating element produces electrical heat. Most electricity is produced by burning coal or by a nuclear reaction—both of which are changes of form. Electric heat also uses changes of form from afar (including disposal of all the waste products). Electricity produced by water (using hydro-electric dams) or wind-powered turbines are exceptions to the normal heat production by change of form.

Solar heat can be produced by solar cells, which convert sunlight directly into electricity. Heat produced this way is not now cost competitive. Solar heat can also be produced by flat-plate collectors, which use water running over a light-absorbing surface. These can effectively heat water up to about 130°F. But, this is less than the over 180°F temperature needed for effective building heating. (An exception is in floor radiant heating, which operates between 90° and 120°F.) Multiple mirrors focusing the sunlight on a central collection device can reach these higher temperatures. Although effective, a large land space in a sunny area is required (but seldom available).

Geothermal heating is also possible in areas where the cracks in the earth's crust bring heat to the surface. The country of Iceland is such a place and uses lots of geothermal energy for heating. Geothermal heating is effective in the few select areas where the geothermal sources are near the point of desired use.

Closed-loop water source heat pumps can operate in most locations to produce cooling from the earth. Here, supply and return pipes are placed vertically in the earth to depths of hundreds of feet. The cooler earth extracts heat from the circulating water.

Heating—unintentional sources of heat production

People, machines, light fixtures, sunlight, and the temperature of outside air will all produce heat within a building. This unintended heat production can be managed by selection of efficient machines and light fixtures, and shading from sunlight. But, all of the rest of sunlight and outside air must be included in heating and cooling calculations.

Heating Production Machines—Use Various Methods

Boilers—heating water for distribution

A boiler is an enclosure to heat water under pressure to produce steam or hot water. Fossil fuels and electrical resistance are the common heat sources. Steam boilers were originally more common, but this is an accident of history. When steam engines were used on-site to produce mechanical power, steam was a waste byproduct used for free heating.

However, steam heat had disadvantages. First, steam was produced and delivered under pressure, which required knowledgeable personnel—called stationary engineers—to monitor and adjust the system to avoid explosions. Also, valves and control points throughout the system were noisy, leaked, and required regular maintenance. Finally, when the steam condensed to liquid water in the distribution system, it had to be drained by gravity or pumped back to the boiler, which affected space and maintenance requirements. Use of hot water—rather than steam—eliminated many, but not all, of these disadvantages.

Heating the ventilation air stream directly

Combustion of fuels can occur in a closed radiator device (heat exchanger) in the air stream. This has the advantage of simplicity of operation—with few moving parts. It has the disadvantage that if the heat exchanger cracks, poisonous combustion gases can be injected into the ventilation air stream. This disadvantage is eliminated if electrical resistance heating is used. A combustion source in the air stream is used in most single-family houses and most commercial ventilation systems for buildings up to about 30,000 square feet. Institutional occupancies, such as healthcare facilities, specifically prohibit this system.

Heat exchangers—maximizing system advantages, eliminating disadvantages

A heat exchanger is a radiator-type device that transfers the heat from a production source to a delivery or storage system to achieve some benefit—or eliminate some disadvantage. For example, a steam boiler could have a heat exchanger in a hot water heat distribution system—making the heat source steam but the distribution system a simpler hot water system. Or, a steam or hot water boiler could have a heat exchanger in the ventilation air stream to eliminate the possibility of any combustion gases entering the ventilation system. Or, a heat exchanger can be used from a hot water boiler to a hot water heating system so that the water within the boiler can be carefully conditioned to avoid buildup of mill scale in the system—thereby increasing the efficiency and lengthening the life of the boiler. Heat exchangers can also reclaim and transfer heat or cooling from exhaust air to incoming make up air to save energy.

Cooling Production—Harder to Achieve with a 20º F Temperature Drop
Change of state produces the cooling

Cooling is a more difficult problem than heating. The temperature ranges are smaller, and the laws of physics are against you. The available cooling sources are fewer, and humidity control must be managed at the same time.

Water freezes at 32°F and human comfort temperatures at about 70°F are sought. This is only about a 40° range whereas heating sources have about a 1,000°F range. As stated above, the laws of physics dictate that heat is a natural byproduct of physical changes of state, which is a disadvantage when you're trying to produce cooling. Only a few chemical reactions produce cooling. However, these are not abundant, economical, or used for building cooling.

Cooling is produced by a change of form—from solid to liquid or liquid to gas. These changes from a more dense form to a less dense form produce cooling. However, to again increase the density of the refrigerant—to start the cooling cycle again—energy is required and heat is produced. Since the production of cooling involves both heating and cooling, effective cooling requires selecting a suitable location for the cooling and for the rejected heat. Or stated another way, cooling production does not actually occur—cooling is only the absence of heat—so it is a location and transportation problem more than a production problem.

Humidity is a further complication. Cooling air decreases the air's humidity carrying capacity. Decreasing humidity can be a desirable goal; however, condensation of humidity is undesirable, so location must be managed.

Cooling Production Machines
Change of state—then moving the heat to a suitable location

Cooling from the surrounding environment

Cooling from the surrounding earth is a very old idea—for example, a root cellar for storing out-of-season vegetables. The cooling from basement walls or landscaped areas on roofs are included in modern cooling system designs. Intake of outside air when it occurs at the desired temperature is similarly part of modern design. Cooling from lakes and streams is possible although frequently frowned upon, since you are ejecting heat to your neighbors.

Evaporation—when humidity conditions are right, cooling occurs naturally

The change in state from liquid water to water vapor produces cooling. An old example is porous earthenware water storage jars, where some of the water seeps through the earthenware, evaporates, and then cools the water within the jar. A similar idea is used for evaporative condensers. Here, the heat-ejecting source (an exterior condenser) uses the evaporation from the surface of the condenser to produce the cooling. The disadvantage with evaporative coolers is that they only function well in a narrow range of temperatures and humidities, so their use is limited.

Absorbers—cooling with steam

An absorber refrigeration machine cools using chemical lithium bromide, water as refrigerant, and steam to separate the lithium bromide and water. This is a four-chamber machine, which uses a four-step process.

1. The refrigerant liquid water is sprayed on a heat exchanger containing the water to be cooled. As it cools, the heat exchanger vaporizes the water and moves it to the next chamber.
2. The water refrigerant vapor is strongly attracted by the lithium bromide and combines to form a diluted solution of water and lithium bromide. This change from vapor to liquid produces heat, which is removed by a heat exchanger in a cooling tower.
3. The dilute solution is pumped to a third chamber and steam drives off the water vapor and a concentrated lithium bromide solution returns to the second chamber.
4. Water vapor refrigerant moves to a fourth chamber where it is condensed to liquid water again using condenser water in a cooling tower.

Absorbers were used in buildings starting in about 1890. When buildings were heated by steam and boilers already existed, absorbers made sense. As hot water or electrical heating systems have taken the place of steam, use of absorbers has declined. One reason for absorbers' early adoption was that centrifugal compressors—used in an alternate refrigeration method—could not then run faster than about 50 rpm. As compressor speed increased (now 1,500 rpm is common), this comparative advantage disappeared.

Compressors and Engineered Chemical Refrigerants

A compressor is a mechanical device that applies pressure to change a refrigerant chemical from a gas (vapor) to a liquid. This change of state produces heat, which must be ejected to a suitable location. Cooling is produced when this liquid refrigerant drops in pressure and expands to a vapor.

Refrigerants

Almost all chemicals will give up heat when changing to a less dense state. Refrigerant chemicals are selected or engineered to change state at a temperature that is useful for the cooling effort. Ammonia was one of the early refrigerant chemicals and is still in use today for food-service freezers. Water, carbon dioxide, and sulfur dioxide were also early refrigerants.

For use in buildings, a temperature change within 2° or 3°F of 55°F in the air stream is sought. This optimizes cooling while minimizing a condensation problem. To achieve change of state at this temperature, engineered blends of the chemicals chlorine and fluorine with hydrocarbons from fossil fuels were developed. These engineered chemicals must be not highly toxic, noncombustible, non-explosive, and non-corrosive. Some examples are:

For reciprocating compressors:
      R-12   dichlorodifluoromethane
      R-22   monochlorodifluoromethane

For centrifugal compressors:
      R-11   trichloromonofluoromethane
      R-113   trichlotrifluoroethane

Big words for complicated chemicals—and these are only a few. A recent edition of the Uniform Mechanical Code lists 47 types of refrigerant.

Compressor Types and Their Uses

Compressors are chosen for energy efficiency, simplicity of operation, ease or absence of maintenance, ability to vary cooling output, optimal size, and sound produced. Different compressor types were developed to optimize one or more of these characteristics.

Reciprocating compressor—strong performer with many sizes, but higher maintenance

A reciprocating compressor is a piston machine—similar to the engine of an automobile. But instead of producing power, an external motor (usually electric) drives the pistons to produce compression. The reciprocating compressor can operate at low speed. It was one of the first compressors and they are still in use today. They range in size from the smallest compressor, such as for a household refrigerator, to the largest commercial installations. These have good energy efficiency and use variable cylinder displacement to vary the cooling output, while maintaining constant speed of rotation. They, however, have many moving parts and, therefore, are high maintenance.

Centrifugal compressor—ease of maintenance but noisier

A centrifugal compressor has a spinning rotor that moves the refrigerant from the center of the rotor outward to produce compression. Centrifugal compressors operate at high speeds and tend to be noisier. They are most commonly used as package units within a chilled water refrigeration and evaporation system. Their energy efficiency is slightly less than the reciprocating compressor; they have fewer moving parts and, therefore, lower maintenance.

Scroll compressor—ease of maintenance for small to midsize uses

A scroll compressor is similar to a centrifugal compressor except the refrigerant enters at the tip of the rotor and is compressed to the center where it exits into a dome at the top of the compressor. These compressors range from the very smallest appliance compressor to midsize commercial compressors of the 5 to 60-ton range.

Helical rotary "screw" compressors—strong performer for larger uses

Helical rotary compressors use two parallel screws to compress the refrigerant along the length of a shaft. This type of compressor was originally used to compress air and has been adapted later to compress refrigerant. Wide use across a range of sizes is not found. Chilled water applications in the 70 to 450-ton range are common. These are energy-efficient, reliable, and can vary the cooling output.

Oil lubrication and hermetic seal—choices that influence maintenance

Compressors have internal moving parts that require lubrication. Compressors will have a mechanism for distributing oil for lubrication, and also continually separating it from the refrigerant chemical. A hermetic seal—a case that encloses both the compressor and the drive motor in one housing—can simplify the lubrication process. It also reduces sound. However, it is sealed at the factory and, in most cases, is not repairable. If it breaks, you replace it.

Heat Ejection Devices
Choosing a suitable location and means to eject heat

Air Cooling-few moving parts, so reliable, but performance limited at high outside temperatures

Air cooling can use convection of air over a heat exchanger, usually assisted with a fan to cool the refrigerant outside the heat exchanger. It has the disadvantage that as the temperature of the refrigerant increases due to load or the exterior temperature increases, the ability to eject heat declines. It has the advantage that the condenser itself has no moving parts, so is simple and reliable. This system is used in many single-family homes and small commercial projects. It can also be used in larger projects when extreme water conservation is a consideration, such as desert operations.

Water cooling—increasingly prohibited

Using the cooler water of wells, rivers, and lakes was once common—a source of cooling that could be obtained for only the cost of pumping. However, since you are discharging the heated water downstream to your neighbors, this is increasingly frowned upon, and frequently prohibited.

Cooling towers—commonly used to let the evaporation of some of the water cool the rest

Cooling towers spray liquid water near the top and a portion evaporates and cools the remaining liquid water. So, the cooling effect of evaporation—not a cooler temperature of the water—produces the cooling. Cooling tower sides have partially open slats to prevent wind from dislodging the water sideways, while still allowing the intended vertical airflow. And fans can be added at the top of the cooling tower to accelerate this airflow. This is the most common method of cooling for midsize and large projects.

Managing the refrigerant chemicals—toxic materials, disposal can be expensive

Residential and small commercial projects use refrigerant chemicals to expand in the heat exchanger. If the heat exchanger cracks, the occupants of the building must be capable of self-rescue to avoid injury from the refrigerant chemical. However, when self-rescue cannot be assumed—such as in facilities housing the extremely old or young, medical facilities, and prisons—the refrigerant cannot be allowed to expand in the air stream. A heat exchanger with a water-based system in the air stream is required instead.

Ejection of waste refrigerant into the atmosphere is increasingly restricted for environmental reasons. When maintenance operations or demolition of the refrigeration machine is required, refrigerant chemicals must be pumped into containers and disposed of at a suitable location off site. If the discarded refrigerant can be recycled, disposal is close to the cost of the required labor. However, when the refrigerant becomes prohibited for environmental reasons, the disposal of the discarded refrigerant has a cost more related to environmental cleanup, which can be shockingly high.

Controlling Humidity—Humidification and Dehumidification

For machines and people—achieved by chemicals and cooling

Humidity control was first introduced to increase the efficiency of manufacturing processes. In about 1900, spinning machines for textiles would frequently jam if the air was too dry. "Air conditioning"—by adding moisture—was used to reduce these breakdowns. Maintaining adequate humidity levels to minimize static electricity that could damage electronic components is a more current example of controlling humidity.

Controlling humidity for the benefit of people is less rigorously and commonly achieved. It was one time thought that people needed 40 to 60% relative humidity. But it is now recognized that no one can sense the difference between 25 and 60% relative humidity. Further, most buildings do not even have a humidistat so existing conditions are unknown.

Chemicals to remove humidity require year-round heating

Desiccants are chemicals that naturally adsorb moisture. An example is the small pouch of chemicals that is included with a shipment of electronic components to adsorb moisture during shipment. Chemicals such as silica gel, activated carbon, activated alumina, and activated bauxites will absorb water and change in physical form but not chemical nature. The absorption process—changing water vapor to liquid water—produces heat. Blowing heated air over the chemicals reverses this process (desorption).

Another chemical system uses salts—chlorides and bromides suspended in liquid. This brine solution is sprayed in the air stream and water vapor is absorbed in the brine solution and dilutes it. It is then later concentrated (in a concentrator) by heating and spraying the solution in the air stream (to evaporate the water but not the brine) that is being ejected outside.

Once boilers were run year-round so dehumidification could be obtained at very low cost, and was common. Now, energy is expensive and boilers either do not run in the warm months or do not exist in buildings at all. So, these methods of dehumidification are rare. Desiccants can be used for very local limited applications, such as dryers on air compressors and pharmaceutical manufacturing equipment, but are not used for dehumidification of the building's cooling system.

Cooling to remove humidity—does not require year-round heating

Since air's ability to hold moisture decreases with temperature, cooling produces dehumidification. The humidification of air will always be a by product of cooling, but it can also be specifically sought. Lowering the temperature of the cooling water or refrigerant in the air stream, even a degree or two, can significantly increase the amount of dehumidification achieved—but at a cost of slight reduction in cooling.

Water or steam to increase humidity

Addition of water or steam into the air stream can rapidly and easily increase humidity. Because addition of humidity is far easier, humidification systems are far more common than dehumidification systems. However, in extremely cold climates, the task becomes quite large. In some freezing temperatures when very dry outside air is taken into the building for fresh air ventilation, the humidification required is huge—to bring it up to normal levels centering around 50%.

We can control humidity, but usually don't

Achieving an ideal humidity—with water removal by cooling, or water addition by injecting water vapor or steam—is fully achievable. In the 1950s, some mechanical systems cooled the air to a lower than desired temperature and then added steam to achieve both the desired temperature and humidity. This idea was achieved at the cost of additional heating equipment and energy cost. Since oil was then two dollars per barrel, energy costs were of little concern. Increased energy cost and the generally lower perceived value of precise humidity control now makes precise humidity control rare. Except when high tech machine considerations exist and humidistats are present (paper mills, pharmaceutical plants, tobacco storage, woodworking), precise humidity control is seldom sought.

Ventilation—Cooling, Odor and Fume Control, Replacing Lost Air

Ventilation is something we are only recently trying to achieve. Castles were drafty, windows leaked, and cracks were everywhere—less ventilation was desired. We now have the ability to seal buildings tightly, and the expectation of cooling makes ventilation standard.

Ventilation has three components:

Circulate air

First is the circulation of the air in the space to even out temperatures, odors, and provide cooling by evaporation. Mechanical ventilation can make it feel 14°F cooler at 50% relative humidity and about 7°F cooler at 100% relative humidity. Before mechanical ventilation systems, this was achieved by using very large rooms, windows, and local fans.

Exhaust undesirable odors and gases

The second component is to exhaust air and undesirable gases from the space. The types of exhaust are:

- General exhaust. Ventilation systems for human habitation require continually exhausting portions of the re-circulating air.

- Toilet exhaust. Toilet exhaust systems are required for odor control. Toilet exhaust systems are required even in buildings with no other mechanical exhaust requirements.

- Process exhaust. Process exhaust removes smoke, laboratory fumes and chemical fumes, and exhaust from industrial operations—such as dust control and removal.

Make up the exhausted air and provide fresh air

Fresh air is required as a companion to general exhaust and is required for all buildings designed for human habitation. Make up air is required to replace air mechanically exhausted or lost for other reasons. The other reasons can include internal combustion sources such as furnaces, hot water heaters, and fireplaces—where air is exhausted to flues—and air lost through openings such as doors and windows.

Any make up air must be fully heated or cooled to reach the temperature of other air in the space. These heating and cooling requirements must be included in the design of the mechanical system. Further, since the exhaust quantities will be variable and not entirely predictable, accommodations—shock absorbers in the fresh air system—must be included. Barometric reliefs or pressure sensors coupled with variable frequency drives can provide this relief.

Moving Air Through Ducts

Air is transported from a central heating, cooling, humidification, and ventilating unit to the points of use through ducts. Ductwork is most commonly made of 18–26 gauge sheet metal, black iron, galvanized steel, or aluminum. For exhausting flames, smoke, and hazardous materials, slightly heavier ductwork is used. Fiberglass and concrete materials are used occasionally.

Ductwork was once fabricated or heavily adjusted by a tradesman on the job site—using sheets of metal stock. Ductwork can now be fabricated off site using continuous roll stock in automated machines. The cost of the finished product fabricated in this way is close to equal to the raw material sheets stock used for job site fabrication—a cost advantage that makes off-site fabrication for orders over about 1,000 pounds desirable and compelling. These automated machines, however, do require computer-aided drawings of each piece to be fabricated—so engineering time and personnel must be allowed for this step.

Velocity and ductwork interior area work together

Velocity times the ductwork cross-sectional area equals the delivered air—cubic feet per minute. Increased velocity will deliver more air but it will also produce more sound. The acceptable velocity in the ductwork is determined considering the acceptable sound, the capacity of the ductwork to withstand pressure, and the speed of travel across heating and cooling coils and filters. Recommended velocities in lineal feet per minute that work with all these considerations are:

Application	Main ducts	Branch ducts	Cooling coils	Heating coils
Radio and TV recording studio	500	400	450	500
Residences	1,000	600	450	500
General offices	1,900	1,500	500	600
Industrial buildings	2,900	2,500	600	700

Friction loss—strictly limits velocity

Air moving through ductwork will contact the side of the ductwork and produce friction. The lowest ductwork surface area for a given volume of air will have the lowest friction. This means round ducts have the least friction, square ducts the next least, and rectangular ducts the most as shown by the following ductwork size and shape comparisons.

Equivalent ductwork sizes to move 1,000 cfm at 500 fpm

Duct size	Cross-sectional area	Ductwork area (sq in) per lineal inch
19 inch round	283 sq in	60 sq in
18" x 18"	324 sq in	72 sq in
37" x 9"	333 sq in	92 sq in
110" x 4.5"	495 sq in	119 sq in

So, moving from round or square to rectangular increases both the cross-sectional area to overcome the additional friction and requires more ductwork material, which increases cost. If you try to increase the flow by trying to "cram more air through the ductwork," friction loss increases greatly. In this same example, at 2,000 cfm the friction loss increases 381% and at 3,000 cfm the friction loss increases 810%.

Other sources of friction loss

Bends—changes of ductwork direction—have the least friction when they are gradual and sweeping. Where a sharp turn is required, turning vanes—curved pieces of sheet metal in the duct—can be added to guide the air around the corner and reduce friction. Mechanical components such as heating and cooling coils and zone control devices in the air stream will also produce friction. They are unavoidable and must be included in the friction loss calculation. Roughness of the ductwork material will also increase friction. Sheet metal has the lowest friction but addition of internal insulation or the use of concrete ductwork will greatly increase friction.

Sealing ductwork to limit leakage—insulating to manage sound and temperature

Ductwork sizing is calculated as if there is no leakage. But ductwork is fabricated in small pieces and joined in the field. Even with the best workmanship, if the joints are not sealed, the system can leak up to 20% of its capacity. Mastic that is field applied by brush over these joints is used to correct this problem. Further, systems used to exhaust smoke—such as a kitchen exhaust or a laboratory hood exhausting radioactive material—have all joints in the ductwork continuously welded.

Ductwork is insulated to minimize thermal loss of air during transportation and to control sweating on the ductwork from cooled air. Insulation is also used to reduce the sound of airflow through the ducts.

Ductwork can have internal insulation applied at the off-site fabrication facility. This has the advantage of being economical and not requiring a later insulating step, and will reduce sound. It has the disadvantage that it increases friction within the ductwork, and in humid environments can allow bacterial growth. For this reason, it is frequently prohibited for healthcare environments. (A limited amount of sound insulation near mechanical units may still be used.)

External insulation can be field applied after the installation of the ductwork. It is more expensive, can be damaged by careless tradesman, and has little sound reduction capability. However, it is the only choice where bacterial growth within the ductwork is a consideration.

Practical limits mean a narrow range of choices for each application

The consideration of velocity, friction loss, and sound impose practical limits. Main ductwork runs start to lose performance at about 100 lineal feet and about 300 feet is the practical limit. After 300 feet, supplemental in-line booster fans must be added—and these fans are noisy.

After the point the air discharges from the ductwork through the grille, the airflow must maintain a velocity of 150–300 fpm. This velocity begins to diminish at 25 feet and stops at about 40 feet.

The other practical consideration is the ductwork size. Ductwork is large and must be considered in the design of the building. And the design of the building will influence the ductwork sizing. For example, high-rise commercial buildings will have a floor-to-floor height of 12'-6". If 9-foot ceilings are needed, this will determine within a couple of inches the height of the ductwork that can be used. Choosing an occupancy that requires larger ductwork may simply be impossible—no matter how much you beg or threaten your designers and contractors.

Piping—an easier transportation problem

The flow of heating and cooling water through pipes follows the same principles of friction, pressure, and velocity as the ductwork. However, since the pipes are always round, for a given capacity there will be a single best size. Sound consideration is minimal and in-line booster pumps are far quieter. Further, piping that delivers an equivalent heating or cooling capacity is far smaller. A supply and return pipe of 1 inch cross-sectional area would equal the heat delivery capacity of ductwork with 5 square feet of cross sectional—so space considerations are of less importance.

Storing heat and cold—even out requirements and reduce equipment size

Heating and cooling needs vary over time. But, if heating and cooling are only produced for immediate use, the mechanical equipment must be sized for the peak load. If heating and cooling can be stored for later use, smaller mechanical equipment can produce the same result.

The first location for storage is the building itself. Before mechanical refrigeration, massive thick masonry buildings tended towards the average temperature of a 24-hour day and therefore, were cooler during the daytime peak temperatures. Modern commercial buildings use the same concept but to a lesser extent. These buildings typically shut off most mechanical systems at night. By varying the timing of the shutoff to match the exterior temperature variations, energy savings can be achieved. And the building will seem "just right" when the office workers return in the morning. (This does require skilled personnel to control the mechanical equipment to match weather predictions.)

Although this saves energy for the overall building, it has very noticeable implications if anyone wants to work during the shutoff hours. That party must pay the cost for the entire building. This restricts off-hour operation for tenants—a very large implication that is easy to overlook. The heated water in a hot water heating system also will have a storage function that will continue to heat even if no new hot water is being provided.

Cooling can be obtained from the earth. That basements are cooler is well known. Mechanical systems can drill and pipe hundreds of feet into the earth and then use the cooling effect of the earth for the mechanical system. Similar systems exist where a below-grade reservoir of water is frozen and then later thawed. This can cycle daily to even out the load on the refrigeration equipment, or in very cold climates a larger reservoir can be frozen using the colder outside air in winter to freeze the ice for cooling in the summer. These systems, however, must estimate the times of use and heat loads when constructing the building. And, later requests for longer hours or higher heat loads may overtax the capacity of the reservoir. Also, upgrade may be economically prohibitive.

Controls—Telling the Heating and Cooling Where to Go

Controls are a system of sensors throughout the building that observe the conditions of temperature, humidity, and ventilation, and then send a signal to remote valves and dampers and mechanical equipment to adjust the existing conditions to the desired conditions. It is a system for maintaining the desired conditions automatically.

Pneumatic systems—once all we had, still reliable

Pneumatic systems use compressed air through small tubing to send a signal from the sensing device, such as a thermostat, to an actuating device, such as a control to start the boiler. There can be some collection relays that gang a few signals together, but it is essentially a point-to-point connection of the sensing and activating device with tubing. The tubing is installed with the construction of the building and any later revision is a renovation effort—so it frequently is never done.

These systems are reliable, and the parts are interchangeable supply house parts, so this system still can be maintained even if parts are discontinued or a supplier company goes out of business. Before personal computers, this was the only system that economically existed, and many are still functioning well after 50 to 100 years. There's no compelling reason to replace such a system, but no pneumatic systems are being installed presently.

Digital electronic systems—more economical control—automated energy management made possible

Widespread use and declining cost of the personal computer—starting in about 1980—made electronic systems feasible. Here, one electronic signal is sent from a sensing device to a central computer. The central computer then sends a signal to an actuating device. How, when, and where the signal is sent is determined by the computer program.

A digital electronic system has several advantages. First, it is more economical to install than the pneumatic system. Once installed, changes can be made by providing different instructions to the computer without any construction changes. Also, more complex instructions can be provided so automated energy management of the entire building is possible. This both increases energy efficiency and reduces the number of personnel necessary to walk the building and make manual adjustments.

The only drawback is that digital systems and their components tend to be proprietary products from a single manufacturer. Delivery of parts and provision of maintenance service can be slow, surly, and expensive. Some vendors will have minimum start-up costs equal to one day's wages for any job—even one taking several minutes to perform. And, the service may be provided weeks later than desired. The business practices of the digital control vendors must be carefully considered before system selection.

Summary

Changing the form of the fuel—by burning—usually produces heat. Since fuel will burn at about 1,000°F—far above the temperatures desired for human use—heating is an easier problem than cooling and was solved first.

Cooling is produced by the change of state of materials from solid to liquid and liquid to gas. When this change in state moves in the opposite direction, heat is produced and it must be discharged to a suitable location. The suitable location will be an exterior air- or water-cooled condenser or a cooling tower.

Since cooling will produce condensation of water and water freezes at 32°F, a narrow range of only about 20°F between the coolant and the desired temperature is practical. This requires larger pipes and ducts for cooling than for heating.

Ventilation is required to cool by convection, exhaust undesirable gases and odors, make up the exhausted air, and provide fresh air to replace the oxygen used. Ducts are large and cause sound and friction loss, and cost must be minimized—so ductwork sizes for a type of building have standardized to within a few inches. Change of use of an existing building to a different type with different ventilation requirements can present costly problems—some of which are insurmountable—such as not enough space for larger ductwork.

Increasing humidity can be readily achieved by spraying steam or water vapor in the air stream. Decreasing humidity can be achieved by desiccants or by cooling. The use of desiccants has been phased out for all but specialized applications. Removal of humidity is a natural byproduct of cooling, but additional dehumidification equipment is seldom added to achieve a precise humidity level. Most buildings up to 30,000 sf do not even have a humidistat, so precise levels of humidity are unknown.

The principles and common practices of heating and cooling production make a narrow range of choices available for each project type and size. For some smaller projects, there will only be one choice. But when more than one choice is available, these principles can assist an informed decision. These decisions can be further guided by knowledge about energy efficiency and the need for skilled maintenance personnel who will have an impact on successful operation for the life of the building.

3.15 HVAC (Heating/Ventilation/Air Conditioning) Systems of Distribution and Control

Seek a narrow range of efficient and effective solutions for each occupancy use

The Heating and Cooling Task

Heating and cooling things
Few requirements. Wide ranges of acceptable temperatures

Most parts of the building—concrete, masonry, and steel—can tolerate a wide range of temperatures—over 100 degrees F—and similar wide ranges of humidity. Contents such as electronic components can have a much narrower range of acceptable temperatures and humidities. But, there is no clear perception of acceptable ranges of temperature and humidity—if they're not damaged it is okay.

Heating and cooling people
People breathe—Required fresh air and exhaust adds complexity and energy work

People have a much narrower range of acceptable temperatures—just a few degrees. But they perceive different combinations of temperature and humidity as being equally comfortable. People also need fresh air, so outside fresh air must be provided—heated and cooled and adjusted for humidity. The amount of fresh air required is one of the driving forces in HVAC design for people. Exhaust is also required both to equalize the pressure produced by this additional fresh air and to control odors and fumes.

Heating Distribution Methods
Conduction and radiation is for heating only—convection is for heating and cooling

Conduction

Conduction heats an object by physically touching the warm heat source, as is done, for example, in radiant floors. The need for physical touching requires many or large conduction surfaces—and is a practical disadvantage. Further, conduction can only provide very limited cooling (about 56°F minimum for the cooling water) without condensation problems. And, it provides no ventilation. (Radiant cooling is used in hospitals where ventilation is separate and humidity is controlled.)

Radiation

Radiation heats the object it strikes without heating the entire space. This can be useful when the spaces are large and open to the outside. But cooling by radiation is not practical. (Heat flows only from hot to cold. But, the sensation of radiant cooling is produced since a cold surface will absorb all the radiant heat that strikes it and reflect none back to the person radiating the heat.) Further negative is ventilation is not possible.

Convection

Convection heats or cools by moving air of the desired temperature and humidity. Heating and cooling, humidity variation, and fresh air and exhaust can be provided. For these reasons, convection is the most common form of heating and cooling. Also, convection air can be filtered to improve indoor air quality.

Ventilation Refers to Airflow
Heating and cooling plus fresh air and exhaust—by convection

Fresh Air can be Vital

Outside fresh air is required for people. The minimum amount of fresh air and exhaust required varies by occupancy type—and is commonly expressed as:

Fresh Air Required by Square Foot or Occupant in cfm (cubic feet per minute)

Retail:	20 cfm per 100 square foot
Public corridors:	5 cfm per 100 square foot
Classrooms, private homes, and theaters:	15 cfm per person
Restaurants, offices, and gyms:	20 cfm per person
	(Figures will vary by code and standard)

These minimum percentages of outside fresh air by occupancy type are specified by code (a 2-page list), but these figures are frequently less than is needed in practice. For specialized applications, such as the portion of the hospital treating highly infectious patients, 100% of all ventilation air must be exhausted. So 100% of the ventilation air is outside fresh air.

For private residences and a few select occupancies, operable windows provide the fresh air. For all other occupancies, the fresh air is provided by mechanically ducted ventilation. Some of the air can be re-circulated, 10–20% typically, but up to 100% of outside air will be continuously added.

Distance separation required between fresh air intakes and exhaust
Common sense—but a frequently overlooked design requirement

Fresh air intakes must bring in pure air. Therefore, the intake openings must be remote—usually 10–15 feet, but sometimes as much as 25–30 feet—from any source of exhaust. Also, the air intakes usually must be a minimum of 10 feet above grade to avoid vehicle exhaust intake. For buildings with multiple mechanical systems, or buildings in dense urban settings, these distance separation requirements can make installation of additional mechanical systems impossible. (And leasing spaces, where the required mechanical system installation is impossible, has caused great economic hardship to many—10 years of lease payments in a space you can not occupy can cause loss of job and bankruptcy.)

Make up air
Replace what is discharged from combustion

In addition to the fresh air requirement for people, outside air must be provided (made up) when air leaves the building for other reasons—so that a pressure balance is maintained. These other reasons include kitchen exhaust, toilet exhaust, and combustion in gas-fired hot water heaters, furnaces, and boilers (also called combustion air). Make up air has lower standards of purity (such as distance separation), few or no requirements for heating, and no requirements for humidity control.

Exhaust Can Be Vital Too
Removal of odors, fumes, and dust

General exhaust

General exhaust is the companion to the fresh air requirement—when fresh outside air is introduced the pressure balance must be maintained by exhausting a similar quantity of the interior air. The exact amount of outside air can also be specified by code—usually to maintain a slight positive pressure in the building (the fresh air is slightly greater than exhaust), so air leakage through cracks and opening is out rather than in—minimizing hot and cold spots.

Toilet exhaust

Mechanical toilet exhaust is required for all occupancies for odor and humidity control. And this includes private residential occupancies that use operable windows for other ventilation requirements. The toilet exhaust systems frequently are required by code to be a separate and independent mechanical exhaust and ducting system from the general exhaust. In other cases, the general and toilet exhaust may be combined.

Kitchen exhaust

Commercial kitchens have a kitchen exhaust system located over a portion of the cooking operations that continuously produce fire and smoke—grills, fryers, and ovens. This is exhausted through welded black iron ductwork using a dedicated exhaust fan. Make up air through a dedicated make up air unit, usually providing some heat, is the required companion to the exhaust system. A small exhaust fan exhausts private residential kitchens but use no dedicated make up air equipment.

Other process exhaust

Exhaust from processes such as laboratory or industrial fumes and dust each can have dedicated exhaust systems. The material and amount of sealing of the exhaust ductwork will vary with the toxic nature and flammability of the exhausting chemicals. For small process exhaust systems (one lab hood of 5 sf), make up air requirements may be ignored. For larger process exhaust systems, make up air provisions must be specifically engineered into the HVAC system.

Plan carefully—change later may be difficult or impossible

These hugely varying requirements produce hugely different mechanical equipment requirements. Once installed, changing to a different occupancy type in later years may be economically impractical or physically impossible. Careful far ranging thought is required when constructing a project so that necessary future flexibility is preserved.

Water's Temperature Stability Influences HVAC Design
Manage what you can afford—then accept compromise

Water causes energy work

Water is the most temperature stable material commonly occurring on earth. It takes more energy to heat one unit of water 1°F than any other material. And the energy to change from ice to liquid and liquid to vapor is huge. The energy required to heat and cool water is one of the driving forces in mechanical system design. And this includes the amount of humidity in the air. It takes far more energy to heat and cool humid air as shown below.

Psychometric charts show the size and possible solutions of the HVAC task
Temperature and humidity and the energy to change

Willis Carrier, the founder of Carrier Air Conditioning, described the relationship among heat and humidity, and energy needed with psychometric charts. They were developed in the early 1900s for industrial applications such as textile spinning machines that would jam if temperature and humidity were not correct, or printing presses that would misalign successive printing colors. Psychometric charts are now used for design of HVAC spaces occupied by people. What they show is that water causes most of the HVAC work.

The amount of energy required to change a pound of air from 55°F to 70°F at different relative humidities in Btu (British thermal units—energy required to raise 1 pound 1 degree F) is:

100% Relative humidity	23–34 Btu (11) per pound of air
50% Relative humidity	18–25 Btu (7) per pound of air
10% Relative humidity	14–18 Btu (4) per pound of air

Water causes most of the heating and cooling work. If high humidity levels must be maintained in a building, more heating and cooling energy will be required.

Optimizing Combinations of Temperature and Humidity

Perceived comfort involves both temperature and humidity

"It's not the heat but the humidity" is an old saying about peoples' intuitive feelings about heat and humidity. But, people will feel "just as comfortable" at a number of combinations of temperature and humidity. In winter, 80°F at 10% percent humidity will feel the same as 70°F at 100% relative humidity—a 10°F difference of equivalent comfort.

The "comfortable" temperature varies with type of people, occupancy, place, and season. Old, inactive men, and women in all climates and most people in cold climates require a hotter temperature to feel comfortable. (A nursing home needs to be hotter than an apartment.) And everyone feels comfortable with about a 3°F higher temperature in winter than summer. But, the relationship among temperature, humidity, and comfort applies in all cases.

The high cost of heating water drives much of mechanical design

The relationship among temperature, humidity, energy, and peoples' perception of identical combinations of humidity and temperature drive much of HVAC engineering. For example, if the temperature of the cooling water in a mechanical system can be lowered from 55°F to the 52°F, more water will be extracted, but less cooling produced. However, since the humidity is less, the occupants will perceive it as being just as comfortable. But the added bonus is that since the building is drier, there will be less buildup of mold and bacteria.

One type of mechanical system using these ideas is called the "face and bypass" system. (Here, a fork in the ductwork before the cooling coil directs some air across the face of the coil, and directs the rest of the air to bypass around the coil.) When the air in both forks is blended together, the air is drier than if the entire amount of the air passed through a warmer coil. These small variations produce large and important benefits in temperature and humidity control.

Mechanical design of occupied space involves complicated heating and cooling calculations—indispensable and required in all cases. Heating and cooling an entire building to an average acceptable temperature is a readily achievable task. But most of the management decisions about different types of mechanical systems and their operation focuses on the amount of fresh air required and delivered. Reduction in the designed amount of outside air provided to a space is frequently attempted to reduce installation costs. Although this will still "meet code," indoor air quality will suffer and stuffiness, a clammy feeling, and possibly mold, may result. Completely shutting off outside air is sometimes done later to save energy. This does not meet code, and the results are even worse.

Evening Out Temperatures in a Building

Achieving even temperature and humidity with zone control

A small range of steady temperatures and humidities are usually desired, but sources of heat and cold are constantly varying. Exterior temperatures, heat gain from the sun, heat gain from occupants, machines, and lights vary with time of year, time of day, location of occupants, operation of machines, and location in the building. And more rooms mean more zones to control.

An old principle was "replace the heat where it is lost." This meant an exterior zone near the windows and an interior zone. This is still a sound principle. But as building insulation improves and the heat within the building from higher occupant densities and more computers and office machines increases, cooling must also be provided. "Adjust the temperature where needed" better describes the new needs. Interior and exterior zones are still highly desirable and frequently used, but more local zone control devices, as described below, should be added.

Controlling installation and operating costs through temperature control

Initial design of a mechanical system anticipates certain hours of use. Mechanical systems can be, but seldom are, designed for continuous full loads. These restricted hours of operation permit smaller, more economical, mechanical systems. Only slight adjustments in the hours of operation are possible while maintaining full systems performance. Once you reach these limits, for example going from a building designed for a single shift to round-the-clock operations, the mechanical equipment upgrades can be economically unfeasible or dimensionally impossible.

Another aspect of cost control is electrical energy costs. Energy usage varies throughout the time of day and day of the week. The heaviest use occurs during normal business hours. Since the power companies' generating capacity is limited, they attempt to even out these demands by charging higher rates at the peak hours. (These are called demand charges and are monitored by demand meters, which record energy usage by time of day. Demand meters are used for commercial, industrial, but not usually residential buildings.)

Building engineers who understand this system can adjust the hours of operation (start running mechanical systems an hour earlier in the morning) or the operation of select mechanical components (stop running the return fans in late afternoon) to minimize energy expense. Power company personnel who know these engineers can phone and offer further cost concessions in times of extreme peak usage—such as a heat wave.

Commonly Used HVAC Systems
Work with customary systems—and the labor available in the project area

Buy factory assembled pre-engineered equipment as much as possible

All mechanical systems are assembled from pre-manufactured components. Factory assembly of these components into pre-engineered designs reduces the equipment cost, design costs, and field installation labor. Further, pre-engineered designs reduce the required skill level of the installation personnel, and increase the number of aftermarket service personnel who will be readily familiar with the equipment.

So it is best to find equipment packages that are closest to your needs. For small residential applications—where electrical voltages are 120 volt—the packaged mechanical equipment will be pre-manufactured and locally stocked. For small commercial applications—where voltages, fuel type, and heating and cooling capacity can produce hundreds of variations for a single unit—"catalog (made to order)" is used. Options from preset menus are selected and a mechanical unit is assembled and shipped, usually within weeks.

Site assembly of pre-engineered components is the next level of difficulty. Site assembly of custom engineered components is the most sophisticated and difficult. Both of these systems require considerable competent design effort, and sophisticated and competent installing tradesman, and subsequent maintenance personnel. Even with competent and diligent office design engineers, the installing tradesmen do much of the design and detailing. Accept this and work with it. If all of these are not or will not be available, a less sophisticated system might be best.

Skilled labor for installation and operation is scarce—match your equipment to the labor available

Skilled labor, both for the initial construction and installation and for the operation and maintenance for the life of the building, is always scarce at the price you are willing and able to pay. A sophisticated site-assembled system in a remote rural area may find that insufficient numbers of skilled installation personnel are available. A person who has never had to attract and retain technical personnel to achieve measurable results can only make the statement, "We can always get more people." Use of normal and customary mechanical systems, wherever possible, should be a goal.

Single Purpose Systems
Desire for economy is sometimes necessary, but future flexibility is limited

Heat and cool things but not people

Buildings for storage, such as warehouses, are intended for use by very few people. Heating only—usually in the form of a unit heater with a heat source such as electrical or gas-fired heat exchanger, and a fan to provide convection—will be used. There are minimal requirements for fresh air or exhaust and no attempt at humidity control. The equipment is stock or catalog (made to order), and installation and maintenance are not sophisticated.

Heat people but not things

Operations that are manned throughout the workday but are too open to permit economical heating can use radiant heating for the occupants. Such "spaces" include bus stops, entrances to hotels, warehouse loading docks, and open-air markets. Commonly, gas-fired or sometimes electric radiant heaters are used. These heat only what the radiation strikes, so are placed to maximize benefit for people. No attempt is made to heat and cool the entire work area or provide humidity control. The equipment is stock or catalog (made to order), and the installation and maintenance are not sophisticated.

Exhaust only is possible

Buildings that contain few people, such as parking garages and agricultural buildings, may need exhaust only. A wall-mounted exhaust fan removes the air and unconditioned outside make up air enters through the doors and other openings. Specific fresh air quantities, heating and cooling, and humidity control are not sought. The equipment is stock or catalog (made to order). Installation is not sophisticated and maintenance is minimal.

HVAC Systems for Human Occupants

Residential is the least complex

Residential buildings include single-family homes, apartments, dormitories, and similar residential settings. Residential buildings provide the fresh air requirements and most of the exhaust requirements by operable windows. Since windows provide the ventilation air, there are two choices for the heating system—radiation and forced air systems.

Radiation

Piped hot water radiation systems using radiators at nearly every window can be used. Convection can improve the distribution by adding a fan to blow air over the radiator heating coils. This is called a fan coil unit or convector. For either system, a thermostatic valve can be added at each radiator or fan coil to provide local zone control. Alternatively, a piped hot water or electrical radiation system can be installed in the floor, or occasionally in the ceiling.

Cooling can also be provided with the same system. For very mild climates, a drip pan can catch the condensation. For most other climates, this drip pan must be piped to a drain. Humidity control is incidental for cooling and cannot be precisely regulated. Since there is piping only with small dimensions, and no ductwork is required, the space required for installation is small. This can permit lower floor-to-floor heights of the structure, which can be a huge cost savings for new buildings and a huge advantage for renovations.

Forced air systems with remote condensers

Single-family residential homes typically have forced air furnaces installed in the building (in warmer climates, sometimes outside). A heat source is usually either electrical or fossil fuel—oil, natural gas, or propane. A cooling coil in the furnace produces the cooling. The heat is ejected to a condenser located outside the building. This is a direct expansion (DX) with refrigerant in the air stream. Therefore, it cannot be used in institutional occupancies (such as hospitals, prisons, and nursing homes).

For warm climates, an air-to-air heat pump system can be used. For cooling, the system operates as described above. For heating, the waste heat from the condenser is routed to the coil in the furnace to produce heat in the building. The system works satisfactorily only to about 20–35°F, and then supplemental heating coils must be added—which defeats the economy of the system. So, air-to-air heat pump systems are usually found only in the southern half of the United States—starting around Tennessee and Kentucky. Water source heat pumps have a larger range.

This forced air system is a single zone system. Fresh air and exhaust quantities are not provided by the system. And, humidity control is incidental to the cooling process, so it cannot be precisely controlled. Humidification can be added with a humidifier. The equipment is pre-manufactured (sold off-the-shelf) and can accommodate areas up to about 3,000 sf. For larger buildings, multiple similar mechanical systems are used. Installation and maintenance labor is usually readily available.

For multi-family residential applications, the forced air system can be used with adequate results only for small buildings—usually less than 10,000 sf. Larger residential buildings or high-rise applications have found these forced air systems troublesome and unsatisfactory—achieving required fresh air separations, routing a forest of pipes and ducts, and maintaining many small systems. Radiation systems described above are preferred, but forced air systems are also used.

Small office and retail spaces—under 3,000 sf are more complex

Small commercial spaces provide the desired and required fresh air and exhaust ventilation quantities solely through a mechanical system. Even if operable windows exist, their ventilation contribution is not counted in the mechanical design. These spaces are typically served by a factory assembled packaged rooftop unit.

Rooftop units

A rooftop unit is a factory manufactured and assembled combination of the heat source—such as electrical coil or gas-fired heat exchanger—an air-conditioning condenser, a blower, and the necessary electrical and electronic controls to make these components work together. This unit delivers the heating, cooling, and ventilation through forced air supply and return ducts—usually mounted on the bottom, but occasionally on the side, of the unit. For the simplest single zone units, a thermostat is the only mechanical component that must be mounted in the building. The package unit is placed on the roof by a crane. Once the electrical, gas, ductwork, and thermostat are connected, the system can be commissioned, tested, and used.

Fresh air can be supplied to the ventilation system by a louvered opening on the side of the unit. This opening can be dampened to make adjustments for the interior pressure in the ventilation system. Or, a thermostat, sometimes called an economizer, can control the damper. More fresh air—up to 100% of the ventilation quantities—can be introduced when the temperature of the outside air is close to the desired interior temperature. This free heating or cooling economizes on the energy costs.

Exhaust quantities can be supplied in two ways. A power exhaust device can be mounted on the rooftop unit, which is synchronized with the fresh air intake. For very small projects and certain occupancies such as a retail store, the building is slightly pressurized by the supply fan supplemented by additional outside air. Exhaust occurs when the exterior doors are frequently opened. The second way is limited to smaller projects and does not work as the project size increases. Further, it is not permitted under many design standards and codes and for many occupancies.

Dehumidification occurs only incidentally to cooling and cannot be precisely controlled. Humidification can be added by a humidifier, but seldom is. These units are catalog (made to order) with delivery times of two-to-six weeks. Installation and maintenance labor are usually readily available.

Rooftop units are made to order from catalog selections

Rooftop units offer a range of combinations of heat source (gas, electric), heat capacity, cooling capacity, volume of supply air delivered, and voltage, phase, and power of electrical service. Each of these characteristics may have up to 15 choices for a single model. The heat source and electrical characteristics will vary independently. But the heating and cooling capacity and supplied air combinations are restricted to paired combinations specified by the manufacturer.

To these combinations can be added options such as the economizer, power exhaust, humidifier, energy efficiency upgrades, and safety features such as automatic shut down in the event of fire alarm activation. Smaller units (under 5 tons capacity) will have few or no offered options. Larger units will have many.

For all but the smallest units with no options, each unit is assembled from catalog specified options and made to order for each project. Delivery times are typically two weeks to two months depending on the size and complexity of unit. Installation of the units can be accomplished with competent, though not highly skilled, personnel.

These units have limits—solving complex problems can be unfeasible

These units are designed for up to about 3,000 sf and work well for single-story buildings with single zones. If a building consists of large open areas with few windows, such as a large retail space, multiple rooftop units can successfully serve spaces over 100,000 sf. But as the number and complexity of zones increases—caused by many windows and doors, more rooms, or variable occupancy heat loads—these systems are less successful. Also, buildings with multiple stories make this system less successful. Air blowers and refrigeration pumps are not designed for the greater heights and distances, so pressure drops can be excessive. Also, the offsets of the multiple ducts and pipes can add additional pressure drops—rendering the overall performance substandard, and subject to frequent breakdowns.

Medium office buildings—up to about 30,000 sf are more complex yet

When the size, number of stories, or complexity in occupancies require multiple zones of control, fewer but more complicated and sophisticated mechanical units are used. These units are catalog (made to order) factory assembled units. The number of options for energy management, energy efficiency, and humidity control are greater and many of these features come standard. Manufacturing delivery times are typically 2 to 4 months.

What is different about these units is that they are designed to accommodate mechanical devices that provide multiple zones from a single package mechanical unit. These zone devices are described in more detail below. A three-story building with 10,000 sf per floor might have two packaged multi-zone rooftop units—instead of the ten that would have been required for single zone units. Since larger mechanical units are more energy efficient and larger units are manufactured of better quality components with more preventive maintenance possibilities, fewer larger units are more economical throughout the life of the building.

These units have some capability to vary fresh air and exhaust quantities but dehumidification is still incidental to cooling. Competent, though not extraordinary, personnel can also install these units. And, maintenance is typically performed by periodic visits of off-site service personnel.

Large commercial buildings—are even more complex

For commercial buildings over about three stories or greater than 150 to 200 feet on the side, the prepackaged factory assembled units described above can no longer be used. Larger systems are custom designed for the project—using individually manufactured components. The components, such as supply fan, return fan, cooling production machine, heat rejection machine (such as a cooling tower, cooling coils, heat production machine, heat exchanger, humidifier, valves and pumps, cooling water treatment equipment, and energy management equipment, just to name a few), will be engineered and manufactured—frequently by different companies. Lead times increase to months or years.

These components are site assembled in an interior mechanical room. For a building such as a high-rise, these mechanical rooms can occupy an entire floor, usually about every 20 floors. On smaller buildings, a portion of the floor may be used. Since this mechanical equipment must take in fresh air, exhaust air, and reject heat, it must be located at least, in part, above-grade, which is more valuable commercial space than a lower level basement.

The complexity of these systems provides as much control as is desired. For these systems, there is supply and return fans as well as separate exhaust fans (return fans usually Do not exist on the smaller systems), so the amount of supply air and pressurization of the building or parts of the building can be controlled. Temperature and humidity can also be controlled. The components of such systems are higher quality and are designed to be disassembled and maintained. These systems will have decades longer life than the smaller systems—and will be more energy efficient.

These benefits do, however, have a cost. The systems are custom designed so competent mechanical electrical engineers are required. "Do it like we did the last one" will probably not produce the desired results. The installing tradesman must be similarly sophisticated. Both theoretical and practical knowledge of the systems and components is required. Obtaining the required number of qualified tradesmen for projects—particularly in remote areas with low population—can be a major project management challenge.

Finally, these systems require similarly sophisticated maintenance personnel full-time and on-site, which is a major cost for the life of the building. Building automation can reduce the number, but not eliminate the need, for these personnel. Attempting to use periodic off-site maintenance personnel can result in poorly functioning equipment, damage to the equipment, and life-threatening malfunctions.

Finer Ventilation Zone Control Within One System May Be Needed
Adjusting for varying needs and preferences

Using an interior and exterior zone as described above is still a sound idea, and is used in most systems. But, further zone control for each of these systems is usually also desired. This can be accomplished by varying the amount or the temperature of the air in each zone.

Variable air volume (VAV) or variable volume and temperature (VVT) zone control devices use a damper in the duct or an in-line box containing a damper to vary the amount of air delivered to the zone—from about 20% to 100% of the maximum quantity. One temperature air is delivered through the ductwork to these devices and a zone thermostat controls the damper. Electrical reheat coils are frequently added to the exterior zone.

This system has the economy of a single duct system with a simple and reliable zone control device. But it has the disadvantage that when little temperature change is required, little air is being delivered, which can produce a stuffy environment. Economically constructed office buildings using only this system can find the occupants falling asleep mid-afternoon. Watch your minimum air quantities so this does not happen to you. Meeting code alone is no assurance of quality.

An older and presently less popular system is a hot deck-cold deck duct system. Here, multiple duct systems each carrying air of different temperatures deliver to a zone volume mixing box. The thermostat controls the amount of air from each duct system to produce an air discharge of a constant specified volume at the required temperature.

Although this system provides good supply air and temperature control, it requires more complicated mechanical equipment and costly multiple duct systems. The space requirements of these ducts will usually mean a greater floor-to-floor height of the building is required—adding additional cost.

Zone temperature control can also be accomplished solely by temperature adjustment coils in each zone. Electrical reheat coils are a common solution with low maintenance, but no cooling is possible. Water coils that can either carry hot or chilled water can provide both heating and cooling. They are, however, far more expensive to install and do require near continual adjustment and maintenance—with occasional building damaging leakage. Continuing adoption of energy management codes restricts the use of reheat coils. Heating or cooling air twice is thought to be unacceptably wasteful.

Radiation heating and cooling zone control may be needed
The choice for many multifamily residential and institutional occupancies

Temperature control in the exterior zone can also be provided by perimeter radiation. Either electric or hot water baseboard radiators or radiant panels in the ceiling can add perimeter heating. Cooling is possible within a very narrow range of temperature and humidity—before undesirable condensation occurs. Perimeter cooling by this method is rare.

Where most of the building consists of an exterior zone, such as apartment buildings, elementary school classrooms, or dormitories—and operable windows substantially provide the fresh air and exhaust—perimeter radiation systems are effective and are typically used. Here, a radiation unit is placed under most windows, as described above.

These radiation units can be fed by a single supply and single return pipe (a two-pipe system). For half the year the pipes supply chilled water and for half a year hot water. The building engineer must determine the exact time of year to change from heating or cooling. And, the drain down and re-supply can take a day. So wrong guesses make the temperatures unsatisfactory for days or a week. This problem can be overcome with separate heating and cooling piping systems (a four-pipe system) but this close to doubles the cost of the mechanical distribution system. Frequently, the designer specifies a four-pipe system, the contractor prices it, the owner falls over with sticker shock, and the two-pipe system is installed.

More Complex and Precise Systems
Still not expensive enough? Then try this

Multiple systems on one project

The systems above are described in their simplest form and many are installed that way. However, many buildings use components of multiple systems. For example, many buildings, regardless of the mechanical system used, ha   radiant heating in the vestibules to the outside. Many office buildings with variable air volume systems add electrical reheat coils to the exterior zone to increase heating capacity and control. Apartment or dormitory buildings with exterior convectors will add kitchen and toilet exhaust systems.

Addition of multiple mechanical system types adds complexity and cost. So, most systems tend to compromise on performance to achieve market rate costs. Humidity control is often abandoned and zone control compromised.

Extremely high standards—where cost is no object

The systems described above are what are being installed in the real world—which satisfies the needs of supply air, fresh air, exhaust air, and temperature and humidity control—balanced with economics and the available installation and maintenance personnel. If applications require extremely high standards, the complexity of system requirements and time and cost of installation increase hugely.

For example, precisely controlled humidity is required for some art restoration. Substantially oversized heating and cooling equipment plus the addition of a boiler for steam humidification, plus supplemental dehumidification cooling must be added.

Medical facilities and laboratories where infection control is crucial can require 100% outside air for supply with 100% exhaust of return air. Humidity control equipment as described above plus perimeter radiation produces a mechanical system that is expensive to install, operate, and maintain.

The extremely high purity required by some facilities, for example in electronics and pharmaceutical manufacturing, can require that the entire ceiling be perforated and deliver supply air, and the entire perforated floor accept the return air. This laminar flow, plus the addition of high purity filters, plus the humidity control described above achieves the desired level of cleanliness. The vast size of the required ductwork can mean that only every second or third floor can be occupied with the rest of the building being devoted to mechanical equipment and ductwork.

Another example is an auditorium designed for orchestras. Here, the ductwork sizes must be vastly increased to reduce the sound of air transmission. The mechanical equipment itself is frequently installed in a separate building separated by vibration isolation mechanisms.

These are but a few examples of the implications for deviating from the normal and customary commercial fresh air, exhaust, and temperature control standards. Such deviations may require a 300–1,000% premium. For select process applications, the premium can be 10,000% or more. If you demand such performance, then be prepared to pay the premium. Unnecessary demands for overly precise performance—such as demands for precise humidity control in a conventional office building—should be recognized early as inconsistent with your purpose and eliminated from the requirements.

System Commissioning, Testing, Adjusting, and Balancing Needed at End of Job

Commissioning

Once all connections are made to the installed equipment, it must be commissioned, which is more involved than just flipping a switch. The steps are:

1. Check nameplates on all of the equipment and motors to ensure that the intended equipment was installed.
2. Check that the electrical power wiring was correctly connected, that power of the intended characteristics is being received at the mechanical equipment, and that the equipment is rotating in the correct direction. (Centrifugal fans can rotate backwards and still deliver air in the correct direction—a most puzzling error).
3. Check that the delivered process gases (fuel and refrigerant) and water to the unit are delivered at the correct pressure and flow—add refrigerant when required.
4. Start up and measure delivered quantities of the air, heat, and cooling and running pressures. Adjust to intended level.

System testing and balancing

Once the mechanical unit itself is performing as intended, an outside independent testing company frequently and similarly reviews the distribution system. The steps are:

1. Substantially repeat the commissioning process described above.
2. Move all dampers to full open position and measure the maximum supply flow at the unit. (This is done by drilling a hole about the size of a pencil in the center part of the ductwork and inserting a probe to the center of the duct that measures the flow. cfm are determined from this reading by use of pre-calculated charts.)
3. Adjust speed of the unit so intended flow is provided.
4. Measure flow at each branch and adjust flow with balancing dampers.
5. At supply grilles, flow is measured with a pyramid shaped hood placed over the grille, and volume adjustments made by a damper by the grille. Where variable volume boxes exist for zone control, the flow is measured in the maximum position, then check and adjust the box to prove the full intended volume range. A "test and balance report" documents these measurements and adjustments and is used to prove the system performs as intended.

Understand the Benefits and Limits of Each System
Each occupancy has its own requirements—later change from one to another may be difficult or impossible

Requirements for supply air, fresh air, heating, cooling, and humidity vary by occupancy type. And, as described above, the method for achieving these requirements also varies by occupancy type. The use of operable windows for fresh air and exhaust quantities in residential occupancies is one example. And space required for very large ducts or very small pipes determines the minimum required floor-to-floor height. So both the type of mechanical system and the dimensions of the building are fixed at the time of original selection of occupancy type.

This means that changing from one occupancy type to another may range from expensive to physically impossible. Even changing from a more to less expensive occupancy type (hospital to dormitory) or acquiring the building from a reputable company that designed and was built by the best personnel, does not guarantee that it will be suitable or even usable for your purpose. Many have acquired buildings not recognizing these facts and have lost their jobs or suffered severe financial hardship. The discussions above should help prevent this from happening to you.

Summary

Heating, ventilating, and air-conditioning systems vary by the intended use and occupancy. The amount of fresh air, exhaust air, humidity control, and zone control are the distinguishing factors. Heating only by perimeter radiation is readily achievable. Heating and cooling together requires forced air systems. And the addition of fresh air by operable windows or ducts adds the burden of heating and cooling the water in this air.

The extreme temperature stability of water and the related humidity control are the driving factors in mechanical system design. In most systems, humidity control is not precisely sought but is rather a consequence of cooling. Since a range of combinations of temperature and humidity will all be perceived as equally comfortable, satisfactory performance can be obtained while only partially adjusting humidity.

Mechanical systems are built from standard components. The more standard the mechanical system, the lower the initial cost of design, installation, and required competence of installation and maintenance personnel. Site assembled mechanical systems have lower operating costs but require higher skill levels from the installing and maintenance personnel. If you have a market rate project where cost is an object, you must use the normal and customary mechanical system choices. These systems are:

1. Private residential
2. Small commercial less than 3,000 sf
3. Medium commercial less than 30,000 sf
4. Large commercial over 30,000 sf
5. Highly specialized and precise systems
6. Exhaust or heat only systems
7. Cost is no object precise high performance systems

The required floor heights, location of fresh air and exhaust openings, and size of electrical service required are specific for each of these types. So change even from a more demanding to less demanding use may be difficult or dimensionally impossible.

Competent and effective mechanical system design is far more complex than the simple description provided above—an entire career can be well occupied with this subject alone. But these few concepts briefly described make the reader more knowledgeable and competent than 95–99% of those involved in the building process—including those with advanced degrees and decades of experience. This knowledge can avoid common and disastrous mistakes and make project success normal.

3.16 Electrical Power—Managing Motion for Useful Purposes

Atoms—the building blocks of all materials—are made of electrons spinning around a central core. Electrical installations in buildings safely manage the flow of these electrons for power and lighting

Forces That Help and Hurt the Motion of Electrons

Current is the flow of electrons—but this flow must be forced

Current, the flow of electrons (measured in amps), helps do the work. (62,510 trillion electrons flowing per second is 1 amp—a fact you do not need to remember.) The flow of electrons is necessary to do the work, yet it alone does not determine the work that is done.

Voltage—potential difference between two points forces the flow of electrons

If a conductor—such as a wire—connects two points with different electrical charges, pressure will cause flow from the greater to the lesser charge. The size of the pressure difference is called the potential difference and is measured in volts. This potential difference alone, however, does no work and produces no power.

Voltage and current together do work

Work (power) measured in watts is the potential (volts) times the current (amps). So a very high voltage and a low current will do the same work as a very low voltage and high current. This makes installation using higher voltages more economical and efficient. Fewer electrons flowing permit smaller wire size and produce less resistance and heat in the wire. This idea is discussed many times below for electrical services, conductor size, and motor efficiencies.

Voltage drop always occurs—and must be managed by conductor size and length

Voltage must remain quite precise for acceptable electrical device operation—within 1% for lighting, 2% for general use, and 3% for motors. Variation beyond these ranges will cause rapid deterioration of lighting ballasts and lamps, and inefficient running or damage to motors. (Motors can tolerate about +/- 10%

for very short periods during start up or load change.) Large diameter conductors and short runs cause the least voltage drop—a principle that affects the distribution of power. Below is an example of voltage drops showing the effect of conductor size:

*Conductor size	AWG 10	AWG 6	AWG 2	0000	750 MCM
% Voltage drop	4.8	1.9	.78	.24	.068

* (120V, 20 amp, direct current, 100 lf conductor. Each conductor size from left to right has approximately twice the cross section of its neighbor.)

Note: AWG is "American wire gauge" and describes the wire diameter for smaller wires—smaller numbers mean thicker wires. MCM is "thousand circular mils" and describes the cross section area of larger wires (cables)—bigger numbers mean thicker wires.

Conductor material, length, diameter, and temperature all affect resistance

Materials have differing resistance to the flow of electrons. This resistance is measured in ohms. An ohm allows passage of 1 amp under the pressure of one volt.

Materials that have low resistance and therefore allow lots of flow are called conductors. Copper and aluminum are the conductors used in building construction. An aluminum conductor has about 50–70% more resistance than a copper conductor. This means that if aluminum wire were used instead of copper, the wire diameter would need to be about 60% larger.

For building construction, these resistances are stated at 77°F. As conductors heat, their resistance increases. Approximately every 5°F rise in temperature produces a 1% increase in resistance. Since temperature rises in components of electrical systems are normally 50 to 100°F, this additional resistance requires both design and operating attention.

Insulating materials—now usually rubber or plastic—have extremely high resistance. Curiously, insulation loses resistance as temperature rises—the opposite of conductors. This is a limiting factor in motor design. As the motor heats up, conductors have increasing resistance but the insulation on the conductors loses resistance—decreasing its ability to insulate as required. So for all electrical conductors (but not all lights) the moral is: cold helps, heat hurts, but this is inevitable and must be managed.

Inductance—advantages to use, disadvantages to manage

When current flows through a wire, it induces (hence the name inductance) a magnetic force to spin around the conductor. The "right hand rule" states that the if the thumb of your right hand points in the direction of the current flow, your fingers in a closed fist will point in the direction of the spinning force around the conductor. And it works in reverse as well. If a magnetic field spin around the conductor is in the direction of your fingers, it will cause current to flow in the direction of your thumb.

This inductance produces much useful electrical work. When the current flows through a conductor, the surrounding inductance can power an electric motor. When a conductor is forced through a magnetic field, current is forced through the conductor and electricity is generated.

But it also causes problems. Alternating current induces a weaker current in the opposite direction—providing another type of resistance (inductive reactance). When many conductors are close, as occurs in electrical wiring in conduit, the inductance of each wire bumps into the other and must be managed. For conductors carrying alternating current, the inductance (where the current lags behind the voltage) both helps maintain the current flow in the intended direction but also reduces usable power. This is discussed in "power factor" and "motors" below.

Capacitance—resists in the opposite direction

Capacitance is the ability of a conductor to temporarily hold a charge. In continuous conductors, such as a wire, resistance (capacitive reactance) is in the opposite direction of inductance discussed above. The current leads the voltage. If inductive reactance and capacitive reactance in a conductor balance, they cancel and the resistance of both the inductive and capacitive reactance disappears. This balance of alternating forces must be managed to make alternating current systems as efficient as possible—capable of doing useful work.

Inductance and capacitance always exist—but are only noticed on larger projects

Inductance and capacitance are laws of physics and exist always and everywhere. On small single-phase projects, the additional resistance caused is handled by increasing the conductor size. (Size for the resistance of the copper material, plus the resistance of the heat caused by current flow, plus a little bit more.) Small projects also typically use small horsepower motors, so power correction complexity is limited. A person working solely on single-family houses may work an entire career without having to take any specific steps or even possibly know about inductance and capacitance—and nothing bad may happen. However, as the project size and complexity of the design increases (on larger projects) inductance and capacitance become important—requiring specific additional machinery for management.

Devices That Help Manage Electricity

Transformers—change voltage

A transformer is a device used to change one voltage to another. It consists of an iron core, frequently in the shape of a square shaped doughnut, with windings of wire on two sides. The difference in number of windings per side determines the amount of voltage change. For example, if there are 100 windings on one side and 200 on the other the voltage will change from 120v to 240v.

Smaller transformers can be air cooled and placed anywhere. They do, however, produce heat, which must be removed, and a characteristic hum, which must be accommodated or accepted. Larger transformers are frequently oil filled and remove heat by fans and radiator fins. These cannot be placed anywhere, but rather require fireproof rooms with accommodation for venting of smoke, which a malfunctioning transformer will produce.

An autotransformer uses a single winding coil, but varies the location of contact on this coil to vary voltage. Some dimming light switches work this way, and another name for this device is a rheostat.

Relays—obtain and send a signal that produces action

A relay is a control device that receives an electrical signal from one source and sends one or more signals to other sources. Relays have terminals for wire connection, a transformer to reduce the voltage, a solenoid (an in-line one directional motor) that closes or opens contacts to send a signal to activate another device or devices. Relays can be fabricated to produce a specific time delay between signal receipt and transmission. These components are assembled in an enclosure measuring (for 120 volts) about the size of a 35mm film canister to the size of a pound of butter.

Capacitors—store a charge

A capacitor can store an electrical charge. A capacitor, sometimes called a condenser, consists of two parallel plates of conducting metal separated by an insulator (these can be wound in a coil like a roll of paper towels). This can be as simple as two pieces of aluminum foil separated by wax paper. Here, a very small charge source can build up a larger charge in the capacitor for quick discharge—as would occur in the flash attachment on a camera.

Capacitors can give a temporary boost to start motors. And capacitors can be used to eliminate spikes in power. (Here, this spike is temporarily stored in the capacitor and then promptly drained to ground to get ready for the next spike.)

Different Industries and Foreign Countries use Different Standards and Names
The meaning is the same, but translation is required

All discussions in this chapter focus on building in the United States of America—so terminology and measurement standards are stated for this use. However, the standards are not universal to all countries and industries. For example, the 77°F baseline temperature for conductors discussed above becomes 70°F in scientific measurement. And this can become a significant design and installation consideration if your building requires installation of scientific equipment and machinery. Similar differences exist for commercial laundry equipment from Sweden, and medical and machine tool equipment from European countries and Japan. They're not wrong; they are just different.

Adjusting for these differences can be readily accommodated during installation—if you know when to look for it. (For example, locked rotor amps for an electric motor are larger than start-up amps, which are larger than running amps. So even if the terms are switched, they can be easily un-switched.) The methods for accommodation are beyond the scope of this discussion, but supervisors and managers who know that this can be a problem can plan to detect and solve it.

Time—Some Huge Ranges

Electricity moves at 186,000 miles per second. This is too fast to measure or to be of any concern in building electrical work. But the impact and the effect of electricity takes place over longer times, which is important. Overcurrent protection fuses that vaporize metal within a fuse have reaction times measured as short as ten thousands of a second. Overcurrent protection breakers, which work by heating up a metal bar, can take a half a second up to 10 seconds to react. Some motors have specific times, such as a half-hour, they can be run at full load without overheating. Transformers may tolerate overcurrent for an hour. Although electricity is instant, the effects of electricity are spread over longer times and must be managed. Just because it is working now doesn't mean it will work in 10 minutes or an hour.

Space—Required for Heat Removal and Safety of Workmen

Whenever energy changes form or does work there will be resistance, which produces heat. Removal of this heat is usually accomplished by allowing some space around the electrical devices for ventilation. This influences the number of wires that can be placed in a conduit, the interior size of electrical gear, and the amount of electrical devices that can be packed into small spaces.

Also electrical devices do require maintenance and service. And electricity can be dangerous. There are therefore specified clearances, usually a minimum of 3–6 feet or greater, around electrical gear that must be allowed for safe work. And this clearance includes both permanent parts of the building and stored materials.

These are not just bureaucratic requirements—they allow for efficient operation of electrical gear and safe servicing. This requires attention both in the design, but particularly in the operation of the completed building. Using the electrical room as a garbage dump or second warehouse is all too common—and should be avoided.

Direct Current Is Controllable and Versatile, Alternating Current Travels Farther

Direct current for short distances—efficient, easily controlled, and can be stored

Direct current flows continuously in one and only one direction. This has a number of advantages and uses. One large advantage is that direct current allows precise speed control of motors—just by changing the flux delivered. No variable transmission mechanism is required, and variations in load and speed will not produce unmanageable overheating.

For this reason direct current motors are used in diesel powered train locomotives. The diesel engine powers a direct current generator, which in turn powers motors by the wheels. (Next time you're stopped by a train take a look and you will see the motors.) These motors struggle under heavy load for minutes from a dead stop to gradually accelerate to the full running speed.

In buildings, direct current motors (an alternating current motor driving a direct current generator—a motor generator set) are used for elevators for their precise and smooth speed control. For similar reasons, direct current motors can be used for cranes, rolling mills, and some fans.

Direct current can also be stored. Capacitors can provide temporary charge storage as described above. Battery storage is also possible. Finally, direct current avoids some of the inefficiency (reduction in useable power) found in alternating current.

For all these reasons, Thomas Edison, one of the early pioneers in electrical device development, preferred direct current generation and distribution for all uses. But this had one huge drawback. Direct current transmission distances are very short—hundreds to thousands of feet—so power plants would have to be located about every three blocks. For this reason, alternating current was chosen. When we do want direct current, we use a motor generator or a rectifier to change alternating to direct current on site.

Alternating current travels far, but introduces inefficiencies that must be managed

Alternating current (in high voltages) can be transmitted great distances—up to hundreds of miles. This permits more convenient location of power plants. Alternating current loses the benefit of speed control and storage capacity of direct current, and has some other qualities that must be managed as well.

Alternating current is produced by rotating a conductor through a magnetic field to generate (induce) current flow. When the conductor cuts through the center of the flow, it generates maximum current in one direction, but when it is outside the flow, it is generating no current. As the rotation continues, maximum flow is produced but in the opposite direction. In our electrical system, this cycle—two peaks and two valleys—is repeated 60 times per second. The power is the "average" of maximum and no power throughout the cycle.

If only one generator and one wiring system are used, it is called a single-phase system. Single-family residential homes and the power outlets in commercial buildings are such single-phase systems. These systems are simple and economical but have limited use when powering larger motors.

A three-phase system uses three separate generators and three separate wiring systems to improve efficiency. Each of these three generators is offset (out of phase) by one third of a cycle. So instead of 60 sets of peaks and valleys in each cycle, you now have 180. This does increase the cost and complexity of electrical installations, but it does increase motor efficiency by about 50–73%. The full load amps for a 10 hp motor illustrates:

Single phase	115 volt	230 volt	*3 Phase*	230 volt	480 volt
	100 amp	50 amp		28 amp	14 amp

These improvements are hard to ignore. Nearly all medium and large motors are three phase.

Power factor—how close you are to maximum power efficiency

The power factor describes (by a percent up to 100%) how close an electrical device is to the maximum possible efficiency. Or stated another way, how much of the electrical energy is doing useful work.

Direct current devices have a power factor of 100%. Alternating current devices such as an incandescent light bulb or an electric heater, produce light and heat by resistance. Current flowing in both directions produces this useful resistance—so the power factor will be close to 100%. (Fluorescent lights do not produce light by resistance and will have a much lower power factor—maybe 50%.)

Devices, such as motors, are intended to do useful work in one direction and the power factor is important. Here the power factor is the difference between the theoretical direct current efficiency in one direction to the achieved alternating current (two direction) efficiency, which will be lower. Efficiencies in the high 80% to 90% are considered good for larger motors. Single phase (smaller motors) will be less.

Transporting Usable Electricity

What the power company brings to you

The power company's methods of generating power are not relevant to the building constructor and owner and manager—so will not be discussed here. But some characteristics of the delivery process do have relevance. Power companies are government granted monopolies, so we have to deal with them. However, they do have very specific requirements for the type and quality of power they must deliver.

First, the power company must very precisely regulate the frequency (60 cycles per second) of the power delivered. This is important since the speed of some motors is governed by the frequency of the power. Second, the power company carefully regulates the voltage delivered. This is important because under or over voltage can burn out larger motors, light fixtures, cause lights to flicker, and cause all devices to operate inefficiently. Finally, they will control the consistency of power delivered in all three phases. This is important since if one phase drops or is lost entirely, the other phases can be overloaded—producing unsafe overheating and destruction of equipment.

When such damage occurs, the power company can be liable for replacement of equipment. And they carefully monitor the quality of their power and know when and where deficiencies occurred. However, you still have to prove it to them. This requires a competent and knowledgeable person from your organization and requires installation of instruments on your project to detect and document the deficiencies.

But if you are a sophisticated user, you are also responsible back to the power company for any variations in inductance and capacitance your operations produce. If the power factor of your equipment is less than certain specifications, sometimes about 85%, you may be required to pay the power company a surcharge on your electrical bill. This covers their cost to correct your deficiencies—so other customers can receive specified power to which they're entitled.

These considerations do not take place on a single-phase project and seldom on a very small commercial project. But if you are graduating from a smaller to a larger project, it is good to know that these rights and responsibilities for both you and the power company do exist.

Long distance transmission requires high voltages

Higher voltages permit smaller conductors with less voltage drop. If the voltage is 10 times as high, the conductor diameter can be about 10 times smaller. Also, for a given amount of current, if the voltage is 10 times higher, the resistance will be 10 times lower. To take advantage of these efficiencies, the voltage of the power leaving the generation plant is quite high—maybe 345,000 volts, and the voltage near your project still will be quite high—maybe 14,800 volts. Transformers successively step down these higher voltages to the point of use at your project. The final transformer that steps down the voltage for your use must be quite close—usually within hundreds of feet of the entrance of the electrical service to your building. The power company owns and maintains this entire network.

Types of Power Delivered—Voltage (120, 240, 277, 480 volts) and Phases (1 or 3)

As discussed above, all power company power is alternating current—60 cycles per second. The voltage and number of phases required is governed by the electrical needs of the project, and will be limited to the type of power company transformer that exists or will be placed within a couple hundred feet of a project.

Single-phase power is delivered to single-family residences and very small commercial buildings;120 and 240 volt connections are possible with this service.

3 phase power with a delta transformer

The delta transformer (so named because the symbol for this type of transformer in electrical wiring diagrams is a triangle, which is also the letter "delta" in the Greek alphabet—*kind of a stretch, but that is the reason*) can provide 120 volt single-phase power and 240 volt three-phase power without the addition of another transformer inside the project. This is an older and currently less popular system. Systems with this transformer typically have no neutral conductor. This restricts the balancing of loads between phases, which reduces the quality of power and the efficiencies of devices.

3 phase power with a wye transformer

The wye transformer (so named because the symbol for this type of transformer in electrical wiring diagrams looks like the capital letter "Y" in the English alphabet—*also a little obscure*) can provide two configurations of power. One configuration provides 120 volt single-phase power and 208 volt three-phase power without the addition of another transformer inside the building. This is presently the most common and popular electrical service configuration for small and midsize commercial projects. Another configuration provides 277 volt and 480 volt three-phase power, but requires a transformer inside the building to provide 120 volt single-phase power. This is popular for commercial installations where the 277 volt power is used for lighting and 480 volt for major equipment power; 480 volt power is also used for industrial buildings with heavier power usage. Systems with this type of transformer typically do have a neutral conductor.

Connecting the power company grid to your project

The owner of the project is responsible for preparing the building to receive the power company's connection—sometimes called the "drop." If the electrical service is to enter the building overhead, the owner of the building will install a "mast"—a pole and conduit containing the conductors to be connected. All necessary interior service work must be completed and first inspected by the municipal authorities, and then by the power company's authorities. Then, cables from the power company's transformer to this drop are installed (and paid for) by the power company.

If the service is to enter underground, the process is similar except the building owner is responsible for installing the empty conduits from the building service entrance underground to the concrete pad that is to receive the power company transformer. The building owner may pull the cables and the power company terminates (makes the final connections), or the power company may do both depending on the city and power company. In either case, the owner is responsible for the cost.

The power company monopoly owes you electrical service (theoretically) for free. However, they do not owe you anything you want. And they strive to make their installation cost balance the utility charges they later receive. So you must be able to competently prove—using plans and calculations—that you need what you are asking for and will produce sufficiently large utility bills. If the power company's payback is borderline, they either may drag their feet processing the installation or demand fairly substantial up-front payments—from two-to-six months wages for a small commercial building. If you know how the system works and have some respect for the position of the power company (tell the truth, present facts to support your request, and Do not get greedy), service can be obtained more rapidly and with significant cost savings.

Electrical Service Entrance on Your Project
Safety, breaking bulk

Service disconnect—shuts off all power

A service disconnect is a switch that can shut off all power to a project. The purpose is to allow quick termination of all power in an emergency, such as a fire, so the firemen can safely work to extinguish the fire. It is the first device in line after entrance by the power company. It may be located on the interior or exterior of the building—within a very short distance (6 to 25 feet) of the service entrance—and access must be unobstructed by multiple locked doors or stored material. For small residential and commercial buildings, only one service entrance with one service disconnect is allowed. This ensures quick and certain shutoff of all electrical power. Very long, skinny buildings can have multiple service entrances of the same voltage. Industrial buildings, which are heavy power users, may have multiple service entrances of different voltages. In both cases, a single service entrance would've been more efficient and safe, but may have been economically unfeasible because of the existing power company distribution network, or the configuration of an existing building.

Overcurrent protection—protects people and equipment from damage

A main circuit breaker or fuse protects the entire project's electrical installation. In the event of an intolerable electrical event—huge overcurrent or short-circuit—that could damage the project's electrical installation, all power to the project can be shut off. This can be part of or next to the main disconnect.

Change of voltage near the point of use and conditioning of power

The power company provides a single voltage at the drop, which can be connected to provide two voltages as described above (120 and 240v, 120 and 208v, 277 and 480v). If additional voltages are desired or required, transformers are added. For larger or more sensitive projects—where the quality of power is critical—power conditioning devices—to detect changes in voltage, frequency, and phasing of power (capacitance and inductance)—can be added as well. (Variations in power can come either from the power company or from the variation in load and demand of the electrical equipment and devices within your project.)

Metering—measuring and charging for power use

Power company meters are installed to assess use charges. A meter is installed very close to the service entrance so that illegal tapping upstream of the meter is dimensionally difficult or impossible. Such violations are visibly apparent.

For small stand-alone or single-tenant buildings, the city and/or power company will specify precise location of the meter. For multi-tenant buildings with the individual tenant responsible for their own power charges, meter banks must be engineered with the original service entrance—and will only have a limited amount of future flexibility. Demands for many smaller tenants, or tenants with usually large power requirements, may be impossible to accommodate later.

Service Entrance Configurations

Single-family residential and small commercial use 100 and 200 amp single phase

For small freestanding projects—where the service entrance is no more than about 50 feet from the farthest point in the project—the meter will usually be mounted on the exterior of the building. A single panel with the main breaker combined provides the overcurrent protection and the main disconnect. The breakers for the distribution branch wiring within the project are also contained within this panel. No transformers or power conditioning equipment are provided. The common sizes are 100 and 200 amps and can be constructed with off-the-shelf components so order times are minimal.

Midsize commercial projects—use standard service sizes

The common service sizes are 200, 400, and 800 amps, which can serve a 3,000 to 15,000 sf building depending on use and electrical loads within the building. The service entrance is similar to the smaller installation, but consists of multiple components: a main disconnect with overcurrent protection in a cabinet, then followed by either multiple panels—each with a disconnect—or multiple disconnect switches with overcurrent protection that then feed the panels. For a 277/480 volt system, transformers can be added to provide 120 volt power. No power conditioning equipment is typically provided. The 200 and possibly the 400 service gear are usually bought off the shelf, but the 400 and an 800 are typically catalog (made to order) and have a short delivery time—on the order of weeks.

Larger commercial and industrial projects—use custom engineered components

Larger projects combine the disconnect, overcurrent protection, transformers, power monitoring instruments, and power conditioning devices in one assembly—called switchgear. For the smallest projects, switchgear can be contained within about a 300 sf room. For larger projects, switchgear will occupy about the size of a midsize single-family house and can be either contained in the building or in a freestanding weatherproof exterior enclosure where one can enter and walk around between the components. These are custom engineered by the manufacturer of the switchgear. Even if the project design engineers schematically outline the requirements of the switchgear, a separate engineering step must follow. This engineering and fabrication time requires 3 to 12 months. And, since the gear is large, it must be sequenced during the construction operations to allow sufficient open space for installation. Space requirements for subsequent installation of repair parts must also be considered. Since the switchgear will provide the permanent power for the building, but can also be used for the construction temporary power, timing is especially critical.

Continuous uninterrupted provision of electricity

Continuous uninterrupted flow of electricity is desirable for all, and critically important for some. For single-family residential and small commercial projects, interruption of electricity is not critical—get flashlights and candles and suffer with the inconvenience. For other occupancies—where interruption is critical—some measures that can be taken in order of cost and effectiveness are discussed below.

Batteries
Simple but heavy and have limited capacity and short useful life

The use of batteries can be a simple and an effective method of providing sufficient power so the building can be safely evacuated and emergency response personnel off-site notified. Some computer battery backup systems have half-hour to an hour capacity sufficient to turn off machines. Battery backup for a limited number of emergency and exit lights to light the exit way typically will last about 90 minutes. Fire alarm and security systems connected to an off-site emergency response center last about 24 to 60 or 72 hours.

A much larger battery backup system is frequently used for telecommunications systems (e.g. phone company and other communication providers). These are intended to maintain the telecommunication portion of the building in operation during a power failure. Here an entire room of the building can be devoted to acid lead batteries. Structural support, fire enclosures, and venting to the outside can be required.

Emergency generators
Emergency generators provide backup of a small portion of the power, but startup is delayed 10 seconds

Emergency electrical generators are typically powered by diesel engines, but occasionally by natural gas. (Natural gas, which could suffer a break in the pipe line, is prohibited for the most critical uses.) These generators are intended to power a portion of the electrical needs of the building only. Exit signs, emergency lighting, and some areas of critical supervisory control, such as communication and fire alarms, may be accommodated, but seldom the entire building.

When power is lost, the emergency generator will automatically start, but this process takes just less than 10 seconds to provide acceptable power. And 10 seconds is too long for any computer-controlled device. The device will shut down and information will be lost. So emergency generators are frequently coupled with battery backup of those pieces of equipment.

Emergency generators generate flue gas, heat, noise, and vibration. For a pad-mounted generator outside the building, these considerations are easily managed. However, if the generator must be installed in the building, accommodation can be huge. Installation of the flue and sufficient pipe insulation to prevent fire can be a difficult routing problem and cost many times the cost of the generator itself—up to four weeks' wages per floor. The heat of the generator must be removed. If this cannot be done by direct venting to the outside, a water cooling system will have to be provided—and the water refrigeration machine will have to be powered by the emergency generator as well. Noise insulation and vibration isolation pads (a steel-framed concrete rectangle resting on springs and/or rubber pads), approximately equal to the weight of the generator, must also be installed. Counting all of these considerations, it can become astronomically expensive at best and physically impossible at worst. Careful thought and planning might best be used before you commit that you can achieve such an installation. Or, alternately, a more feasible design solution should be sought early in the project development.

Critical power
Critical power requires use of two power grids to produce uninterrupted power

When no interruption of power is acceptable—such as a hospital using computer-controlled patient monitoring machines for patients in surgery—a critical power system can be used. Here, the building is connected to two completely independent power grids. When one power grid fails, an automatic transfer switch instantly switches to the other grid so there is no interruption in power. Typically, only the critical portions of the building are fed with critical power, not the entire building.

Installation of such a system is expensive both for a project and for the power company, and will only be done when the critical needs exist, and/or when the project owner is willing to pay an unusually high premium to the power company.

Overcurrent Protection, Grounding for Safety
Safety of people and machines

Overcurrent protection avoids damage to electrical components, occupants, and contents

All electrical conductors—wires, cables, and bus bars—are sized and capable of tolerating a specific amount of heat due to resistance. If overheated, due to excessive instant or continuous load, the insulation may melt or the conductor vaporize. If the electrical flow occurs in a completely unintended direction—connecting a conductor to an inappropriate location, or massive malfunction of an electrical device—a short circuit, which can cause instant vaporization of conductors, can also occur.

Overcurrent protection handles both of these conditions. One such device is a breaker, which consists of a partially sprung bimetal bar (two metals laminated together). As this bar is heated, one of the metals will expand more than the other and, at some point, spring shut and open the circuit. This has the advantage that it is reusable—as soon as the bar cools down, the breaker can be reset at no cost and with no replacement parts. It has the disadvantage that it is slow to react—up to minutes to fully heat up and trip.

Another such device is a fuse, which uses a metal bar designed to vaporize quickly before the conductor is damaged. Response time can be extremely rapid—in fractions of the second—but replacement parts must be kept on hand. In a larger commercial or industrial installation where there is large number of different types of fuses, this can require management attention for inventory control.

Single-family residential and small commercial use almost exclusively breakers for overcurrent protection. Larger commercial and industrial installations will use a combination of fuses and breakers. Some of the larger fuses can contain a fusible portion combined with the spring-operated breaker. Some can be disassembled for installation of replacement parts.

Sizing of the breakers is determined both by the size and the timing of the anticipated electrical load. A quick surge can occur when the main disconnect breaker is turned on when there is abundant power available from the power company. This must be temporarily resisted. Lighting and convenience power loads will tend to be more steady and even. Motor loads—where start-up loads are 4 to 6 times running loads, and running loads can vary—require special consideration.

Grounding—disposes of a fault into the earth

When an electrical fault occurs, it must be safely allowed to travel to ground—the earth. For small, single-family residential and commercial projects, a metal conduit is used as a ground—traveling back to the service entrance. The service entrance can be grounded to the water service entrance pipe, which enters the earth. Here, a bonding jumper, which is a cable that goes around the meter, is required to ensure that any gaskets or pipe compounds used in installation of the meter do not interrupt the electrical flow. Instead of grounding to the water pipe, a dedicated ground rod can be driven into the earth and the ground wire connected.

For small and midsize projects, an additional ground wire can be run through the conduit with the electrical conductors. For industrial projects, a ground bus system can be installed at least in the areas housing machinery with heavy electrical requirements—large motors or heating devices. Here, a grid of electrical buses (square conducting metal bars) can be installed throughout the area. And the electrical devices are connected to this bar. Grounding rods connected to this bus are driven into the earth and/

or connected to the structure in multiple locations. The purpose of such a system is to immediately and locally dispose of any faults that occur—to protect people and the machines.

A separate grounding system can also be installed in areas that have lighter electrical loads but use explosive gases. Here, each and every metallic component—doors and windows and metal tables—is connected to a ground system to prevent arcing of static electricity, which could produce an explosion.

Distributing Electricity Around Your Project

A good goal is to have the highest quality power, the least resistance, and least voltage drop in the distribution system. Larger cables and higher voltages will have less resistance and voltage drop. So larger cables—feeders—serve the individual distribution panels. Step-down transformers from a higher voltage, if used, are located close to the point of use—usually less than 100 feet. The small electrical devices—small motors, appliances, and lighting—are connected to these panels.

Providing separate lighting panels and power panels can assist the quality of the power at these panels. In this way, the variable power loads will not affect the voltage of the lighting devices.

Raceways

A raceway is a long, metal enclosure for the conductors. Raceways protect the conductors from mechanical damage after installation. In addition, raceways must have space to permit dissipation of the heat of the conductors. To dissipate this heat and prevent mechanical damage during installation (stripping off the insulation while pulling the cables), raceways can only be filled to about 40% of their space capacity. And raceways can only contain conductors of a single voltage. (A raceway that has a metal subdivision—in effect two raceways attached together—can contain one voltage in each portion of the raceway.) The common raceways are electrical metal tubing (EMT), rigid conduit, manufacturer fabricated raceways, buss duct, and flexible conduit.

EMT (electrical metal tubing)—light duty interior

EMT is a thin-walled steel tubing used for the branch wiring (wiring closest to the point of use) for above grade interior areas without moisture, chemical, or explosion hazards. Tubing is usually less than two inches, with 3/4" diameter most common. Connection of pieces uses coupling pieces—either a set screw where a screw holds the pipe, or a compression fitting where the whole coupling screws down to hold the pipe by compression. EMT can be cut, bent, and coupled by hand without power-assisted equipment.

Rigid conduit—more resistant to damage

Rigid metal conduit is thicker-walled steel tubing used for branch wiring subject to moisture, chemical, or explosion hazards, and for some underground and concrete encased applications. In larger diameters, it is also used for feeders (wiring closest to the service entrance). The common trade sizes are up to six-inch diameter. Connection of the pieces is by a threaded male-female coupling where both the coupling interior and the piping exterior are threaded. Rigid conduit requires power-assisted equipment for cutting and bending. These power-assisted operations require more time, more space, and do produce waste oil from the fabricating machines. This means that this work should be fully completed, and the equipment removed, early in the project.

Manufacturer fabricated raceways—more flexibility for later changes

When frequent changes to the number and location of power outlets with minimal disturbance of the surrounding operations is sought, manufactured raceways are sometimes used. Instead of the round tubing described above, these are long, square boxes with a removable cover and provision for addition of frequent penetrations—up to one foot on center.

These raceways can be cast into the concrete floor to form a grid work over the entire floor. If the raceway is split with a metal divider, all of the phone, data, and power wiring for interior office partitions can be fed through this grid work. Outlets can be added after occupancy without opening the ceilings or walls or significantly disturbing the occupants of the office. For power distribution, this still works well. However, after deregulation of the phone companies (who used to have all phone lines terminating in one central location) and addition of computer networks, a grid work pattern that is directed towards one central location is not well matched to these new networks.

Another system, frequently added after occupancy, is a surface mounted raceway. It is sometimes called by one manufacturer's name "wire mold." This also is a long box with a removable cover and knockout openings. A manufacturer designs all of these raceways as a complete system. Every component—raceways, terminations, couplings, bends, outlets, and other fittings are designed and manufactured by a single company. Connections are usually made by screwing or bolting these components. There are hundreds of components per system. And if you add colors, multiply the hundreds times the number of colors. So, once you start the system you're stuck for life. If a system or part of the system is later discontinued, as has happened with many sub-floor raceways, adaptation of aftermarket parts or custom fabrication of components may be required—at significant cost and time.

Buss duct—flexibility for industrial use

A buss duct is a manufactured square raceway that contains the conductors as part of the assembly. The conductors are square, un-insulated metal (usually copper) bars permanently fixed to the interior of the raceway. A skilled electrician can make connections at virtually any point along the duct. Buss ducts are typically found in industrial applications.

Flexible conduit—accommodate imperfection and reduce vibrations

Flexible steel conduit, frequently coated with a plastic or rubber coating, can be used for the last few feet (usually less than 6 feet) of connection to equipment or lights. It also can be used for tight and twisting runs, such as the interior of cabinets. Flexible conduit can readily accommodate the minor angle and dimensional imperfections that accompany all work. It can also isolate the vibrations from equipment, such as a motor, from the rest of the raceway system.

Mechanical attachment—keeps raceways attached and maintains grounding

Mechanical attachment of the raceway to the structure is an important possibility. For single-phase installations, the conduit functions as the grounding system—even one loose coupling can defeat the grounding system. The continuity of the ground is maintained by attachment of the raceway system to the structure at specified intervals.

For larger numbers of conduit or larger conduit diameters, independent support structures are required. "Trapezes" are horizontal metal bars suspended from the structure above, or structural steel supports from the columns or floor structure. Since these all take space and larger conduits requiring longer bends also takes space, these conduit runs and related support structures must be designed early in the project—before installation of some other larger components, such as the HVAC ductwork that makes them dimensionally impossible. This frequently means a shop drawing, of this routing and the structure around it, is made before installation of any work. Those graduating from a smaller project to larger projects should be aware of the importance and related time and personnel for this additional step.

The environment around the raceway—defending against water, chemicals, and fire

Water, fire, explosion, concrete, earth, and mechanical impact all deteriorate or damage a raceway system. Protection is done by selection of the raceway system as described above, but also by the fittings and devices attached to these raceways. Gaskets are added to reduce vapor transmission. Explosion-resistant fittings must be cast (not stamped), which can increase their size 500 percent. Critical underground locations such as high voltage lines and feeders serving fire pumps, can be concrete encased (usually tinted red) to protect against mechanical damage. This protection of the raceways is critical, and has huge cost and material delivery impacts.

Conductors—Pathways for Electrical Motion

Copper vs. aluminum

Conductors are long, slender pieces, made either of aluminum or copper that conduct electricity. Conductors consist of wire (a single conductor in insulating jacket), cable (multiple conductors in one insulating jacket), or buss bars (rectangular conductors with no insulation).

Aluminum has the desirable characteristic of being cheaper, lighter, and stronger in tension. But it has the undesirable characteristics that, first, it is about a 50 to 70% less effective conductor so must be larger than copper to accommodate the same load. It also has severe drawbacks that the connections between aluminum conductors expand and contract more—and oxidize and corrode. If properly secured by a clamping compression fitting, aluminum conductors may be safely and effectively used. However, if a single connection anywhere in the project is imperfect, a fire can start. This is a level of quality control that is practically unachievable.

For this reason, aluminum conductors are usually used for larger conductors that must be hung longer distances between supports. Few connections are needed and these can be visually inspected. Aluminum conductors are either discouraged or specifically prohibited in other locations; then copper is used instead.

Connection of conductors to devices

In a single-phase system, a hot (line voltage) conductor is connected on one side of a device and a neutral on the other—a supply and return to allow the flow of electrons. In a three-phase system, a connection can be made between 2 phases or between 1 phase and a neutral. The neutral provides the advantage that the load on one phase does not influence another phase.

Conductor to conductor connection—methods and devices

There are four joining methods to conductors, or a conductor to service gear or equipment:

Twisted wire with cap

Small wire sizes (AWG 18-AWG 6) can be joined by twisting the two wires together followed by twisting on a cap such as a wire nut. This is done manually without power-assisted tools. Visual inspection of the joint after installation is not possible.

A bolt compressed clamping system

For connection of larger conductors (AWG 14–500 MCM) to service gear or equipment, a clamping fitting is used. This consists of a lug (to permit bolting to the equipment) connected to a clamping device. The conductor is inserted in the clamping device and a bolt compresses and secures the conductor. This is frequently called a solderless connection. If two conductors are to be joined, similar sets of clamping arrangements are used. This is frequently called a split bolt connection.

Compression (a metal jacket)

The compression fitting is similar to the solderless connection described above except the cable is secured by compression of the metal jacket around the conductor. This jacket is similar to the metal cylinder that connects the eraser to a wood pencil. A special crimping tool is required.

Welded connection

As the name implies, the conductor is joined by welding. A common use is to join a grounding conductor to the building structure.

Insulation of Conductors—Resisting Electrical Flow, Defending Against Water, Heat, and Chemicals

The insulation on conductors must resist mechanical damage, chemical attack, moisture, and heat—so there are different installation types that are strongest in each of these capacities. The capacity of the insulation is shown by a four place symbol on the jacket of the insulation. The first is the material of the insulation (T = thermoplastic, R = rubber), and the second is the operating temperature (H = 167 F, HH = 194 F both operating temperature at full current load), third is moisture resistance (W = wet), and fourth is the outer jacket (N = nylon). For example, THHW means moisture and heat resistant thermoplastic, and THHN means heat resistant thermoplastic.

The insulation is also color-coded to indicate its installed use—always white or natural gray for neutral, green for grounding. But black, red, blue, brown, yellow, or orange all can be used for line voltage. Knowing the labeling and color-coding system is useful in evaluating installed electrical devices. But it also has importance in project management. Since there are multiple insulation jackets (which are difficult or impossible to fully see after installation in conduit), and color coding for line voltage is not completely uniform, it can be a wise decision to standardize wire and insulation types for an entire project (even if in some locations some small additional cost is incurred), so that inadvertent and undetectable mistakes are not made.

User Disconnects and Controls—for Safety and Efficiency

Disconnects—local power shut offs

To safely maintain and service electrical equipment, a convenient and effective means of disconnecting the power to a device must be provided. The specific location and dimensions of the disconnect in relation to the equipment is regulated, but the principle is that it must be very close—within feet—and in visual contact of the service personnel so they can ensure that it's off and it doesn't get turned on during service operations. All serviceable equipment, such as heating devices and motors, require such a disconnect.

For the very smallest motors and devices, the wall plug can simply be removed. For slightly larger devices—motors up to about 2 hp the manual toggle switch similar in principle to a light switch is sufficient. Larger devices require a magnetic starter, which uses a pushbutton that activates a solenoid to close the switch. Who provides such starters—the mechanical, plumbing, or the electrical contractor? The answer requires a piece-by-piece determination in the estimating and purchasing stage of project management. There is no standard practice or uniformly right answer, and since even midsize starters can cost over a week's wages and there are hundreds of starters on a project, imprecise definition is a common mistake. It can consume a good part of the profit on a project or cause you to lose your job!

Motors and motor control centers—control and protection

Larger motors require a means to turn them on and off, but have other demands as well. The electrical load of a motor is variable. Start up current is typically four-to-six times the running current. The running current will vary with the load imposed on the motor. And if the rotor of the motor locks due to heavy load, the current will increase until the motor is damaged or an overcurrent protection device is tripped. There are several ways to deal with this variable current requirement of motors.

Fractional horsepower motors (3/4 hp or less) start with full current and may or may not have a device to shut the motor down if overheated. Motor speed and power delivered will vary under load.

Motors may also have multiple windings that can be energized in sequence. For example, a 20 hp motor could have two windings. The first winding is energized activating a 10 hp motor and once up to speed, the second winding is energized to produce the full 20 hp.

Motors may also be started with variable voltage. Here, an autotransformer is combined with the motor to start at very low voltage and increase to a higher voltage as the motor starts and increases in speed. Such a starter contains an on/off switch, usually an overcurrent protection device, and autotransformer, if used, and instrumentation and relays to sense the condition of the motor and activate the appropriate devices at the appropriate time. The smallest devices may be 8 inches on the side and can be purchased as stock items. Larger devices can be about the size of a residential refrigerator and are custom engineered for the project.

Where multiple motors exist, a motor control center containing many controllers can be fabricated as one connected assembly. Similar to switchgear, these are engineered by the manufacturer, so months to a year must be allowed for engineering and fabrication.

Electrical Load Calculation
Finding a reasonable estimate of what will happen when

There are many electrical devices on a project, each operating at different times with different demands when in operation. If all were run, or worse yet, all were started at the same time, the electrical load and therefore, the service size demanded, would be huge. This instant start and continuous use is a highly improbable or almost impossible event. Calculation of electrical load involves estimating how much less than the maximum is certain and probable.

The electrical load for each device—lights, motors, and heaters—under start up and continuous load can be known from the manufacturer's data on the equipment. Estimating the amount and kind of usage requires application of rules and judgment.

Diversity and demand factors—reduce estimated service size

These describe in percentages from 0–100% how much of the time an electrical device will be in use. If two loads cannot possibly be on at the same time, for example, a mechanical unit that can heat or cool but not both at once, only the larger of the two electrical loads will be counted. For retail and industrial spaces, where all the lights will typically be on at once, the demand factor is 100%. For load calculations for residential duplex receptacles, a demand factor of 25% may be assumed the rule. For usages where reliable estimates are more difficult, 75% usage may be assumed. What you definitely know you can calculate, what you do not know for sure is usually specified by rule. When the calculation is done, you need some provision for future expansion and a safety factor of about 20%. That is to say, a 100-amp panel would only be permitted to serve an 80-amp load.

It is useful to know that service size for a building is calculated based on some assumptions of use. It is not adding up all the electrical loads in the building, nor is it adding the capacities of all the breakers in the electrical service gear. Remodeling and changes of use within these assumptions is possible, but further revisions are limited or impossible.

Bigger is more efficient and cheaper per unit delivered

Higher voltages permit smaller conductors. Larger service gear and motors run more efficiently. This permits lower installation and operating cost per unit of electrical work delivered. There are approximately 50% savings (per unit of achieved electrical capacity) in going from a 230 volt to a 460 volt system, a 25 hp to a 100 hp motor, or a 25 KVA to a 250 KVA transformer. The project size and type heavily influence the design of the electrical system. But when it is a choice, knowing that bigger is better can produce huge initial and long-term cost savings.

The Design and Engineering Role of an Electrical Contractor

More than any other trade, the electrical contractor is responsible for portions of the project field engineering and design. If one has a theoretical knowledge of electricity and a practical knowledge of electrical materials and methods (two very large ifs), the electrical code becomes a how-to manual—a recipe book. So, this requires the electrical contractors personnel down to installing tradesmen to review, understand, calculate, and engineer parts of the installation. Further, vendors hired by the electrical contractor will engineer, design, and fabricate the switchgear and motor control centers.

No matter how good your design and specifications you are only halfway done. The other half is done by the knowledge and work of the electrical contractor. Engaging the electrical contractor early in the design process can significantly accelerate the schedule, solve problems before they become problems, decrease cost, and increase serviceability of the installed work.

Summary

Electrical power is the flow of electrons forced by the difference in potential to do useful work. This flow is resisted by the natural resistance of the conducting material increased by heat. This causes voltage drops that must be managed. This flow is most efficient and these resistances the least with large diameter conductors and high voltages.

The electrical design should start with the largest conductors and highest voltages possible and move towards the point of service entrance, successively decreasing the conductor size and sometimes the voltage, to the point of use. For buildings, alternating current is used for most purposes. Direct current, which has the capacity to precisely control the speed of a motor without overheating and without the need for an additional transmission device, is used for elevators and some industrial equipment.

A power company provides power to the project with very specific voltages and frequencies. They own and maintain the grid and network up to the point of your service entrance drop.

The electrical service entrance consists of: a disconnect to shut off all power to the building in an emergency, overcurrent protection to protect the electrical installation from damage caused by heavy usage or unexpected surges from outside the project, a break of bulk for distribution, and sometimes power conditioning equipment and transformers. On the smallest project, this can be as simple as a single panel with the main breaker. On a larger project, it can expand to custom-fabricated switchgear the size of the single-family house.

The power is distributed around the project in conductors enclosed in raceways. Both must be selected to withstand varying exposures to earth, concrete, water, chemicals, fire, and explosion. Size, costs, engineering time, and fabrication time can vary hugely in response to these accommodations. An additional means of overcurrent protection and disconnect is provided by closeness—being within a few to, at most, a hundred feet—of the final point of use for all equipment over about 3/4 hp and for heating devices.

Bigger is better—more efficient to install and run—but, bigger means the work is more complex and that more knowledge is required. And this knowledge is not obtained from a single source, and it can not be completely delegated. "We hire good consultants to handle that" is wishful thinking and a recipe for failure. Good installations require management by all involved with the project. And, this requires some knowledge of some electrical facts to know who to hire, how to manage them, and what is needed. This chapter helps provide such knowledge, and helps achieve project success.

3.17 Electrical Lighting—Managing Light Levels, Colors, and Contrast

Even if you do not want to, or think you can or should, you will have influence, up to complete control over lighting design. A little knowledge will help

What Is Light?

Light is the middle part of the electromagnetic spectrum

Light is the visual portion of the electromagnetic spectrum. This spectrum has different wave lengths, which produce different effects and results. Longer wave lengths produce radio, television, and microwave signals. Wave lengths just longer than the visible spectrum—infrared wave lengths—produce heat. The visible spectrum has wave lengths of 4,000 (red), then yellow, green, blue up to 7,600 angstroms (violet). (An angstrom is very small—about one trillion of an inch. A fact you Do not need to remember!) Shorter still wave lengths are x-rays and gamma rays.

Lighting is the visible spectrum. But visible light sources will also produce some infrared and ultraviolet, which can sometimes interfere with communication signals such as radio. (A concern about low strength signals is not normal in commercial construction.) But the spillover effects of the other parts of the electromagnetic spectrum must be recognized and managed—with light fixture selection and location. A good rule is to take the light you want and manage the rest of the spectrum that comes with it!

Brightness—how much light is there?

Brightness is the amount of luminous flux (light energy) at or on a surface. One common measure is the foot candle—the light energy one candle will produce on a one square foot surface one foot away. Another name for the foot candle is a lumen. And, a lux is 1/10 of a foot candle or lumen.

Up to about 100 foot candles produces continual increase in visual performance—both color and detail perception. However, except for small areas of detail work, increases above 100 foot candles produce little further benefit and increase fatigue. Eventually, it becomes painful.

Color—how is it measured and described?

Color is measured and described in three ways. The first is chromaticity (correlated color temperature), which refers to heating a metal to a specified temperature—measured in degrees Kelvin (centigrade minus

273 degrees to absolute zero) and then measuring the color produced. A second is called the color rendering index (CRI). This compares—in percentages up to 100—how closely the light source resembles incandescent. These numbers were developed by surveying the reactions of human subjects asking, "How closely does it resemble an incandescent light?" and is a widely accepted measure. The comparisons of these measurements for common light sources are:

Lamp type	Correlated color temperature (degrees kelvin)	Color rendering index (CRI)
Incandescent	3,000	100
Fluorescent warm white	3,020	52
Florescent cool white	4,190	62
Mercury clear	5,750	16
Metal halide	3,990	62
High-pressure sodium	2,100	21
Low-pressure sodium	1,740	-44

(Low-pressure sodium is almost all yellow—making the appearance of other colors so bad that it rates a negative number.)

These are averages. When extreme color correctness is sought, the proportions of each wave length (color) produced by a light source can be obtained either from the manufacturer of the lamp or evaluated in a testing laboratory; 3,500 K is now considered an adequate compromise between light quality and cost for interior lighting.

Occasionally, color will be described with verbal descriptions—"blue northwest sky," "uniform overcast sky," "average mixture of sunlight and skylight," and "candle flame." These casual sounding names actually correspond to precise color temperatures.

Light of certain wave lengths must be reflected off a pigmented surface capable of reflecting that wave length or the color is not seen. Both the correct light source and reflective surfaces are required to see a color.

Technical Note: *Only lighting engineers' and some interior designers' daily work requires this much detailed discussion about color. But the rest of us are sometimes asked to manage and decide such matters. The few ideas above give the concepts that reduce intimidation and make these informed decisions possible.*

How Do We Form a Picture from the Light We See?
The eye does not snap a picture like a camera but rather constructs an image from many changing clues gathered over time

Detail is perceived by the eye in the small center portion—at angles of only a couple degrees—called a fovea. The vision to about 30° is adequate though less precise, and lesser peripheral vision extends to about 170°. The eye moves about 10 times per second to construct a composite image from a collection of snapshots.

Color is seen better at higher light levels

The eye has two sensing devices: cones, which are good at low light levels but have poor color sensitivity, and rods, which work at higher light levels and have better color sensitivity. So, we have very poor color perception in low light levels, particularly at night. And to change from use of rods to cones is instant from dark to light, but about 60 times slower from light to dark—taking up to an hour for full adaptation. This is familiar for anyone entering a dark theater during the daytime—where it can take a few minutes of adaptation to even find the seats. Upon leaving the theater, the adaptation to the lighter condition is instant, but may be uncomfortable.

Contrast is essential for vision
More light helps but only to a point—higher contrast required at lower light levels

The eye requires contrast to see. You can read this page because there are dark letters on light paper. This contrast is essential and improves to a point, but increased contrast produced by higher light levels is fatiguing. So contrast can be far higher at lower light levels. For example, the moon might have a contrast ratio to the surrounding night sky of 5,000,000 to 1, and we see the new moon with no discomfort.

Another form of excessive contrast is glare. Here, the angle of reflectance of the light causes what might otherwise be acceptable contrast to become focused in an undesirable location—becoming excessive. Reflection angles over 30 degrees can begin to produce glare on some surfaces. At over 60 degrees most, and over 80 degrees virtually all, surfaces produce glare. Rougher surfaces will increase the angle at which glare occurs, but not eliminate it altogether.

The Eye Puts It All Together

The workings of the eye described above—constant motion and changes in response to contrast and changes in light levels—influences how our eye assembles an image and how we provide lighting to assist this.

> *Time of viewing*—The more time we have to evaluate an image, the better the reaction will be. And more time will allow some reduction in the light level and contrast, while still producing the same result.

> *Size of object viewed*—The larger the object, the faster and better the reaction will be at a given light level. One instinctively moves an object closer to the eye for this reason.

> *Contrast*—Increase in contrast—to a point—will increase perception. Common desirable levels of contrast for interior lighting conditions range from 3 to 1 for a task in the immediate surround, 10 to 1 for a task in the far surround, and 40 to 1 anywhere in the field of vision.

> *Amount of light reflected*—More light up to the point of discomfort, again, means better perception. The light level and contrast work together. If the amount of light reflected is extremely low, the contrast can be greatly increased.

All four of these factors are interactive as described above. But the time of viewing and the size of the object viewed are not easily controllable—so we design lighting in response to them. Light fixture design focuses on contrast and the amount of light provided and reflected.

Human factors are important

In addition to the engineering considerations of vision discussed above, we all have certain perceptions of what light levels should be for certain settings. The saying "stay out of dark alleys" indicates our instinctive association between light levels and security. Increased light levels will also tend to make people talk louder. Lower light levels are used for a quieter mode in some restaurants. And some current zoning ordinances dictate that about 1/2 foot candle is the maximum amount of light one property can discharge on another—an engineering definition of good neighborliness!

Light Sources

Light from the sun

Daylight, sometimes called natural light, implies that it is somehow superior or preferable to other light forms. It can produce even color rendition, which is valued when color correctness is important, such as matching samples in the printing industry.

But it's not always superior. Natural light is gone at night, varies with time of year, time of day, and cloud cover. So, when predictable lighting at desired times is essential, as it is in most work environments, daylight must be supplemented with light produced by electricity.

Making Light—Electricity Makes Something Glow

Incandescent lamps—use a glowing wire

An incandescent lamp is a hot wire in a bottle. It consists of a base, a filament (usually tungsten), and a glass bulb. The bulb is filled with either nitrogen or argon—unreactive gases—at atmospheric pressure. This is the simplest type of light. It is the original type developed by Thomas Edison. (The correct term for a replaceable device that produces light is lamp. Incandescent lights are more commonly referred to as bulbs and fluorescent lights as tubes.)

They work when line voltage, usually at 120 volts, flows through the filament causing resistance, heat, and light. When operating, pieces of the tungsten filament are constantly leaving the filament and blackening the bulb. The blackening will reduce light output by about 25%. And when the filament is reduced by 25%, it breaks and the light instantly stops.

Weak points of incandescent lamps

1. Short lamp life—The useful rated life of some lamps is: 25 watt 2,500 hours, 60 watt 1,000 hours, and 200 watt 750 hours.
2. High heat production—The light and heat produced by lamps is:

Lamp	Light (visible) %	Infrared light %	Heat %
25 watt	8.7	85.3	6
60 watt	7.5	73.3	19.7
200 watt	10.2	67.2	22.6

3. They give way more heat than light.
4. Not energy efficient—A 25-watt lamp produces 11 lumens per watt, a 100-watt lamp about 16 lumens per watt, and 1,000-watt lamp 23 lumens per watt. All are low efficiencies.

Strong points of incandescent lamps

1. Even colors favoring the warm end of the spectrum—Color correctness and warm hue are favored for residential and hospitality uses.
2. Versatile—Incandescent lights come in a wide variety of bases, bulb sizes, textured and tinted glass, shapes, and wattages.
3. Easily dimmed—Can be easily dimmed from 0–100% by varying the voltage, using the simplest of dimmers.
4. Not temperature or time sensitive—Incandescent lamps can operate in any temperature, and can be turned on and off at any time without shortening lamp life.
5. Low fixture cost and no auxiliaries—No auxiliaries such as ballasts, starters, or transformers are required, so the initial light fixture and following maintenance costs can be low.

Tungsten halide lamps—a smaller and hotter incandescent light

The incandescent light has one variation—instead of argon or nitrogen, the lamp is filled with a halogen compound such as iodine, bromine, fluorine, or chlorine. These chemicals cause a regenerative cycle in which the tungsten leaving the filament is sucked back and bonded to the filament again. This both increases the filament life and reduces the blackening of the glass. This permits the light to work at a higher temperature, which in turn permits greatly shrinking the size of the lamp—to less than 1/2" across. This can be useful in or around tight spaces such as cabinet work.

Glowing Gas Produces the Light—Fluorescent, Mercury Vapor, and Sodium Vapor

Fluorescent lamps—an interior lighting workhorse

A fluorescent lamp consists of electrodes and a glass enclosure, which is filled with a reactive gas. The electrodes initiate and maintain a flow of electrons. The flow of electrons causes electrical activity within the gas that produces electromagnetic radiation.

Several aspects of this process must be managed. First, the starting voltage to initially excite the gas is higher than the running voltage. Second, with the alternating current power source, the flow of electrons is interrupted 60 times per second, which can cause flicker of the lights. Finally, the arc column at the electrode has a negative resistance—meaning that as it heats up the electrical resistance drops. If not regulated, this decrease in resistance will produce an increase in current that could destroy the lamp within a fraction of a second. Management of these aspects requires auxiliary electrical devices—ballasts, transformers, capacitors, and frequency converters that are used as described below.

The fluorescent lamp was introduced in the 1930s. A fluorescent lamp has the components described above. The glass enclosure contains a few drops of mercury. When the electron flow vaporizes and excites this mercury, it gives off ultraviolet radiation. When nothing further is done, the lamp is used for sun tanning and vegetable inspection. But when phosphor coating on the interior of the glass is added, the ultraviolet light causes theses phosphors to glow—visible light. Additional chemicals can be added to the phosphors to improve the evenness of the light produced.

The reactions that produce the light are temperature sensitive. This means first that the diameter of the tube cannot be too large or it will cool and the desired reaction will stop. These lights are designed to work at room temperatures of 70–80°F. They work progressively worse, then eventually stop, at colder temperatures. Enclosures that retain the heat around the lamps—and lower temperature ballasts—can extend the working temperature range only a little. Both the lamp and the ballast deteriorate with age—with a noticeable decrease in light output, increase in flicker, and eventual instant failure.

The auxiliary that can manage some of these problems consists of a ballast to perform the required electrical regulation (described above). It can also include a capacitor to improve the power factor and a frequency converter to change the 60 cycles per second line voltage delivered to as high as 25,000 cycles per second—to reduce the apparent flicker.

Weak points of fluorescent lamps

1. Color correctness—Fluorescent lamps favor the blue-green colors, and the light produced is not evenly distributed across the color spectrum. There are noticeable spikes of colors at certain wave lengths. Addition of other chemicals to the phosphors—for "warm," "deluxe," and "full spectrum" offers only partial improvement.

2. Not versatile—The tube diameter is limited by temperature as described above. Further, energy efficiency of the lamp increases for longer tubes and smaller diameters—another limitation on tube shape.

3. Temperature and time sensitive—In addition to the temperature sensitivity described above, fluorescent lights cannot be efficiently turned on and off frequently. They work most efficiently if left on for a minimum of three hours. More frequent cycling will reduce efficiency and shorten lamp life.

4. Radio frequency interference—Fluorescent light fixtures can produce radio interference for surrounding electronic equipment. This can occur with extremely sensitive equipment within 10 feet of the fluorescent fixture—such as in radio stations and laboratories with sensitive electronic equipment. For normal commercial installations, this concern can be safely ignored.

5. Dimming limited—Manufacturers claim that fluorescent lights with specialized ballasts and dimming equipment can be dimmed from 30–100% of capacity. Although this may technically be true, user reaction has found the results generally unsatisfactory. If you want good dimming, choose another type of lighting system.

Strong points of fluorescent lamps

1. Energy efficient light producer—A 48" 40-watt lamp will produce about 76 lumens per watt. However, the required auxiliary also uses power—reducing the light output per watt by about 20%.
2. Less heat production per light production—The fluorescent lamp produces: light 16.5%, infrared 37.5%, heat 46%. This is about double the light produced per watt by an incandescent lamp.
3. Long lamp life—The lamp life of a fluorescent lamp will range from 12,000 to 20,000 hours.

Neon lamps
Usually used for decoration and signs

A neon light is similar to a fluorescent light, except that it is filled with neon gas, which glows pinkish red. Addition of helium can produce pinkish white. The glass can be tinted to produce other colors. Due to a high striking (starting) voltage, neon lights can work in colder temperatures.

Mercury vapor lamps
Usually used for industrial and exterior use

The mercury vapor lamp is about the size of a lipstick case and contains some mercury. Unlike the fluorescent lamp—where the mercury gas glows—for mercury vapor lights, the arc itself produces the light.

Weak points of mercury vapor lamps

1. Color correctness—These lamps heavily favor the blue and green colors. Red is almost nonexistent and ultraviolet is high. This makes them suitable for landscape lighting and less suitable for other applications. Phosphors can be added to the interior of the lamp to improve color correctness.
2. Not versatile—The lamp comes in one configuration with different outputs—all very close in size and shape.
3. Long start and restart times—Starting and achieving full light output takes about five minutes. Once shut off, it must cool down for three to five minutes before restart. This can be a serious drawback for security lighting.
4. Position sensitive—The lamp works well in the vertical but poorly in the horizontal position.

Strong points of mercury vapor lamps

1. Energy-efficient light producer—Metal halide lights will produce about 50 to 60 lumens per watt. From this must be subtracted about 12 percent for the energy use of the auxiliary transformer.

2. Long lamp life—The stated lamplight will be around 24,000 hours, but actual usage can frequently be longer, with some reduction in the light output.

3. Higher wattages mean fewer fixtures—Lamp wattages in the 400–1,000 watt range can be obtained, permitting greater spacing between fewer fixtures. This can be an advantage when the cost of the mounting device, such as a parking lot light pole, and the labor cost to replace lamps are both considerable. If halogens are added, the light efficiency can increase to 100 lumens per watt. The color rendition improves, but the restrike time can increase to 15 minutes.

Sodium vapor lamps
Mostly used for parking lots and highways

Sodium vapor lights are similar to mercury vapor, except sodium rather than mercury is used. The lamp is about the size of a cigarette. It is about 100% more efficient than a mercury lamp, and 25% more efficient than a mercury lamp with halogens added. But 15–75 watts per fixture must be subtracted for the power of the auxiliary. It is not position sensitive. It takes about 10–20 minutes to start and reach full capacity. Restriking requires a 3–4 four minute cool down.

The light of a low-pressure sodium lamp is almost exclusively yellow. Reflected colors may appear grayish or difficult to see at all. High-pressure sodium lamps reduce but do not eliminate this deficiency.

Summary—Lamps

Incandescent lights used heavily in residential applications are energy inefficient, simple, versatile, color correct, and flexible. Fluorescent lights used in commercial applications are more energy efficient, but worse in all other ways. Mercury and sodium lights are used for industrial and exterior lights. These choices are based on engineering facts, local custom, local fixture supplies, and the knowledge of local tradesmen. So, changing a lamp type can be resisted and slow. Pick this fight carefully.

Directing Light—Managing Light Location and Contrast

Lighting originates from a single point and radiates to many points in all directions. But it is desired in only some of these points and directions. Reflectors are used to redirect the light to these desired locations.

Reflectors—Direct and Focus Light, Manage Heat

The amount of light reflected is influenced by the type of material, color of material, roughness of material, and angle to the light source. Reflectors are installed in back of the light source. The percent reflection (directly back) of materials commonly used as reflectors is:

Material	Light reflected straight back
Aluminum polished	85%
Aluminum matt	80%
Stainless steel polished	55–65%
Porcelain enamel shiny	60–80%
Porcelain enamel matt	60–83%
White wall surfaces	70–90%

Adding color can reduce the reflectivity down to near zero. As the angle of reflectance decreases from 90 degrees (straight on) to zero degrees (light parallel to the surface), the amount of reflection increases for all materials and roughness. At about 80 degrees, all materials including black become a reflector—as one knows from driving along the blacktop road when the sun is low.

Reflectors are shaped in three ways:

1. *Semicircle*—A semicircle can reflect light ranging from a complete scattering of the light to complete focus at one point—by varying the distance of the light source from the reflector—similar to the way a handheld magnifying glass can focus sunlight on a point.
2. *Parabola*—A parabola is a curved shape that has the property that a properly located light source will reflect light parallel and in one direction. The headlight of a car is one such example. Some lighting needs will have only one of these requirements—such as the spotlight in a theater—but most need a combination of spot and diffuse lighting. So these reflectors need a complex curve combining parts of a semicircle and parts of a parabola.
3. *Irregular reflectors*—If diffuse light, rather than a combination of focused and diffuse light is required, sometimes the entire interior of a fixture will be an unengineered reflector. A suitable reflecting material is chosen and a combination of flat and angle surfaces with an imprecise purpose form the interior of the fixture. An economical 2 x 4 fluorescent fixture is one such example. The imprecise reflection by the reflector must be supplemented with a light fixture lens for some applications.

Lenses and Diffusers—Further Focuses Light and Manages Glare

Even if the reflector were fully capable of directing the light to the desired location, there would still be one problem: the contrast between the light fixture and the surrounding area would be too great for comfort. To reduce this contrast and further manage and distribute the location of light, lenses in front of the light sources are used, as described below.

Translucent material

The amount of light transmitted is influenced by the material, and color and texture of the material, as follows:

Material	Transmission %	Reflection %
Clear glass	80–92	8–10
Acid etched glass	82–88	7–9
Sand blasted glass	77–81	11–16
Solid white glass	12–38	40–66
Textured glass	57–90	7–24
Mirrored glass		80–90

What isn't transmitted or reflected is heat and reduces light output. The glass will also slightly change the path of the light rays producing some diffusion and glare reduction. A frosted incandescent light bulb, flat colored plastic sheets in a 2 x 4 fluorescent fixture, and glass lampshades are examples.

"Egg crate" and parabolic lenses

The egg crate lens, as the name implies, is a grid work of flat vertical slats forming boxes between a half-inch to 2-1/2 inches on a side. This reduces glare by directing light rays directly down through the grid. A variation is the parabolic grid where, instead of flat slats, the slats are curved in the partial shape of a parabola, which focuses the light downward more effectively.

Prismatic lens

These are flat plastic sheets covered with small clear plastic pyramids. These refract the light, while not markedly decreasing transmission.

Shades

These reduce glare by markedly decreasing light levels and partially redirecting the light. Residential fabric or paper lampshades are examples. Perforated metal is more common in commercial fixtures.

Indirect light—reflect it all

To manage contrast and glare, the light source can be obscured from vision and all light reflected off the other surfaces in the room. It can also be effective for dramatic effect and mood lighting. But every time light is reflected, some light is converted to heat and lost. This method does not have maximum efficiency. And, it can be difficult to reflect sufficient light for effective detailed task lighting.

Photometric Diagrams Show How Much Light Goes Where

The combination of reflectors and lenses will produce a light pattern both within the light fixture, sometimes in back of it, and on the surface to be illuminated. For commercial fixtures, the manufacturer will measure these light values and produce a map called a photometric diagram. This resembles the geographical topographic map with lines showing the location of equal light levels. And they show both the illuminated surface and the wasted light that is reflected and lost in back of the fixture. For parking lots using multiple light poles, many fixture manufacturers (if you agree to buy their fixtures) will produce a photometric diagram showing the achieved light levels for every point on your site.

Cautionary note: Although few think they are responsible for intentionally designing lighting, they make decisions that matter. Knowing that the material, color, and roughness of the fixture reflector and lens, and that all surfaces in the room influence lighting quality will assist correct decisions.

Light Fixtures—Assembling the Components in a Useful Housing

Light fixtures consist of a source of light, auxiliaries to make the light work, reflectors and lenses, and a housing. The correct name for a light fixture is technically luminaire (a French word for light fixture) but few know this or use the term.

Light fixtures must:

1. Make light of a suitable color and quantity, direct it where required, and manage glare.
2. Control the heat within and around the fixture.
3. Resist the environment—such as water, chemicals, ultraviolet light, mechanical damage, and vandalism.
4. Balance the economies of initial cost, operating energy cost, and the maintenance cost to change lamps and other parts.

Four jobs of the light fixture housing

The light fixture housing encloses and assembles the lamp, auxiliaries if any, reflectors, and lens. The fixture housing must perform four functions:

1. ***Manage heat for proper performance of the lamp***—In almost all cases, the task is to direct the heat generated by the lamp to a suitable location. If there is a non-critical and large area behind the fixture, such as with the suspended light in a factory, heat may be acceptably dissipated in this direction. In other cases, such as landscape lighting, if additional heat on the lighted subject is not objectionable, heat may be directed with the light. One exception is fluorescent light fixtures for colder temperatures where they may design the light fixture housing to retain the heat generated. Heat management is essential for proper operation and useful life of a fixture, and the method and direction of heat management must be determined before the fixture can be selected.

2. ***Resist the environment surrounding the fixture***—Resistance to chemicals, and water liquids or vapors is accomplished by selection of the housing material and coating on this material, followed by gasketing. This can range from a simple cork lens washer for a residential shower fixture to multiple plastic and rubber gaskets at every opening and penetration of the light fixtures, so that it can operate under water—such as a swimming pool light. Resistance to ultraviolet light is done largely by the coating on the fixture housing. Resistance to explosion usually requires heavier and larger cast, not stamped, housings and full gasketing.

3. ***Resist mechanical damage***—Resisting the mechanical impact from objects that occur in an industrial environment or vandalism is accomplished first by increasing the thickness and reinforcing the fixture housing. Much of the required improvement focuses on the lens—changing from glass to plastic, such as polycarbonate. Substantial concealment of most of the fixture parts in a concrete or block wall, and covering the lens with metal bars or grills, offers further improvement. All of these are impact and vandalism resistant. Aggressive damage—such as by firearms—will still occur.

4. ***Appearance***—The demands for specific appearance can range from nonexistent in industrial applications to the most critical criteria in some high-end retail, restaurant, and hotel uses. This gap is so great it usually is not bridged—the fixture is either of good lighting performance but indifferent appearance or the opposite, indifferent performance but good looking. When both characteristics are demanded, such as for museums or showpiece theaters, cost and delivery time can increase 1,000 to 5,000 %.

Cautionary note: Awareness of the reason for importance of these four tasks helps manage fixture selection.

Age and Dirt Must Be Considered
Old age is no fun—and grime doesn't pay

All the discussions above about energy efficiency and color correctness of lamps are for new lamps out of the box, but this doesn't last. Lamps will lose about 25% of their light output over their life. And the distribution of light colors changes over this time as well. Expensive color correct lamps gradually become less correct. And the normal accumulation of dust and grime on the light fixture reflector and lens can reduce the light output by 50%. Cleaning and relamping can manage this total 75% reduction in light output, but at around 10 years of service, complete fixture replacement for a moderately priced interior fixture becomes an economic alternative to continued maintenance. The useful life of an exterior fixture may be 50–100% longer. Decorative fixtures valued for their appearance, not specific lighting performance, may have a useful life equal to the life of the building.

Controlling Lights

Switching

Line voltage switching—simple, but number of fixtures on a switch is limited

With line voltage switching, the current that powers the lights flows through the switch. Flipping this switch provides the power and turns on the lights. This is a system used in all normal houses, light commercial, retail, and offices. It is simple and requires no special equipment or devices, but it has one limitation. Since the current for all the fixtures controlled by a switch flow through this switch, the number of fixtures that can be controlled by a single switch is limited by the current carrying capacity of the conducting wire and the switch. This means that only about six 2 x 4 fluorescent fixtures can be controlled by one switch. It also means that if you wish to remodel and change the switching arrangement, you must rewire the line voltage (power) to the light fixtures.

Low voltage switching—allows many fixtures on one switch

In this system, powering of the light fixture and switching of the light fixture are separated. The fixtures are powered by normal line voltage—120 or 277 volt. How the line voltage is circuited does not restrict the switching possibilities. Switching is accomplished by a low voltage 12 or 24 volt signal to each fixture. The number of fixtures that can be controlled by a single switch vastly increases to the point where, for most uses, it can be considered unlimited. Remodeling switching can be accomplished by changing the switching control wires only—not the line voltage power wiring to the fixtures.

Dimming—varying the quantity of light from a fixture

Varying the quantity of light produced by a fixture can first be accomplished by activating part or parts of the lamp or lamps. A three-way incandescent light is one example. This light has two independent filaments. The first, the second, or both filaments at once can be energized to produce three different light levels. Similarly, a 3 tube fluorescent light fixture with two ballasts can energize 1, 2, or 3 lamps to produce three different light levels.

Light levels can be altered by dimming. Here, a dimming switch alters the voltage delivered to all lamps in a fixture. Dimming from 0 to 100% works well for incandescent fixtures, but poorly for fluorescent fixtures, and not at all for other gaseous discharge fixtures.

Automatic Control
Several methods, but most have limitations

Time clocks—simple, but can only handle a few circuits. Also must be manually reset

A manual time clock is a line voltage switch commonly used to activate signs and security lighting. Here, a clock face is powered by a small motor and pegs are placed at the desired on and off times on the clock face. As the wheel rotates, the pegs trip a switch that activates the lights. The two limitations are first, since line voltage flows through the time clock, the number of light fixtures that can be controlled by a single time clock is extremely limited—usually only one or two. Second, changing the activation times throughout the year requires someone to remember to do this at the appropriate time. If multiple time clocks are used at one location, the result can be uneven and confusing—Is anyone there? Are they out of business? Or are some of the lights broken?

Photocells—simple but imprecise and can be fooled

A light-sensing photocell mounted on a light fixture can activate the fixture. This has the advantage of simplicity of operation, but the disadvantage of imprecise control. For example, the parking lot lights may not activate at the same time or the time desired—such as lighting until the end of a work shift. And the photocell can be confused by a buildup of grime on the sensor or lower lighting conditions such as during a thunderstorm. When close enough is good enough, photocell activation may be satisfactory.

Occupancy sensors—simple but not too smart

Occupancy sensors switch a light by sensing—usually with an infrared beam—the presence of motion in the room. After a time delay—when no motion takes place—the lights are turned off. This can prove a minor inconvenience when a motionless person reading at a desk or sitting on a toilet may cause the lights to inappropriately turn off. Also, the absence of lighting in an area can be a security concern. Finally, fluorescent light fixtures are intended to be run continuously for hours and do not function well when frequently turned on or off. The design cycle time for fluorescent light fixtures is three to five hours, but this could be shortened to minutes with an occupancy sensor—reducing efficiency and shortening the life of the fixture.

Lighting control panels overcome these problems

Lighting control panels can provide the desired type and quality of control and overcome the obstacles described above. In one simple example, a lighting control panel can activate all of the signs or all of the security and parking lot lighting for an entire shopping center at a time controlled by the owner of the shopping center. Similar interior lighting controls can be used in an industrial facility to match the activities and shifts in the plant.

A combination of time clocks, photocells, and dimming can more precisely control light levels in a more complicated building. For example, in a building with many floor to ceiling windows, the light levels can be changed each time the sun goes behind a cloud or moves throughout the day around the building—to brighten and dim fixtures so that the light levels remain constant with no activities required by the occupants. Such a system has a higher initial cost and does require more knowledgeable maintenance personnel throughout the life of the building.

Lighting Design

Common practice in the real world

The common lighting design practice in the real world for most buildings is a four-step process.

1. ***Light level selection***—The required quantity of light for the size of objects to be viewed and the time available for viewing is selected. A guide to these quantities is shown below.

Type of lighting	Average foot candles
Residential kitchen general	10
Residential kitchen sink, range, work counter	50
Residential dining	10
Residential bedrooms	5
Residential halls	5
Office general	20–30
Office detail work	50–100
Office corridors	10–20
Industrial assembly	30–50
Industrial detail work	100–500
Parking lots	2–5

These are recommended light levels developed by illumination engineers based on scientific study and experience. There are frequent attempts by politicians—in the name of energy efficiency—to demand a reduction in these light levels. Since they neither do much detail work nor follow the rules they set for others, unworkable requirements do not affect them. But our eyes and how we see have not changed.

2. ***Manage contrast and glare***—Contrast is required for vision, but is only good to a point and then becomes counterproductive. The recommended maximum levels of contrast are:

Task	Maximum brightness ratio
Between task in the adjacent darker surface	3–5 to 1
Between task and more remote darker surface	10–20 to 1
Between light fixtures and surface adjacent to them	20 to 1
Anywhere in the normal field of view	40 to 1

Management of this contrast is done both by the fixture reflector and lens, but also by selecting surfaces in the room that have acceptable light reflectance. Recommended light reflectance levels are:

Surface	Recommended light reflectance
Ceiling	80–90%
Walls	40–60%
Desks, bench-top machines and equipment	25–45%
Floors	Not less than 20 %

So it is not just the fixture that does the job. It is the combination of the reflector, lenses, and the color and roughness of the reflecting surfaces in the room that manages contrast.

3. ***Pick a fixture***—Fixtures are selected based on the efficiency of light production, color of light produced, heat management of the fixture, and resistance to environmental considerations as discussed above. The common choices tend to be: residential—predominantly incandescent (compact fluorescents are selected by some who do not mind the inferior color and have made decisions on energy efficiency on emotion rather than engineering information). Office and light industrial—predominantly fluorescent. Larger industrial and warehouse with higher ceilings use some fluorescent and more mercury and sodium vapor lamps. Exterior lighting uses mercury and sodium vapor lamps.

4. ***Space the light fixtures evenly***—Light fixtures are typically arranged using only rules of thumb based on past experiences—perhaps a light fixture, three ceiling tiles, and then another light fixture. This distribution will give approximate light levels and average management of glare.

This is how it's done in the real world, which includes probably 99% of projects constructed. The builder, the architect, or an electrical engineer who is not a lighting engineer may do these layouts. And the results as you'd expect are just okay, and sometimes unsatisfactory. We all have worked in spaces where there is either insufficient light or excessive glare that requires makeshift measures—bringing a light from home or taping paper on the edge of a fixture.

Design by Lighting Engineers

Huge improvement is possible with lighting engineers. Their design approach is different and far more effective than the approach described above. A more dramatic and pleasing appearance can result, as well as more efficient lighting and less visual fatigue for the occupants. One particularly demanding lighting engineering problem is a sports stadium. Here, a small fast moving ball must be seen extremely well by the players and very well by the spectators. And since their angle of view is different, background contrast, reflection, and glare are also different for the players and spectators. Different light levels are required in the stands, corridors, foodservice, restrooms, and parking lots—and all of these light levels must be made to work together side-by-side. A lighting engineer experienced in this type of work is your only hope of success. Similar demanding tasks exist in assembly occupancies, such as churches and concert halls.

Lighting engineers, however, will want influence on the light reflecting qualities of all the surfaces in the space—and architects and interior designers may not take well to an engineer dictating paint colors. Since the selected fixtures will probably be higher performing in many categories, their costs will be higher.

Finally, since the use of a lighting engineer is so rare, finding one will be difficult. Major cities may only have a few and smaller cities may have none. An expert from afar can be slow, expensive, and a real pain to manage.

Lighting Economics—Seldom an Easy Single Right Choice

Purchasing fixtures—inefficient and annoying supply house practices

The discussions above illustrate that buying fixtures can be far more complicated than one would imagine. Discussions of photometric diagrams, chromaticity of the lamp, the coating on the metallic housing, and the efficiencies of auxiliaries exhaust all but the most determined. Most will say, "It can not be that complicated, just tell me what to do." And, the light fixture supply houses will—but not to your advantage.

Most commercial light fixtures are not sold directly to the consumer. They are sold through supply houses. And some supply houses will have an exclusive or preferred ability to sell some brands or types of light fixtures. Supply houses will attempt to get some of their exclusive products specified. For a large "specified and bid project," the light fixture supply houses will assemble the entire job into a "light fixture package." They will neither itemize the cost per fixture type, nor will they provide any technical information before bid time—attempting to make substitutions ("breaking the spec") impossible. And they will only give approximate pricing until hours before bid time, and a final price minutes before the general contractors' bids are due to the owner.

By behaving as haggling bazaar merchants, they hope to conceal up to 1,500% markups on fixtures they believe they control. This costly and counterproductive "dance" can be avoided if the contractor participates in the specification process. A couple of renditions of ruling out any fixture for which line item cost will not be furnished, changes attitudes and rationalizes the process. Only the party who ultimately buys and pays for the fixtures can gain this cooperation. It is worth participating in the process.

Lifecycle cost—fixture cost (initial and replacement), energy costs, and maintenance are all important

The total cost to purchase, replace if necessary, operate, and maintain the fixture for the entire life is more important for light fixtures than for many other components. The operating energy is a higher portion of the initial fixture purchase price, and maintenance costs can be astronomical as described below.

The cost of purchase of a light fixture is easy to understand. But light fixtures get damaged or break, and some future remodeling may be required. So it is extremely important that a light fixture, or one functionally identical, will be available for many years to come. If not, satisfactory replacement of one fixture in the room may only be possible by replacement of all such fixtures. The further a fixture is from standard, the more likely that it will be discontinued.

Energy efficiency is also easy to understand. It is the cost of electricity needed to run the fixture—including both lamps and auxiliaries.

Maintenance of the light fixtures is a significant consideration that is not so easy to understand. The estimated useful life of the lamp, its replacement cost, and the cost of the ballasts and transformers can be well known. The labor to install these replacement components, however, can vary widely—from a single man screwing in a light bulb in less than a minute, to a crew of three with a powered lift taking 3-hours.

An inventory of replacement parts is a consideration as well. There are literally tens of thousands of different lamp types with a 10,000% cost range. If your facility requires more than about 10 of the most standard types, inventory management will become a problem. Lamps may only be available from certain supply houses, so multiple supply houses may be required for all your lamp needs. Either a large inventory will be required, delays in lamp replacement accepted, or maintenance personnel taking a half day off to travel to a distant supply house to obtain one light bulb. The decision to avoid these problems is made when you pick the fixture.

Summary

Lighting uses a portion of the electromagnetic spectrum. When we obtain light we also obtain other parts of the electro magnetic spectrum—ultraviolet and infrared—mostly heat. Management of this heat in and around the fixture and compensation for the heat in the HVAC system is a task that demands awareness and attention.

Time of viewing and size of an object influence the effectiveness of seeing, but both of these are beyond the builders' control. The amount of light reflected and contrast that also influences effectiveness of seeing, are within the builders' control and are the focus of lighting design. The light source, reflector, lens, and reflectance of everything else in the room work together to manage light levels and contrast.

Lamp types vary hugely in the types and evenness of color produced. Color correctness of lamp types are balanced with the economics both in energy use and the maintenance cost of lamp replacement to select a compromise that is "good enough."

Lighting economics requires consideration of the initial cost of the fixture, the cost and availability of replacement of this fixture, the power cost to run it, and the maintenance and servicing costs to replace lamps and auxiliaries. Selection of the fixture commits you to these costs for the life of the fixture so careful selection is advisable.

Line voltage switches, dimmers, photocells, occupancy sensors, and manual time clocks control lighting on small simple projects—with limited flexibility and "just satisfactory" results. Larger projects can improve these results with low voltage switching and lighting control panels.

99% of building lighting design is by rules of thumb and general guidelines, not specific lighting engineering. So, the designer may be you. Knowledge of the few ideas presented in this chapter will move you to the head of the class—probably more knowledgeable than all other members of the building team. And if your project requires design by lighting engineers, the same knowledge will help you evaluate their proposals and secure the benefits their knowledge and skill offers, while maintaining the economies your organization demands. In either case, your effectiveness at achieving project success will be greatly enhanced.

Index

About the Author

J.F. McCarthy

J.F. McCarthy has worked as a general contractor in the United States for 36 years—during the second half of the 20th century and first half of the 21st century. He continues to work now, and hopes to work a good while longer.

Completed projects include: single-family homes, low-rise residential (apartments, nursing homes), hi-rise residential, municipal buildings (city halls, police and fire stations), schools (preschools, grade and high schools, and universities), offices (both entire office buildings and tenant build-outs), retail and restaurants, historical restoration, civil structures (sewage treatment plants, spillways, and retaining structures), process manufacturing plants, and medical (inpatient human hospitals, outpatient facilities, and in and outpatient drug rehab and psychiatric facilities, professional offices, dental offices, and veterinary hospitals). So far, there have been no locks and dams, bridges, tunnels, power plants, pipelines, or large road projects.

A construction education was assembled. At the start of the J.F. McCarthy's career, formal education in construction or construction management was not yet offered. Three years of trade school (drafting and blueprint reading, estimating, and scheduling), a bachelors of science at a university (engineering and architecture subjects), followed by an MBA were done instead. And most of this was done at night school, while working during the day.

The difference between the classroom and the workplace produced frustrations for the author and undoubtedly aggravation for the teachers. "No one does it that way" "Why does this work, when theory says it should not?" and "How is it really done?" were not always welcomed or well answered at the time. Reading, seminars, and help from coworkers over 30 years have better answered these questions.